Sams **Teach Yourself**

Windows
PowerShell®

in **24**
Hours

 800 East 96th Street, Indianapolis, Indiana, 46240 USA

Sams Teach Yourself Windows PowerShell® in 24 Hours

Copyright © 2015 by Pearson Education, Inc.

ISBN-13: 9780672337284

ISBN-10: 0672337282

Library of Congress Control Number: 2015900973

Printed in the United States of America

First Printing May 2015

Trademarks

All terms mentioned in this book that are known to be trademarks or service marks have been appropriately capitalized. Sams Publishing cannot attest to the accuracy of this information. Use of a term in this book should not be regarded as affecting the validity of any trademark or service mark.

Warning and Disclaimer

Every effort has been made to make this book as complete and as accurate as possible, but no warranty or fitness is implied. The information provided is on an "as is" basis. The author and the publisher shall have neither liability nor responsibility to any person or entity with respect to any loss or damages arising from the information contained in this book.

Special Sales

For information about buying this title in bulk quantities, or for special sales opportunities (which may include electronic versions; custom cover designs; and content particular to your business, training goals, marketing focus, or branding interests), please contact our corporate sales department at corpsales@pearsoned.com or (800) 382-3419.

For government sales inquiries, please contact governmentsales@pearsoned.com.

For questions about sales outside the U.S., please contact international@pearsoned.com.

Editor-in-Chief
Greg Wiegand

Acquisitions Editor
Joan Murray

Development Editor
Sondra Scott

Managing Editor
Kristy Hart

Project Editor
Andy Beaster

Copy Editor
Keith Cline

Indexer
Cheryl Lenser

Proofreader
Katie Matejka

Technical Editor
Jeff Wouters

Publishing Coordinator
Cindy Teeters

Cover Designer
Mark Shirar

Compositor
Gloria Schurick

Contents at a Glance

Table of Contents

Part V: Putting Windows Powershell to Work

About the Author

Timothy Warner is an IT professional and technical trainer based in Nashville, Tennessee. Tim became acquainted with information technology in 1982 when his dad bought the family a Timex Sinclair 1000 home computer and he taught himself BASIC programming. Today he works as an author/evangelist for Pluralsight and shares Windows PowerShell knowledge with anyone who'll listen at his Two Minute PowerShell blog: http://2minutepowershell.com. You can reach Tim directly via LinkedIn: http://linkedin.com/in/timothywarner.

Dedication

To all my students, past and present.
Thank you for giving me a professional calling,
and I hope that my work helps you attain your goals.

Acknowledgments

The Windows PowerShell community is a terrific group of people. Thank you, Jeffrey Snover, Bruce Payette, and Lee Holmes et al. for giving the world Windows PowerShell. Thanks to all the PowerShell experts in the world for being so kind and willing to share your knowledge. I seek to emulate your actions every day.

It may take a village to raise a child, but I know that it takes a large office full of talented professionals to publish a book. To that end, I want to thank my wonderful editor Joan Murray for having faith in my abilities. Thanks to my publisher, Greg Wiegand, for being so receptive to my ideas.

Editorial and production staff rarely receive the credit they deserve. Thanks so much to Windows PowerShell MVP Jeff Wouters, my technical editor, for being so thorough with the manuscript. Truly, this book is at least twice as good as it originally was thanks to you.

Thanks to Keith Cline, my copyeditor, for making my writing easier to follow. Keith knows that I gave his editing skills quite a workout, for sure. Sorry, Keith!

I extend my gratitude as well to Andy Beaster, my production editor, and to the ever-helpful Cindy Teeters for streamlining the entire book publishing process. Andy and Cindy are professionals in every sense of the word.

Thanks to my family, friends, and colleagues for your never-ending love and support. Finally, thank you, my reader. I hope that this book helps you accomplish your next professional goal.

We Want to Hear from You!

As the reader of this book, you are our most important critic and commentator. We value your opinion and want to know what we're doing right, what we could do better, what areas you'd like to see us publish in, and any other words of wisdom you're willing to pass our way.

We welcome your comments. You can email or write to let us know what you did or didn't like about this book—as well as what we can do to make our books better.

Please note that we cannot help you with technical problems related to the topic of this book.

When you write, please be sure to include this book's title and author as well as your name and email address. We will carefully review your comments and share them with the author and editors who worked on the book.

Email: consumer@samspublishing.com

Mail: Sams Publishing
         ATTN: Reader Feedback
         800 East 96th Street
         Indianapolis, IN 46240 USA

Reader Services

Visit our website and register this book at informit.com/register for convenient access to any updates, downloads, or errata that might be available for this book.

Introduction

"Try not. Do...or do not. There is no try"

—Yoda, *Star Wars Episode V: The Empire Strikes Back*

Hello, and welcome to the world of Windows PowerShell. I'm your instructor, Tim Warner. To me, it's a good sign that you're actually reading this Introduction (so few readers of tech books do, in my experience). Perhaps your first question is, "What's in it for me?" and I'm here to give you those details with minimal muss and fuss.

If you work as a Windows systems administrator or hope to in the future, learning Windows PowerShell is no longer an option. Likewise, if you plan to advance your career in IT administration, you need to know your way around Windows PowerShell scripting and automation. This, then, is what's in it for you: By learning how to harness Windows PowerShell, you make yourself a more effective and valuable Windows systems administrator. And if you have value in the IT workplace, you have a means of having a stable, lucrative career and an equally stable and lucrative life.

Who Should Read This Book

The first thing I do when I teach "stand up" training classes is to get a feel for my student. What is your background? What do you hope to get out of this training? As I wrote this book, I had the following audiences in the forefront of my mind:

▶ **Microsoft certification candidates**: I'm here to tell you that if you don't understand Windows PowerShell, you have a high likelihood of failing your Microsoft Certified Professional (MCP) exams. And I'm not just talking about Windows Server 2012 R2 certification, either. Microsoft Learning stresses PowerShell-based administration in all of their products nowadays, so you simply cannot escape the technology, no matter how hard you might try.

▶ **Windows systems administrators**: I'm sure that you've been aware of Windows PowerShell over the past several years, and maybe you've been avoiding learning the technology because the tech appeared too "programmy" or math heavy. Let me assure you that by the time you complete this book, you won't be afraid of that anymore because you'll be convinced how much easier PowerShell makes your life as a "boots on the ground" sysadmin.

▶ **IT newcomers**: If you are working on a transition into full-time IT work, whether you're entering IT from an unrelated field or preparing to graduate from trade school or college, then welcome! You have an advantage in learning Windows PowerShell at the outset of your IT career because you'll be able to seamlessly integrate PowerShell automation into your vision of IT.

If you find that you don't belong in any of the previous three classifications, don't worry about it. Set your sights on learning as much as you can and, above all else, having fun, and you'll be fine.

How This Book Is Organized

These "24 Hour" books begin with the premise that you can learn a technology (Windows PowerShell, in this case) by studying the material in 24 one-hour sessions. Maybe you can use your lunch break as your training hour; then again, the hour after your children finally fall asleep at night might work better.

In any event, allow me to present hour-by-hour details on how I structured the content:

▶ Hour 1, "Getting to Know Windows PowerShell," makes the case that knowing Windows PowerShell is mandatory and not optional for Windows systems administrators. You'll also learn how PowerShell works from an architectural/design standpoint.

▶ In Hour 2, "Installing and Configuring Windows PowerShell," you understand the Windows PowerShell release cycle, backward-compatibility basics, and how to upgrade your installed Windows PowerShell version.

▶ In Hour 3, "Mastering the Windows PowerShell Help System," you learn how to learn Windows PowerShell. Believe me, this chapter is one of the three most important chapters of the book because you'll use the help system every day.

▶ In Hour 4, "Finding and Discovering Windows PowerShell Commands," you master the **Get-Command** cmdlet. This is the second of the three most important chapters, again based on how often you'll use these skills.

▶ In Hour 5, "Thinking in Terms of Objects," you use **Get-Member** to list the methods and properties of PowerShell objects. This hour completes the "triad" of three core chapters that comprise your foundational understanding of Windows PowerShell.

▶ In Hour 6, "Mastering the Windows PowerShell Pipeline," you begin to understand that in Windows PowerShell, you're always working from within a command pipeline, and you also recognize that in a PowerShell pipeline, you're almost always dealing with objects.

▶ In Hour 7, "Sorting, Filtering, and Measuring Windows PowerShell Output," you learn how to cut down your output to separate only the data you need.

▶ In Hour 8, "Managing Windows PowerShell Providers," you learn how you can access and browse various data stores, from environment variables and the Registry to the certificate store and Active Directory, in the same way that you browse your file system from the command line.

▶ In Hour 9, "Formatting, Exporting, and Converting Windows PowerShell Output," you pick up some valuable skills on creating submission-quality output of your PowerShell pipelines.

▶ In Hour 10, "Implementing One-to-One Windows PowerShell Remoting," you get a grip on the wonderful remoting architecture in Windows PowerShell. Here we examine how to set up remoting and establish remote sessions with other Windows computers on our network.

▶ In Hour 11, "Implementing One-to-Many Remoting," you learn how to send PowerShell commands and even entire scripts to an unlimited amount of target computers in parallel. This chapter demonstrates the raw power you have at your fingertips when you use PowerShell to manage your Windows networks.

▶ In Hour 12, "Deploying PowerShell Web Access," you learn how to set up PowerShell to be accessed from any remote device—even mobile phones and tablets from outside your corporate firewall. This is a cool technology, for sure.

▶ In Hour 13, "Multitasking Windows PowerShell," you discover the Windows PowerShell jobs architecture, in which you can send simple or complex PowerShell operations to the background of your session. By mastering jobs, you (and PowerShell) can multitask with aplomb.

▶ In Hour 14, "Harnessing Windows PowerShell Workflow," you take the next step with PowerShell jobs and learn how to design and deploy durable PowerShell tasks that respond to state changes, such as system reboots. Very cool stuff here.

▶ In Hour 15, "Introducing WMI and CIM," you finally come to terms with two acronyms many Windows systems administrators hear all the time but rarely understand: Windows Management Instrumentation (WMI) and Common Information Model (CIM). By the end of this chapter, you'll be crystal-clear on how to fetch system state data from the WMI repository by using PowerShell code.

▶ In Hour 16, "Searching and Filtering with Regular Expressions," you put your string searches on steroids by learning how to use the .NET Framework's regular expression syntax to perform highly specific find and replace operations on your data—all with PowerShell code.

▶ In Hour 17, "Installing and Managing Software with OneGet," you learn how to install and manage software, all from the PowerShell console command line. If you've used command-line software package management in Linux or OS X, what you learn during this hour will be immediately familiar.

▶ In Hour 18, "Desired State Configuration Basics," you learn what will doubtless become the next generation of Windows Server systems configuration: Desired State Configuration, or DSC, in Windows PowerShell.

▶ In Hour 19, "Introduction to Windows PowerShell Scripting," you take everything you've learned over the previous 18 hours of training and apply that knowledge toward code reuse. In other words, you'll learn the basics of writing, configuration, and running Windows PowerShell script files.

▶ In Hour 20, "Making PowerShell Code Portable with Modules," you build upon what you learned in the preceding hour of training concerning PowerShell scripts and target that knowledge toward packing your code into modular...well, modules.

▶ In Hour 21, "Managing Active Directory with Windows PowerShell," you embark on a four-hour journey of PowerShell domain-specific management. Here the "domain" is Active Directory Domain Services (AD DS) itself.

▶ In Hour 22, "Managing SQL Server with Windows PowerShell," you learn how to use the SQL Server PowerShell module and SQL Management Object (SMO) to interact with SQL Server databases and objects through PowerShell code.

▶ In Hour 23, "Managing SharePoint Server with Windows PowerShell," you learn how to create SharePoint farm objects (web application, site collection, list, and so forth) by using the SharePoint Server 2013 PowerShell snap-in.

▶ In Hour 24, "Managing Microsoft Azure with Windows PowerShell," we complete the training by applying Windows PowerShell to Microsoft's public cloud service: Azure.

Conventions Used in This Book

In my experience as an author and a teacher, I've found that many readers and students skip over this part of the book. Congratulations for reading it. Doing so will pay off in big dividends because you'll understand how and why we formatted this book the way that we did.

Try It Yourself

Throughout the book, you'll find Try It Yourself exercises, which are opportunities for you to apply what you're learning right then and there in the book. I do believe in knowledge stacking, so you can expect that later Try It Yourself exercises assume that you know how to do stuff that you did in previous Try It Yourself exercises.

Therefore, your best bet is to read each chapter in sequence and work through every Try It Yourself exercise.

About the Bitly Hyperlinks

Whenever I want to point you to an Internet resource to broaden and deepen the content you're learning, I provide a uniform resource locator (URL, also called an Internet address) in the following form:

```
http://bit.ly/uaKpYD
```

You might wonder what the heck this is. The way I look at the situation, if I were reading this title as a print book and needed to type out a URL given to me by the author, I would rather type in a "shortie" URL than some long, crazy URL with all sorts of special characters, you know what I mean?

The most important thing I have to tell you concerning the bitly short URLs is that the ending part is case sensitive. Therefore, typing the previous URL as, say, http://bit.ly/UaKpyD isn't going to get you to the same page as what I intended.

About the Code Images

For most Try It Yourself exercises, you'll see one or more source code images that are annotated with alphabetic letters. The Try It Yourself steps are then cross-referenced with parts of each code image. Hopefully, you find this format convenient to your learning. Remember not to fall into the trap of blindly copying the provided code; instead, remember that learning to program requires (yes, requires) lots and lots of trial and error.

That actually is a point well worth repeating: To become effective with Windows PowerShell, you need to use it daily. Don't complain about retyping my code examples. Instead, look at it as an opportunity for you to practice.

System Requirements

You don't need a heck of a lot, computer-wise, to perform all the Try It Yourself exercises in this book. However, if you do not meet the necessary system requirements, you are stuck. To that end, make sure that you have the following met prior to beginning your work:

- ▶ **A Windows-based computer**: Technically, you don't need a computer that runs only Microsoft Windows. For instance, I use VMware Fusion to run Windows 8 virtual machines (VMs) on my OS X computer. No matter how you slice it, though, Windows PowerShell has *Windows* in its name for a reason, so you'll be stuck at the starting gate unless you have a Windows machine at your disposal.

▶ **An Internet connection**: In learning Windows PowerShell, you'll be hitting the Web all the time to gain additional insight, obtain code examples, and so forth. Moreover, because Windows PowerShell doesn't ship with local help files, you'll need an Internet link to download those at least once.

▶ **A VM network and an Azure subscription**: You can build a two- or three-node practice network for free. Windows 8.1, for instance, includes Hyper-V. You can also download Oracle VM VirtualBox to deploy a VM-based network. Microsoft is kind enough to offer full-feature evaluation editions of their software, so you shouldn't have to pay big bucks for licenses. Along those lines, Microsoft offers trial subscriptions of their Microsoft Azure subscription service. As I wrote this book, I made sure that replicating my network environment was as painless as possible for you because I want you to work through every single example in the book to maximize your learning.

Design Elements Used in This Book

Some code statements presented in this book are too long to appear on a single line. In these cases, a line-continuation character (➡) is used to indicate that the following line is a continuation of the current statement.

NOTE

Items of Interest

Notes offer interesting information related to the current topic.

TIP

Useful Tidbits

Tips offer advice or show you an easier way to perform a task.

CAUTION

Potential Pitfalls

Cautions alert you to a possible problem and suggest ways to avoid it.

Okay, that's enough of the preliminaries. It's time to learn how to use Windows PowerShell.

HOUR 1

Getting to Know Windows PowerShell

What You'll Learn in This Hour:

▶ Why you should learn Windows PowerShell sooner rather than later

▶ How Windows PowerShell developed over time

▶ What components make up the Windows PowerShell product family

▶ How to use Windows PowerShell to easily gather system information

Hi there. In the span of my career as a technical trainer and systems administrator, I've had the chance to interact with thousands of other Windows administrators. To that point, I cannot count how many times many of these administrators said something akin to the following to me:

▶ "I know that I need to learn Windows PowerShell, but I'm afraid and intimidated."

▶ "Programming involves math, and I can't stand math. Windows PowerShell feels like programming to me."

▶ "I lost out on promotions at work because I didn't know Windows PowerShell."

▶ "I've been dragging my heels on earning my Windows Server 2012 certification because I've been avoiding learning Windows PowerShell."

Do any of these sentiments sound familiar to you? If so, take heart; you are not alone. My purpose in writing this book is to give you the confidence and skills you need to become proficient in Windows PowerShell. As an instructor, I take the approach of getting your hands dirty with the technology at the same time we learn the theory. After all, with a product like Windows PowerShell, the practice is at least as important as the theory.

To set the stage for our training and for the rest of this book, let's begin by considering the manifold reasons why learning Windows PowerShell is not an optional task for the twenty-first century Windows systems administrator.

Why You Should Learn Windows PowerShell

Frankly, if you were to put pencil to paper (or fingers to the keyboard, to be more contemporary), you could probably generate a pretty thorough list of reasons why it is crucial to your career success to learn and master Windows PowerShell. However, for convenience, let's start with the reasons outlined in the following sections.

The Technology Is Not Going Away

Windows PowerShell has been around since 2006, and Microsoft has invested steadily in the technology ever since. Stated simply, Windows PowerShell is here to stay, and we need to get accustomed to that fact. I hope you take heart in the idea that by learning Windows PowerShell, you are actually making your work easier to perform through automation. After all, how much do you enjoy creating hundreds of Active Directory user accounts manually, or pushing configuration files to a thousand servers by hand?

Within Microsoft Corporation, their published Common Engineering Criteria (CEC) documentation mandates that all Windows product teams ensure that the majority of each feature's functionality can be accomplished by using Windows PowerShell in addition to using a corresponding graphical tool. The long story short is that we had better get used to it, because Windows PowerShell is here to stay, and it represents the future standard for Windows systems administration.

Some Tasks Can Be Accomplished Only with Windows PowerShell

In Microsoft's enterprise server product portfolio, which includes products such as System Center, Exchange Server, Lync Server, SharePoint Server, and many others, we have historically noted that there exist some administration and configuration tasks that can only be performed by using Windows PowerShell.

From what I've seen in my work, Microsoft still provides a graphical user interface (GUI) for the more mundane tasks; for higher-impact, potentially destructive actions, however, it's Windows PowerShell all the way. To my mind, this makes it all the more important for us to understand how Windows PowerShell works, get comfortable with the technology, and lose any intimidation we may retain concerning the shell.

Windows PowerShell Is One Interface to Rule Them All

One of the many things so brilliant about Windows PowerShell is the uniformity of its command syntax. As you'll learn while you work through this book, PowerShell cmdlets (pronounced *command*-lets) consist of a verb-prefixsingularnoun syntax that is at once easy to remember and intuitive to apply.

In case you wondered what I meant by "prefixsingularnoun": each PowerShell command should have a short prefix that serves both to easily identify the command as well as to prevent name collisions with commands from other sources.

That's why, for instance, all the Active Directory cmdlets use the AD noun prefix, the SharePoint Server cmdlets use SP, and so forth.

The singular noun naming is intended to make it easier for us administrators to remember; it's a pain asking yourself "Is it Get-Service or Get-Services?" all the time.

Here's the kicker: Once you get the hang of discovering and using Windows PowerShell cmdlets, you'll find your productivity ramp up exponentially with all Microsoft technology. Consider: You might have basic skills with the Exchange or Lync graphical management tools, but by knowing Windows PowerShell, you'll find yourself performing Exchange or Lync administration from the command line in a much more powerful and efficient manner.

So, the upshot is Windows PowerShell presents a consistent, level playing field for all your Windows systems administration needs. The day will come when you can fully manage your Windows network by using only Windows PowerShell.

You Won't Pass Your Certification Exams Without Windows PowerShell Knowledge

Microsoft added Windows PowerShell-related questions to their IT pro certification exams a long time ago. However, there was a time when it was enough simply to identify which cmdlet went with which administrative task. No more, my friend!

The bottom line is that if you are seeking certification in any contemporary Microsoft product, such as Windows Server 2012 R2/vNext or Windows 8.1/10, you are very likely not to pass your exams unless you have a comprehensive knowledge of Windows PowerShell.

For instance, I recall seeing questions on my SharePoint Server 2013 certification exams that required me to evaluate several lines of Windows PowerShell script code and to choose my answers based on which parts of the code required modification. You simply aren't going to be able to answer these questions correctly recognizing only cmdlet names.

You Can "Future-Proof" Your IT Career by Mastering Windows PowerShell

I challenge you to consult an online IT job search site and count how many Windows systems administrator job postings mention Windows PowerShell. The bottom line is that IT departments can now see how much Windows PowerShell benefits them.

For one thing, think of the human-error equation. Why risk botching up your production systems through human error when you can script out multistep administrative tasks in Windows PowerShell and have the scripts run with 100% accuracy every time?

Even if a job posting doesn't mention Windows PowerShell explicitly, you'll certainly give yourself a leg up as a job candidate by showing off your Windows PowerShell skills and abilities.

Brief History of Windows PowerShell

In operating system terminology, a shell is a command-line interface (CLI). Historically in Microsoft Windows, administrators relied on command.com (in Windows consumer systems) and Cmd.exe (in Windows NT-based systems) to perform actions from a keyboard-only session.

In UNIX/Linux/OS X, the Bash shell and its related variants have served administrators well for a long, long time. We can write so-called shell scripts that automate repetitive actions, and then run the scripts either ad hoc or on a predefined schedule.

Shell scripts in Windows are just as important as those in Linux environments, but Microsoft saw that it needed to offer administrators more programmatic flexibility. So along came the Windows Script Host (WSH), Visual Basic Scripting Edition (VBScript), and a host (pun intended) of other lightweight, interpreted scripting languages.

Sadly, the VBScript experiment didn't prove too fruitful, because the language itself was the vector of many vulnerabilities and security exploits. Of course, there is also the problem that what we can do with one line of Windows PowerShell often requires 30+ lines of VBScript to accomplish the same task.

One key reason why PowerShell is so much more efficient than VBScript is because Microsoft went through the trouble of coding the most common administration tasks (using .NET languages) and building them into PowerShell core cmdlets. In most cases, we can run a PowerShell one-liner that saves us from researching and building a 200 line VBScript file. I'm grateful to Microsoft for that, personally!

Monad Manifesto

In 2002, the now Microsoft Distinguished Engineer Jeffrey Snover (pronounced *Snow-ver*) published the Monad Manifesto, a white paper outlining a completely revamped method for administrative automation in Windows. Figure 1.1 shows you what Jeffrey looks like.

FIGURE 1.1
Jeffrey Snover, the inventor of Windows PowerShell.

TIP

What Is a Monad?

What became Windows PowerShell began life as a new technology called Monad (pronounced *MOH-nad*) in 2002. The term *monad* derives from the work of the seventeenth-century mathematician and philosophy Gottfried Wilhelm Liebnitz, who defined a monad as the fundamental element of physical reality.

You would be well advised to read the Monad Manifesto, which is freely available at http://bit.ly/1paKsJa (direct PDF download). It's amazing to me how much of that vision in 2002 has been delivered in full by the time of this writing in the fall of 2014.

Monad became Windows PowerShell v1.0 in 2006. Table 1.1 describes the Windows PowerShell version history.

TABLE 1.1 Windows PowerShell Version History in a Nutshell

Windows PowerShell Version	Release Date	Associated Operating Systems	Standout Features
1.0	2006	Windows Server 2003, Windows Server 2008, Windows XP SP2, Windows Vista	Initial release
2.0	2009	Windows Server 2008 R2, Windows 7	Remoting, jobs, modules
3.0	2012	Windows Server 2012, Windows 8	Updatable help, IntelliSense, snippets, resumable sessions, automatic Foreach, member enumeration
4.0	2013	Windows Server 2012 R2, Windows 8.1	Desired State Configuration, exportable help, network diagnostics
5.0	2014	N/A (Public preview as of this writing)	OneGet, out-of-band hardware management, classes

Don't freak out if you don't understand the "standout features" given in Table 1.1. In due time, you'll know what all this means and more.

For now, note the following:

▶ Windows PowerShell is on a fast-paced release cycle.

▶ Windows PowerShell releases are loosely coupled with Windows operating system releases.

Defining PowerShell

You know, with all this preliminary information, we never formally defined what Windows PowerShell is. Pshaw! According to my good friend Wikipedia:

Windows PowerShell is a task automation and configuration management framework from Microsoft, consisting of a command-line shell and associated scripting language built on the .NET Framework.

I chose to include the previous definition because I find it concise and accurate. I do want to stress, though, that Windows PowerShell is first and foremost a management shell, with the automation aspects following close behind.

The issue with that definition is that it probably won't do you much good if you have no idea what the .NET Framework is.

The .NET Framework is an abstraction layer that sits between your applications and your operating system and underlying device drivers and computer hardware. The short statement is that the .NET Framework allows software developers to tap into any aspect of a Windows system's hardware and software that is exposed via the .NET Framework.

One of the great beauties of Windows PowerShell is that we Windows administrators don't have to know a lick of C# or VB.NET programming. Windows PowerShell cmdlets are actually compiled .NET classes, so we can leverage the power and scope of the .NET Framework by issuing easy-to-use Windows PowerShell cmdlets. The great power of PowerShell (so to speak) lies in its simplicity. You can leverage the power of the .NET Framework in a non-programmy way that systems administrators like.

As you'll see before too long, the Windows PowerShell team leveraged all the best parts of various command shells, scripting languages, programming languages, and advanced mathematics in developing Windows PowerShell. For instance, you'll find that many of your favorite commands work in Windows PowerShell (almost) exactly as they do in their original environments.

Understanding the Windows PowerShell Components

This section discusses the three primary tools for crafting and executing Windows PowerShell code:

▶ Windows PowerShell console (powershell.exe)

▶ Windows PowerShell ISE (powershell_ise.exe)

▶ Windows PowerShell host applications (first and third party)

Windows PowerShell Console

The Windows PowerShell console is a command-line interface (CLI) that is sometimes called a *REPL* (pronounced *REP-uhl*) interface. This acronym signifies the four basic tasks of an interactive shell: First, the Windows PowerShell runtime environment *reads* the code that you've submitted to it and makes sure that your syntax passes muster.

Second, the runtime *evaluates* the code and determines the most efficient and secure execution plan. At its base, Windows PowerShell is an interpreted scripting language in which the Windows PowerShell runtime parses your script code line by line.

Third, Windows PowerShell *prints* the results into the standard output, which is typically the computer screen. However, Windows PowerShell gives you almost unlimited flexibility in redirecting output. You can push output to HTML, XML, plain text, PDF... the list goes on and on.

Fourth and finally, Windows PowerShell *loops* by passing control back to the user and waits for further instructions.

The upside to the console is that it is a fast way to "get in and get out" with Windows PowerShell code. The downside is that the console doesn't include the fancy code-help assistance that is offered by the Windows PowerShell ISE. Figure 1.2 shows you a screenshot of a representative Windows PowerShell session.

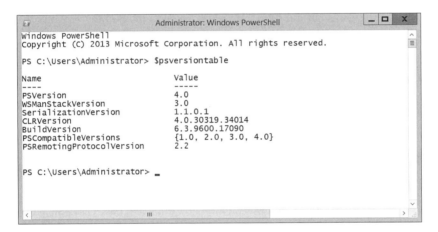

FIGURE 1.2
The Windows PowerShell console is fast and convenient, with abundant help available, even when errors occur.

TIP

Starting a PowerShell Console Session

My own preferred way to start a Windows PowerShell console session is to right-click the Windows PowerShell icon either from the Start screen, Start menu, or taskbar, and then select **Run as Administrator** from the shortcut menu. Figure 1.3 shows you what the taskbar jump menu looks like.

FIGURE 1.3
Because a portion of your systems administration will require elevated privileges, it's general best practice to start Windows PowerShell sessions as an administrator.

CAUTION

Run Windows PowerShell as Administrator

It is technically possible for you to run Windows PowerShell as a standard Windows user, but I suggest that you always start your Windows PowerShell sessions as an administrator.

The reason for my suggestion is simple: The last thing you want is for an important script to bomb out halfway through because Windows PowerShell doesn't have the permissions it needs to accomplish such-and-so a task. Even a task as mundane as updating the local PowerShell help files requires an elevated user token.

Remember that Windows PowerShell has potential access to the deepest nether regions of your system's hardware and software; such a degree of access typically requires administrative permissions.

PowerShell Integrated Scripting Environment

The Windows PowerShell Integrated Scripting Environment (ISE) is, as its name implies, an integrated scripting environment that helps you to compose, debug, manage, and run Windows PowerShell .ps1 script files.

An ISE is a scripting language counterpart of an integrated development environment (IDE) that traditional programmers use to code their programs. Because Windows PowerShell is an interpreted scripting language instead of a compiled programming language like C#, we have the ISE terminology. Figure 1.4 shows you the Windows PowerShell ISE interface.

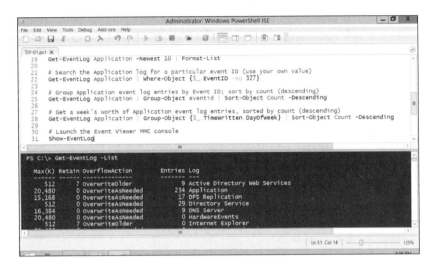

FIGURE 1.4
The Windows PowerShell ISE.

The ISE includes many IDE features that Windows PowerShell scripters will find useful, including the following:

▶ **IntelliSense code completion:** This feature helps you learn cmdlet syntax as you type.

▶ **Code highlighting:** You can tell at a glance where your cmdlets and parameters are, as well as if you made a typing mistake.

▶ **Code folding:** You can click to expand and collapse related script elements, like functions, for easier browsing in long script files.

▶ **Debugger:** You can step through your scripts line by line to detect and resolve problems.

▶ **Multipane interface:** You can view and edit multiple Windows PowerShell script files simultaneously. Those tabs actually represent separate, isolated Windows PowerShell sessions.

▶ **Snippets:** You can access a library of built-in "starter" code constructs to help you create a potentially complex script more efficiently.

ISE Disadvantages for System Administrators

Wow. The ISE offers us a lot, doesn't it? You might be wondering whether the ISE has any disadvantages for us Windows systems administrators. Yes, there are a few:

▶ **Inconsistent keyboard shortcuts:** The Ctrl+C keyboard shortcut we use as a "break" command in the Windows PowerShell console doesn't work that way in the ISE; instead, in the ISE you'll need to use the Stop button on the toolbar to break script execution.

▶ **Cumbersome for interactive use:** If you need to get in and get out quickly with Windows PowerShell, you're better off using the console than starting the bulky ISE application.

▶ **Not installed on Server OS by default:** Although you'll find the Windows PowerShell ISE available immediately on Windows client operating systems, the tool must be installed manually on Windows Server systems. The good news is that this task is easily accomplished in Windows Server 2012 R2 by issuing a single line of Windows PowerShell:

```
Install-WindowsFeature PowerShell-ISE
```

We'll use the Windows PowerShell ISE later on in this book, after you've obtained your proverbial sea legs with the Windows PowerShell console.

For those of you already experienced with the PowerShell ISE, you may want to consider some worthwhile add-ons like ISESteroids (http://www.powertheshell.com/isesteroids/), which "supercharges" the ISE environment.

PSReadLine (https://github.com/lzybkr/PSReadLine) brings several of the ISE features to the normal PowerShell console.

Other First- and Third-Party Windows PowerShell Hosts

As an experiment, open the Windows PowerShell console and type the following command:

```
$host
```

The **$host** system variable gives you metadata concerning the current Windows PowerShell host environment. Remember that Windows PowerShell is a runtime environment that always is hosted by a parent process.

Some Microsoft management tools are actually Windows PowerShell host applications. Take the Active Directory Administrative Center (ADAC) on Windows Server 2012 domain controllers, for example.

Take a look at Figure 1.5; do you see the PowerShell History pane? Whenever you use the ADAC GUI, Windows actually runs corresponding Windows PowerShell commands and echoes them in the History pane.

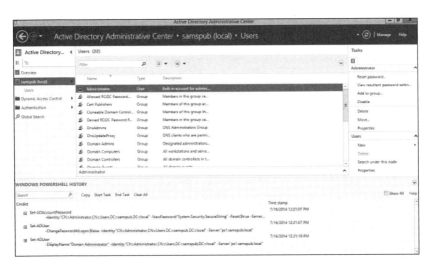

FIGURE 1.5
Active Directory Administrative Center. Note the Windows PowerShell History pane that I've highlighted in yellow for your convenience; ADAC is one of several Windows PowerShell host applications made by Microsoft.

As it happens, Microsoft publishes the API for Windows PowerShell. This allows third-party developers to create their own Windows PowerShell host applications. Here are a few examples for you to check out at your convenience:

- **Idera PowerShell Plus**: http://bit.ly/1qGY9fn

- **Sapien PowerShell Studio**: http://bit.ly/1qGYf6t

- **Quest PowerGUI**: http://dell.to/1qGYqyO

Investigating the Power and Simplicity of Windows PowerShell

The powershell.exe console host application "lives" in the directory path C:\Windows\System32\ WindowsPowerShell on 64-bit systems. This means that you can call the console host directly by using a Start menu/Start screen shortcut, or you can invoke it from the traditional Cmd.exe command prompt session by typing the following:

```
powershell
```

Assuming that you have the ISE installed, you can start the ISE from a command prompt session (Cmd.exe or PowerShell.exe) by issuing the following command:

```
ise
```

You can actually switch between Cmd.exe and PowerShell.exe easily. Try the following simple procedure:

1. Start an elevated Cmd.exe session; you can do this on Windows Server systems by using **Windows+R** to invoke the Run dialog box and typing **cmd**. Of course, there exist several different ways to accomplish this task—don't take my approach as the only one.

2. Invoke the Windows PowerShell console host by typing **powershell**.

3. Now, from within PowerShell, return to the Cmd.exe environment by typing **cmd** again.

4. To leave the Cmd.exe interpreter and resume your Windows PowerShell session, type **exit**. Notice the PS at the front of the console prompt; this is your visual indicator that you are in a Windows PowerShell session.

TRY IT YOURSELF

Getting Event Log Information with Windows PowerShell

In this exercise, you'll dive into learning Windows PowerShell by firing up a console session and using the **Get-Eventlog** cmdlet. Don't be intimidated by the sometimes strange syntax we'll see. Everything will be fully explained to you in time, and before long it will all be second nature to you anyway.

So for now just sit back, type code, review the output, and enjoy the ride without worrying about the fine syntax details. More will be revealed, I promise!

By the way, the code we use in this Try It Yourself exercise works in any version of Windows PowerShell, so feel free to work through the following steps on your Windows server or client computer. Enjoy!

1. Open an elevated command prompt. The specific method for doing this varies a bit depending upon your operating system. The general instructions on Windows client systems are to (a) press the Windows key on your keyboard; (b) type **cmd** and press Enter; (c) right-click the resulting Cmd.exe icon; and (d) select **Run as Administrator** from the shortcut menu.

2. Now that you are in an administrative Cmd.exe session, you can start Windows PowerShell by typing **powershell** and pressing Enter. By the way, it's implied that you should press Enter after every command from now on, okay?

   The reason why I'm having you enter Windows PowerShell from the Windows command prompt is simply to remind you that it can be done this way. Having options is great, right?

   You can tell that you're in a Windows PowerShell session because the command prompt is prepended with (appropriately enough) PS.

3. Okay, let's get down to business. We'll start by viewing all the event logs on our system. We do this with the **Get-EventLog** cmdlet along with the **list** parameter:

```
Get-EventLog -list
```

Although I show you cmdlets in title case, it's important for you to know that cmdlets are not case sensitive. Therefore, you can get the same result by typing **GET-EVENTLOG**, **get-eventlog**, or **GeT-eVeNtLoG**. The **Get-EventLog-list** statement gives us a tabular view of all event logs on our system, along with some pertinent metadata like their maximum log file size and the number of entries contained therein.

4. If you want to view the entries in a specific log, such as the Application log, we can issue the following statement:

```
Get-EventLog -LogName Application
```

5. Whoa! The previous command gave us a *lot* of information, wouldn't you agree? Let's try viewing only the most recent five entries, shall we? Try this:

```
Get-EventLog -LogName Application -Newest 5
```

6. That's a little better, right? However, the tabular view is a bit cramped onscreen. Why don't we format the output in a more eye-friendly way onscreen:

```
Get-EventLog -LogName Application -Newest 5 | Format-List
```

Figure 1.6 shows the difference in output. That strange vertical bar character you used is called the pipe. You can access the pipe character by holding Shift and typing the key above Enter on your keyboard. We use pipe a lot in Windows PowerShell to chain commands together.

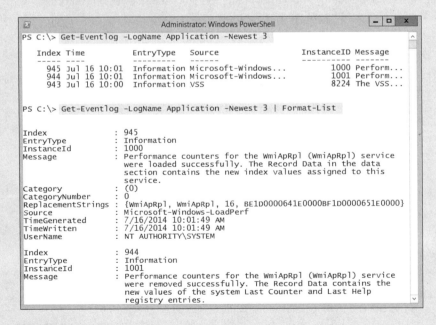

FIGURE 1.6
You can view Windows PowerShell output in several different ways.

7. To save yourself some typing, press the up-arrow key on your keyboard; notice that this allows you to access previously typed commands.

Let's assume that you want a printed record of this Application event log output. To do that, you can add a third link to your Windows PowerShell pipe chain:

```
Get-EventLog –LogName Application –Newest 5 | Format-List | Out-File "C:\
events.txt"
```

8. Finally, you can open your newly created text log file in Notepad directly from our Windows PowerShell session:

```
Notepad C:\events.txt
```

9. To exit your Windows PowerShell session and return to Cmd.exe, type **exit**. Type **exit** a second time to close the Cmd.exe command window. You're done!

Summary

We began this hour by reviewing the myriad reasons why learning Windows PowerShell is mandatory if you plan to have any kind of longevity as a Windows systems administrator in the twenty-first century.

We then undertook a brief history of Windows PowerShell. Again, I want to remind you to read Jeffrey Snover's Monad Manifesto and refer to it as we proceed through the rest of this volume. I think you'll share my amazement at how much of Jeffrey's vision for administrative automation has been realized in Windows PowerShell.

By now, you have a solid grasp on how to get in and out of the Windows PowerShell console host. I gave you a bit of a tease on the other popular hosts such as the ISE and Active Directory Administrative Center. In time, you'll be a master of any Windows PowerShell host, I assure you.

Finally, you got some experience in actually running some live Windows PowerShell commands. If you found typing out the commands to be awkward, take comfort in the fact that you aren't alone.

It will doubtless take time before running Windows PowerShell statements feels like second nature. Actually, I heard Jeffrey Snover give a talk once in which he admitted that he does a fair amount of fumbling around when he uses Windows PowerShell. This is coming from the inventor of the technology!

Q&A

Q. Why do people say that Windows PowerShell is faster than GUI tools? It takes me what seems like forever to learn how these commands work!

A. Here's the deal: With Windows PowerShell, you make an up-front investment. Yes, you'll find that accomplishing a particular task (for example, installing a Windows Server 2012 feature) may feel cumbersome and take several minutes to do initially by using Windows PowerShell instead of the Server Manager GUI.

However, this up-front time investment pays huge dividends when, once you've mastered the syntax, you can perform the task in seconds with Windows PowerShell either by working interactively in the Windows PowerShell console or (even better) by running a stored .ps1 script that already contains perfect, infinitely reproducible syntax.

Q. I noticed that I can get directory listings by running the dir command in Windows PowerShell. However, when I use my favorite switches with the command, such as dir /w, I get an error. What gives?

A. The Windows PowerShell team created aliases for most of the command Windows and Linux command shell internal commands. Specifically, **dir** in Windows PowerShell is an alias for the native **Get-ChildItem** cmdlet. So, you cannot use the Cmd.exe parameters in Windows PowerShell. Sorry about that!

Q. Isn't the Windows PowerShell console dangerous? I mean, every time you press Enter, you're actually doing something, or potentially doing something, on your system.

A. This is true, to a point, and is one reason why it is advisable to use the Windows PowerShell ISE when you want to double- and triple-check your code before submitting it to the interpreter.

On the other hand, there exists a nifty switch parameter called **–WhatIf** that takes the "bite" out of any Windows PowerShell statement. For instance, try this out on your system:

```
Stop-Service Spooler -WhatIf
```

As I'm sure you can guess, the Stop-Service cmdlet is used to stop running Windows services. The Spooler service refers to the Print Spooler service, which allows your system to submit print jobs. However, the **–WhatIf** parameter simply instructs Windows PowerShell to parse your command and let you know what would happen whether you actually ran it. Pretty neat, eh?

Workshop

Spend some more time using the Get-EventLog cmdlet that you learned about during this hour's Try It Yourself exercise. How can you obtain syntax help concerning this cmdlet?

See whether you can figure out how to export a comma-separated value (CSV) file showing the most recent 25 entries from your system's Security log. Make liberal use of the **–WhatIf** switch parameter to test your syntax in advance.

Quiz

1. Which of the following commands displays the identity of the current Windows PowerShell host?

    a. host

    b. $host

    c. hostname

2. Why is it suggested to run Windows PowerShell as an administrator?

    a. Windows PowerShell won't run without administrative privileges.

    b. Many actions you take in Windows PowerShell require administrative privileges.

    c. Actually, you should always run Windows PowerShell as a standard user.

3. How can you tell at a glance that you are running a Windows PowerShell console session?

    a. The Administrator label in the window title bar

    b. The greater than (>) symbol that appears at the end of your command prompt

    c. The PS that appears in front of your command prompt

Answers

1. The correct answer is B. We use the **$host** system variable to ascertain the current Windows PowerShell host. Figure 1.7 shows you this command in action.

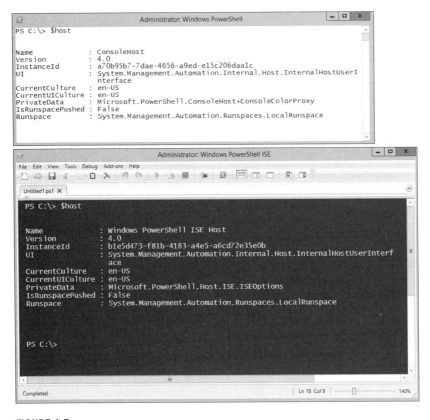

FIGURE 1.7
The **$host** system variable lets you know the identity of the current Windows PowerShell host application. You can see the console host on the top and the ISE host on the bottom.

2. The correct answer is B. The best practice is to run Windows PowerShell under administrative privileges wherever possible because many administrative tasks simply won't work without having administrative access.

   You can quickly check to see whether you are running a Windows PowerShell session as an administrator. If Administrator appears in the title bar, you're all set. Otherwise, you're running the console as a standard user and you should kill that session and start with the proper privileges.

3. The correct answer is C. By default, a PS, standing for PowerShell, appears at the front of your command prompt in a Windows PowerShell console session.

HOUR 2
Installing and Configuring Windows PowerShell

What You'll Learn in This Hour:

- ▶ How to quickly determine the current Windows and PowerShell versions on your computers
- ▶ How to install the "latest and greatest" version of Windows PowerShell
- ▶ How to customize your Windows PowerShell environment; specifically, the console and the ISE

Hey there! Welcome back. In the preceding hour, you developed an initial familiarity with Windows PowerShell, that most wonderful administrative automation environment. This hour will take your understanding to a new level, first by inventorying our systems to figure out which versions of Windows PowerShell we can run, and then how to install the bits if they aren't there to begin with.

You'll then learn how to tweak and tune the console and Integrated Scripting Environment (ISE) environments to suit your preferences. To be sure, as a newcomer, you probably aren't sure what your preferences are. However, in time, you'll come to rely on this knowledge and you'll find that the first thing you do when you administer a new system is to customize the Windows PowerShell environment to help you be as comfortable and efficient as possible. Let's get to work.

Determining Your Windows PowerShell Environment

You'll recall that Windows PowerShell has limitations both in terms of the .NET Framework version and host operating system version that is required. Windows PowerShell is an administrator-friendly and (largely) programming code-free portal into the .NET Framework. To get your feet wet, let's review the Windows PowerShell-.NET Framework version matchup by studying Table 2.1.

TABLE 2.1 Windows PowerShell and .NET Framework Versions

Windows PowerShell Version	Required .NET Framework Version
3.0	4.0
4.0	4.5
5.0	4.5

Of course, the next obvious question is, "How can I tell which version of the .NET Framework I have installed on my system?" First off, know that your computer can host multiple versions of the .NET Framework. This is because Microsoft technologies are written to a particular .NET version, so by definition you'll likely need different versions available concurrently on the same system.

Determining Your .NET Framework Version

To figure out which versions of the .NET Framework you have installed on your system, follow these steps:

1. Open up an elevated PowerShell session and issue the following command:

```
Get-Item -Path "HKLM\SOFTWARE\Microsoft\NET Framework\Setup\NDP\*"
```

2. What we're doing here is programmatically accessing the Registry by using a PowerShell provider—pretty neat, eh? Take a look at Figure 2.1 to see my output from a Windows 8.1 workstation that has several .NET Framework versions installed.

To install a particular version of the .NET Framework if you don't have it, run an online search engine and submit the following string, substituting for *X* the .NET Framework version you're interested in:

```
download .NET Framework X
```

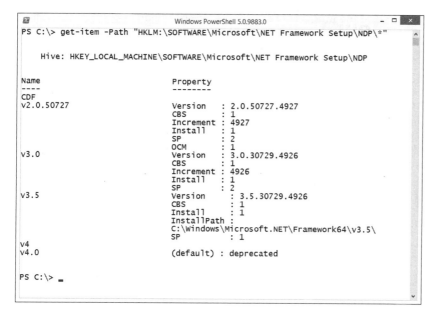

FIGURE 2.1
We can use Windows PowerShell's Registry provider to list installed .NET Framework versions.

Determining Your Windows Version

No, I'm actually not joking by giving you the aforementioned chapter heading. Nowadays it can be tricky to determine easily which version of Windows you're running. Sure, the Start screen makes it pretty easy to figure out if you're running Windows 8 instead of Windows 7. But how do you know whether you have Windows 8.1 installed? Do you have the "update" installed as well? Are you running Windows Server 2012 or Windows Server 2012 R2?

Windows PowerShell is finicky about which versions of Windows it supports. For instance, Windows PowerShell v5 runs only on the following systems:

▶ Windows Server 2012 R2

▶ Windows 8.1 Enterprise

▶ Windows 8.1 Professional

Thus, the release to manufacturing (RTM) versions of Windows Server 2012 and Windows 8 are left out in the proverbial cold in terms of their capacity to run Windows PowerShell v5. And Windows 7? As they say on Long Island, "Fuhgetaboutit."

Windows PowerShell v3 and v4 are much more liberal it its system requirements. You can run v3 on Windows Server 2012, Windows Server 2008 R2, Windows 8, and/or Windows 7.

Again, the question comes up: How can we efficiently query which particular version of Windows we're running? Follow these steps:

1. Open the Run dialog box, type **cmd**, and press **Enter**. You don't need to have elevated command prompt privileges for this exercise.

2. Type **ver** to get the Windows build version. Cross-reference your result with Table 2.2 to get your Windows version.

TABLE 2.2 Windows OS Version Numbers

Windows OS Version	Ver Output
Windows Server 2008 R2 SP1	6.1.7601
Windows 7 SP1	6.1.7601
Windows Server 2012	6.2.9200
Windows 8	6.2.9200
Windows Server 2012 R2	6.3.9600
Windows 8.1	6.3.9600

3. Now type **powershell** to invoke the Windows PowerShell interpreter. Next, type the following command to retrieve the current Windows PowerShell version:

```
$PSVersionTable.PSVersion
```

Figure 2.2 shows you what all this looks like.

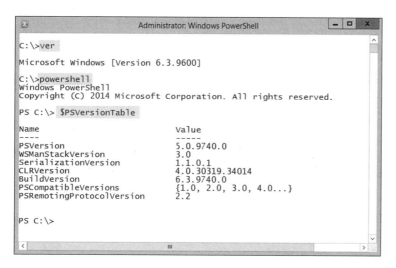

FIGURE 2.2
You can query your Windows and PowerShell version numbers, all from the convenience of the command prompt.

NOTE

Assumptions About Your Windows OS and Windows PowerShell Versions

As you know, Windows PowerShell runs on several Windows versions, including those that are no longer supported by Microsoft. (Windows XP comes immediately to mind.) In the name of keeping this book current and in-scope, I will assume unless explicitly stated otherwise that you run either Windows Server 2012 R2 or Windows 8.1. Conveniently, those are the only two Windows versions that support Windows PowerShell v5.

That said, the vast majority of Windows PowerShell you'll learn in this book is applicable to any version of Windows PowerShell from version 2 onward. I'll let you know when we cover features that are exclusive to version 5, and along the way you'll certainly become familiar with the major new features of PowerShell v3 and v4 as well.

Installing the Latest Version of Windows PowerShell

Okay, let's assume that your system runs Windows 8.1 and your Windows PowerShell version is 4.0. How can you get the latest and greatest Windows PowerShell version? Should you trust that Windows Update will take care of that update for you?

Not necessarily. Although Microsoft initially rolled out new Windows PowerShell releases with corresponding Windows operating system releases, the Windows PowerShell release cycle is now independent of the OS in the form of the Windows Management Framework, or WMF.

The cool thing about WMF is that the Windows PowerShell team can continue to enhance Windows PowerShell and get those changes to us administrators without having to wait for a new version of Windows to come around the pike.

As of this writing, Windows PowerShell v5 is in Public Preview mode, which means that anybody can download and install the product even though it hasn't yet been "baked into" a Windows OS version.

WMF Components

When you install WMF, you receive the following parts and pieces:

▶ Windows PowerShell runtime environment (including all supporting modules, snap-ins, providers, and so forth).

▶ Windows PowerShell ISE. (This is crucial to take advantage of IntelliSense help for new cmdlets, net snippets, and so on.)

▶ Windows Remote Management (WinRM) components. (Remoting is a core functionality of Windows PowerShell.)

▶ Windows Management Instrumentation (WMI) infrastructure and Server Manager provider.

▶ Other components that are new with this version. (For instance, WMF 4.0 gives you the Desired State Configuration binaries.)

Microsoft is not known for their user-friendly URLs. So, to locate the download page for the appropriate WMF version you're interested in, fire up your favorite search engine and perform the following query, substituting for *Y* your target WMF version:

```
download Windows Management Framework Y
```

Installing the WMF

The Windows Management Framework comes in 32-bit (x86) and 64-bit (x64) editions. Specifically, the installer has a .msu extension and can be installed simply by double-clicking it and following the prompts.

As you can see in Figure 2.3, the WMF looks and behaves like a standard Windows Update standalone installer, which it actually is.

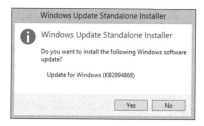

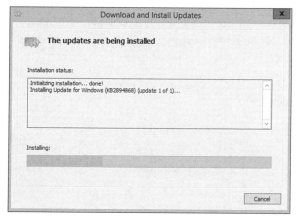

FIGURE 2.3
The Windows Management Framework is a standalone Windows Update package with the .msu extension.

A Word of Warning

As nice as it is to run the "latest and greatest" Windows PowerShell version, please (and I can't stress this enough) perform due diligence and research compatibility before upgrading Windows PowerShell on production servers. Remember that products like SharePoint Server and Exchange Server expect to work with particular Windows PowerShell versions, and the last thing you want to have to do is troubleshoot broken functionality as a result of a Windows PowerShell version upgrade.

In addition to performing the requisite online research, perform at least a couple trial installations on nonproduction servers or on your administrative workstation to ward off any other potential "ghosts in the machine"; you'll be glad you did.

If you have need to install WMF on several systems, you may want to consider using Group Policy Software Installation or System Center Configuration Manager (SCCM) to deploy the .msu package in a more efficient manner.

Customizing the Windows PowerShell Console

At this point, you know of at least a couple ways to start the Windows PowerShell console. I've also stressed how important it is that you run Windows PowerShell console sessions with elevated credentials. But now that you've started Windows PowerShell in a console, what next?

Well, for one thing, you'll want to customize the environment so that it's easier on your eyes and more conducive to your administrative workflow.

To access the console options, you must open the Control menu, which is located in the upper-left corner of the console window (see Figure 2.4). Select **Properties** from the menu to access the console's Windows PowerShell Properties sheet.

FIGURE 2.4
The command menu, circled, is the hidden way to unlock all the Windows PowerShell customization options. I opened the Edit menu in this screenshot to show you the QuickEdit commands.

Let's take a look at the console options a page at a time, beginning with the Options tab shown in Figure 2.5.

- ▶ **Cursor Size:** This setting is unimportant, in my opinion. You can make the blinking cursor larger or smaller. Who cares, right?

- ▶ **Command History:** The Buffer Size property determines how many previous commands are "remembered" by the console. I suggest bumping this up as much as you dare. The Number of Buffers setting determines how many separate buffers (which is to say, Windows PowerShell console sessions) are allowed. Enabling the Discard Old Duplicates option ensures that your command history doesn't waste space with duplicate entries. Recall that we access the command history in the console by pressing the up-arrow key.

- ▶ **Edit Options:** I suggest you enable both of these options so that you can use your mouse to perform copy and paste operations within the console window. You'll learn how this function works in an upcoming Try It Yourself exercise.

FIGURE 2.5
The Options tab of the Windows PowerShell Properties sheet.

Next, let's move to the Font tab, shown in Figure 2.6.

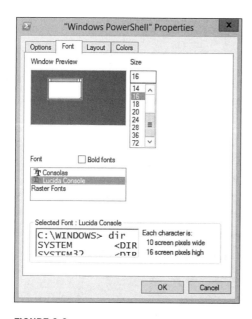

FIGURE 2.6
The Font tab of the Windows PowerShell Properties sheet.

Here I recommend that you choose the Lucinda Console font for Windows PowerShell, chiefly because this font make it easier to distinguish some of the more optically troublesome punctuation marks such as the single quote (') and the backtick/grave accent (`). I tend to boost the font to 14 or 16 points to reduce the need to squint at my monitor; your mileage may vary.

Third, we'll examine the important Layout tab, shown in Figure 2.7.

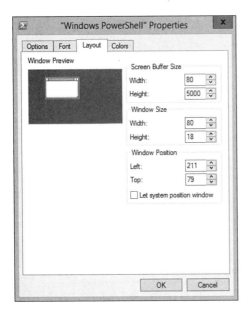

FIGURE 2.7
The Layout tab of the Windows PowerShell Properties sheet.

- ▶ **Screen Buffer Size:** The Width parameter specifies how many characters are stored horizontally. The Height value determines how many lines of output can be accessed via vertical scrolling. I suggest you "super size" this value so that you can have detailed access to your console output.

- ▶ **Windows Size:** If your screen buffer width is set to a larger value than window size width, your code will cause horizontal scrolling, which in my opinion is undesirable. Set the Window Height option to whatever is comfortable given your current monitor.

- ▶ **Window Position:** I normally don't mess with these settings, instead preferring to use my mouse to manually position the console window on my monitors.

The best power-user tip I have for you with regard to setting Windows PowerShell layout options is to make the screen buffer width and the window size width the same size. Doing this ensures that neither your code nor output is cut off on the right side of the window. You can see what I'm talking about by looking at Figure 2.8.

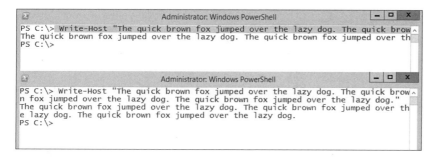

FIGURE 2.8
In the top line, the screen buffer width is 200, and the window size width is 80. In the bottom line, I set both values to 80. Quite a difference in terms of code legibility, wouldn't you agree? By the way, I highlighted the Write-Host statements to make them easier to differentiate from their output.

Finally, let's check out the Colors tab, shown in Figure 2.9. Select **Screen Background**, and then click a color swatch to change the background color; do the same for **Screen Text** to change the color of your text.

The pop-up text colors are relevant for output that is overlaid on the console screen, such as when you press F7 to access your previous command buffer. As a matter of fact, try that right now; the F7 shortcut will likely prove useful to you in the future.

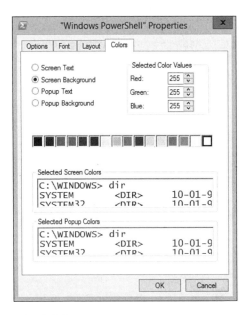

FIGURE 2.9
The Colors tab of the Windows PowerShell Properties sheet.

▼ TRY IT YOURSELF

Customizing the Windows PowerShell Console

In this Try It Yourself exercise, you'll customize your Windows PowerShell console environment to suit your preferences. To complete this exercise, you need a Windows PowerShell shortcut icon on your system's taskbar. This behavior occurs by default in Windows Server 2012. On Windows 8 systems, press the **Windows** key to go to the Start screen and type **powershell** to locate the icon. Next, right-click the icon and select **Pin to Taskbar** from the pop-up menu.

Work through the following steps to complete the exercise. Have fun!

1. Right-click the Windows PowerShell icon on your taskbar. From the Jump list, right-click the Windows PowerShell icon and select **Properties** from the shortcut menu. What we're doing is modifying the behavior of this shortcut so that it obeys our custom preferences whenever we left-click the icon from now on.

2. Let's start by configuring Windows PowerShell console to start with elevated privileges by default. On the Shortcut property tab, click **Advanced**. In the Advanced Properties dialog, select **Run as Administrator**, and then click **OK**. Figure 2.10 shows the interface.

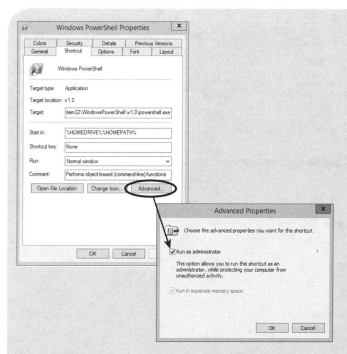

FIGURE 2.10
You can configure the Windows PowerShell console to start with elevated privileges by default.

3. Navigate to the Font tab and set the environment to use Lucinda Console at 16 points.

4. Navigate to the Colors tab and set the screen background to gray and the screen text to black. Just for grins, set the pop-up text to a wacky color.

5. Navigate to the Layout tab and set the screen buffer width and window size width to **80**. Change the screen buffer height to **5000**.

6. Navigate to the Options tab and ensure that **QuickEdit Mode** and **Insert Mode** are both enabled.

7. Click **OK**, and then left-click the Windows PowerShell icon on your taskbar. Verify that the console session picked up your changes. Issue a few token Windows PowerShell commands:

```
Write-Host "Hello world!"
Get-Service | Where-Object {$_.Status -eq "Stopped"}
$host.version
```

8. Now press **F7** to review your command history. Use the up-arrow and down-arrow keys to move through the list, and press **Enter** to invoke an old command. Press **Esc** to dismiss the command history window. Figure 2.11 shows this interface. By the way, this recent commands menu will pick up any adjustments you made to the pop-up text or background.

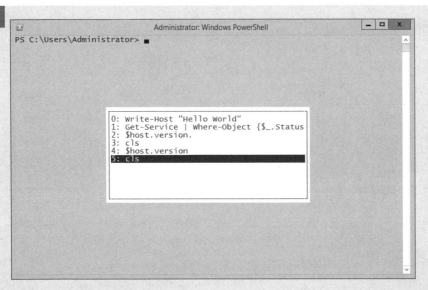

FIGURE 2.11
The F7 keyboard shortcut is a handy alternative to using the up-arrow and down-arrow keys alone to access previously typed Windows PowerShell commands.

9. Finally, experiment with Quick Edit mode. Open Notepad and type out the following:

```
Write-Output "Now is the time for all good men and women to come to the aid of
their country. The quick brown fox jumped over the lazy dog."
```

We'll get into the details later, but it's considered PowerShell best practice to use Write-Output instead of Write-Host to present text to the user. For one thing, Write-Output puts its output in the pipeline, and Write-Host doesn't.

If you want to substitute my old typing class boilerplate for something else, so much the better. Now select that statement in Notepad and copy it to your Windows Clipboard.

10. In your Windows PowerShell console, right-click your mouse on a new line. See what happened? This is the magic of Quick Edit mode in action. You can put literally anything—some cool Windows PowerShell one-liner you found on the Internet, say, or some long directory path—onto the Clipboard and easily integrate it into your console session with no typing required.

Make sure to press **Enter** after you've pasted that statement to see what happens. Notice that the text wraps properly because you sized your window buffer appropriately? Incidentally, the Write-Host cmdlet is useful to print output to the screen.

11. To work in reverse, open the console Control menu and click **Edit > Mark**. Now highlight the Write-Host statement in the console window and press **Enter**. You just copied that statement back into the Clipboard.

12. Go back to Windows Notepad and choose **Edit > Paste**. You're done!

Customizing the Windows PowerShell ISE

The Windows PowerShell Integrated Scripting Environment (ISE) truly deserves a chapter all to itself. So for our purposes in this hour, we'll stick to learning how to install the tool, start it up, and change some of the most popular options.

Verifying That the ISE Is Installed

The fastest way to check whether you have the ISE installed on your system is to type **ise** from your Windows PowerShell console session. If the tool starts, it's installed—simple as that.

The reason I bring this up is that although the ISE is normally installed by default on Windows client operating systems, it is not installed automatically on all Windows Server installations.

On your Windows Server computers, issue the following Windows PowerShell command from a console session:

```
Get-WindowsFeature –Name *ise*
```

As I'm sure you can detect intuitively, **Get-WindowsFeature** is used to query Windows Server roles and features, and ***ise*** performs a wildcard search on role/feature names. Check out Figure 2.12 to see what the interface looks like if you do have the ISE installed.

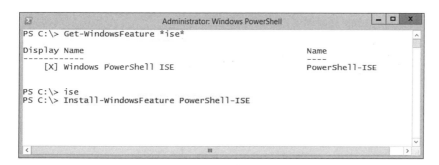

FIGURE 2.12
You may need to use some Windows PowerShell kung-fu to install the Windows PowerShell ISE.

Windows PowerShell Versus PowerShell

You may have noticed that I habitually refer to Windows PowerShell as Windows PowerShell and not just PowerShell. Why is this? Basically, I'm respecting Microsoft's trademark.

You see, if you run a search at the United States Patent and Trademark Office website (tmsearch. uspto.gov), you'll learn that while Microsoft owns the trademark on *Windows PowerShell*, several other companies claim rights to the word *PowerShell* alone when used in particular contexts.

Therefore, although you can certainly get away with calling Windows PowerShell just PowerShell in friendly conversation, you'll be adopting the Microsoft-preferred approach if you use Windows PowerShell. Just thought you'd want to know.

If your Windows Server system doesn't have the ISE installed, another line of Windows PowerShell comes to your rescue:

```
Install-WindowsFeature –Name PowerShell-ISE
```

Mandatory ISE Tweaks

Okay, perhaps I'm being a bit overdramatic by labeling the following Windows PowerShell ISE customizations as "mandatory," but they are such for me.

First of all, click **Add-Ons > Commands** to turn off the Commands add-on. As nice as that functionality is (and you'll learn all about how to use it later in the book), right now it serves as a distraction that we'll want to be rid of. You can always click **Add-Ons > Commands** again to toggle the tool back on.

Second, notice the following buttons on the toolbar, which are called out in an annotation in Figure 2.13. You can get their ToolTip names by hovering your mouse over them:

- ▶ Show Script Pane Top
- ▶ Show Script Pane Right
- ▶ Show Script Pane Maximized

These buttons enable you to change the orientation between the Script pane, which is where you work on your Windows PowerShell code and optionally save your work as .ps1 script files, and the Console pane, which functions almost exactly like the traditional Windows PowerShell console window.

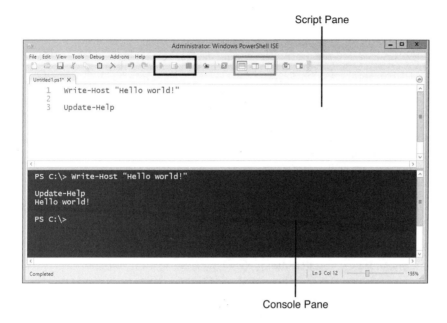

FIGURE 2.13
Our "tricked-out" Windows PowerShell ISE console.

Personally, I prefer having the Script pane on top and the Console pane on the bottom, but your mileage may vary.

For our third customization, let's open the Options dialog box by clicking **Tools > Options**. Navigate to the General Settings tab and ensure that **Show Line Numbers** in the Script pane is selected. Believe me, using line numbers when you author Windows PowerShell scripts makes documentation and troubleshooting *so* much easier. Make any other customizations as you see fit and click **OK** when you're done.

One more cool trick: Hold down **Ctrl** and scroll your mouse wheel. This is a quick and excellent way to zoom your Script and Console pane output in or out to your liking. I use that shortcut in the ISE all the time.

In the Script pane, type some innocuous Windows PowerShell such as the following:

```
Write-Host "Hello, Windows PowerShell ISE!"
$PSVersionTable
```

Returning to the toolbar, notice the following buttons, which I've again called out in Figure 2.13:

- ▶ Run Script (F5)
- ▶ Run Selection (F8)
- ▶ Stop Operation (Ctrl+Break)

Try using the **Run Script** and **Run Selection** options so that you can get a feel for their difference. In essence, pressing F5 or clicking Run Script will execute everything in your Script pane. Be careful with this option!

By contrast, you can use your mouse to select certain lines in the Script pane (or simply place your cursor in a single line) and then press **F8** or the **Run Selection** button to execute only the selected lines of Windows PowerShell code.

Finally, the Stop Operation button is useful to halt the execution of a long-running operation. In the Windows PowerShell console environment, we can use the Ctrl+C shortcut, but in the ISE, this shortcut performs the standard Windows Copy command instead.

Summary

In this hour, we "wrestled the bear" a bit and learned how to wrangle the Windows PowerShell console and ISE to suit our workflow and personal preferences. At this point, you know how to access the customization options for the console and ISE, and I've given you some great tips for optimizing your environment for maximum legibility.

In your career as a Windows systems administrator and budding Windows PowerShell expert, you may find that you're not the only person at your organization who uses Windows PowerShell. Therefore, I want to get you thinking sooner rather than later of how you can leverage Microsoft best practices to make your Windows PowerShell code and environment as team friendly as possible.

To that previous point, understand that if you aren't the only user of your system, then changing Windows PowerShell defaults may affect the other users' experience as well. That's why in time you'll learn how to leverage the Windows PowerShell profile to give you both customization power and flexibility.

In the next hour, though, you'll learn how to use the Windows PowerShell help system. Understanding how to read the help is perhaps your most important skill to master; trust me.

Q&A

Q. Can I customize the standard Windows command prompt the same way that I can customize the Windows PowerShell console?

A. Absolutely! In fact, you'll discover that the Properties pages for Cmd.exe are the same as those for Windows PowerShell. This underscores the fact that although their console options are similar, Cmd.exe and PowerShell.exe are two completely separate and independent executable program files.

I didn't go into detail here because we haven't yet covered PowerShell object members, but in time you'll learn how to programmatically change all aspects of the PowerShell console host. This serves to further decrease your reliance on graphical user interfaces.

Q. In the Windows PowerShell console Properties (specifically the Font tab), I see only three fonts to choose from. Can I change the default font to something else?

A. Yes and no. Sadly, changing the default font in the Windows PowerShell console is extremely difficult to do because the console is coded in such a way as to maintain compatibility with Cmd.exe, which in turn maintains compatibility with ancient Windows command shells.

I mean, you can search the Internet, and you'll find some tutorials that show you how to hack the Windows Registry to force the Windows PowerShell console to display your custom font. However, I advise against these procedures on general principle. After all, you need your console host to be as rock solid and stable as possible on production systems.

However, start the ISE, click **Tools > Options**, and check out the Colors and Fonts tab, shown in Figure 2.14. Here you can go wild tricking out all the fonts, colors, and styling within the application.

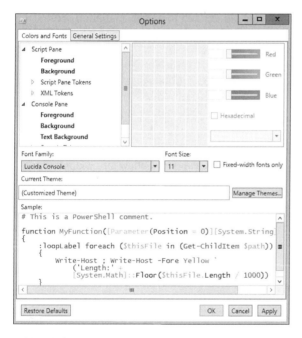

FIGURE 2.14
You can customize fonts to a granular degree from within the Windows PowerShell ISE environment. From within the Windows PowerShell console, though? Not so much.

Workshop

By using your curiosity and some Internet research, see how you can customize the Windows PowerShell environment by using only Windows PowerShell code.

I'll give you a little hint: the **RawUI** object, nestled deep inside the **$host** system variable, goes a long way to giving you an answer to this question. For instance, try out the following one-liner:

```
$host.UI.RawUI.WindowTitle="My Windows PowerShell Console"
```

Quiz

1. You can install Windows PowerShell v5 on Windows 7 systems.

   a. True

   b. False

2. Which of the following Windows PowerShell cmdlets is used to display output on screen directly?

   a. Write-Host

   b. Get-Host

   c. Write-Output

   d. Get-WindowsFeature

3. To ensure that your Windows PowerShell console code doesn't get cut off or run outside the window border, you should set your screen buffer width and window size width...

   a. Such that the buffer width is larger than the window size width

   b. Such that the window size width is larger than the window size width

   c. Independently of each other

   d. To the same size

Answers

1. The correct answer is B. As Windows PowerShell (and the .NET Framework) matures over time, the list of supported Windows versions gets increasingly thin. Windows PowerShell v5 is supported only on Windows Server 2012 R2 and Windows 8.1 systems.

2. The correct answer is C. You should use Write-Output when you need to communicate with the PowerShell user or script runner. Although some PowerShell admins use Write-Host, this isn't best practice because Write-Host doesn't write objects to the pipeline.

   The suggested guidance for Write-Host is to use it only when you want to display semi-formatted informational text, disclaimer text, and so forth. As it happens, you can add parameters to Write-Host to change the foreground and background colors of the output to make them stand out better for the user.

3. The correct answer is D. By setting the screen buffer width and window size widths to the same value, you ensure that your Windows PowerShell code and output "wraps" when it reaches the right border of the console window.

HOUR 3

Mastering the Windows PowerShell Help System

What You'll Learn in This Hour:

▶ How Windows PowerShell command syntax works

▶ How to keep Windows PowerShell help up-to-date

▶ How to understand Windows PowerShell help article syntax

▶ How to perform offline help file updates

An old mentor of mine once taught me, "Being skillful isn't necessarily about having knowledge in your head all the time. Rather, it's about knowing where to go to look up the knowledge when you need it."

Those words have proven themselves to be useful in my life. In a default installation of Windows PowerShell, we get hundreds of cmdlets out of the box. Once you start adding first- and third-party features, that cmdlet list gets into the thousands.

It's inconceivable that you'll remember them all, or even the vast majority of the Windows PowerShell vocabulary. To that end, it is crucial that we master the Windows PowerShell help system. Once you know your way around help, it will be trivial to discover cmdlets and learn how they work with a minimum of muss, fuss, or greasy aftertaste.

Anatomy of a Windows PowerShell Cmdlet

Strictly speaking, there exist a number of different Windows PowerShell "commands." For instance, we have

▶ **Cmdlets:** Windows PowerShell commands that are written in a compiled .NET programming language

▶ **Functions:** Windows PowerShell commands that are written natively in Windows PowerShell

▶ **Workflows:** Long-running, durable PowerShell commands that can survive system restarts and respond to other environmental changes

- ▶ **Configurations:** Windows PowerShell scripts that orchestrate Desired State Configuration (DSC) settings

- ▶ **Classes:** PowerShell v5 gives us the ability to create honest-to-goodness .NET classes, which are code blocks that provide a specific interface

Nevertheless, for our purposes, the primary Windows PowerShell command type is the cmdlet (pronounced *command-let*).

Take a look at Figure 3.1, and we'll discuss the structure of a typical cmdlet.

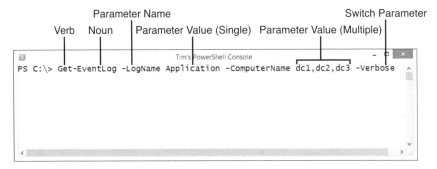

FIGURE 3.1
Anatomy of a typical Windows PowerShell cmdlet.

NOTE

What's in a Name?

The Windows PowerShell team really used their heads when they named the cmdlet. If you perform an Internet search for whatever administrative task you need to perform (for instance, "create a domain user account") and add the word *cmdlet* to your search, you'll be pleased to discover that the vast majority of your search results will be Windows PowerShell related.

The Windows PowerShell team created a new word with cmdlet, and I for one am glad that they did.

First of all, observe that all cmdlets, at least in theory, take the following form:

```
ApprovedVerb-PrefixSingularNoun
```

I can't overstate how important the prefix is to a PowerShell command. Number one, a prefix serves to uniquely identify a command and mitigate the possibility of name collisions with another command. Number two, prefixes give administrators better discovery of PowerShell commands. For instance, we can run the following statement to retrieve all the Active Directory commands on a Windows Server domain controller:

```
Get-Command -Noun AD*
```

CAUTION
_____

Watch Spacing

Please don't make the mistake of putting a space between the verb and the noun. Likewise, don't use an incorrect separator character such as the underscore. It's verb-hyphen-noun, okay? Microsoft publishes a list of verbs that are officially approved for Windows PowerShell.
_____

Open a Windows PowerShell console and submit the following command to retrieve a list of approved verbs for your current Windows PowerShell version:

```
Get-Verb | Sort-Object -Property Verb
```

Don't get hung up on the fact that not every approved verb is actually a verb; you'll occasionally see some inconsistencies within Windows PowerShell. "Verbs" such as *New* or *Where* are rare exceptions to the rule.

Also, PowerShell normally alerts you if or when you load a module whose vendor made the mistake of ignoring PowerShell approved verbs. We'll see that behavior in Technicolor when we cover PowerShell-based SQL Server administration.

Noun Behavior in Windows PowerShell

I want to make two more points concerning the noun portion of cmdlet names. First, remember that nouns and parameter names are (almost) always given in the singular person. Thus, if you issue

```
Get-EventLog -List
```

you'll get a run of all the event logs that are present on the target system. However, if you run

```
Get-EventLogs -List
```

you'll get an error message. Nouns are singular! In the real world, you will run across vendor PowerShell modules that disobey the "singular noun" rule, much to your frustration.

Second, most cmdlet nouns are named with a brief prefix that denotes which module they come from. For example, on Windows Server 2012 domain controllers, you'll find commands such as the following:

```
Get-ADUser
Get-ADComputer
```

The AD prefix obviously denotes Active Directory. In SharePoint Server 2013, Microsoft's enterprise content management platform, those cmdlets are all prefixed with SP. Get it?

Now, then, let's refer back to Figure 3.1 and walk through each component of a Windows PowerShell cmdlet.

A *parameter* is an option that is passed to a cmdlet that alters how the cmdlet behaves. Parameters never have spaces, and they are always prefixed by the hyphen. There is also never a space between the hyphen and the parameter name.

Parameters can be required or optional, named or positional. We'll cover what that stuff means momentarily when we delve into the Windows PowerShell help system.

Each parameter has one or more *values*. For instance, in Figure 3.1, we see the **LogName** parameter accepts a single value (the log name to be viewed), and the **ComputerName** parameter accepts one or more values. One way to give a cmdlet multiple parameter values is a comma-separated list with no spaces in between the value elements.

Finally, *switch parameters* are parameters that function like an on/off switch (hence their name, I suppose). In Figure 3.1, you either want verbose output or you don't.

Updating the Windows PowerShell Help Library

You can obtain help for any Windows PowerShell cmdlet by issuing one of the following commands:

- ▶ **Get-Help** *cmdletname*
- ▶ **help** *cmdletname*
- ▶ **man** *cmdletname*

"Wow. There are three different help commands? What's the deal with that?" you may wonder. Actually, there's some smoke and mirrors going on here. Take a look at Figure 3.2. You can see that Get-Help is an honest-to-goodness cmdlet, Help is a function, and that the Linux-friendly **man** command is an alias for help.

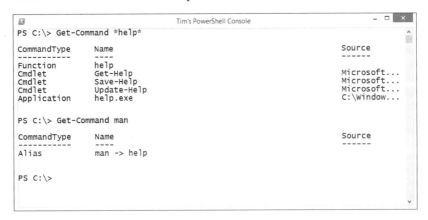

FIGURE 3.2
The Windows PowerShell help commands involve some behind-the-scenes trickery.

Specifically, the Help function simply runs Get-Help, piping the results to More, giving you a friendly, page-at-a-time display. The PowerShell team added this "more" functionality to make PowerShell intuitive to "old salt" Cmd.exe and Command.com (!) administrators who habitually used | **more** from the Windows command prompt.

Have you run Get-Help on your system? If not, try the following:

```
Get-Help -Name Get-Service
```

Don't be surprised if you see the same output as shown in Figure 3.3; it's by design.

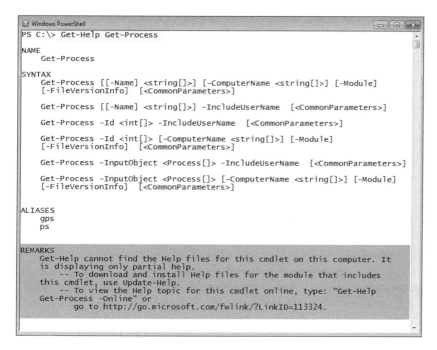

FIGURE 3.3
As of Version 3, Windows PowerShell doesn't ship with local help files.

Understanding Updateable Help

Microsoft ships Windows PowerShell without local help files because the environment is almost constantly changing. Therefore, "locking" the help files of a released Windows PowerShell version will definitely result in outdated help and information that is no longer valid.

As of version 3, Windows PowerShell help is fully updateable. You can update the help files across all installed modules, or you can selectively update individual modules.

To that end, you have three options for viewing Windows PowerShell command help on your computer, and all of them require an Internet connection.

You can use the **Online** parameter to fetch the help article directly from Microsoft web servers. For instance, try the following:

```
Get-Help -Name Get-Service -Online
```

The **Online** option pops open your default web browser and points you to the latest and greatest online version of that particular help article.

You can also simply browse to the TechNet library at technet.microsoft.com and search for our target cmdlet directly, or you can perform an Internet search, making sure to specify the word *cmdlet* in our search string to ensure that you get great results.

Finally, you can simply update your local help library with the most recent version available from Microsoft. Try this:

```
Update-Help
```

Bingo! You should get into the habit of running Update-Help regularly (say, every week or two) on your systems to ensure that the local Windows PowerShell help files are current with their online counterparts.

Note that Update-Help actually performs a help file check only once every 24 hours. So, if you run Update-Help three times in a day, only the first run of the command did anything. However, adding the **Force** switch parameter to the cmdlet will indeed perform a true version check with Microsoft web servers.

Viewing Help Content

Now that you have local help files installed, try out some of the different ways to view help content so that you get a feel for them:

```
Get-Help -Name Get-Help
```

Running Get-Help with the name of a cmdlet gives you a "standard" help file that flies past you onscreen pretty quickly. Remember that I said that help is a function that essentially modifies how the **Get-Help** cmdlet works. Try this:

```
Help Get-Help
```

Is that better? You can now use the spacebar key to scroll through the help article one screen at a time. If you actually read the help article, you'll see that there exist other useful parameters in this cmdlet, but we'll examine those later on in this hour of training.

I use the –ShowWindow parameter most of the time when I look at PowerShell help files because I have a dual-monitor setup and it's nice to have my console on one screen and the help file on the other. Try this:

```
Get-Help -Name Get-Service -ShowWindow
```

Updating Help on Offline Systems

So far, you've learned how to keep your local Windows PowerShell help files current. All well and good, you respond. But what about your secure servers that don't have Internet access?

Well, some Windows systems administrators would argue that you should be running Windows PowerShell from your administrative workstation and not your servers, but for now I'll entertain the thought that you do in fact need to update the Windows PowerShell help on an offline system. How do you do that?

It's pretty simple, actually. Here's the stepwise approach:

1. Run Save-Help on an online system.

2. Put the saved Windows PowerShell help files in a shared location, a USB thumb drive, or another location.

3. On the offline system, run **Update-Help** with the **–SourcePath** parameter.

Pulling down Windows PowerShell help to a local folder couldn't be easier:

```
Save-Help -DestinationPath "c:\savedhelp"
```

Figure 3.4 shows what the saved help looks like. It's basically a bunch of Extensible Markup Language (XML) and Microsoft compressed Cabinet (.cab) archives.

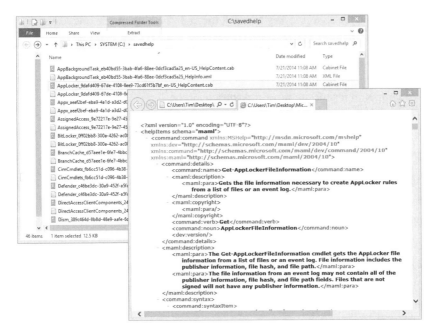

FIGURE 3.4
Saved Windows PowerShell help files aren't much to look at, but they can be useful in secure network environments.

You now go to the offline system and run Update-Help, but this time, specify the location of those previously saved help files:

```
Update-Help -SourcePath \\server1\savedhelp
```

Understanding Windows PowerShell Help Syntax

As I've said before, running **Get-Help** or Help along with a cmdlet name gives you the "standard" help output. However, I suggest that you add the **Full** parameter to retrieve the entire contents of the help file. Try this:

```
Get-Help Get-Eventlog -Full
```

A full Windows PowerShell help entry is broken down into the following parts:

▶ **Name:** The name of the cmdlet. So far, so good.

▶ **Synopsis:** A one-sentence description of what the cmdlet does.

- ▶ **Syntax:** Lists the parameter sets associated with the cmdlet. You'll learn about parameter sets momentarily.

- ▶ **Aliases:** Lists any built-in aliases for this cmdlet, if present.

- ▶ **Description:** A more comprehensive explanation of the cmdlet's functionality.

- ▶ **Parameters:** A blow-by-blow listing of each parameter along with its relevant metadata.

- ▶ **Inputs:** Whether this cmdlet can accept input from another cmdlet appearing earlier in the pipeline.

- ▶ **Outputs:** The data type that this cmdlet puts out of the Windows PowerShell pipeline.

- ▶ **Notes:** Miscellaneous information that didn't fit into any of the previous sections of the help document.

- ▶ **Examples:** One or more real-world use cases of the cmdlet in question.

As nice as all this information is, in my experience I'm most interested in quickly seeing the examples so that I can learn how to actually use a given cmdlet. We can "short-circuit" Windows PowerShell help into displaying only the examples thusly:

```
Get-Help Get-EventLog -Example
```

Defining Parameter Sets

The toughest part of comprehending Windows PowerShell help articles is figuring out what the heck *parameter sets* are and how the syntax works.

Here's the deal: Oftentimes, a cmdlet can be used in two or more fundamentally different ways. Take the Get-EventLog cmdlet, for example. The Syntax portion of its help file looks like the following:

```
SYNTAX
    Get-EventLog [-LogName] <String> [[-InstanceId] <Int64[]>] [-After
    <DateTime>] [-AsBaseObject] [-Before <DateTime>] [-ComputerName
    <String[]>] [-EntryType <String[]>] [-Index <Int32[]>] [-Message <String>]
    [-Newest <Int32>] [-Source <String[]>] [-UserName <String[]>]
    [<CommonParameters>]

    Get-EventLog [-AsString] [-ComputerName <String[]>] [-List]
    [<CommonParameters>]
```

These are two parameter sets. The first one, which obviously contains far more parameters than the second, is used to delve into particular event logs on one or more computers.

The second, shorter, parameter set is used to simply retrieve a list of available event logs on one or more systems.

You can tell if a parameter accepts multiple values by looking for a nested set of square brackets within the datatype. For instance, many cmdlets include a –ComputerName parameter whose data type is listed as <String[]>. The inner square brackets represent an array of values.

Also, when the parameter name and its data type are not themselves enclosed within a single set of square brackets, then this is a required parameter. In the first parameter set for Get-EventLog, you have to provide a value for –LogName or PowerShell will stop in its tracks and prompt you for that value.

CAUTION

Do Not "Mix and Match" Parameter Sets

The thing to remember about parameter sets is that parameters within each cannot—I repeat, cannot—be "mixed and matched." For instance, if you run the following:

```
Get-EventLog –LogName Security –List
```

you'll get an error because the **LogName** and **List** parameters belong to separate parameter sets.

More Information About Parameters

Speaking of cmdlet parameters, the best way to learn about them in my humble opinion isn't so much trying to comprehend the syntax in the parameter sets as it is running **Get-Help** with the **–Full** option.

If you do that and browse the help article's Parameters section, you'll see the following bits of metadata concerning each parameter (this is what's called the attribute table):

▶ **Data Type:** This determines the type of data (string, integer, and so on) that is allowed to be given as a parameter value.

▶ **Required:** This determines whether the parameter is required or optional when used within a parameter set.

▶ **Position:** This determines whether you can pass in a parameter value based on its position in your cmdlet syntax; in this case, you don't need to specify the parameter name.

▶ **Default Value:** This determines what, if anything, Windows PowerShell fills in as a default parameter value if you don't specify it yourself.

▶ **Accept Pipeline Input:** This determines whether you can pass data from another cmdlet into this one.

▶ **Accept Wildcard Characters:** This determines whether you can use the asterisk (*) and other wildcard characters with the parameter.

NOTE

But How Do I Know What the Cmdlet Is Called?

All this talk of how to get cmdlet help is great, but you need to know the cmdlet name to get the help, right? Yes and no. In the next hour, you'll spend a lot of time learning the easiest and most efficient ways to discover the cmdlets you need to accomplish your goals.

In the meantime, if you don't know the specific name of the cmdlet you need help on, try using wildcards. Remember that the asterisk (*) wildcard has been around for a long time in Windows; the symbol represents any number of unknown characters. Try the following Windows PowerShell statements to get a feel for how to find cmdlet help files when you don't remember the specific cmdlet name:

```
Get-Help *process*
Get-Help *printer*
Get-Help *help*
Get-Help Get-*
```

Let's use Get-EventLog again as a way to understand required and positional parameters. First, notice that the first parameter set in Get-EventLog help looks like this:

```
[-LogName] <String>
```

Confusing, I know. As I stated briefly earlier, the fact that the parameter and data type coupling isn't itself surrounded by square brackets means that this is a required parameter. For instance, try running the following:

```
Get-EventLog
```

You'll be prompted for input at pipeline position 1, won't you? That's because, at least in this particular parameter set, Get-EventLog requires the name of a particular log to view.

Now, try this command instead:

```
Get-EventLog Application
```

Did it work? Yes, it did. This is because **LogName** is a positional parameter. In the parameter set syntax, positional parameters have the parameter name enclosed in square brackets. (I told you that it is, generally speaking, easier to understand parameters by reading the Full help.)

TIP

Use Named Parameters

My strong suggestion to you is to use named parameters (which is to say, the parameter name and its value) instead of positional parameters. When you explicitly declare your parameter names, you can put them in any order you want. For instance:

```
Get-EventLog -Newest 3 -LogName Security
```

The previous example didn't "blow up" even though we already established that **LogName** is a positional parameter in position 1. You don't have to worry about getting your parameter values in the right order when you name them. In time, after you've mastered the parameters of a cmdlet, you can do stuff like this:

```
Get-EventLog Application -Newest 10
```

You'll be able to do this because you'll understand precisely *why* you're running the cmdlet in that way.

▼ TRY IT YOURSELF

Investigating Windows PowerShell Help

In this Try It Yourself exercise, you'll practice using Windows PowerShell help and begin to let some of the concepts and procedures I've been teaching you sink in. Work through the following steps to complete the exercise.

1. If you haven't already done so, fire up an elevated Windows PowerShell console session. Remember that if the window title bar doesn't say Administrator, you aren't in an elevated session.

2. Make sure that you've downloaded the latest and greatest Windows PowerShell help files from the Microsoft servers:

   ```
   Update-Help -Force
   ```

3. Let's start by looking up help articles that have something to do with system processes:

   ```
   Get-Help process
   ```

   In Hour 4, "Finding and Discovering Windows PowerShell Commands," you'll learn all about discovering cmdlets. One way to do that, actually, is to run **Get-Help** along with a keyword, as we just did here. The reason this works is that Microsoft supplies a help article for every cmdlet that they ship in the product. In case you aren't in front of your computer right now, Figure 3.5 shows you this output.

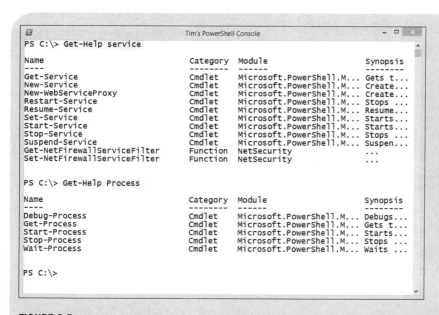

```
                              Tim's PowerShell Console            -  □   x
PS C:\> Get-Help service

Name                        Category  Module                    Synopsis
----                        --------  ------                    --------
Get-Service                 Cmdlet    Microsoft.PowerShell.M... Gets t...
New-Service                 Cmdlet    Microsoft.PowerShell.M... Create...
New-WebServiceProxy         Cmdlet    Microsoft.PowerShell.M... Create...
Restart-Service             Cmdlet    Microsoft.PowerShell.M... Stops ...
Resume-Service              Cmdlet    Microsoft.PowerShell.M... Resume...
Set-Service                 Cmdlet    Microsoft.PowerShell.M... Starts...
Start-Service               Cmdlet    Microsoft.PowerShell.M... Starts...
Stop-Service                Cmdlet    Microsoft.PowerShell.M... Stops ...
Suspend-Service             Cmdlet    Microsoft.PowerShell.M... Suspen...
Get-NetFirewallServiceFilter Function NetSecurity               ...
Set-NetFirewallServiceFilter Function NetSecurity               ...


PS C:\> Get-Help Process

Name                        Category  Module                    Synopsis
----                        --------  ------                    --------
Debug-Process               Cmdlet    Microsoft.PowerShell.M... Debugs...
Get-Process                 Cmdlet    Microsoft.PowerShell.M... Gets t...
Start-Process               Cmdlet    Microsoft.PowerShell.M... Starts...
Stop-Process                Cmdlet    Microsoft.PowerShell.M... Stops ...
Wait-Process                Cmdlet    Microsoft.PowerShell.M... Waits ...


PS C:\>
```

FIGURE 3.5
You can use Get-Help to discover cmdlets if you don't remember their exact names.

4. Let's do page-at-a-time help. You can press spacebar to page through the document, or you can press Ctrl+C to bail out of the help pages.

```
Help Get-Process
```

5. How many parameter sets do you see for Get-Process? If you're running Windows PowerShell v5, like I am, you should see a whopping six different parameter sets.

6. Now let's try something new. Type **Get-Help Get-Process**, a hyphen, and then press **Tab**:

```
Get-Help Get-Process -<tab>
```

Keep pressing **Tab**. This is one of the best Windows PowerShell shortcuts in existence, let me tell you. You can use Tab to cycle through parameters! Not only does this help you find the parameter you need quickly and easily, but it also helps you minimize (or avoid) typing errors. Press **Tab** until you hit Examples, and then press **Enter**.

```
Get-Help Get-Process -Example
```

7. If you study the **Get-Process** parameter sets, you'll see that you can look up services by name or by ID. Try the following:

```
Get-Process -Name powershell -fileversioninfo
```

8. Observe that in the previous example we added the **fileversioninfo** switch parameter to add some variety. Run the Get-Process statement again, this time without the fileversioninfo flag, and make a note of the process ID given. You can then look up this process by its ID value:

```
Get-Process -Id <idvalue>
```

Accessing Additional Command Help

I'll bet you $20 to a stale jelly donut that you had no idea that the Windows PowerShell help system was so comprehensive. And we're not even finished with it!

Windows v3 brought forward some excellent advances to the command help functionality. Let's take a closer look at the following useful help extensions:

▶ The "About" files

▶ The –**ShowWindow** parameter

▶ The **Show-Command** cmdlet

The "About" File Library

Windows PowerShell has its own collection of conceptual help files; these documents are affectionately called About help files. Run the following statement to retrieve a list of all of them:

```
Get-Help about_*
```

Yes, that's an underscore (_) between "about" and the rest of the article title. To load up one of the files, you can leverage your newfound skills with the Windows PowerShell help system. For example, let's read the documentation on using aliases in Windows PowerShell:

```
Get-Help about_Aliases
```

NOTE

Study Conceptual Help System

I cannot stress enough how informative this conceptual help system is. Invest time in studying this documentation; doing so will pay off huge dividends as you gain more expertise with Windows PowerShell. Look at Figure 3.6 to get an idea on how you can export the list of About help topics to a text file.

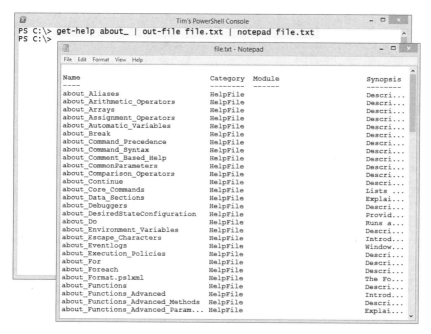

FIGURE 3.6
By leveraging the Windows PowerShell pipeline and the Out-File cmdlet, you can easily export a list of About help files to a text file for easy reference. Remember that Windows PowerShell is not case sensitive, so Get-Help, GET-HELP, and get-help are all functionally equivalent.

The –ShowWindow Parameter

ShowWindow is an optional parameter of Get-Help that makes it worlds easier to parse the help file syntax while you work.

Suppose, for example, that you need to learn how to find and stop a Windows service by using Windows PowerShell. When you run **Get-Help Stop-Service**, you find it awkward (at the least) to try commands out "ping-ponging" between the help and your console session.

Instead, try this:

```
Get-Help Stop-Service -ShowWindow
```

Figure 3.7 shows the output. The window that appears gives you the full help article in an uncluttered, easy-to-use format that won't interfere with what you're doing with the Windows PowerShell console.

FIGURE 3.7
The **ShowWindow** parameter forces help topics into a separate window. If you have a two-monitor setup, you'll be sitting in the lap of luxury as you work in a live Windows PowerShell console session in your other monitor. No clutter!

The ShowWindow window has a zoom slide in the lower right that you can click to zoom the text in or out; personally, I prefer to hold down Ctrl and scrub my mouse wheel to do the same thing.

The Find box enables you to quickly jump to a particular location in the help file, and the Settings button enables you to pare down on the number of sections you see in the window.

The Show-Command Cmdlet

The super-cool **Show-Command** cmdlet is a Windows PowerShell v4 feature that displays Windows PowerShell command options in a graphical window.

To see for yourself, try this:

```
Show-Command -Name Get-EventLog
```

If you examine the help file for **Show-Command**, you'll learn that **Name** is a positional parameter. So, you could feasibly do this instead:

```
Show-Command -Name Get-EventLog
```

Take a look at Figure 3.8 and cross-reference those annotations with the following descriptions of the command window interface:

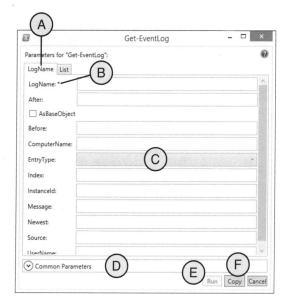

FIGURE 3.8
The Show-Command window gives you a graphical front end to using cmdlets.

▶ **A:** Parameter sets are conveniently separated into tabs.

▶ **B:** Required parameters are marked with an asterisk.

▶ **C:** Other parameters have standard graphical controls, and multivalued options are allowed.

▶ **D:** Common parameters can be added to any cmdlet and are used for debugging, code improvement, and risk mitigation.

▶ **E:** The Run button executes the cmdlet based on what you entered into the command window.

▶ **F:** The Copy button puts the cmdlet syntax into the Windows Clipboard; you can then paste into your session at your leisure.

The Show-Command window isn't exactly online help, but I thought it useful to add it to this part of the book because it gives you an opportunity to apply everything you've learned thus far about cmdlet structure and function.

▼ TRY IT YOURSELF

Taking Windows PowerShell Help to the Next Level

Let's imagine that you want to create a new alias in Windows PowerShell such that typing np will start Windows Notepad. How do you get there from here? Why not take advantage of Windows PowerShell help to give you the assistance you need at this point.

Work through the following steps to complete the exercise. You'll find the solution file, TIY-Hour02a.txt, in the book's companion files archive.

1. First of all, how can you find out which cmdlet you use to create a new alias? Try this:

   ```
   Get-Help *alias*
   ```

   This invocation of Get-Help lists the help files that Windows PowerShell has on hand for anything with alias as part of its name. Well, doggone it—there *is* a **New-Alias** cmdlet!

2. Before you drill into using the **New-Alias** cmdlet, let's take a moment to peruse the conceptual help document on aliases:

   ```
   Get-Help about_aliases -ShowWindow
   ```

3. Let's get some syntax and usage help for **New-Alias** by putting the full help document in a separate window we can display along our Windows PowerShell console window:

   ```
   Get-Help New-Alias -ShowWindow
   ```

   Pay particular attention to the **Name** and **Value** required parameters, which map to the alias name and target command, respectively.

4. Now that you have the cmdlet syntax under your belt, let's actually craft the command by using the pop-up command window:

   ```
   Show-Command New-Alias
   ```

5. Fill out the **Name** and **Value** parameters as shown in Figure 3.9. Note that you'll also select the **Confirm** switch parameter just for grins. This is a good option to specify in a Windows PowerShell command that changes data.

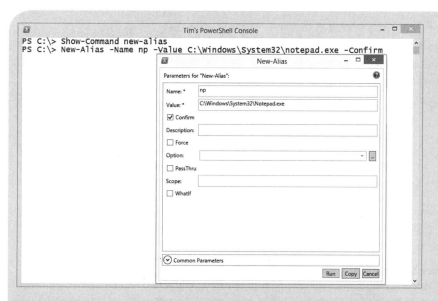

FIGURE 3.9
The Show-Command window is a great educational tool, and also helps you prevent syntax errors in your Windows PowerShell code.

Click **Copy** in the dialog box to copy your code to the Clipboard, and then click **Cancel** to close the window and return to your Windows PowerShell session.

6. Right-click inside your Windows PowerShell console to paste in the command that you saved from the Show-Window dialog box. Press **Enter** and you'll see the following confirmation output:

```
Confirm
Are you sure you want to perform this action?
Performing the operation "New Alias" on target "Name: np Value:
C:\Windows\System32\Notepad.exe".
[Y] Yes  [A] Yes to All  [N] No  [L] No to All  [S] Suspend  [?] Help
(default is "Y"):
```

Press **Enter** to accept the default response (Yes). The good news is that for the rest of your time in this particular Windows PowerShell session, you can type np to start Windows Notepad. The bad news is that your custom alias will disappear from PowerShell when you close this session. You'll learn how to make your custom aliases persistent later on in the book.

Summary

Take a deep, cleansing breath and give yourself a hearty clap on the back—you've come a long way toward becoming a competent Windows PowerShell user. The blood, sweat, and tears that you exert mastering Windows PowerShell command syntax will be immeasurably useful once you start diving into doing real work at the Windows PowerShell command line.

In the next hour, you'll take everything you learned in this hour about cmdlets and apply it to the practical question of how you can find the cmdlet you need for any administrative occasion. See you then!

Q&A

Q. I like the ShowWindow parameter. Can I use it to force other command output into an easy-to-read window?

A. Well, why don't you experiment with Windows PowerShell and try it out for yourself? Sadly, the **ShowWindow** parameter exists only as a parameter of Get-Help. That said, you can redirect Windows PowerShell command output to a variety of formats. For instance, try this:

```
Get-Service | ConvertTo-HTML | Out-File -FilePath "getservice.html"
```

You'll find the getservice.html Web page in your current working directory. Open the file in your favorite Web browser and examine the results!

Q. Can you tell me more about the "common parameters" that are part of every Windows PowerShell cmdlet?

A. Sure. Here are the common parameters that are included in Windows PowerShell v5:

▶ **Debug:** Displays programmer-level detailed information about the actions performed by the command

▶ **ErrorAction:** Specifies how the cmdlet should respond to a non-fatal execution error

▶ **ErrorVariable:** Stores error messages in a variable

▶ **OutVariable:** Stores output objects in a variable

▶ **OutBuffer:** Accumulates a certain number of objects in the buffer before forwarding them to the next command in the pipeline

▶ **PipelineVariable:** Stores the value of the current pipeline element in a variable

▶ **Verbose:** Displays administrator-level detailed information about the actions performed by the command

▶ **WarningAction:** Determines how the cmdlet responds to a warning

▶ **WarningVariable:** Stores warning data in a variable

▶ **WhatIf:** Describes the effect of a command instead of actually executing it

▶ **Confirm:** Prompts the user for confirmation before running the command

Remember to study the internal conceptual help for the common parameters:

```
Help about_CommonParameters –ShowWindow
```

Once you reach the point of writing your own Windows PowerShell scripts and modules, you'll want to take advantage of the common parameters to give your users a better experience with your code.

Q. You said that help is not an alias of Get-Help, but a function. How can I see what the help function actually does under the hood?

A. Great question. Run the following command to take a peek at the source code that underlies the Help function:

```
(Get-Command Help).Definition
```

You'll learn all about the Get-Command cmdlet in the next hour. In this code, **definition** represents a property of the **Help** object. If you scroll to the last line of the code output (which probably looks like so much gibberish to you at this point), you'll see this:

```
Get-Help @PSBoundParameters | more
```

Basically, what that code says is, "Run Get-Help feeding in whatever parameter the user supplies, and pipe the output to 'more.'"

Workshop

Using your burgeoning Windows PowerShell-fu and your Internet research skills, figure out a way to display a list of all help files that deal with Windows PowerShell remote management.

Quiz

1. Which of the following commands enables you to download Windows PowerShell help files from a network share location?

   a. Get-Help

   b. Update-Help

   c. Save-Help

2. Which of the following commands would a Linux systems administrator be most likely to try when calling the help file for a Windows PowerShell cmdlet?

   a. man

   b. help

   c. Get-Help

3. The use of parameter sets is optional in Windows PowerShell.

   a. True

   b. False

Answers

1. The correct answer is B. You'd use **Save-Help** to download the Windows PowerShell help files from the Internet, and then put the files on a network share. Then, you'd run **Update-Help**, specifying the **SourcePath** parameter to download the offline help files to the local system.

2. The correct answer is A. All else being equal, a Linux systems administrator would probably choose **man** (short for *manual*), because this is the way to obtain command help on UNIX and Linux systems. As you know, **man** is an alias for **Get-Help**, and is one example among many of the care that the Windows PowerShell team took in making Windows PowerShell as shell- and environment-agnostic as possible.

3. The correct answer is B. Parameter sets describe the ways that a Windows PowerShell cmdlet can be applied. You must use the parameters specified in a single parameter set when you use a Windows PowerShell command.

HOUR 4

Finding and Discovering Windows PowerShell Commands

What You'll Learn in This Hour:

▶ How Windows PowerShell commands are packaged

▶ Locating Windows PowerShell commands

▶ Running external commands

Having emerged from the preceding hour, in which you learned how to comprehend and use Windows PowerShell help, you are undoubtedly champing at the bit to discover specific Windows PowerShell commands to be productive with. By the end of this chapter, your Windows PowerShell powers will reach another level.

Your ability to locate the correct cmdlet for the job will be limited only by your imagination, or at least your ability to articulate what you need to do. For instance, do you need to install a role on one of your servers? No problem. Manage your Dynamic Host Configuration Protocol (DHCP) leases from a command line? Consider it done. Let's get to work.

How Windows PowerShell Commands Are Packaged

By now you understand what a cmdlet is. But how are cmdlets made available to your computer? Well, in two principal ways:

▶ The snap-in

▶ The module

Understanding Snap-Ins

In Windows PowerShell nomenclature, a *snap-in* is a compiled dynamic link library (DLL) that contains PowerShell commands. The potential problem with snap-ins is they must be registered (installed) on a system before use and implements cmdlets and Windows PowerShell providers.

The snap-in model was replaced with the module model in Windows PowerShell v2, but you'll find that many of the core Windows PowerShell features were written as snap-ins.

As inconvenient as they are for us, PowerShell "end users," snap-ins make a lot of sense when your PowerShell commands reach deeply to the nether regions of the .NET Framework. Because snap-ins represent compiled code, they run faster than do modules, which are basically just plain text script files.

To see what snap-ins you have registered on your system, open an elevated Windows PowerShell console session and issue the following command:

```
Get-PSSnapin -Registered
```

You can leave out the **registered** parameter to see available snap-ins. However, you can add a registered snap-in to your current Windows PowerShell session by using **Add-PSSnapin**. For instance, the following statement loads the Microsoft SharePoint Server 2013 snap-in:

```
Add-PSSnapin –Name Microsoft.SharePoint.PowerShell
```

For completeness, I'll let you know that the **Remove-PSSnapin** cmdlet is used to remove a snap-in from your session. Remember, though, that each Windows PowerShell console session is an island unto itself in terms of loaded snap-ins or modules. Specifically, each PowerShell session represents a runspace that serves as host to any loaded modules, defined variables, aliases, and so forth. Unless you've saved those artifacts elsewhere, they all disappear from the runspace as soon as you close that session.

Consequently, you'll need to include the **Add-PSSnapin** statement to your profile script in order to autoload the snap-in to new Windows PowerShell console sessions.

Understanding Modules

Starting in Windows PowerShell v2, the module is the preferred way to package Windows PowerShell cmdlets and providers.

NOTE

Because this book is IT pro and not developer-centric, we don't need to delve into the details concerning modules other than saying that they are, in general, easier to use and manage than snap-ins. For one thing, we don't have to register any DLLs (at least not directly; some modules do register DLLS in the background during module load). In point of fact, you can simply drag and drop a module file to your computer to start using its enclosed commands.

To retrieve a list of modules that are available on your system, run the **Get-Module** cmdlet, specifying the **ListAvailable** parameter:

```
Get-Module -ListAvailable
```

Where Does Windows PowerShell Find Modules?

You might wonder how Windows PowerShell "knows" which modules have been loaded onto a particular computer. As it happens, a Windows PowerShell-provided environment variable named **$PSModulePath** stores the default search locations for modules. From a Windows PowerShell console session, run the following command:

```
$env:PSModulePath
```

As long as your module exists in one of those directory paths, you'll have seamless access to that functionality. And yes, you can in fact add your own entries to the **$PSModulePath** environment variable. You'll learn how to do that later on in the book. Be patient!

You'll find that your installed module list on a server grows as you add new roles, features, and additional software. For instance, promoting a Windows Server computer to an Active Directory Domain Services (AD DS) domain controller gives you the ActiveDirectory module. Installing SQL Server 2012 provides you with SQL Server Windows PowerShell functionality. And so on.

Working with Windows PowerShell Modules

Our next concern is learning how to tap into the modules that we have available on our system. Prior to Windows PowerShell v3, you had to manually import a module before its functionality became available to you.

For instance, suppose that you wanted to install a server role on a Windows Server 2008 R2 domain controller. After starting an elevated Windows PowerShell console session, you'd need to load the Server Manager module:

```
Import-Module -Name ServerManager
```

Of course, the first question is how did we know that the Server Manager module was called ServerManager and not something else? For now, just take comfort in the fact that as long as you're running Windows PowerShell v3 or later, modules are autoloaded for you whenever you reference a command contained in that module, and the module is stored in a PSModulePath location.

To test out module autoloading, let's first verify that we don't have the Server Manager module loaded into our session:

```
Get-Module
```

Good. Now we need to find the command to install a new Windows feature by invoking **Get-Help** or **Get-Command** along with the –Name parameter and the asterisk (*) wildcard character:

```
Get-Help -Name *feature*
Get-Command -Name *feature*
```

As you can see in Figure 4.1, the cmdlet we need to install a Windows feature is **Install-WindowsFeature**. Okay, let's run help on that:

```
Get-Help InstallWindowsFeature –ShowWindow
```

Recall that the –ShowWindow parameter of Get-Help pops the help file into a separate window for easier browsing. It's an optional parameter, but one that I use all the time during command discovery.

Try another run of Get-Module and what do you see? That's right—the Server Manager module has been loaded into your session, and you have full access to all the commands that the module exposes. Note that some modules include additional commands that you don't see because your user account has no privilege to them.

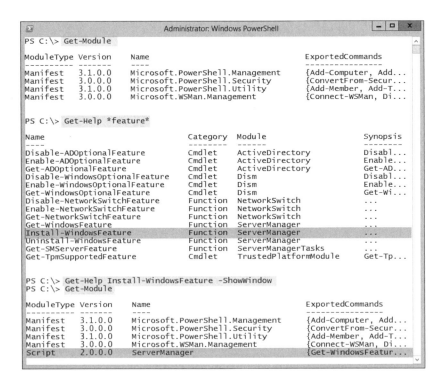

FIGURE 4.1
Module autoloading means that we can access Windows PowerShell commands without the administrative burden of having to remember to import specific modules. What you're seeing here is that we start out without the Server Manager module loaded into our session. Then, once we retrieve help concerning one of the Server Manager cmdlets, Windows PowerShell autoloads the entire Server Manager module for us.

How many commands are contained in the ServerManager module? Why not pipe the **Get-Module** results into the **Measure-Object** cmdlet?

```
Get-Module –Name ServerManager | Measure-Object
```

Measure-Object is an excellent tool to have in your belt. Whenever you need to perform a count, it's there for you. Measure-Object can also give you sums, minimum values, and maximum values—read the help file for yourself and get comfortable with its parameters.

On my Windows Server 2012 R2 system, I show seven commands. Pretty light! However, try the following on one of your domain controllers:

```
Get-Module -Name ActiveDirectory | Measure-Object
```

Hmm. I have 147 commands. How about the total number of commands from all available modules and snap-ins? By the way, the semicolon in the next command statement is called a continuation character. Here the semicolon allows us to run more than one command in the same segment of the PowerShell pipeline:

```
Get-Module -ListAvailable | Import-Module ; Get-Command -CommandType cmdlet |
Measure-Object
```

Wow. I see 665, and mine is a "vanilla" Windows Server 2012 R2 domain controller with no additional features or software installed. The theme here is that we will probably never master the identification and usage of even the majority of Windows PowerShell commands.

Installing RSAT Tools on Windows 8.1

The general best practice advice for Windows PowerShell administration is that you should be performing most of your work not directly on your servers, but instead on your administrative workstation.

By leveraging the Remote Server Administration Tools (RSAT) and Windows PowerShell remoting, you can do most or all of your work directly from your Windows 8.1 domain-joined workstation.

Now before you say, "Tim, what are you doing? This is a PowerShell book, not a Windows book!" let me explain. Besides giving us the GUI administration tools, the RSAT also gives us the associated PowerShell modules that comprise the various and sundry Windows Server roles and features.

Thus, you need the RSAT in order to access these server modules...understood?

What Is the RSAT?

The Remote Server Administration Tools (RSAT, pronounced *ARE-sat*) is an optional download for Windows client operating systems that gives you the graphical user interface (GUI) management tools and associated Windows PowerShell modules for Windows Server roles and services.

The gotcha is that there exist several RSAT packs, and you need to make sure you're download-ing and installing the correct one. For instance:

- **RSAT for Windows 7 SP1:** You can manage Windows Server 2008 R2, Windows Server 2008, and Windows Server 2003 servers from Windows 7 SP1. No Windows Server 2012 or Windows 8 allowed.

- **RSAT for Windows 8:** You can manage Windows Server 2012 computers from Windows 8. No Windows Server 2012 R2 or Windows 8.1 supported here.

- **RSAT for Windows 8.1:** You can manage Windows Server 2012 or Windows Server 2012 R2 servers from a Windows 8.1 (not Windows 8 RTM) workstation.

Before we go any further I want to put in a plug for PowerShell remoting, which we'll learn all about later. With remoting you connect directly to your servers and run commands remotely on those boxes, obviating the necessity of the RSAT toolkit.

▼ TRY IT YOURSELF

Installing the RSAT Tools

In this Try It Yourself exercise, you'll download and install the Remote Server Administration Tools for Windows 8.1. This will allow you to access Windows PowerShell commands to manage Windows Server 2012 R2 server systems. Follow these steps to complete the exercise.

1. Run a search engine query for **download RSAT Windows 8.1** to locate the proper download page. I would give you a direct URL, but Microsoft has the bad habit of changing their Web page addresses on a regular basis.

2. On the RSAT download page, click **Download**. Select either the 64-bit (x64) or 32-bit (x86) .msu Microsoft Update standalone installation package, as appropriate, and click **Next**.

3. After the file has been downloaded to your Windows 8.1 system, double-click the .msu file and follow the prompts to install the tools. You'll be prompted to restart your computer once the installation completes.

4. After your reboot, make sure you log in to your Windows 8.1 computer with domain admin-istrative privileges. You can customize the RSAT tools and associated Windows PowerShell modules that are loaded on your system by opening the Programs and Features Control Panel, clicking **Turn Windows Features On or Off**, and browsing to the Remote Server Administration Tools entry, as shown in Figure 4.2.

5. Pop open an elevated Windows PowerShell console session and run the following:

```
Get-Module -ListAvailable
```

You'll see several server-related module entries, depending on the RSAT tools enabled in Control Panel.

6. Windows Server 2012 R2 has Windows PowerShell remoting enabled by default. So, for instance, you can run the following command to enumerate all Active Directory user accounts on your domain controllers:

```
Get-ADUser -Filter *
```

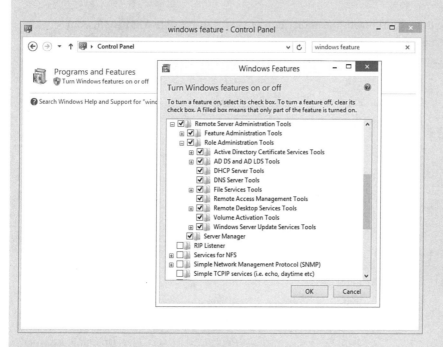

FIGURE 4.2
In Windows 8.1, you can disable unnecessary RSAT tools (and their associated modules) through the Control Panel interface.

Locating Windows PowerShell Commands

Alrighty then! It's time for us to move to the main event of this hour of training: specifically how we can discover the cmdlets we need to accomplish our Windows systems administration tasks. Good stuff here—fasten your seat belts.

Verbs and Nouns, Revisited

Recall that Windows PowerShell cmdlets have the standard syntax:

```
ApprovedVerb-PrefixSingularNoun
```

The Windows PowerShell team actually standardized the "legal" verbs in the Windows PowerShell language to make it easy for us administrators to correctly guess command names. Retrieve a list of approved verbs by running the following command sequence, which first gathers all the verbs, and then sorts them alphabetically by verb name:

```
Get-Verb | Sort-Object Verb
```

Because I believe that your knowing as many of these verbs as possible will benefit your Windows PowerShell skills greatly in the long run, I'd like to give you the list here in this book. These verbs are current as of Windows 8.1:

Add	Exit	Pop	Skip
Approve	Expand	Protect	Split
Assert	Export	Publish	Start
Backup	Find	Push	Step
Block	Format	Read	Stop
Checkpoint	Get	Receive	Submit
Clear	Grant	Redo	Suspend
Close	Group	Register	Switch
Compare	Hide	Remove	Sync
Complete	Import	Rename	Test
Compress	Initialize	Repair	Trace
Confirm	Install	Request	Unblock
Connect	Invoke	Reset	Undo
Convert	Join	Resize	Uninstall
ConvertFrom	Limit	Resolve	Unlock
ConvertTo	Lock	Restart	Unprotect
Copy	Measure	Restore	Unpublish
Debug	Merge	Resume	Unregister
Deny	Mount	Revoke	Update
Disable	Move	Save	Use
Disconnect	New	Search	Wait
Dismount	Open	Select	Watch
Edit	Optimize	Send	Write
Enable	Out	Set	
Enter	Ping	Show	

You can count up the approved verbs easily enough; there are 98 on my Windows 8.1 system:

```
Get-Verb | Measure-Object
```

Where Did the Verb-Noun Syntax Come From?

Jeffrey Snover and the Windows PowerShell team took some of the best parts of the UNIX/Linux command shells when they developed Windows PowerShell. But what about the verb-noun command format?

As it happens, the PowerShell team "borrowed" that command format from the DIGITAL Command Language (DCL), the super old-school command language used on OpenVMS-based mainframe/mini-computer systems. According to Snover, the verb-noun format works better than noun-verb because the former is skewed more toward IT administrators than programmers. After all, systems administrators tend to think of action first, while programmers tend to think of objects (nouns), and then actions (methods) afterward.

TIP

I'm sure I said this before, but it bears repeating: Windows PowerShell commands and parameters are *not* case sensitive. Therefore, you don't have to waste time capitalizing. In fact, the only reason I do use capitalization for you in this book is to improve readability. While we're on the subject, you should make use of tab completion and Intellisense in the Windows PowerShell ISE; you'll find that your cmdlet and attribute references are "automagically" capitalized.

Getting Familiar with Get-Command

The **Get-Command** cmdlet, which also can be referenced with the alias **gcm**, is our best friend in terms of Windows PowerShell command discovery. If you're looking for a list of all aliases, by the way, try Get-Alias. Onward, then...

Suppose, for instance, that you want to use Windows PowerShell to manage services on your Windows 8.1 system. Let's try:

```
Get-Command service
```

That didn't help, did it? That's right. Equally important to **Get-Command** in your cmdlet discovery efforts is liberal use of the asterisk (*) wildcard character. (Incidentally, the "star" character is pronounced *ASTER-isk*, not *ASTRICK* or some other verbal abomination. Database administrators also call the asterisk *splat* because the shape is reminiscent of a bug splatted on your window.)

Okay, let's try the command again, this time padded with asterisks and using the command gcm alias for Get-Service:

```
gcm *service*
```

Aha! Now we're cooking with gas. Parsing the results brings us to **Get-Service**, which we can then bring into action to discover more commands. For instance, what if we wanted to manage the Remote Registry service? We could do the following:

```
Get-Service
```

Then parse the results list for the appropriate entry. But why do that when we know that the Remote Registry service has the word *registry* in it? Try this instead:

```
Get-Service *registry*
```

Good deal. Figure 4.3 shows you what all this output looks like, by the way.

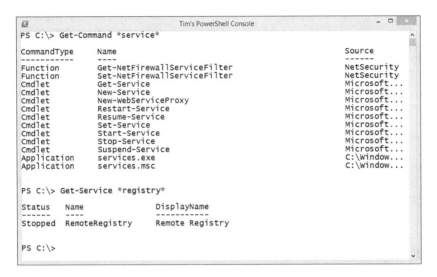

FIGURE 4.3
The Get verb, the Get-Command cmdlet in particular, and the asterisk wildcard represent your Windows PowerShell command discovery toolset.

TIP

Incidentally, I suggest you be cautious with "wrapping" your keywords with asterisks because you don't know, in most cases, if other characters appear before or after your keyword. For example, the following command won't give you your expected results:

```
Get-Service registry*
```

Using asterisk wildcards for command searches is okay when you truly don't know the full name of a PowerShell object, but if you know the name, type it. You consume extra system resources when you (over)use the asterisk in filtering operations.

So far, so good? Now let's interrogate particular Windows PowerShell modules for commands. For instance, let's see what functionality is available in the ActiveDirectory module on a Windows Server 2012 R2 domain controller:

```
Get-Command -Module ActiveDirectory
```

How did I know that Get-Command had a **Module** parameter? Well, you should know the answer to that question, my friend!

```
Get-Help Get-Command
```

What you'll notice when you examine the Active Directory cmdlets is that the noun portion is prefixed with AD. In Windows PowerShell, the noun prefixes accomplish two goals:

- ▶ They identify their parent module. (AD stands for Active Directory.)

- ▶ They prevent name collisions. (Two modules both may have a **New-User** cmdlet, but only Active Directory has **New-ADUser**.)

If you know the cmdlet prefix, you can run **Get-Command** along with the **Noun** parameter. Check this out:

```
Get-Command -Noun AD*
```

The preceding command easily rounds up all the Active Directory cmdlets without our having to know the name of the parent module. A good practical example of this is the SharePoint 2013 PowerShell snap-in, which has the funky name Microsoft.SharePoint.PowerShell. Because all the SharePoint commands have the prefix SP, it's a lot easier to run this to gather up all the SharePoint commands. The gcm alias for Get-Command saves us some typing as well:

```
gcm -Noun SP*
```

What if you want a list of all the **Get** commands that pertain to Windows PowerShell?

```
Get-Command -Verb Get* -Noun PS*
```

Differentiating Get-Command and Get-Help

At first blush, the command discovery capabilities of **Get-Command** may seem strikingly similar to those of **Get-Help**, which you learned how to use in a previous chapter. Well, yes and no.

Here's the deal: **Get-Help** retrieves help articles for commands, whereas **Get-Command** selects the commands themselves. To be sure, the results of the following commands look pretty similar at first:

```
Get-Command *service*
Get-Help *service*
```

In other words, if you need to find a command that allows you to stop a service, either **Get-Command** or **Get-Help** leads you to **Stop-Service**. That said, remember that Windows PowerShell works in a schema called the pipeline, and the results of a cmdlet execution are one or more objects, not simply blocks of text like we see in UNIX/Linux.

Here's the summary statement: Get-Command gives general metadata about a command, whereas Get-Help retrieves the help file and all the useful information contained therein. To demonstrate the difference, run the following two commands one after the other and compare their very different output:

```
Get-Command -Name Get-Process
Get-Help -Name Get-Process
```

▼ TRY IT YOURSELF

Discovering Windows PowerShell Commands

This Try It Yourself exercise will give you a chance to experiment with discovering Windows PowerShell commands in a safe environment. Specifically, you'll discover ways to manage system processes by using Windows PowerShell.

Perform the following steps in an elevated Windows PowerShell console to complete the practice session.

1. Start by learning which Windows PowerShell commands deal with processes:

   ```
   Get-Command *process*
   ```

   Of course! You could have guessed that **Get-Process** gives you a list of all running processes on your computer. Are you getting the hang of this Windows PowerShell thing, yet?

2. I wonder whether any aliases exist for **Get-Process**? Of course you can (and should) read the help file that includes this information. However, you can also try these commands (do them in order):

   ```
   cd alias:
   dir | Where-Object { $_.Definition -eq "Get-Process" }
   ```

   What the heck is going on here? Figure 4.4 shows the output for this. The first command shifts our context to the Alias PSDrive, which makes all available command aliases available to us in much the same way that a file system makes directories and files available to us. Don't worry; you'll learn all about PowerShell providers and PSDrives in the next hour.

   The second line of code uses the Dir alias (which actually references **Get-ChildItem**), filtering the output to show all aliases that are mapped to **Get-Process**. Pretty neat, isn't it?

   The ps alias is poignant because ps is the name of the equivalent command on UNIX/ Linux systems.

3. Get a run of all processes on your system (make sure to try the ps alias as well):

   ```
   Get-Process
   ```

   That's a lot of information! Here are the default data columns that are returned by **Get-Process**:

- ▸ **Handles:** The number of memory handles opened by the process
- ▸ **NPM(K):** The amount of nonpaged memory, given in kilobytes
- ▸ **PM(K):** The amount of paged memory, given in kilobytes
- ▸ **WS(K):** The working set, given in kilobytes
- ▸ **VM(K):** The amount of virtual memory used by the process
- ▸ **CPU(s):** The amount of processor time consumed by the process
- ▸ **ID(K):** The process ID (PID) of the process
- ▸ **ProcessName:** The name of the process

4. It's most helpful for me to see processes organized by a metric in descending order. For instance, let's view all processes by decreasing CPU; we can also choose the properties we want to see, as well as retrieve the "top" 10 entries:

```
Get-Process | Select-Object ProcessName, CPU -First 10 | Sort-Object CPU
➥-Descending
```

If the preceding pipeline looks complex, let me break it down into its three constituent components:

- ▸ First, we get a list of all processes running on the system.
- ▸ Second, we filter out the first 10 processes, bringing along only two properties: ProcessName and CPU. When we learn how to use Get-Member a bit later in this book, you'll learn that sometimes the label of a property isn't the same as it's name, but take this information at face value for now.
- ▸ Third, we perform a descending sort on the CPU property.

Remember that the Windows PowerShell help system is our friend:

```
Get-Help Get-Process -Examples
Get-Help Select-Object -Examples
Get-Help Sort-Object -Examples
```

5. Open an instance of Windows Notepad:

```
notepad
```

Next, look up the process properties for Notepad:

```
Get-Process -Name *notepad*
```

6. The easiest way to investigate the properties (data attributes) of a Windows PowerShell object is to pipe the cmdlet into **Get-Member:**

```
Get-Process -Name *notepad* | Get-Member | more
```

7. If you carefully read this admittedly daunting list of properties, methods, events, and aliases, you'll find a method named **kill**. Gee, I wonder what effect that method has on a process.

We can capture any Windows PowerShell object into a variable. Variables are defined by using the dollar sign ($) and a unique name. You can then use what programmers call *dot notation* to invoke the **kill** method:

```
$np = Get-Process -Name Notepad
$np.kill()
```

▶ For more detailed information on how to capture any Windows PowerShell object into a variable, refer to Hour 5, "Thinking in Terms of Objects."

You should have seen the running Windows Notepad application disappear. Don't be alarmed; we killed the running process, we didn't delete the actual application.

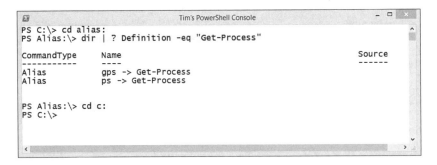

FIGURE 4.4
You can make liberal use of aliases along with PSDrives to discover which aliases are mapped to a given command. Here the question mark (?) is an alias for Where-Object, and –eq is how Windows PowerShell represents equality (=).

TIP

Don't Forget About Tab Completion

I want to underscore what a critical habit using tab completion in Windows PowerShell is. PowerShell Most Valuable Professional (MVP) Jason Helmick advises "exercising your pinkie finger" so that it will be at-the-ready to press Tab as you enter Windows PowerShell code. In Windows PowerShell v5, tab completion is supported for most everything: commands, parameters, file paths, and the like. For instance, type the following and start pressing **Tab** repeatedly:

```
Get-
```

You should find that Windows PowerShell cycles through all the **Get** commands that are available on your system. Now type **Get-Eve** and press **Tab** to complete **Get-Event**, and then press **Tab** again to complete **Get-EventLog**.

Press the spacebar, a hyphen, and then press **Tab** several more times. Now you're cycling through parameters. Type **L** and **Tab** to complete **LogName**, and then add another space and hyphen.

Pressing Tab repeatedly one final time cycles through parameter values—in this case, the event logs that are available on your computer. This is powerful stuff, my friend, and I'm sure you don't want to miss it.

Running External Commands

Although the so-called DOS command shell, Cmd.exe, has many similarities, at first blush, to the Windows PowerShell console host, they are two totally separate executable program files. Therefore, you can't expect to fire up Powershell.exe and run **ver** to get the Windows version; nor can you start Cmd.exe and type **$host.version** with success.

Nonetheless, the Windows PowerShell team understood that many of us "old dog" Cmd.exe experts will want to run our favorite compiled executable command-line tools like **ping**, **ipconfig**, and **tracert** in Windows PowerShell, and they made accommodations for us.

You'll find that you can run the following statements, with parameters and all, with 100% success in a Windows PowerShell console:

- ► `ping -a -n 2 executrain.com`

- ► `netstat /?`

- ► `ipconfig /displaydns`

- ► `net use * \\server\share`

This is a big deal, when you think about it, because Windows PowerShell has its own syntax for dealing with directory paths, parameters, and the like. The team at Microsoft put a lot of effort into replicating "old school" functionality. The idea is that if we are accustomed to using ping to test Layer 3 connectivity, we should be able to continue using the tool. By the way, Windows PowerShell includes a cmdlet that extends upon ping's functionality; it's called Test-Connection.

All this being said, there are a few "gotchas" when dealing with external commands in Windows PowerShell. Essentially, here our options in encapsulated form:

- ► External command in environment path

- ► Invoke-Item

- ► The call operator

- ► The stop parsing symbol

Let's discuss each of those options in turn.

External Command in Environment Path

As long as the external command you want to run exists in a directory that is part of your system's PATH environment variable, Windows PowerShell will execute the command as if it were a Cmd.exe session.

You can check your PATH environment variable contents by querying the environment variable PowerShell provider drive:

```
$env:path
```

This is the pathway used by Windows PowerShell when you run your favorite command-line tools; the built-in programs all exist within system directories or directories already present in your search path.

Invoke-Item

We can use the Windows PowerShell cmdlet **Invoke-Item** to run the default action on an external command or file. For instance, let's say that I have an Adobe Portable Document Format (PDF) file in my C:\pdfs directory that I want to open by using Windows PowerShell.

Because I have Adobe Reader installed on the system and that program is associated with PDF files, I can use the following Windows PowerShell statement to open the PDF directly:

```
Invoke-Item -Path "C:\pdfs\mypdfdocument.pdf"
```

TIP

Technically, I didn't need the quotation marks there because my directory path didn't contain spaces. However, I suggest that you habitually use quotes with strings in all cases to be safe.

The Call Operator

When we prefix an invocation to an external command with the ampersand (&), Windows PowerShell evaluates your statement as a command instead of as a .NET Framework object as usual.

For example, if you were to try the following method for starting Internet Explorer from a Windows PowerShell console, the statement would generate an error:

```
iexplore
```

However, if you use the invocation operator, it works. (As a general rule, remember to use spaces.)

```
& "C:\Program Files\Internet Explorer\iexplore.exe"
```

You can even experiment with passing single parameters to external commands this way; for instance, the following statement opens Internet Explorer and loads the Bing home page:

```
& "C:\Program Files\Internet Explorer\iexplore.exe" www.bing.com
```

When you want to start submitting multiple parameters to an external command, things can get hairy pretty quickly. Let's suppose that you want to start Internet Explorer with extensions disabled and open the Google home page.

You can parameterize the parameters, as it were, in the following way:

```
$ie = "C:\Program Files\Internet Explorer\iexplore.exe"
$extoff = "-extoff"
$url = "www.google.com"
```

Now when you run the command with the invocation operator, you just plug in your variables:

```
& $ie $extoff $url
```

Now, as it happens, you can pass multiple arguments to Internet Explorer without having to do the parameterization. Nonetheless, it's a good skill to have in your tool belt if and when you find yourself needing to launch a complex external command from Windows PowerShell.

The Stop Parsing Symbol

Windows PowerShell v3 introduced the "stop parsing" symbol (**--%**), which instructs the Windows PowerShell parser to stop interpreting the following input as PowerShell code.

Let's take icacls, for example. This is an old command-line utility with which we can view and modify the discretionary access control lists (DACLs) on folders and files.

The following statement grants the user Chad Modify permissions on a folder named docs; we also specify container inherit (OI) and object inherit (OI) parameters:

```
icacls .\docs /grant Chad(CI)(OI)M
```

TIP

By the way, the .\ means that the docs folder exists in my current working directory.

Anyway, as you can see in Figure 4.5, issuing icacls from within Windows PowerShell results in a lot of so-called blood on the screen. The PowerShell parser got hung up on interpreting the **CI** and **OI** parameters, specifically the parentheses.

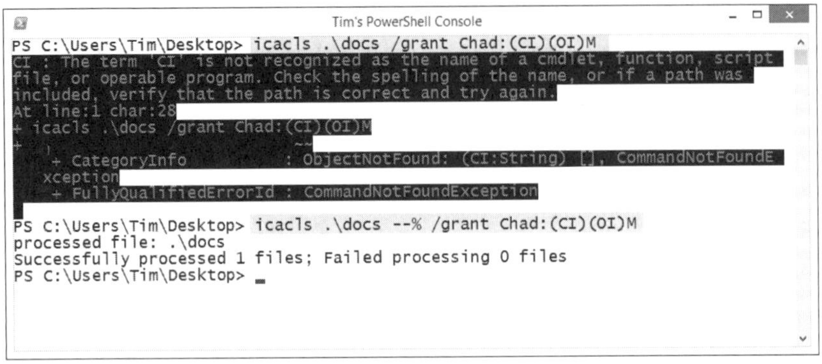

FIGURE 4.5
Windows PowerShell can get all bungled up in terms of trying to parse symbols in external commands. The stop parsing symbol comes to the rescue.

Now let's invoke the "stop parsing" command right before we issue our parameters:

```
icacls .\docs --% /grant Chad(CI)(OI)M
```

Success! By the way, you'll want to study the conceptual help document on parsing to get a deeper grasp on how Windows PowerShell comprehends your code:

```
Get-Help about_parsing -ShowWindow
```

Summary

By now I think you have a clear picture as to how Windows PowerShell commands "arrive" to your systems. We covered the difference between snap-ins and modules, and you are familiar with how Windows PowerShell v3 and later autoload modules whenever you reference individual commands within them.

You also learned how to set up your administrative workstation for Windows PowerShell management by installing the RSAT tools. This information will come to the forefront later in this book when we cover Windows PowerShell remoting.

Finally, you invested valuable time in learning how to discover Windows PowerShell commands and run external commands from within Windows PowerShell.

In the next part of this book, we'll wade into yet-deeper conceptual waters, learning all about what Windows PowerShell objects are and how the pipeline works. Great fun (and illumination!) will be had by all, I assure you.

Q&A

Q. How can I get a list of all available verbs and their relative counts? I want to see which verbs are most "popular" in Windows PowerShell.

A. Sure thing. You already have the skills necessary to answer this question, actually. Remember that we use **Get-Command** to retrieve cmdlets and **Sort-Object** to count them up. The following statement introduces the **Group-Object** cmdlet, which is useful to group objects in the Windows PowerShell pipeline:

```
Get-Command -CommandType cmdlet | Group-Object –Property Verb |
Sort-Object –Property Count -Descending
```

As you can see in Figure 4.6, the five most often used verbs in Windows PowerShell v5 are as follows:

▶ Get

▶ Set

▶ New

▶ Remove

▶ Add

And no, the irony and humor are not lost on me that the third most popular Windows PowerShell verb isn't a verb at all!

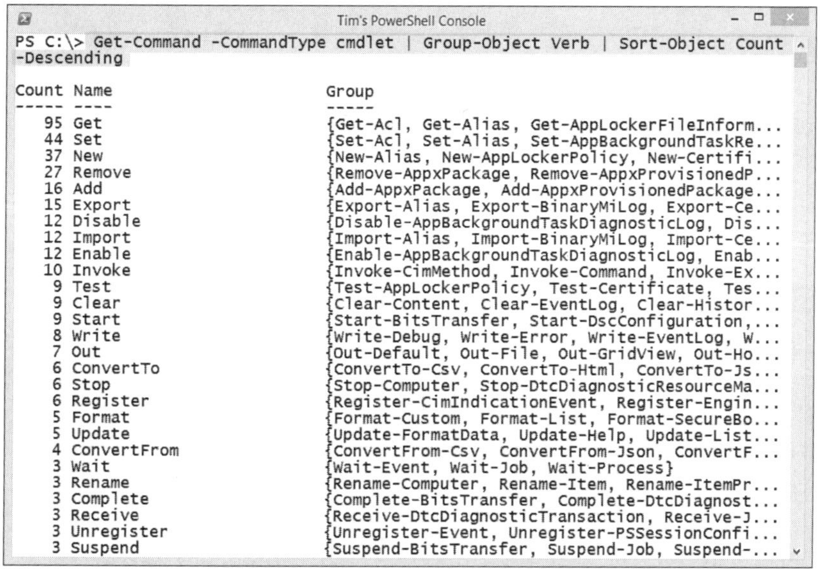

FIGURE 4.6
It should come as no surprise to you that Get is the most frequently used verb in Windows PowerShell.

Q. I know that I use Get-Command –module to retrieve cmdlets from Windows PowerShell modules. But what if I want to see commands from a snap-in instead?

A. Although Windows PowerShell prides itself on its consistency, the "snap-in thing" is an exception to that rule. Confusingly, we use **Get-Command –module** with snap-ins as well as with modules. So to retrieve all the commands resident in the SharePoint Server 2013 snap-in, we would issue the following Windows PowerShell statement. For reference, Get-Command also has a –PSSnapin parameter:

```
Get-Command -Module Microsoft.SharePoint.PowerShell
```

Q. When I'm actively searching for Windows PowerShell commands, I build up quite a command history. Can you please recap the ways that I can use to access previously used commands in a single Windows PowerShell session?

A. Sure thing! Remember that we set the command history buffer (number of buffers as well as the number of 'remembered' commands per buffer) in the Windows PowerShell console Properties pages. That said, here are your options for recalling previous commands in a session:

▶ **Up arrow:** Each tap of the key will give you a previously issued statement.

▶ **F7:** Invokes the command history buffer. Click within the window and use arrow keys to find the command you need. Press **Enter** to execute the command.

▶ **Get-History:** You can also use the alias history, and use **Clear-History** to dump all contents from the session command history buffer.

Workshop

Using your skills with Windows PowerShell command discovery and the help system, figure out a way to export a list of all stopped services on your system to a comma-separated value (CSV) file named stopped-services.csv.

Quiz

1. We use the _____ cmdlet to enumerate the properties and methods that are associated with a given Windows PowerShell object.

   a. Get-Command

   b. Get-Member

   c. Get-History

2. The Windows command prompt console and the Windows PowerShell console are located in the same directory in Windows.

   a. True

   b. False

3. The **TotalCount** parameter of the **Get-Command** cmdlet retrieves the total number of commands from a specified module.

   a. True

   b. False

Answers

1. The correct answer is B. We use **Get-Member** to enumerate, or list, the attributes (properties) and actions (methods) that are associated with a given Windows PowerShell object.

2. The correct answer is B. The PowerShell.exe executable is located in the path C:\Windows\System32\WindowsPowerShell\v1.0. The Cmd.exe executable is located in the path C:\Windows\System32. This quiz question is intended to reinforce the fact that the "DOS prompt" and the PowerShell prompt are totally separate programs.

3. The correct answer is B. Remember to read the help file! Doing so will tell you that the **TotalCount** optional parameter can be used to retrieve a specified number of commands. For instance, the following statement gives us 10 alias commands. Note that you could use the pipeline to perform filtering and sorting if you want to pull back specific aliases.

```
Get-Command -CommandType Alias -TotalCount 10
```

Thinking in Terms of Objects

What You'll Learn in This Hour:

► The problem with UNIX and Linux
► What an object is
► Discovering object members
► Putting objects into action

Let's learn about objects! One of the biggest mantras you'll hear from Windows PowerShell aficionados is this statement, "In PowerShell, everything is an object." By the conclusion of this hour, you'll understand in detail not only why the statement is absolutely true, but also how foundational the concept is to your mastering the language.

We'll begin our consideration of Windows PowerShell objects by stepping back into the time machine and examining, from a high level, how data is output and processed in UNIX/Linux operating systems. We'll then cover the necessary programming concerning "programmer stuff" like classes, objects, properties, and methods. Finally, we get to the good stuff—applying our newfound knowledge of objects to Windows PowerShell.

The Problem with UNIX/Linux

As you know by now, many of the members of the Windows PowerShell team studied UNIX and UNIX-like operating systems like Linux very closely as they architected Windows PowerShell.

I think their goal in their survey of other programming/scripting languages was to cherry-pick the best features, adapt them to Windows PowerShell, and then tweak functionality to make the features even easier to use by non-programmers.

It's certainly true that you can do some mighty powerful things with Linux. (I'll just use *Linux* from now on, but know that I'm referring to UNIX, Linux, and all *NIX variants.) By using the pipeline, which you'll learn all about in the next hour, you can do stuff like the following:

▶ Get a list of all running processes

▶ Filter the return list to show only processes that meet particular criteria

▶ Modify the filtered list to show only particular data columns

▶ Send the "massaged" process list to yet another program

That's pretty cool, isn't it? We'll do all this and more with Windows PowerShell as we continue our lessons in this book. However, what I want you to understand if you don't know this already is that Linux is a file-based operating system. This means that all items, whether they are honest-to-goodness text files or return values of a command like ps, are simply flat text. In Linux even hardware such as disk drives are represented as files in the file system. Quite a paradigm shift when we're coming from a Windows perspective, right?

What does this fact mean for the busy Linux administrator? Well, for starters, it means that all of the cool things we need to do to our aforementioned process list (searching, filtering, sorting, and so forth) requires that we pipe the output of one Linux command into another command, and so on down the (pipe)line until we have the data we need.

One of the biggest pain points with Linux and its text-object approach is that you're feeding data into completely separate programs, each of which has its own syntax and behaviors. For instance, to perform those process management tasks in my earlier example, you have to be familiar with the following Linux tools at the least:

▶ ps

▶ grep

▶ awk

▶ sed

By contrast, consider how Windows PowerShell behaves. We've already covered facts like PowerShell command syntax is entirely uniform and predictable. That's awesome.

What's just as nice is that because Windows PowerShell treats all items as objects, each with their own data types, methods, and properties, we have so much more flexibility and control over the objects' behavior and outputs than we do in Linux.

I wouldn't expect you to be bowled over with joy at this point. To be sure, you might not even know what an "object" is as it relates to computer programming in general and Windows PowerShell in particular. Let's get to that point immediately.

What Is an Object?

The Windows PowerShell documentation defines an *object* as a collection of data that represents an item. To me an object is a data structure that could very well be looked at as we examine a database table with rows and columns.

Fire up an elevated PowerShell console prompt and issue the following command:

`Get-Service`

In case you're reading this book apart from your computer, let me give you the partial output of that command from my Windows 8.1 workstation:

```
PS C:\> Get-Service

Status     Name                DisplayName
------     ----                -----------
Stopped    AdobeARMservice     Adobe Acrobat Update Service
Stopped    AdobeFlashPlaye...  Adobe Flash Player Update Service
Stopped    AeLookupSvc         Application Experience
Stopped    ALG                 Application Layer Gateway Service
Stopped    AppIDSvc            Application Identity
Running    Appinfo             Application Information
Running    Apple Mobile De...  Apple Mobile Device
Running    AppMgmt             Application Management
```

Take a look at the output; it looks like a table, right? You see three columns:

▶ **Status:** Shows the running state of the service

▶ **Name:** "Short" programmatic name for the service

▶ **DisplayName:** "Friendly" name for the service

These columns in the output are formally known as properties; they define attributes or descriptive metadata about an object. By the way, each row in the output, in this example Windows services, represents an object. Finally, the entire list of services returned by command like **Get-Service** is known as a collection.

To make these points easier for you to visualize, check out Figure 5.1.

NOTE

The vocabulary terms I gave you are very important and will recur throughout the rest of this book.

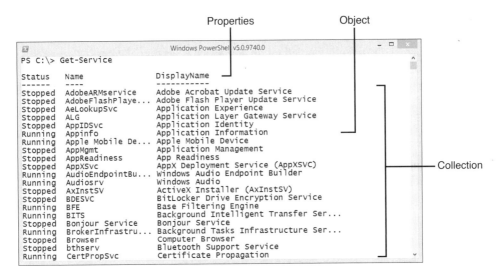

FIGURE 5.1
Remember that in Windows PowerShell, all data is represented as an object.

A Bit of (Important) Historical Background

I understand that this is not a programming book, per se. Nonetheless, I would be remiss as your instructor if I didn't take the time to explain some of the foundational principles in object-oriented programming (OOP, pronounced *oh-oh-pee* or *oop*).

The best way to walk you through the concept is by using a visual aid. Spend a moment studying the generic class diagram in Figure 5.2.

Imagine you wanted to design a computer program that simulates different kinds of cars. Would you create a definition for each car individually and re-create all the behaviors and attributes of each car from scratch? Of course not; you'd create a single blueprint for the car's design (call it a template), and then you'd use that template to instantiate, or bring into existence, specific instances of the car model.

I've actually given you the greatest benefit of object orientation. You can save yourself tons of time and effort by employing code reuse instead of "reinventing the wheel" with your code.

Specifically, the code reuse with classes comes through what's called inheritance. You can either instantiate exact copies of class blueprints and then modify the individual instances, or you can define a subclass that is a blueprint based upon a parent blueprint. Pretty cool stuff, indeed.

In Figure 5.2, observe that we created a template Car object. The formal name for an object template is class. In Windows PowerShell, the class is also known as the data type; you'll learn how to view an object's parent class momentarily.

Next, note that we can split the functionality of our car class along two lines: descriptions of individual attributes of the car, stuff like its name, color, and so forth. We also can define particular actions that the car can perform, stuff like turning the engine on or off, accelerating, braking, and steering. All standard stuff, wouldn't you agree?

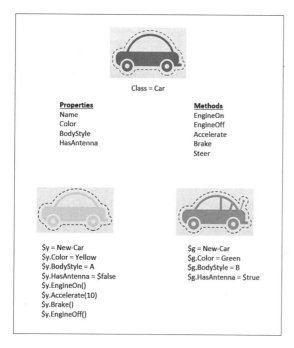

FIGURE 5.2
A traditional educational class diagram, like those used in programming classrooms around the world.

The bottom part of Figure 5.2 is where the true magic happens: We can instantiate, or duplicate, all the properties and methods from the parent class as many times as we want, no code rewrites necessary! Isn't that great?

In Figure 5.2, I'm using PowerShell conventions like variables that begin with a dollar sign. Note, however, that we access the properties and methods by using what is known in the programming world as dot notation. We'll get into that aspect more at a later time in this hour.

Referencing Individual Objects

As you know, running PowerShell commands like **Get-Service** result in a collection in which each row of data represents an individual object.

We can reference those individual objects within a collection easily enough by specifying a parameter such as –**Name**:

```
PS C:\> Get-Service -Name alg

Status      Name                    DisplayName
------      ----                    -----------
Stopped     alg                     Application Layer Gateway Service
```

The preceding statement returns a single row that represents the Application Layer Gateway Service service. We could also write the query using the **DisplayName** property, but we need to use quotation marks and get the spelling of the service name exactly:

```
PS C:\> Get-Service -Name "Application Layer Gateway Service"

Status      Name                    DisplayName
------      ----                    -----------
Stopped     ALG                     Application Layer Gateway Service
```

Here are two questions you probably have now. Even though the answers will become apparent in time, here are the short answers:

▶ Can I use single quotes instead of double quotes?

Yes, you can use single quotes or double quotes to delimit strings, but make sure that you don't mix them up 'like this."

▶ How did you know that **Get-Service** had a **Name**?

The default output of **Get-Service** gives us both Name and DisplayName as columns. You can safely assume that referencing one or more of those column names in your Windows PowerShell will bring back the desired results.

Now let's turn our attention to how we can dig deeper into Windows PowerShell objects.

Discovering Object Members

Windows PowerShell gives us three columns of data back about our Windows services when we run **Get-Service**. However, there is actually much more service data that PowerShell is tracking, but just hiding from you in the default output. How can we see that additional data?

In my experience, one of the most common things you'll do when discovering PowerShell commands is piping command output to **Get-Member**. The **Get-Member** cmdlet returns a collection that describes all of the metadata (properties, methods, and events) concerning that object.

Try the code in Listing 5.1.

LISTING 5.1 Collection Describing Metadata

```
Get-Service | Get-Member


TypeName: System.ServiceProcess.ServiceController

Name                        MemberType    Definition
----                        ----------    ----------
Name                        AliasProperty Name = ServiceName
RequiredServices            AliasProperty RequiredServices = ServicesDependedOn
Disposed                    Event         System.EventHandler Disposed(System....
Close                       Method        void Close()
Continue                    Method        void Continue()
CreateObjRef                Method        System.Runtime.Remoting.ObjRef Creat...
Dispose                     Method        void Dispose(), void IDisposable.Dis...
Equals                      Method        bool Equals(System.Object obj)
ExecuteCommand              Method        void ExecuteCommand(int command)
GetHashCode                 Method        int GetHashCode()
GetLifetimeService          Method        System.Object GetLifetimeService()
GetType                     Method        type GetType()
InitializeLifetimeService   Method        System.Object InitializeLifetimeServ...
Pause                       Method        void Pause()
Refresh                     Method        void Refresh()
Start                       Method        void Start(), void Start(string[] args)
Stop                        Method        void Stop()
WaitForStatus               Method        void WaitForStatus(System.ServicePro...
CanPauseAndContinue         Property      bool CanPauseAndContinue {get;}
CanShutdown                 Property      bool CanShutdown {get;}
CanStop                     Property      bool CanStop {get;}
Container                   Property      System.ComponentModel.IContainer Con...
DependentServices           Property      System.ServiceProcess.ServiceControl...
DisplayName                 Property      string DisplayName {get;set;}
MachineName                 Property      string MachineName {get;set;}
ServiceHandle               Property      System.Runtime.InteropServices.SafeH...
ServiceName                 Property      string ServiceName {get;set;}
ServicesDependedOn          Property      System.ServiceProcess.ServiceControl...
ServiceType                 Property      System.ServiceProcess.ServiceType Se...
Site                        Property      System.ComponentModel.ISite Site {ge...
Status                      Property      System.ServiceProcess.ServiceControl...
ToString                    ScriptMethod  System.Object ToString();
```

Wow. There is a lot of output! Don't be alarmed, though; I walk you through it all gently in the following sections.

Data Type

Notice the TypeName: field at the top of the output. This represents the underlying .NET class that defines the objects returned by the command. In the case of **Get-Service**, the underlying .NET data type is

```
System.ServiceProcess.ServiceController
```

Normally, I use the rightmost component of the data type when I'm building PowerShell pipeline sequences; you'll understand that more when we get to the pipeline in the next hour. Thus, I say that Get-Service returns ServiceController objects.

For now, know that perhaps the best way to get documentation on the PowerShell classes is to put the entire string into Google.

The first result will likely be the Microsoft Developer Network (MSDN) documentation library. As you can see in Figure 5.3, you can bypass a lot of the "programmer speak" and view everything you wanted to know about the members of the class.

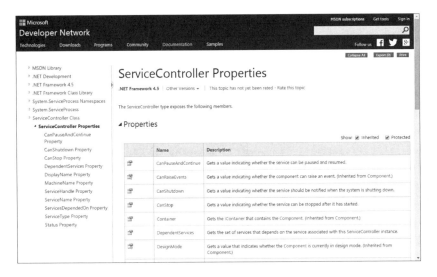

FIGURE 5.3
.NET classes that you can use in PowerShell aren't well documented internally, so turning to MSDN is often your best bet.

For now, all I want you to know about the data type is that it references the parent class that defines the members of a particular object.

Member Type

Now we're really getting into the thick of things. In object-oriented programming, each object has two fundamental descriptors: properties and methods. Properties define the descriptive/functional attributes of an object.

For instance, notice that for Windows services there is a **Status** property, which specifies whether a service is running or stopped.

Some cmdlets have special properties defined for them called **AliasProperties**. An **AliasProperty** is simply a "shortcut" to another property name.

In the **Get-Service** membership, **Name** is an **AliasProperty** for the **ServiceName** property. So, you can reference the same data (here, the Windows Search service) by using either of the following statements:

```
Get-Service -Name wsearch
Get-Service -ServiceName wsearch
```

That's some cool trickery, isn't it? The official **ServiceName** property for the Search service is Windows Search, yet Windows PowerShell was able to correctly resolve the inconsistency. Those developers in the PowerShell product team thought of almost everything, didn't they?

The second fundamental aspect of an object is the method. A method represents some action that the object can take. Again, to use **Get-Service** as an example, you can invoke the **Start** and **Stop** methods to easily start and stop a Windows service, respectively.

Try the following on a noncritical service. (I'm going to use the Print Spooler service as an example.) In the first line, we put the Print Spooler object instance into a variable. (This is the most common way to "play with" PowerShell objects.)

```
$spool = Get-Service -spooler
```

Next, we can stop the service by invoking the **Stop()** method:

```
$spool.Stop()
```

To check the service's run state, let's just have PowerShell tell us about the contents of our variable:

```
$spool
```

Of course, you can use the **Start()** method to restart the service. Feel free to do so, unless you don't like printing, as I don't.

How Do Objects Come to Be?

Understand that the members of a Windows PowerShell object don't just magically appear. For built-in cmdlets like **Get-Service** or **Get-Process**, the Windows PowerShell team used a .NET programming language to create the object classes that represent Windows services or processes. The programmer gets to choose which properties, methods, and events that he or she wants to expose to the end user.

What's cool is that if you have an interest in learning .NET programming, you can extend upon built-in PowerShell object classes and even create your own!

Now, I recognize that the Windows PowerShell hotshots in my audience will say, "Tim, we have the **Start-Service** and **Stop-Service** cmdlets already!"

True, true. As with all things Windows related, there are many ways to skin a cat. And I say that proverbially; we have four cats in our household.

Getting to Know Get-Member

In all likelihood, you'll run **Get-Member** so often that it's probably best for you to get into the habit of using its alias, **gm**. For example:

```
Get-Process | gm
```

As you seek to discover what's possible with PowerShell objects, you'll find yourself "piping to **gm**" reflexively. That's how we do it!

For completeness' sake, make sure to check out the full help for **Get-Member**:

```
Help Get-Member -ShowWindow
```

Scroll through the help output until you get to the **-MemberType** parameter. This optional parameter makes our lives easier when we need to investigate only particular aspects of an object.

For instance, if we wanted to view only the properties available with **Get-Process**, we could run Listing 5.2.

LISTING 5.2 Properties Available with Get-Process

```
PS C:\> Get-Process | gm -MemberType Properties

    TypeName: System.Diagnostics.Process

Name                      MemberType      Definition
----                      ----------      ----------
Handles                   AliasProperty   Handles = Handlecount
Name                      AliasProperty   Name = ProcessName
```

```
NPM                     AliasProperty  NPM = NonpagedSystemMemorySize64
PM                      AliasProperty  PM = PagedMemorySize64
VM                      AliasProperty  VM = VirtualMemorySize64
WS                      AliasProperty  WS = WorkingSet64
__NounName              NoteProperty   System.String __NounName=Process
BasePriority            Property       int BasePriority {get;}
Container               Property       System.ComponentModel.IContainer C...
EnableRaisingEvents     Property       bool EnableRaisingEvents {get;set;}
ExitCode                Property       int ExitCode {get;}
ExitTime                Property       datetime ExitTime {get;}
Handle                  Property       System.IntPtr Handle {get;}
HandleCount             Property       int HandleCount {get;}
HasExited               Property       bool HasExited {get;}
Id                      Property       int Id {get;}
MachineName             Property       string MachineName {get;}
MainModule              Property       System.Diagnostics.ProcessModule M...
```

The –**MemberType** property is an example of an enumeration. In an enumeration, the Microsoft .NET Framework development team predefines a list of valid values for that property, which we can get to by using PowerShell. As you can see in the previous output, there are more property types available in Windows PowerShell than **property** and **AliasProperty**. Perhaps we'll discuss some of the lesser-used property types later in the book.

If you want to see methods available with **Get-Process**, you can do the same thing, as shown in Listing 5.3.

LISTING 5.3   Methods Available with Get-Process

```
PS C:\> Get-Process | Get-Member -MemberType Method

   TypeName: System.Diagnostics.Process

Name                        MemberType Definition
----                        ---------- ----------
BeginErrorReadLine          Method     void BeginErrorReadLine()
BeginOutputReadLine         Method     void BeginOutputReadLine()
CancelErrorRead             Method     void CancelErrorRead()
CancelOutputRead            Method     void CancelOutputRead()
Close                       Method     void Close()
CloseMainWindow             Method     bool CloseMainWindow()
CreateObjRef                Method     System.Runtime.Remoting.ObjRef CreateOb...
Dispose                     Method     void Dispose(), void IDisposable.Dispose()
Equals                      Method     bool Equals(System.Object obj)
GetHashCode                 Method     int GetHashCode()
GetLifetimeService          Method     System.Object GetLifetimeService()
GetType                     Method     type GetType()
InitializeLifetimeService   Method     System.Object InitializeLifetimeService()
```

Kill	Method	void Kill()
Refresh	Method	void Refresh()
Start	Method	bool Start()
ToString	Method	string ToString()
WaitForExit	Method	bool WaitForExit(int milliseconds), voi...
WaitForInputIdle	Method	bool WaitForInputIdle(int milliseconds)...

Remember that methods define concrete actions that we can perform on an object. Again, by far the most common way to work with objects is to "pack" them into a variable. You can look at a variable as an in-memory placeholder for data on which you can read from and write to.

Putting Objects into Action

Now that you understand a little bit about objects, properties, and methods, what can you actually do with them? All this object-oriented theory is wonderful, but we are systems administrators here, not programmers. We need stuff to do in a practical context.

You're probably waiting to get your hands dirty with the technology. Good for you; that's why you purchased this book.

Before you start the next Try It Yourself exercise, fire up the PowerShell Integrated Scripting Environment (ISE) and set up the interface like you see in Figure 5.4.

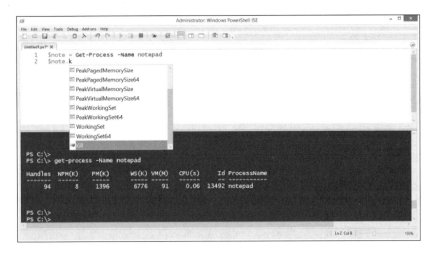

FIGURE 5.4
Windows PowerShell ISE, all fired up and ready to help you learn to master objects.

TIP

Remember to start the ISE as an administrator by right-clicking its icon and selecting **Run as Administrator** from the shortcut menu.

I think you'll agree with me in short order that the ISE makes it much easier to view and interact with object members than the console host does. The functionality is called IntelliSense, and it will "automagically" reveal commands, parameters, and values for you as you type. Awesome!

One more thing: Make sure that you temporarily relax your computer's script execution policy in the ISE before you begin work:

```
Set-ExecutionPolicy -ExecutionPolicy Bypass
```

You can (and should) reset it to a more reasonable policy once you're finished with your practice:

```
Set-ExecutionPolicy -ExecutionPolicy RemoteSigned
```

TRY IT YOURSELF

Working with Object and Members

In this Try It Yourself exercise, you'll learn how to manage processes with PowerShell by discovering, viewing, and tweaking object members.

1. Start Windows Notepad on your system and keep it running. You don't have to add any data to a document; we're concerned with the Notepad process itself.

2. How can we refer to Notepad programmatically with PowerShell? Try this:

```
Get-Process
```

Remember that in the ISE when you type in the script (white) portion, your command isn't automatically run. Place your cursor within the line and then either press **F8** or click the **Run Selection** button in the ISE toolbar.

You'll observe that Microsoft gives you approximately eight columns in the collection output by default. Specifically, look down ProcessName until you find notepad.

3. Cool. To "play with" Notepad, you'll want to pack it into a variable. Let's do that now:

```
$np = Get-Process -Name notepad
```

Wait! How could I use **name** as my parameter when the **Get-Process** output uses **ProcessName**? Let's investigate:

```
Get-Process | Get-Member
```

Aha! Do you see what's going on? The PowerShell team defined an **AliasProperty** (shortcut) called **Name** that we can substitute for the clunkier **ProcessName** property.

You also should have seen a *lot* of IntelliSense as you created your **$np** variable. For instance, as soon as you typed the first parameter dash, a drop-down showed you a list of all possible parameters. After you selected **–Name** and pressed the spacebar, another drop-down gave you a rundown of all active processes on the system.

4. Just to prove that our **$np** variable, which represents the Notepad application, is an object that has the same members as the parent class (**System.Diagnostics.Process**), let's run a **gm** on the variable directly:

```
$np | gm
```

5. Let's have some fun. To retrieve the current value in a property, we use good old-fashioned dot notation. You'll see a property called **MainWindowTitle**; let's give this a try:

```
$np.MainWindowTitle
```

If your system is set up like mine, the result will be "Untitled-Notepad" or something like it. Let's change the value:

```
$np.MainWindowTitle = "My File"
```

Whoops! You should have seen some "blood" on the screen. As it happens, many Windows PowerShell properties are read-only.

6. Let's focus in on another property. The **BasePriority** property is a read-only property that determines how much relative CPU power is devoted to the process. Let's get the current value:

```
$np.BasePriority
```

That isn't helpful, though. What does the number mean? Remember what I told you earlier: Run a Google search on the parent class of the object. If you look up the MSDN page for System.Diagnostics.Process, you'll learn that a BasePriority of 8 is normal priority, and that a BasePriority of 4 is idle (low priority).

Thus, if we could remove the **readonly** flag on the property, we could lower the Notepad process's priority, as follows:

```
$np.BasePriority = 4
```

Don't worry; you'll get plenty of opportunity to actually modify property values as we work through the other lessons in this book.

7. How about a method? **Kill()** looks pretty interesting:

```
$np.Kill()
```

Poof! You should see that Notepad was closed. Aren't you glad I asked you not to add data to your Notepad file?

Summary

If you made it through this hour relatively unscathed, my hat is off to you. In my own career, it took a long time before the principles of object-oriented programming began to make sense and allowed me to see their great utility.

The great power afforded to us by the Windows PowerShell object model will become increasingly apparent to us as we start to link the output of one command to the input of another in the pipeline. Later still, we'll make use of variables, objects, and members all the time in developing useful Windows PowerShell scripts that automate the work that we undertake every day.

Once again, I want to stress that you should not beat yourself up if you feel a bit of information overload at this point. The skills you are building will become increasingly sharp with practice. Also, we'll begin using these principles throughout the rest of the book.

Q&A

Q. When I run Get-Service, I want to see the Name property first, then the Status, and then the RequiredServices to show dependencies. I don't want to see the DisplayName. How can I do that?

A. Great question. To be sure, we don't have to content ourselves with the default columns, but to do this we'll need to go into territory we haven't formally covered yet. Try the following:

```
Get-Service | Select-Object -Property Name, Status, RequiredServices
```

If you've used Structured Query Language (SQL) with relational database systems, you should be right at home with the **Select-Object** cmdlet. Essentially, we are taking the full service list and running it through a filter in which we specify a comma-separate list of only those columns we want to see in the output.

Q. I don't like the default tabular display output in either the ISE or the Windows PowerShell console. What other output options are there?

A. You're opening a can of worms here! We'll cover all the available output types later in the book, but for starters you can try piping your command output to **Format-Table** with the **–AutoSize** switch parameter. The **–AutoSize** switch stretches each column to its full width, barring any limitations you have on your console dimensions:

```
Get-Service | Format-Table -AutoSize
```

Q. Do individual object members (such as the DisplayName property of the Get-Service object) have members of their own?

A. Indeed they do. Try the following, and feel free to substitute any noncritical Windows service for what I use in this simple example:

```
$s = Get-Service -Name wsearch
$s.DisplayName
$s.DisplayName | Get-Member
```

I show you some partial output from my Windows 8.1 system here:

```
PS C:\> $s.DisplayName | Get-Member


   TypeName: System.String

Name            MemberType    Definition
----            ----------    ----------
Clone           Method        System.Object Clone(), System.Object ...
CompareTo       Method        int CompareTo(System.Object value), i...
Contains        Method        bool Contains(string value)
CopyTo          Method        void CopyTo(int sourceIndex, char[] d...
EndsWith        Method        bool EndsWith(string value), bool End...
Equals          Method        bool Equals(System.Object obj), bool ...
GetEnumerator   Method        System.CharEnumerator GetEnumerator()...
GetHashCode     Method        int GetHashCode()
GetType         Method        type GetType()
GetTypeCode     Method        System.TypeCode GetTypeCode(), System...
IndexOf         Method        int IndexOf(char value), int IndexOf(...
IndexOfAny      Method        int IndexOfAny(char[] anyOf), int Ind..
Insert          Method        string Insert(int startIndex, string ...
IsNormalized    Method        bool IsNormalized(), bool IsNormalize...
LastIndexOf     Method        int LastIndexOf(char value), int Last...
LastIndexOfAny  Method        int LastIndexOfAny(char[] anyOf), int...
```

Do you see what's going on here? The **DisplayName** property itself is an instance of a .NET class (blueprint) called **System.String**. In turn, the **String** class includes a whole bunch of methods that allow us to do stuff with that string object. When PowerShell experts like Jason Helmick say, "In Windows PowerShell, everything is an object," they aren't kidding!

Workshop

The only way you're going to truly master Windows PowerShell is by working through challenges. Here is a sequence of tasks that I'd like you to complete. Remember that it isn't "cheating" if you need to look back in this hour (or consult another reference, particular the PowerShell internal documentation) to get an answer.

The following workshop task sequence presumes that you are running Windows PowerShell v4 or later on Windows 8.1 or Windows Server 2012.

1. Determine what kind of object is produced by **Get-Disk**.

2. What **Get-Disk** properties store the make and model of your computer's fixed/removable hard drives?

3. List the methods included in the **Get-Disk** object.

Quiz

1. A _____ defines the actions that an object can perform.

   a. property

   b. event

   c. method

   d. class

2. Why do Windows PowerShell users typically use variables when investigating and modifying the members of an object?

   a. Doing so is mandatory.

   b. Doing so makes working with properties and methods more convenient.

   c. Doing so prevents dot notation from being used on the system and causing instability.

3. When you run **Get-Service**, the list of services returned is known collectively as an object.

   a. True

   b. False

Answers

1. The correct answer is C. A method is functionality programmed into an object that specifies actions that it can perform. By contrast, an event member specifies what actions can happen to the object itself. Finally, a property describes the object in some way.

2. The correct answer is B. Although it's not required to pack PowerShell objects into variables, doing so makes it far easier to "pin down" the object temporarily while you do your work on it. Recall that we use dot notation to access the members of an object variable.

3. The correct answer is B. The entire output table is called a collection. Specifically, **Get-Service** returns a list of objects that are all instances of the **ServiceController** parent .NET class.

Mastering the Windows PowerShell Pipeline

In the previous hour, I told you, "In Windows PowerShell, everything is an object." True, true. In this hour, I have another geeky aphorism for you:

> *If you understand how the pipeline works, then you truly "get" Windows PowerShell.*

This hour, we start by examining the power of the Windows PowerShell pipeline from a high level. After you have the basics down, we'll drill deeply.

This is some tough conceptual and practical work, I must warn you. However, I assure you that taking the time to master the pipeline will reap enormous dividends in terms of your future efficiency as a Windows systems administrator. Let's get started.

Understanding How the Pipeline Works from a High Level

If you have at least intermediate expertise with Windows, you've probably run a Cmd.exe statement such as the following:

```
Dir | more
```

True, you might not have any earthly idea how that statement worked under the hood, but you knew that it will give you a directory listing based on your current working directory and display only a screen full of information at a time.

Going further, I can tell you now that the Windows command shell and the Linux Bash command shell allow you to feed output from one command into another all day long, but you get nowhere near the power that you do with Windows PowerShell.

In Cmd.exe pipes, for instance, the output from the first command exits an interface called StdOut and is received through the pipeline by the second command's StdIn. Linux works the same way.

Why isn't this powerful? Because the output and input don't have any "personality," that's why! It's all flat text. This is why you really need to understand stuff like text parsing and regular expressions to do anything remotely powerful with the Windows Cmd.exe or Linux pipelines.

But I get a bit ahead of myself. In Windows PowerShell, the pipeline exists as a method to string together commands, which is the very same thing the pipeline does in other command shells. However, we'll recall from our training thus far that all data in PowerShell are .NET objects, each of which contains a suite of properties, methods, and events.

From a functional standpoint, the object-based nature of Windows PowerShell means that we can parse, filter, sort, export (the list goes on) our object data as broadly or granularly as we want, provided that the commands in the pipeline understand the data being received. More on that in just a second.

Brief Case Study

Let's imagine that you're a Windows systems administrator for a busy company. One of your colleagues calls you in a panic, saying, "There's a process on server01 that's eating up all its CPU and messing up user access to their home folders. Find and kill the process—now!"

Because you're already in the server room, you log on to the affected server, fire up an elevated PowerShell console, and run the following command to isolate the problematic process:

```
Get-Process | Sort-Object –Property CPU –Descending
```

In doing this, you discover that the lob1 process is indeed consuming way too much central processing unit power. You scratch your head and think to yourself, "Now, how did Tim say you should kill a process with PowerShell? Oh yeah, just remembered," and you type the following:

```
$p = Get-Process –Name lob1
$p.Kill()
```

Does that work? Well, yes it does. But could you have done the job with a PowerShell "one-liner" instead of two lines of code. PowerShell power users are constantly on the hunt to find ways to do more with less code. You know, let's determine whether another cmdlet exists that we could use with the pipeline instead:

```
PS C:\> get-command -Noun *process*

CommandType      Name                  Source
-----------      ----                  ------
Cmdlet           Debug-Process         Microsoft.PowerShell.Management
Cmdlet           Get-Process           Microsoft.PowerShell.Management
Cmdlet           Start-Process         Microsoft.PowerShell.Management
Cmdlet           Stop-Process          Microsoft.PowerShell.Management
Cmdlet           Wait-Process          Microsoft.PowerShell.Management
```

Ah yes, we have **Stop-Process**. That's convenient. Let's pretend that the lob1 process was still running. We could try the following to stop the process:

```
Get-Process -Name lob1 | Stop-Process
```

You should know, however, that the previous one-liner performs a "close," not exactly a "kill." You could add the –Force switch to simulate a true process termination, like so:

```
Get-Process -Name lob1 | Stop-Process -Force
```

Alternatively, you can invoke the kill() method in one line instead of two by enclosing the Get-Process call in parentheses like this:

```
(Get-Process -Name lob1).Kill()
```

Windows PowerShell gives us so much creative freedom in how we do our work—I love it!

After-Action Review

Now let's spend a moment describing how the PowerShell pipeline worked in the preceding example from a high level; afterward, we'll delve into the gory details.

First, we did this:

```
Get-Process | Sort-Object -Property CPU -Descending
```

I think you know by now that **Get-Process** returns a collection of **System.Diagnostics.Process** objects that correspond to all running processes on the computer. How can we confirm? Pipe the cmdlet to **Get-Member**:

```
Get-Process | Get-Member
```

At the risk of repeating myself too much, we use Get-Member to determine (a) the type of object being returned in the pipeline; and (b) the methods and properties exposed by that object.

Let's consult the full help for **Get-Process**. (Let's look at the online version to make sure we have the latest copy.)

```
Get-Help Get-Process -Online
```

Scroll past the parameter section of the file and you'll come to an Inputs and Outputs section.

NOTE

This is crucial, because it tells us not only the object types that the cmdlet outputs, but also the types of objects that **Get-Process** accepts from preceding cmdlets in the pipeline. Make a note of this, please.

Now look at the full help file for **Sort-Object** and observe the object type it uses as an input. You should see System.Management.Automation.PSObject. Don't get bogged down by all the "System... blah" stuff. Look at the rightmost object name. I can tell you that **PSObject** is about as generic a .NET object as can exist in PowerShell.

Essentially, you can pipe just about any PowerShell object into **Sort-Object**, and **Sort-Object** will do its best to sort on any property or properties that you specify as parameters. Make a little bit of sense?

Now let's examine the second pipeline we used in the foregoing example:

```
Get-Process -Name lob1 | Stop-Process
```

Okay. We already know that **Get-Process** outputs **Process**, **FileVersionInfo**, or **ProcessModule** objects depending on how you use the command. Open the help for **Stop-Process** and you'll learn that it indeed expects **Process** objects as input.

There is a bit more to the story, as there always is, but I hope you get the main ideas:

▶ PowerShell "tries" to make pipelining as easy on the administrator as possible.

▶ Objects entering the pipeline must have a compatible data type (object type) to be successfully received and processed by the subsequent command in the pipeline.

Finally, I will let you know parenthetically that Windows PowerShell actually has several pipelines. The primary pipeline with which we're concerned with in this book is called the output pipeline (analogous in the roughest way to StdOut in the Cmd.exe world). The others, which we won't discuss here, are as follows:

▶ **Error pipeline:** Used to catch and channel error messages

▶ **Warning pipeline:** Used to catch and channel warning messages

▶ **Verbose pipeline:** Used to handle a lot of output

▶ **Debugging pipeline:** Used to "peek under the hood" when troubleshooting pipeline code

Understanding in Depth How the Pipeline Works

That **Get- | Stop PowerShell** one-liner is one that you'll probably use all the time in your work as a systems administrator. For this section, in which we dig deeply into how the PowerShell pipeline works under the hood, choose an innocuous service on your computer (I'm going to pick on the Print Spooler service) and run the following statements:

```
Get-Service -Name *spool*
Get-Service -Name spooler | Stop-Service
Get-Service -Name *spool*
```

How did it work? Did you verify that the service was originally running, and then was stopped as a result of your brilliant use of the PowerShell pipeline? Good. Of course, you can run the following statement to restart the service:

```
Start-Service -Name spooler
```

First, Data Types

Actually, the specific example isn't at all important. What we're concerned with is learning exactly what the object data looks like where the pipe (|) character exists.

NOTE

According to Wikipedia, the notion of the pipeline and its accompanying vertical bar character representation were created in 1973 by Douglas McIlroy, an American UNIX pioneer. McIlroy chose the vertical bar simply because it physically resembled an actual pipeline. Of course, the behavior of the PowerShell and UNIX pipelines also shares a metaphorical link with physical pipelines.

For starters, here is a truncated extract of the **Get-Service** command help:

```
OUTPUTS
    System.ServiceProcess.ServiceController

        Get-Service returns objects that represent the services on the
computer.
```

Okay. This isn't news to us. We know by now that **Get-Service** "spits out" **ServiceController** objects. You can pipe to **Get-Member** if you want to refresh your memory of its properties and methods.

Now, here is the same section of the help file for **Stop-Service**:

```
INPUTS
    System.ServiceProcess.ServiceController or System.String

        You can pipe a service object or a string that contains the name of a
service to Stop-Service.
```

Well, isn't that special? As it happens, the **Stop-Service** cmdlet natively expects **ServiceController** objects. Of course, the PowerShell team did this intentionally; after all, both cmdlets deal with system services.

The bad news is that all your pipeline work won't be this seamless. The good news is that there is (almost) always a way around this problem. For example, you can hack the PowerShell pipeline to custom-fit inputs and outputs; you'll learn about that later on in this hour.

Second, Parameters

The true "secret sauce" to what makes the PowerShell pipeline so awesome is what is called parameter binding. When you pipe two PowerShell commands together, the object type is what allows the possibility of data flow to occur. That's step one.

But what PowerShell does next is revolutionary: it looks for a match on parameter values and/or property names. What do I mean? Let me explain.

Again, take a look at this abbreviated help from **Stop-Service**:

```
-InputObject <ServiceController[]>
    Specifies ServiceController objects representing the services to be stopped.
Enter a variable that contains the objects, or type a command or expression that
gets the objects.

    Required?                       true
    Position?                       1
    Default value
    Accept pipeline input?          true (ByValue)
    Accept wildcard characters?     false
```

One of the biggest benefits you're going to get by studying this book is the crucial value of reading the full help file for PowerShell commands. In the previous extract, we see a parameter called **InputObject**.

The <ServiceController[]> specifies the expected object type, and the square brackets [] denotes an array of values. In other words, we can pass more than one service into this cmdlet.

So far, so good. The **Required?** and **Position?** values are **true** and **1**, respectively, which means that we must specify a value for **InputObject** immediately when declaring this command.

My astute readers will say, "Ah, we must be using positional parameters, because we haven't been specifying the **InputObject** parameter name!" Good work, my friend. The following statements are identical:

```
Stop-Service -InputObject spooler
Stop-Service spooler
```

For me, the most important line here is "Accept pipeline input?," which we see is set to **true** (**ByValue**) for **Stop-Process**. We'll worry about what **ByValue** means in the next section. The **true** tells us that PowerShell can, and most likely will, use this parameter for binding the two cmdlets together.

Check out Figure 6.1 and I'll recap before I turn you loose on a Try It Yourself exercise.

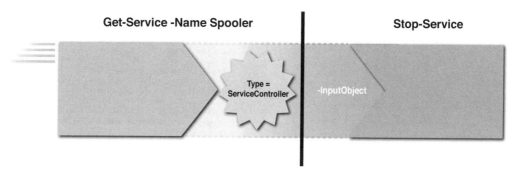

FIGURE 6.1
Parameter binding is the true "magic" behind the Windows PowerShell pipeline.

Look at the arrow in Figure 6.1; this reminds us that the Windows pipeline always moves from left to right. In a later hour, you'll learn how to iterate through a collection of objects, which translates into cycling through the same pipeline repeatedly.

I created the **Get-Service** and **Stop-Service** shapes in an intentionally complementary way. As you'll learn in the upcoming Try It Yourself exercise, not all PowerShell commands write to the pipeline.

In this example, PowerShell chooses to bind the output of **Get-Service** to the input of **Stop-Service** by using the **ServiceController** object itself. This reference is made on the **Stop-Service** side by means of the **–InputObject** parameter.

Examine this snipped from the **Stop-Service** help file:

```
-Name <String[]>
    Specifies the service names of the services to be stopped. Wildcards are
permitted.
```

The parameter name is optional. You can use "Name" or its alias, "ServiceName", or you can omit the parameter name.

```
Required?                  true
Position?                  1
Default value
Accept pipeline input?     true (ByPropertyName, ByValue)
Accept wildcard characters? true
```

What this tells us is that **Stop-Service** can also bind to string data from the preceding command, specifically the object's name. You'll find in PowerShell that almost every object has a property (or **AliasProperty**) called **name**. Figure 6.2 shows the parameter binding in action in this case.

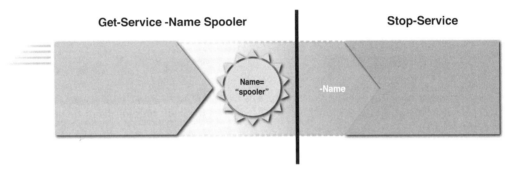

FIGURE 6.2
Sometimes parameter binding can take advantage of a shared property name.

▼ TRY IT YOURSELF

Investigating the Windows PowerShell Pipeline

In this Try It Yourself exercise, imagine you are tasked with generating an HTML report that displays all the stopped services on your computer. After generating the report, we'll tease apart the pipeline for troubleshooting and educational purposes. They are one and the same anyway, right?

To get started, open an elevated PowerShell console.

1. Let's refresh our memory as to the members of **Get-Service**, shall we?

   ```
   Get-Service | Get-Member
   ```

2. It's been a while since we played with object methods, so try the following to generate a variable to hold all system services whose status is equal to Stopped. We'll then display the contents of the variable. Here is partial output from my Windows 8.1 computer:

```
PS C:\> $srv = Get-Service | Where-Object -Property Status -eq "Stopped"
PS C:\> $srv

Status    Name               DisplayName
------    ----               -----------
Stopped   AdobeARMservice    Adobe Acrobat Update Service
Stopped   AdobeFlashPlaye... Adobe Flash Player Update Service
Stopped   AeLookupSvc        Application Experience
Stopped   ALG                Application Layer Gateway Service
Stopped   AppIDSvc           Application Identity
Stopped   AppReadiness       App Readiness
Stopped   AppXSvc            AppX Deployment Service (AppXSVC)
Stopped   AxInstSV           ActiveX Installer (AxInstSV)
Stopped   BDESVC             BitLocker Drive Encryption Service
Stopped   Bonjour Service    Bonjour Service
```

You are going to learn all about the **Where-Object** cmdlet and the comparison operators in a later lesson; you can ignore them for now. All that matters is that you now have all the stopped services packed into a variable named **$srv**.

3. Before you proceed, let's check out what's popping in terms of datatype, properties, and methods with **$srv**:

```
$srv | Get-Member
```

Cool. So we know (actually, we already knew; remember that repetition is a core principle of adult education) that the **$srv** variable consists of a bunch of **ServiceController** objects, each with a **Name** property, among so much more data.

4. As it happens, PowerShell includes a nifty parameter called **Out-File** that is handy for quickly snagging a textual representation of whatever data resides in the pipeline. Try this:

```
$srv | Out-File -FilePath stopped-services.txt
```

To open the file, type:

```
Notepad stopped-services.txt
```

5. You know what we need to do next, right? Yes, indeed: consult the **Out-File** help file and look for the inputs, the outputs, and pipeline-aware parameters. Here is truncated output:

```
INPUTS
    System.Management.Automation.PSObject

        You can pipe any object to Out-File.


OUTPUTS
    None

        Out-File does not generate any output.
```

Yikes! The **PSObject** input type means that **Out-File** will accept just about any kind of PowerShell object under the proverbial sun. However, there are no outputs. We can prove this to ourselves by trying to pipe **Out-File** to **Get-Member**:

```
$srv | Out-File test.txt | Get-Member
```

This command should generate an error, and it underscores what I told you earlier; namely, some PowerShell commands don't participate in the pipeline at all, some commands don't have an output, some commands don't accept pipeline input, and some commands have both inputs and outputs.

6. By the way, what kind of parameter binding do you suppose took place in this example? Again, parse the **Out-File** help file:

```
-InputObject <PSObject>
    Specifies the objects to be written to the file. Enter a variable that
    contains the objects or type a command or expression that gets the
    objects.

    Required?                        false
    Position?                        named
    Default value
    Accept pipeline input?           true (ByValue)
    Accept wildcard characters?      false
```

Easy enough. You'll learn before too long if you haven't already that **PSObject** is a great object to work with because it's so flexible.

Passing Data Through the Pipeline

You understand that a parameter is a way to modify the run state of a Windows PowerShell command. Parameters can be passed positionally:

```
Get-EventLog Application
```

Or they can be passed by name:

```
Get-EventLog -LogName Application
```

Under the proverbial hood, most parameters have three key attributes:

- ▸ **Name:** This is the "friendly" name of the parameter
- ▸ **Value:** This is the specific setting for the parameter
- ▸ **Data type:** This is the object data type used for the parameter

I said "most" parameters because with switch parameters, the name and the value are one and the same. For instance:

```
Get-ChildItem C:\Windows -Recurse
```

I say all of this as a setup for the point that Windows PowerShell binds parameters internally either by using parameter values or by using parameter names.

NOTE

This bears repeating. When performing parameter binding in the pipeline, PowerShell always tries to bind **ByValue** first, and then **ByPropertyName** second if it can't find a match by value.

Don't Forget About the "About" Help Files!

Unfortunately, it's too easy to overlook the incredible resource that is the about_ help file library that's built in to Windows PowerShell.

You can learn a great deal about how PowerShell works internally by reading some of these documents. Get a list of 'em all:

```
Get-Help about_*
```

For our purposes in learning about the PowerShell pipeline, I draw your attention to the following files in particular:

- ▶ about_pipelines
- ▶ about_parameters
- ▶ about_objects

Happy studying.

Parameter Passing by Value

If you read the help for a PowerShell command and a particular parameter accepts pipeline input by value, then this indicates that you can pipe any value to the parameter, provided the incoming parameter value has a data type that's expected by the receiving command.

Parameter Passing by Property Name

In my experience, PowerShell can make a binding based on values in the vast majority of cases. However, cases certainly arise when PowerShell must go to, as my colleague and PowerShell guru Don Jones says, "Plan B."

Let's take the following example. Imagine you were diagnosing a malware infection on your user's computer, and in so doing you found a rogue service named winders_updatte. (Yeah, sometimes malware authors aren't the best spellers.)

It's one thing to stop the service, but an even better idea is to stop the underlying process that is mapped to the service. So, we have the following pipeline:

```
Get-Service -Name winders_updatte | Stop-Process
```

Will this work? Earlier in this hour, we reviewed the help for **Stop-Process**, so you already know that the cmdlet looks for **Process** objects as input. You'll recall also that **Stop-Process** has a parameter named **–InputObject** that does indeed accept pipeline input by value. Sadly, the data type required here is **Process**, not **ServiceController**. Nuts! Parameter binding by value isn't going to work in this case.

On to plan B. **Stop-Service** has a **–Name** parameter that expects the **String** data type. For example:

```
-Name <String[]>
    Specifies the process names of the processes to be stopped. You can
    type multiple process names (separated by commas) or use wildcard
    characters.

    Required?                        true
    Position?                        named
    Default value
    Accept pipeline input?           true (ByPropertyName)
    Accept wildcard characters?      true
```

When PowerShell attempts to do parameter binding by property name, it examines all the properties of the incoming objects (in this case, **ServiceController**), and looks for a property with a matching name and data type. Believe it or not, it isn't any more complicated than that.

Look at Figure 6.3 to see the members of **Get-Service**.

As you can observe in Figure 6.3, the **–Name** parameter in **Get-Service** and the **–Name** parameter of **Stop-Process** have the same exact parameter name and datatype, so we (should be) good to go with this command sequence.

What's good about the property name binding method is that it opens up a lot of pipelining possibilities that might not have worked otherwise. What's bad about this binding method is that you sometimes get unexpected results.

In our example here, the malware service has the name winders_updatte. This is the value that will be sent across the pipeline into **Stop-Process**. If there indeed exists a service with the exact match on that name, the pipeline should work. However, if the underlying service has another name, the pipeline breaks, and we're hosed.

FIGURE 6.3
PowerShell can make use of the Name/ServiceName string property to bind Get-Service to Stop-Process.

We'll revisit parameter binding (of both the ByValue and ByPropertyName varieties) much more as we proceed through the rest of this volume. In the meantime, I just want you to embrace the following take-home messages:

▶ The data (object) types must match on both sides of the pipeline for data to flow.

▶ PowerShell first attempts to match parameters by value (data type) only.

▶ Failing that, PowerShell looks for matching property name (and data type) on each side of the pipeline.

▶ Sometimes even a parameter match can result in unexpected results.

TIP

Don Jones often advises that if you get unexpected results in a pipeline expression, remove the rightmost element and pipe the rest to **Get-Member**. If you see a member list, at least you know that the output is pipeline-aware. You can also view the output objects' data type and property list.

I think you'll agree with me that the **ByValue** parameter binding method is pretty intuitive. However, the **ByPropertyName** is tougher. So, I'd like you to work through the following Try It

Yourself exercise to give yourself some practice. Note that this exercise requires that you have access to multiple computers in an Active Directory Domain Services (AD DS) environment. If this requirement is too steep, study all the steps in the exercise anyway to enhance your learning.

▼ TRY IT YOURSELF

Experimenting with Pipeline Parameter Binding

In this exercise, your goal is to generate a list of services from multiple Windows domain computers. You'll use a comma-separated value (CSV) format file as input.

1. Create a text file named servers.csv that contains the following data:

```
computername,role
dc1,domain controller
dc2,domain controller
mem1,file server
sql1,sql server
sp1,sharepoint server
exA,exchange server
```

If you have a smaller network in your lab, substitute the hostnames of your actual computers. Remember that this process will work seamlessly only in an Active Directory domain environment.

2. Now start an administrative PowerShell console session. You'll leverage the nifty **Import-Csv** cmdlet to perform the data input. (Don't forget to study the help file for **Import-Csv**!) I also want you to echo the contents of the **$servers** variable so that you can see the output. Finally, pipe to **Get-Member**:

```
$servers = Import-Csv -Path .\servers.csv
$servers

computername                          role
-----------                           ----
dc1                                   domain controller
dc2                                   domain controller
mem1                                  file server
sql1                                  sql server
sp1                                   sharepoint server
ex1                                   exchange server


$servers | Get-Member

    TypeName: System.Management.Automation.PSCustomObject
```

```
Name            MemberType    Definition
----            ----------    ----------
Equals          Method        bool Equals(System.Object obj)
GetHashCode     Method        int GetHashCode()
GetType         Method        type GetType()
ToString        Method        string ToString()
computername    NoteProperty  System.String computername=dc1
role            NoteProperty  System.String role=domain controller
```

Pay particular attention to the presence (and spelling) of the **Computername** string parameter of **Import-Csv**. We'll need to call it into action in just a moment.

3. Now for the moment of truth—piping the results of our **$servers PSCustomObject** objects into **Get-Service**:

```
$servers | Get-Service
```

Ugh. Did your screen "bleed red," as PowerShell expert Jason Helmick often says? Yeah, me too. Here's the problem: As we expect, PowerShell attempted a parameter bind by value first.

Well, take a look at Figure 6.4 to see what happened.

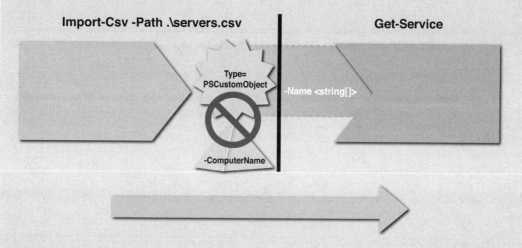

FIGURE 6.4
The Get-Service cmdlet assumed the Import-Csv output was string objects, and erroneously attempted to bind to its own –Name parameter. Bad news.

4. What we do now is switch to "plan B" and force PowerShell to do a property name bind instead. By "plugging up" the **–Name** parameter on the **Get-Service** side, PowerShell then attempts to do a property bind between its own **–ComputerName** property and the matching **–ComputerName** property on the **Import-Csv** file.

For proof, check out the output of the **Get-Service** help file:

```
Get-Help Get-Service -Parameter ComputerName


-ComputerName <String[]>
    Gets the services running on the specified computers. The default is the
    local computer.

    Type the NetBIOS name, an IP address, or a fully qualified domain name of
    a remote computer. To specify the local computer, type the computer name,
    a dot (.), or "localhost".

    This parameter does not rely on Windows PowerShell remoting. You can use
    the ComputerName parameter of Get-Service even if your computer is not
    configured to run remote commands.


    Required?                      false
    Position?                      named
    Default value                  Local computer
    Accept pipeline input?         true (ByPropertyName)
    Accept wildcard characters?    false
```

Now let's take a quick look at the members of the **Import-Csv** object:

```
Import-Csv -Path .\servers.csv | Get-Member


   TypeName: System.Management.Automation.PSCustomObject

Name         MemberType   Definition
----         ----------   ----------
Equals       Method       bool Equals(System.Object obj)
GetHashCode  Method       int GetHashCode()
GetType      Method       type GetType()
ToString     Method       string ToString()
computername NoteProperty System.String computername=dc1
role         NoteProperty System.String role=domain controller
```

Can you see what's going on? We have a match on property name (**ComputerName**) and data type (**string**) on both sides of the pipeline. So, data flows and all is well. Here's the code, by the way:

```
Import-Csv -Path .\servers.csv | Get-Service –Name *
```

The asterisk is, in effect, a placeholder that says "return all service names." You'll learn more about the so-called splat operator in the next couple hours of training.

"Forcing" Objects Through the Pipeline

Before I wrap up this hour, I want to spend a little time discussing how we can resolve the issue of parameter values/properties simply not lining up properly. As it turns out, you can actually massage PowerShell command output to sort of "force" data through the pipeline successfully.

Case Study

As a case study, let's suppose that you have been handed a CSV file containing a roster of newly hired employees. Your task is to create Active Directory user objects for the new personnel as efficiently as possible.

Here's the fictional CSV file, named newhires.csv:

```
Netname,FirstName,LastName,EmailAddress
qbirnum,Quentin,Birnum,qbynum@timwarnertech.com
sharter,Susan,Harter,sharter@timwarnertech.com
mlove,Michael,Love,mlove@timwarnertech.com
```

We already covered the fact that the **Import-Csv** cmdlet produces "custom" objects that resemble, but aren't exactly, string objects. I also showed you the membership of those objects by piping the statement to **Get-Member** like so:

```
Import-Csv -Path .\newhires.csv | Get-Member
```

Now let's fire up the full help for **New-ADUser**. I'll show you only the relevant data here (specifically inputs, outputs, and properties that pertain to those in the CSV file):

```
INPUTS
    System.Nullable`1[[System.DateTime, mscorlib, Version=4.0.0.0, Culture=neutral,
    PublicKeyToken=b77a5c561934e089]]
    System.Nullable`1[[System.Boolean, mscorlib, Version=4.0.0.0, Culture=neutral,
    PublicKeyToken=b77a5c561934e089]]
    System.Security.SecureString
    Microsoft.ActiveDirectory.Management.ADAuthenticationPolicy
    Microsoft.ActiveDirectory.Management.ADAuthenticationPolicySilo
    System.Security.Cryptography.X509Certificates.X509Certificate[]
    System.String
    Microsoft.ActiveDirectory.Management.ADKerberosEncryptionType
    Microsoft.ActiveDirectory.Management.ADUser
```

```
Microsoft.ActiveDirectory.Management.ADPrincipal[]
System.String[]
```

OUTPUTS
   System.Object

Yikes! That's a lot of inputs, all of which are way beyond our grasp because we know that **Import-Csv** doesn't output any of those wacky Active Directory-related data types. Perhaps the **System.String[]** input will work here? Because **New-ADUser** is the end of the pipeline, we don't particularly care about outputs.

Now we'll have a look at the pertinent **New-ADUser** parameters. The **–GivenName** string parameter should line up with the CSV file's netname field:

```
-GivenName <string>
```

Required?	false
Position?	Named
Accept pipeline input?	true (ByPropertyName)
Parameter set name	(All)
Aliases	None
Dynamic?	true

The **–GivenName** string property should match up with the FirstName column in the CSV file:

```
-GivenName <string>
```

Required?	false
Position?	Named
Accept pipeline input?	true (ByPropertyName)
Parameter set name	(All)
Aliases	None
Dynamic?	true

Likewise, the **New-ADUser –SurName** property should link with the LastName field in the file:

```
-Surname <string>
```

Required?	false
Position?	Named
Accept pipeline input?	true (ByPropertyName)
Parameter set name	(All)
Aliases	None
Dynamic?	true

Finally, we have the **EmailAddress** string property to hook into the CSV file's EmailAddress field. It's great that the column names match here—what a relief...or is it?

```
-EmailAddress <string>
```

Required?	false
Position?	Named
Accept pipeline input?	true (ByPropertyName)
Parameter set name	(All)
Aliases	None
Dynamic?	true

You'll observe that all of the aforementioned **New-ADUser** properties accept pipeline input only by property name. Hmm. Time to test:

```
Import-Csv -Path .\newhires.csv | New-ADUser
```

Man—blood all over the screen again, as shown in Figure 6.5.

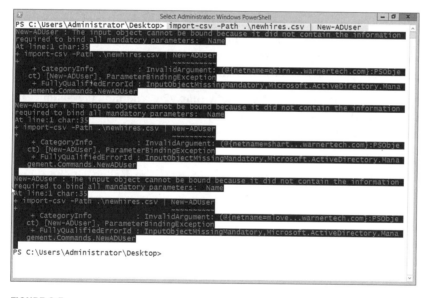

FIGURE 6.5
The error messages tell us that PowerShell can't find any properties in the Import-Csv output that matches property names in Get-ADUser.

TIP

The solution to this problem is simultaneously simple and complex. Remember that to do property name-based parameter binding, the parameter names and data types must match exactly. The data type part is covered; it's all string data.

As it happens, though, we can employ custom properties to manually map properties from **Import-Csv** to corresponding properties in **New-ADUser**. Yes, indeed!

Introducing Hash Tables

In computer programming, a garden-variety variable contains a single unit of data. An array is a special type of variable that can simultaneously store multiple data elements. We can consider a variable as an individual mailbox, and an array as a free-standing cluster of mailboxes like you might find at an apartment building.

In PowerShell a hash table (also spelled hashtable) is yet another kind of array. Specifically, a hash table is an associative array that contains a collection of key/value pairs. Hash tables are a great way to present more complex, organized data. We denote a hash table generically in our PowerShell code this way:

```
$hashtable_name = @{key1 = item1; key2 = item2;...}
```

By way of trivia, the "hash" in hash table doesn't refer to cryptographic hashes as much as it does to culinary hash. You see, we "chop and mix" data elements in PowerShell hash tables in much the same way that you might prepare hash in your kitchen.

Yes, it's true that we can fix our particular problem trivially simply by renaming the column headers in newhires.csv to match the **New-ADUser** property names. However, you are learning here, so the simplest approach is not the preferred one here.

Now I'm just going to go ahead and throw the following ugly PowerShell statement at you and then explain it a little bit afterward. Because of the amount of code we're dealing with here, I'm doing this is in the PowerShell ISE:

```
Import-Csv -Path .\newhires.csv |
Select-Object -Property * , `
@{name='samAccountName';expression={$_.netname}}, `
@{name='GivenName';expression={$_.firstname}}, `
@{name='Name';expression={$_.lastname}}, `
# @{name='EmailAddress';expression={$_.emailaddress}} |
New-ADUser
```

The two ways to do a line break in your code are as follows:

▶ The grave accent (`), also called the backtick character

▶ The pipe (|) operator

For detailed information on PowerShell scripting, including how to manage line breaks, refer to Hour 19, "Introduction to Windows PowerShell Scripting."

The first part of the pipeline should be immediately understandable. The middle part employs the **Select-Object** cmdlet and specifies we want to pull all property values from the CSV file. We use the comma in PowerShell as a command separator when we want to do more than one action in the same part of the pipeline.

The hash tables begin on the third line. Let's look closer at the first one:

```
@{name='samAccountName';expression={$_.netname}},  `
```

Here, **name** and **expression** are the keys, and are arbitrary for our purposes here. We do need to be consistent with their names within the context of this script, however. The values match the properties expected in **New-ADUser**. So **samAccountName** is a required property that, in this case, we are hand-mapping to the netname field in the CSV file.

The dollar sign underscore (**$_**) variable is a shortcut way of referring to the current object in the pipeline. Here, we parse the CSV file and connect everything in the **netname** column to the **samAccountName** property in **New-ADUser**.

And so on for the next two hash tables.

NOTE

You'll notice that I commented out my hash table for the EmailAddress field by placing an octothorpe (#) character in front of the line. I included this line only as reference; we don't need it here because the column header name in the CSV file is already EmailAddress.

Summary

Hey, you deserve a hearty, congratulatory clap on the back for completing this lesson. Arguably, the object and pipeline concepts are the most difficult to grasp in all of Windows PowerShell, especially for those of us who are IT pros and not software developers.

The great news is that if you are beginning to comprehend objects, properties, and how the pipeline works, you are well on your way to mastering Windows PowerShell.

You also deserve a break. In Hour 7, "Sorting, Filtering, and Measuring Windows PowerShell Output," you learn how to filter and sort PowerShell output, which is decidedly less brain-cell intensive.

Q&A

Q. **You spoke of arrays and hash tables briefly in this hour. I know I'll learn them in depth later, but what is the key difference between an array and a hash table?**

A. As I explained, an array is a special type of variable that holds more than one data element. For instance, here is a simple array that contains a bunch of strings:

```
$array = "New York", "Tennessee", "South Carolina"
```

As you would expect, PowerShell includes methods whereby we can interact with individual elements in the array, and subtract elements, and so forth. However, notice that the array elements are not named; they simply exist as-is.

By contrast, a hash table is useful when we need to work with more than one data element by name. Look here:

```
$states = @{"Region1" = "New York"; "Region2" = "Tennessee"; "Region3" =
➥"South Carolina"}
```

Q. **Is there a fast way to know what's going on inside the pipeline at any point?**

A. You're thinking logically, that's for sure. You should get to the point, given enough time and experience, that you can put your finger on the pipe character and either know outright what kind of object exists there, or you can find out. For instance, let's imagine that the following pipeline expression gave us trouble:

```
Get-Service -Name Wsearch | Stop-Process
```

Remember the old mantra: "When in doubt, remove the last element from the pipeline and pipe to **Get-Member**."

```
Get-Service -Name Wsearch | Get-Member
```

Doing so will tell you precisely the object data type and all the parameters that are available for binding. You can quickly look up individual properties in the help by using the **–Parameter**... parameter:

```
Get-Help Stop-Process -Parameter InputObject
```

Q. **Look, I don't have a lot of time, and I can't remember the parameter name I'm searching for. How can get a list of only the parameters for a given cmdlet?**

A. Sure, no problem. Here we can apply the asterisk wildcard character. For instance, the following statement retrieves just the parameters of the **Get-ChildItem** cmdlet:

```
Get-Help Get-ChildItem -Parameter *
```

Here's a wonderful PowerShell one-liner that brings back a list of only parameters that accept pipeline input, as well as how they do so. Awesome!

```
Get-Help Get-Process -Parameter * | Where {$_.pipelineInput -Like 'true*'} |
➥Select Name, PipelineInput
```

The preceding example is good also because it exposes you to the **Where-Object** and **Select-Object** cmdlets, both of which you'll become intimately familiar with in the next hour of training.

Workshop

Start up four instances of Windows Notepad on your system. By using only Windows PowerShell, learn everything you can about the processes. Determine whether you can kill all four processes at once.

Similarly, figure out a way to get a list of running services on your system, sort them alphabetically by service name, and output to an HTML report. We haven't covered all those steps in this book yet; I'm challenging you to use your PowerShell-fu and research skills to get the job done. I believe in you.

Quiz

1. When you pipe objects, PowerShell attempts to associate the piped objects with one of the _____ of the receiving command.

   a. objects

   b. outputs

   c. parameters

   d. methods

2. The Linux and Cmd.exe shells pipe _____, whereas Windows PowerShell pipes only _____.

   a. text, objects

   b. text, parameters

   c. objects, text

   d. objects, parameters

3. What does the **$_** mean in the following Windows PowerShell expression?

   ```
   Get-Service | Where-Object { $_.Status -eq "Stopped" }
   ```

   a. All items in the pipeline

   b. Items in the pipeline with a string data type

   c. Current item in the pipeline

Answers

1. The correct answer is C. Remember that the onus is on the receiving command to map one of its parameters to either the incoming object directly (by value), or to a matching property name (by property name).

2. The correct answer is A. The most immediate differentiator between pipelining in UNIX, Linux, and Windows' own Cmd.exe is that these command shells pipeline flat text. By contrast, Windows PowerShell pipelines fully functional data structures called objects.

3. The correct answer is C. The **$_** automatically created variable is used as a shorthand method for iterating through each object in a collection. Actually, the **$_** shortcut is synonymous with the **$PSItem** automatic variable. Therefore, we can rewrite the previous statement like this:

```
Get-Service | Where-Object { $PSItem.Status -eq "Stopped" }
```

Sorting, Filtering, and Measuring Windows PowerShell Output

What You'll Learn in This Hour:

▶ How to sort your PowerShell output

▶ How to extract only the PowerShell output you need to see

▶ How to measure various properties of PowerShell output

Windows PowerShell has many more output streams than you are probably aware of. For instance, try the following command from an elevated PowerShell session:

```
PS C:\> Get-Command -Verb out
```

CommandType	Name	Source
Cmdlet	Out-Default	Microsoft...
Cmdlet	Out-File	Microsoft...
Cmdlet	Out-GridView	Microsoft...
Cmdlet	Out-Host	Microsoft...
Cmdlet	Out-Null	Microsoft...
Cmdlet	Out-Printer	Microsoft...
Cmdlet	Out-String	Microsoft...

Remember that **gcm** is a popular alias for **Get-Command**. Under the hood, all your commands, whether they are single cmdlets or complex pipelines, exit the pipeline by default through **Out-Default**, which pipes to **Out-Host**. Here, try these:

```
Get-Process |Out-Default
Get-Process | Out-Host
```

I want to start this hour this way for two reasons:

▶ In the next hour, we revisit these concepts when we examine how to format, export, and otherwise "massage" PowerShell output.

▶ In this hour, we're concerned with manipulating output mainly for onscreen display.

Specifically, we'll start this hour of training by learning how to generate PowerShell output in our preferred sort order. Then I'll teach you how we can cut down on the output volume by using filtering. Finally, you'll learn how to use **Measure-Object** to obtain all sorts of cool metadata concerning our PowerShell object output.

Sorting Output

How would you display the top 10 processes on your computer, ordered by their CPU utilization? Try this:

```
Get-Process
```

I'd like to introduce you to the **Sort-Object** cmdlet. Examine the syntax of the command:

```
Sort-Object [[-Property] <Object[]> ] [-CaseSensitive] [-Culture <String> ]
[-Descending] [-InputObject <PSObject> ] [-Unique] [ <CommonParameters>]
```

TIP

Remember that you can see the syntax of a command by viewing the cmdlet's help.

You see that we can sort by one or more properties. How do we know we can sort on more than one object property? Remember that the [] in the parameter data type (here, the –**Property** parameter) denotes an array.

Also observe the –**Descending** switch parameter. This denotes an inverse, or Z to A, sort. Where is the corresponding –**Ascending** switch? It turns out we don't need it because PowerShell defaults to an ascending sort. Try this:

```
Get-Process | Sort-Object -Property Name
```

Next, try this and observe the difference:

```
Get-Process | Sort Name -Descending
```

If you examine the –**Property** parameter in the help file, you'll learn that it's positional, so we don't have to specify the –**Property** parameter name; most PowerShell professionals don't.

Also, you can see (and read in the help file) that **Sort** is an easy alias for **Sort-Object**.

Discovering Property Names

All this sorting stuff is cool, but how do we know the names of the columns by which we want to sort? **Get-Process** has a particularly gnarly set of columns, even in its default **Out-Host** view:

```
PS C:\> Get-Process

Handles  NPM(K)    PM(K)      WS(K) VM(M)   CPU(s)     Id ProcessName
-------  ------    -----      ----- -----   ------     -- -----------
    370      21     4796       1480   125     1.16   9596 AAM Updates Notifier
    246      24    26948      24676   189     2.80   7988 Acrobat
    162      19     2744       3036    95    16.05   1572 AppleMobileDeviceS...
    182      22     4424      14564   138     0.08   9336 ApplePhotoStreams
    426      24     5088       7188   124     6.89   4624 APSDaemon
    161       9     6716       7540    38   172.47   6948 audiodg
    456      23    12464      11716   132    10.34   6012 CameraHelperShell
    423      26    14016       6576   193     0.45   2928 chrome
```

Look at the CPU(s) column—I thought that parentheses weren't allowed in property names. Also, these values aren't in bytes, but kilobytes. What's going on?

As always, we should pipe to **Get-Member** to reveal all properties:

```
PS C:\> Get-Process | Get-Member -MemberType Properties


   TypeName: System.Diagnostics.Process

Name          MemberType     Definition
----          ----------     ----------
Handles       AliasProperty  Handles = Handlecount
Name          AliasProperty  Name = ProcessName
NPM           AliasProperty  NPM = NonpagedSystemMemorySize64
PM            AliasProperty  PM = PagedMemorySize64
VM            AliasProperty  VM = VirtualMemorySize64
WS            AliasProperty  WS = WorkingSet64
__NounName    NoteProperty   System.String __NounName=Process
BasePriority  Property       int BasePriority {get;}
```

I'm showing you only a partial list of properties to save white space in this book. The bottom line is you'll observe **AliasProperty** definitions for the columns found in the default output. The PowerShell team also is doing some beneath-the-covers trickery to convert bytes to kilobytes and so forth.

NOTE

The bottom line: We can learn the columns that we want to sort by simply by examining the properties of the given object. I know that I'm repeating that point a lot, but it bears repeating because the concept is so foundational to mastering Windows PowerShell.

Another point to ponder: PowerShell is, in largest part, *not* a case-sensitive language. You'll see in the help that if you do need to run a case-sensitive sort, you can tack on the **–CaseSensitive** parameter to your expression.

Sorting on Multiple Criteria

Thus far, we know that **Sort-Object** accepts one or more columns, and applies an ascending sort by default. We can reverse the sort by specifying the **–Descending** parameter.

What if we need to sort on multiple criteria? For example, how could we get a list of services sorted first by their running state, and then by name?

First off, piping **Get-Service** tells you that the "running state" of a service is defined by the **Status** property, and the name of the service is given by the **Name** alias. Try this:

```
Get-Service | Sort-Object -Property status, name
```

What happens here is that **Sort-Object** performs an ascending sort by **Status**, and then for matching **Status** values (of which there are many in this example), we perform a secondary ascending sort.

Naturally, your next question is, "Can I apply an ascending sort to one property, and a descending sort to another property?" The answer, sadly, is no, at least not conveniently. Sure, if you do enough Google research you may find a hacky "solution," but as of Windows PowerShell v5, the product team hasn't given us this capability out of the box.

Adding Grouping to the Mix

The **Group-Object** (aliased to **Group**, reasonably enough) is great when you have a lot of repetition in your output and want to separate the output based on a grouping level.

For example, use the following command (or the alias **cd** for those of you with prior Cmd.exe experience) to set your current location to the \windows\system32 directory:

```
Set-Location c:\windows\system32
```

Now run a general directory listing. (The common aliases for the **Get-ChildItem** cmdlet are **dir** or **ls**.)

```
Get-ChildItem
```

There's a lot of content in that directory, agreed? Let's check our members:

```
Get-ChildItem | Get-Member
```

The output is interesting because you'll see two types of .NET object types:

- **DirectoryInfo**, which represents folder objects
- **FileInfo**, which represents file objects

For file objects, you'll see **Name**, **Extension**, and **Count** properties, among others. Let's try to group the directory contents by extension:

```
Get-ChildItem | Group-Object –Property extension
```

That's not the cleanest output because PowerShell gives us the object collection in what appears to be a random order. Once we add **Sort-Object** to the pipeline, everything becomes much better:

```
PS C:\Windows\System32> Get-ChildItem | Group-Object –Property extension |
Sort-Object -Property count -Descending

Count Name                    Group
----- ----                    -----
2393 .dll                     {accessibilitycpl.dll, ACCTRES.dll, acledit....
 498 .exe                     {aitagent.exe, aitstatic.exe, alg.exe, appid...
 120 .NLS                     {C_037.NLS, C_10000.NLS, C_10001.NLS, C_1000...
 105                          {0409, AdvancedInstallers, AppLocker, ar-SA...}
  29 .lrc                     {igfxrara.lrc, igfxrchs.lrc, igfxrcht.lrc, i...
  29 .resources               {Gfxres.ar-SA.resources, Gfxres.cs-CZ.resour...
  21 .msc                     {azman.msc, certlm.msc, certmgr.msc, comexp....
  19 .cpl                     {appwiz.cpl, bthprops.cpl, desk.cpl, Firewal...
  15 .ax                      {bdaplgin.ax, g711codc.ax, ksproxy.ax, kstvt...
  13 .rs                      {cero.rs, cob-au.rs, csrr.rs, djctq.rs...}
  13 .xml                     {ApnDatabase.xml, AppxProvisioning.xml, loca...
  12 .dat                     {dfpinc.dat, dssec.dat, FNTCACHE.DAT, ieapfl...
  10 .tlb                     {activeds.tlb, amcompat.tlb, msdatsrc.tlb, m...
   9 .searchconnector-ms      {connectedsearch-appcmd.searchconnector-ms, ...
```

Filtering Output

Now that we're ready to address the tasks of filtering PowerShell output, I must tender a disclaimer: Those of you with prior experience with using Structured Query Language (SQL) or Windows Management Instrumentation Query Language (WQL) to interact with relational databases and the WMI repository, respectively, are going to have somewhat of an advantage here, at least at first.

The advantage is conveyed by the fact that the PowerShell team indeed studied SQL as they "cherry picked" the best features from different programming languages, scripting languages, and command shells in developing the original specification for Windows PowerShell. For instance, in SQL you might run the following query to pull selected data from a fictional Employees table:

```
SELECT empid, firstname, lastname, hiredate
FROM employees
WHERE hiredate > 01-01-10
ORDER BY hiredate -asc;
```

Let me summarize the SQL keywords at play here and what they are doing:

▸ **SELECT** retrieves row data **FROM** one or more tables.

▸ **WHERE** performs row filtering on one or more criteria.

▸ **ORDER BY** performs ascending and/or descending sorts.

The good news here is that we have the **Select-Object**, **Where-Object**, and **Sort-Object** PowerShell cmdlets that correspond neatly to the three aforementioned SQL statements!

Using Select-Object

You'll rarely see PowerShell power users specify the entire **Select-Object** cmdlet. Instead, you'll see them use either the **Select** or ? aliases. The alias is taking on a new and vital importance in your PowerShell education, isn't it?

Nonetheless, while aliases provide great convenience at the PowerShell console prompt, they are less useful in scripts. Please avoid aliases in your scripts and use full cmdlet and parameter names instead to maximize your code's readability and compatibility.

Let's return to our old standard reference cmdlet, **Get-Process**. We already know that running the command as-is brings back a subset of properties that the original developers (in this case, the PowerShell product team) deemed most useful for us to see.

That said, we can now use a powerful combination of **Get-Member** and **Select-Object** to return only properties that WE want to see, and in our preferred sequence to boot.

Compare the output of the following example with what you get if you run **Get-Service** with no additional commands:

```
Get-Service | Select-Object -Property ProcessName, Id, cpu, ws
```

Hey, Have You Been Using Tab Completion?

I haven't made too big of a deal of it so far, but I wanted to remind you that you should be growing increasingly accustomed to using PowerShell tab completion. Remember that PowerShell v3 and later allow you to tab-complete just about everything, even value data. For instance, type the following and then repeatedly press the **Tab** key (making sure to add a space after **–Name**):

```
Get-Service -Name
```

Isn't that cool. Tab completion not only is faster because you're doing less typing, it also makes it much less likely that you'll misspell or actually forget what a command, method, or property name is. Please rely on tab completion whenever it's available. You'll find in your experience that most objects support tab completion, but some haven't yet been updated (as surprising as that is) to take advantage of the capability.

The **Select-Object** cmdlet includes the **–First** and **–Last** parameters, which accept integer values and specify the number of desired objects from either the start or end of the array, respectively. To wit:

```
PS C:\> Get-Process| Sort-Object -Property ws -Descending | Select-Object -First 5

Handles  NPM(K)    PM(K)      WS(K) VM(M)   CPU(s)       Id ProcessName
-------  ------    -----      ----- -----   ------       -- -----------
    295      68   379520     369348   868 2,034.69     5036 chrome
    209      46   305460     305256   484    64.08    12100 chrome
   1678     114   158192     201892   514 1,424.98     4440 chrome
    791      50   210280     180316   827    26.53     6868 powershell
   1116      61    86416     158556   622   282.09     9832 WINWORD
```

In summary, **Select-Object** behaves in much the same way that **SELECT** does in SQL. With the latter, we specify column names from one or more target tables. With the former, we specify properties from the current object(s) in the pipeline.

Using Where-Object

Where-Object performs horizontal (row-level) filtering in your pipeline. Whereas **Select-Object** allows you to customize the properties that are returned by PowerShell, **Where-Object** gives you the power to control the output volume.

Here's a quick example that shows how we can use **Where-Object** (aliased to where or ?)

```
PS C:\> Get-Process | Select-Object -Property ProcessName, cpu, ws | Where-Object
{ $_.cpu -gt 50 } | Sort-Object -Property cpu -Descending
```

ProcessName	CPU	WS
chrome	2046.390625	375738368
chrome	1428.203125	206757888
svchost	1471.125	131334144
Dropbox	607.765625	123338752
chrome	529.96875	95666176
SnagitEditor	1359.796875	89669632
mbamservice	644.21875	81158144
dwm	966.953125	72392704
svchost	1281.640625	71282688
MsMpEng	739.546875	65445888
mbam	788.578125	64946176
System	2096.015625	10842112

Cool. Let me break down this pipeline for you, step by step:

1. We retrieve all process objects active on the current system.

2. We filter out all columns (properties) except ProcessName, CPU, and WS.

3. We extract the rows that contain CPU values above 50.

4. We sort the output on the CPU property, descending.

As you can see, the **Where-Object** command requires that you construct an expression—more on that in a moment. In the meantime, try the following one-liner out and let me know if it works:

```
Get-Process | Select-Object -Property ProcessName, ws |
➥Where-Object {$_.cpu -gt 50} | Sort-Object -Property cpu -Descending
```

Did it work? Why or why not? Well, it should not have worked, and the reason comes down to the pipeline (once again). In the select portion of the pipeline, we remove the CPU column from the output. Therefore, the **Where-Object** doesn't even see it, and its expression always evaluates to null. Thus, no output.

Now there are some other things we could do to fix the above problem. By putting the Where-Object expression before Select-Object, we filter out unneeded rows before we cut down the number of properties we see in the output.

Some cmdlets include a –Filter parameter that enables you to perform filtering at that point instead of having to connect to a Where-Object expression. This speaks to the "filter left" PowerShell best practice suggestion, and reduces the number of objects that need to be processed further down the pipeline.

CAUTION
___

The take-home message here is that you need to be careful if/when you combine **Select-Object** with **Where-Object**, and as always you need to be mindful of exactly what data exists in each phase of your Windows PowerShell pipelines.
___

What Is a "Working Set," Anyway?

The **Get-Process** output is certainly cryptic to any but the most experienced and hardcore of geeks. First of all, the **WorkingSet** (WS) property defines the number of memory pages that were recently referenced by the process. This value is given in kilobytes (KB). In layman's terms, higher values mean that the process may be more RAM-hungry than other processes.

The CPU property also gives us (to me, anyway) unexpected output. My initial assumption would be that the property should give us a CPU utilization counter that ranges from 0 to 100, like Task Manager does. Nope.

Instead, the CPU property of the **Get-Process** command gives us the amount of time that the process has occupied on all system processors, given in seconds.

Comparison Operators in PowerShell

Look at the following PowerShell statements: does their syntax make sense to you?

```
Get-Module -ListAvailable | ? { $_Name -notlike "Microsoft*" }
Get-Command | Where-Object { $_.CommandType -ne "cmdlet" }
```

The previous **Where-Object** expressions involve our old friend $_, but I'm speaking in particular of the funky references to **–notlike** and **–ne**.

Also, notice in the previous code I "padded" the expression in the Get-Command pipeline with spaces, and didn't do that for the Get-Module statement. Personally, I like to add leading and trailing space in my expressions to give them "breathing room" and to make the code more legible for others to comprehend.

These are what are called comparison operators, and they, as you would expect, serve to compare two values and return a Boolean **$true** or **$false** result. Here's the grand list:

▶ **-eq** (equal to)

▶ **-ne** (not equal to)

▶ **-gt** (greater than)

▶ **-ge** (greater than or equal to)

▶ **-lt** (less than)

- ▸ **-le** (less than or equal to)

- ▸ **-like** (wildcard comparison)

- ▸ **-notlike** (wildcard comparison)

- ▸ **-in** (contained in an array)

- ▸ **-notin** (not contained in an array)

- ▸ **-contains** (contains the specified value)

- ▸ **-notcontains** (does not contain the specified value)

NOTE

The foregoing isn't a complete list; see the help file about_Comparison_Operators for the full information.

You might be familiar with the traditional mathematical comparison operators such as =, >, <, and so forth. The PowerShell team explicitly chose these textual representations to avoid conflict with the mathematical symbols in other contexts.

For example, in Linux and Cmd.exe you can redirect output by using the greater than symbol:

```
dir > cdrive.txt
```

We can actually do this in PowerShell as well; hence you see the need for alternatives.

The best way for you to get comfortable with using these comparison operators is to actually use them. To that point, work through the following Try It Yourself exercise on that very subject.

▼ TRY IT YOURSELF

Playing with PowerShell Comparison Operators

In this Try It Yourself exercise, you'll gain some experience in using PowerShell comparison operators "on their own" as well as in the context of the pipeline.

To complete this exercise, work from an elevated PowerShell console session.

1. Let's begin by running some simple expressions, all of which return either Boolean true or false. I won't give you the answers here; half the fun is thinking about the expected result and then comparing your idea with the actual output:

```
2 + 3
50 - 5
33 * 3
100 / 4
```

```
8 -ge 8
8 -lt 6
4 + 2 * 3 * (20 / 3)
```

The last expression was interesting because it reminds us of the order of mathematical operations. (Remember the old mnemonic PEMDAS?) Feel free to put parentheses around any expression or subexpression that you need PowerShell to evaluate first.

2. Now let's try some more interesting examples:

```
"Spam" -eq "spam"
"Spam -ceq "spam"
```

What did you see? You can prepend c to your comparison operator to make it case sensitive. By default, string comparisons are not case sensitive.

3. Let's do more with strings:

```
"abc" -ne "abc"
"Windows PowerShell" -like "*shell"
```

The –like operator is excellent when you need to use fuzziness in your expressions. For instance, combining –like with the asterisk in the last example says, "Does 'Windows PowerShell' match on any word ending in 's-h-e-l-l'?"

4. On to more generic examples:

```
"abc", "def" -contains "def"
"def" -in "abc", "def"
```

5. And now we'll consider a few practical situations where the use of comparison operators helps us with our PowerShell expressions.

For instance, here we can retrieve a list of PowerShell commands available on our system that are of the **CommandType** cmdlet:

```
Get-Command | Where-Object {$_.CommandType -eq "cmdlet"}
```

6. What if we need to retrieve any PowerShell command that includes the string **clear** in its name?

```
PS C:\> Get-Command | Where-Object {$_.name -like "*clear*"}
```

CommandType	Name	Source
-----------	----	------
Function AssignedA...	Clear-AssignedAccess	
Function	Clear-BCCache	BranchCache
Function	Clear-BitLockerAutoUnlock	BitLocker
Function	Clear-Disk	Storage

```
Function      Clear-DnsClientCache                      DnsClient
Function      Clear-FileStorageTier                    Storage
Function      Clear-Host
Cmdlet        Clear-Content
Microsoft...
Cmdlet        Clear-EventLog
Microsoft...
Cmdlet        Clear-History
Microsoft...
Cmdlet        Clear-Item
Microsoft...
Cmdlet        Clear-ItemProperty
Microsoft...
Cmdlet        Clear-KdsCache                            Kds
Cmdlet        Clear-Tpm
TrustedPl...
Cmdlet        Clear-Variable
Microsoft...
Cmdlet        Clear-WindowsCorruptMountPoint            Dism
```

If you're anything like I am, you'll be using the asterisk wildcard operator all the time. After all, given how many thousands of PowerShell commands exist in the world today, I daresay nobody has all their names memorized, including Jeffrey Snover, the creator of Windows PowerShell.

NOTE

If you've ever played the awesome game Minecraft, you know that the cardinal rule in that game is never to dig straight up or straight down lest you find yourself in a lava pool.

With Windows PowerShell, the equivalent mantra is "filter left, format right." What this means is that the formatting commands that you'll learn about in the next couple of hours terminate the pipeline in most cases.

Therefore, you want to put your filtering commands as far to the left in the pipeline as possible, and then save the filtering, exporting, and converting commands for the end.

Measuring Objects

One of the features of Microsoft Excel that I especially enjoy is its ability to rapidly give me measurement data based on my selection. Take a look at Figure 7.1 to see what I mean.

We can do all of this and more by invoking the **Measure-Object** cmdlet. Here is the syntax from the command's first parameter set, which is the one that I use all the time:

```
Measure-Object [[-Property] <String[]>] [-Average ] [-InputObject <PSObject>]
[-Maximum ] [-Minimum ] [-Sum ] [<CommonParameters>]
```

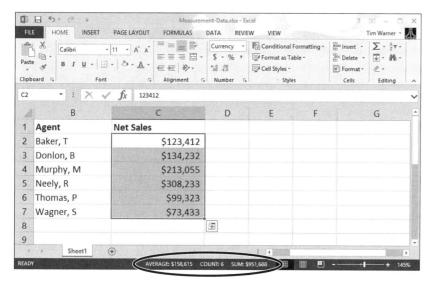

FIGURE 7.1
Microsoft Excel provides easy access to common measurement data.

The foregoing syntax doesn't tell us this directly, but **Measure-Object** (aliased to **measure**) performs the count operation by default. For instance:

```
PS C:\> Get-ChildItem -Path "C:\Windows\System32" | Measure-Object

Count     : 3397
Average   :
Sum       :
Maximum   :
Minimum   :
Property  :
```

Delving Deeper into Measure-Object

How about we try a more interesting example? Imagine we had a CSV file named student-grades.csv that had the following contents:

```
Lastname,grade
Abbott,81
Barclay,77
Miller,92
Night,66
Potter,80
Singleton,96
Williams,54
Zion,90
```

Now let's build a pipeline:

```
PS C:\Users\Tim\Desktop> Import-Csv -Path .\student-grades.csv |
➡Measure-Object -Property grade -Average -Maximum -Minimum

Count     : 8
Average   : 79.5
Sum       :
Maximum   : 96
Minimum   : 54
Property  : grade
```

"Cool beans!" as we used to say in the 1980s. You may be wondering two things, like I did at first:

▶ How does the **–Property** parameter work?

▶ How did PowerShell know we wanted to work on the grade field in the CSV file?

To the first point, let's consult the **Measure-Object** help:

```
PS C:\Users\Tim\Desktop> Get-Help Measure-Object -Parameter Property

-Property <String[]>
    Specifies one or more numeric properties to measure. The default is the
    Count (Length) property of the object.

    Required?                    false
    Position?                    1
    Default value                Count
    Accept pipeline input?       false
    Accept wildcard characters?  false
```

Aha. We learn that the **–Property** parameter is positional in the first position, and that it defaults to performing a count. Mystery solved. We also see that the parameter expects a string value.

Honestly, I wonder whether the help file's statement that the **–Property** parameter doesn't accept pipeline input is an error. It's crucial to note that the PowerShell help system is not infallible by any means. In point of fact, one of the beauties of updateable help in PowerShell is that we see those fixes as they are made by the Windows PowerShell team.

At any rate, let's see the data that comes out of the **Import-Csv** part of the pipeline:

```
PS C:\Users\Tim\Desktop> Import-Csv -Path .\student-grades.csv | Get-Member

    TypeName: System.Management.Automation.PSCustomObject
```

```
Name            MemberType    Definition
----            ----------    ----------
Equals          Method        bool Equals(System.Object obj)
GetHashCode     Method        int GetHashCode()
GetType         Method        type GetType()
ToString        Method        string ToString()
grade           NoteProperty  System.String grade=81
Lastname        NoteProperty  System.String Lastname=Abbott
```

Okay. So PowerShell dynamically creates a **NoteProperty** for each column header in the CSV file. The data type is string, which is completely compatible with the data that **Measure-Object** expects.

What Measure-Object Is and What It Isn't

We need to keep in mind that **Measure-Object** is excellent at giving us numeric statistics, but it won't tell us anything else about our data.

For instance, to continue our preceding example, how could we generate a report that lists the students with the top three grades? Like this:

```
$csv = Import-Csv -Path .\student-grades.csv
$csv | Sort-Object -Property score -desc | Select-Object -First 3
```

```
Lastname                             grade
--------                             -----
Singleton                            96
Potter                               80
Zion                                 90
```

You can use the **Measure-Object** command to calculate text file statistics as well. Let's imagine that we have the following text file, boilerplate.txt:

Lorem ipsum dolor sit amet, consectetur adipiscing elit. Sed et nulla mattis, luctus libero at, semper dolor. Aenean sed arcu a metus tincidunt mollis. Curabitur consectetur, arcu at rhoncus rhoncus, ante sem cursus mauris, sed lobortis erat dui sit amet odio. Duis nec sollicitudin nunc, sed lacinia ante. Sed egestas quis lorem tristique aliquam. Proin scelerisque vulputate leo, in ornare mi sodales sed. Sed quis quam finibus velit placerat auctor. Quisque aliquam justo dolor, ac rutrum elit tincidunt a. Quisque molestie cursus justo vitae dictum.

Aliquam ornare nunc sit amet purus lobortis elementum. Quisque ornare rhoncus pellentesque. Quisque a quam vehicula urna ultricies ornare. Maecenas vel mi vitae ipsum tristique dapibus vitae in libero. Maecenas a turpis et magna facilisis tempus. Aliquam maximus placerat pulvinar. Maecenas vitae mauris a lorem vestibulum porttitor et eu eros. Donec vestibulum lectus in diam volutpat, a sollicitudin augue vehicula. Integer sed sapien sed metus dictum imperdiet. Phasellus luctus et urna id pharetra. Aliquam quis congue nulla. Etiam in condimentum mauris. Ut euismod lorem at aliquet convallis. Proin a nibh laoreet, lobortis eros eu, ultricies arcu.

NOTE

By the way, I obtained that boilerplate text from the nifty website lipsum.com; I use it all the time when I need "dummy" data for my classes or books.

Anyhow, check out the following PowerShell one-liner:

```
PS C:\Users\Tim\Desktop> Get-Content -Path .\boilerplate.txt |
Measure-Object -Word -Line -Character

            Lines              Words            Characters
            -----              -----            ----------
                2                181                  1206
```

That's a pretty neat trick, isn't it? I suggest that you read the help file and test out the examples for **Get-Content**; it's a particularly useful command that we'll spend more time with later on in the book.

Summary

So, how do you feel about your Windows PowerShell skills thus far? As your teacher I'm overjoyed, because now we can start to write more complex PowerShell code and I'm confident that you understand what we're doing.

In the upcoming hours, you'll learn how to access several data providers, including the file system, Windows Registry, and certificate store. We'll then revisit some of this hour's material as you learn how to format, convert, and export PowerShell data. Stay tuned, and congratulations on the great work you've done.

Q&A

Q. All this talk of comparison logic makes me think of the if/then construct in other scripting and programming language. Does Windows PowerShell support conditional logic?

A. Indeed it does. For example, let's say we wanted PowerShell to take action depending on the status of your computer's Server service. We could try the following mini-script (best authored in Windows PowerShell ISE) shown in Figure 7.2:

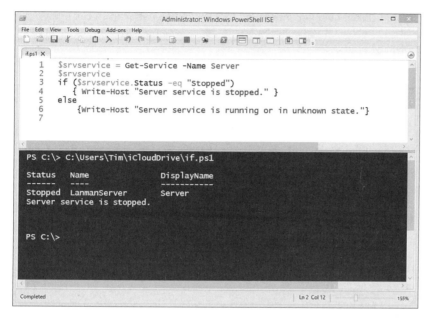

FIGURE 7.2
Windows PowerShell fully supports conditional and branching logic.

You'll learn all about the **if** statement later in the book, but for now I want to briefly walk you through the code, line by line:

▶ **Line 1:** We define a variable to hold the desired service object in memory.

▶ **Line 2:** We echo back the contents of the variable for reference.

▶ **Line 3:** We use parentheses around our **if** expression; remember that all expressions evaluate to Boolean true or false.

▶ **Line 4:** We put the action logic in curly braces ({}); the Write-Host cmdlet writes general output to the screen.

▶ **Line 5:** We can use else or else if, depending on our needs.

▶ **Line 6:** We code what we want to happen if the **if** statement evaluates to false.

Q. Can you really not sort one property ascending, and another property descending in Windows PowerShell?

A. Nice use of the Boolean NOT in your question! Anyhow, I believe I mentioned that it is possible but not necessarily convenient (at all) to perform ascending and descending sorts on the same data.

Example 5 in the **Sort-Object** help file shows us how we can use hash tables to force Windows PowerShell to show us the services on our computer in descending **Status** order and ascending **DisplayName** order:

```
Get-Service | Sort-Object -Property @{Expression="Status";Descending=$true},
➡@{Expression="DisplayName";Descending=$false}
```

I'll leave it to you to figure out how that pipeline works.

Q. I forgot which command the question mark (?) is an alias for. Can you please remind me?

A. Use **Get-Alias** to retrieve a list of all system-generated and user-created alias mappings on the local system:

```
PS C:\> Get-Alias

CommandType     Name
-----------     ----
Alias           % -> ForEach-Object
Alias           ? -> Where-Object
Alias           ac -> Add-Content
Alias           asnp -> Add-PSSnapin
Alias           cat -> Get-Content
Alias           cd -> Set-Location
Alias           chdir -> Set-Location
Alias           clc -> Clear-Content
Alias           clear -> Clear-Host
Alias           clhy -> Clear-History
Alias           cli -> Clear-Item
Alias           clp -> Clear-ItemProperty
Alias           cls -> Clear-Host
Alias           clv -> Clear-Variable
Alias           cnsn -> Connect-PSSession
```

See? The question mark is an alias for **Where-Object**. Incidentally, you can always look at PowerShell's internal About documentation if you need to remind yourself of all the comparison operators supported in the language:

```
Help about_Comparison_operators -full
```

Workshop

Flex your Windows PowerShell muscles by figuring out how to generate a list of hotfixes that are currently installed on your computer. Going further, display only the security updates.

Adding one more layer of complexity, generate a report on your installed security updates that sorts descending on installation date and then ascending on hotfix ID.

Quiz

1. Will the $events1 and $events2 variables return identical results?

```
$events1 = Get-Eventlog -LogName System -Newest 1000
$events1 | Group-Object -Property source -noelement | Sort-Object -Property
➥count
-Descending

$events2 = Get-Eventlog -LogName System -Newest 1000
$events2 | Sort-Object -Property count –Descending | Group-Object -Property
➥source
-noelement
```

   a. Yes

   b. No

2. What is the purpose of the multiplication in the following PowerShell statement?

```
Get-Process | Where-Object { $_.WorkingSet -gt 25000*1024 }
```

   a. To convert the output to kilobytes

   b. To convert the output to bytes

   c. To ensure that processes with high working set values are captured in the results

   d. To exceed the maximum working set value

3. Which of the following commands uses –First and –Last parameters to easily capture the head/tail of the PowerShell output?

   a. Where-Object

   b. Select-Object

   c. Sort-Object

Answers

1. The correct answer is B. You have to pay attention not only to the data that's in the pipeline, but also the order in which you operate on that data. In the **$events1** procedure, we perform a grouping first and then sort second. We do the opposite in **$events2**; try this out on your computer to get a feel for how the output difference manifests itself. Here the output difference probably isn't a big deal. However, you will run into cases where it may cost you valuable time and money to make this kind of pipeline error.

2. The correct answer is A. Read the help file for **Get-Process** and you'll learn that the **WorkingSet** property is given in bytes. Windows administrators tend to think in terms of kilobytes, megabytes, and gigabytes, so instructing PowerShell to multiple the **WorkingSet** value by 1,024 gives us results in KB instead of B.

3. The correct answer is B. The following command retrieves the five processes on my system with the highest working set values, expressed in kilobytes:

```
PS C:\> Get-Process | Sort-Object -Property WorkingSet -Descending |
➥Select-Object -First 3

Handles  NPM(K)    PM(K)      WS(K) VM(M)    CPU(s)      Id ProcessName
-------  ------    -----      ----- -----    ------      -- -----------
    278      74   514048     511364   837    570.77   16272 chrome
   1777     220   213704     294776   649  2,105.70   12864 chrome
   1099      64   301896     251248   897     69.44    6868 powershell
```

Once again, we need to be careful to place **Sort-Object** first in the pipeline, because if we run **Select-Object** first, we'll just feed the first three processes returned by PowerShell to **Sort-Object**.

Managing Windows PowerShell Providers

What You'll Learn in This Hour:

▶ What are providers?

▶ Introduction to default PSDrives

▶ Using the FileSystem provider

▶ Using the Alias provider

▶ Using the Registry provider

▶ Using extended providers

This hour of training is all about lifting a veil of mystery from your eyes. "So *that's* why that works the way it does in Windows PowerShell!" is what I hope to hear from you.

Here we concern ourselves with accessing common data stores on our computer—the file system, certificate store, and the Registry, among others—all by using only Windows PowerShell.

What Are Providers?

In Windows PowerShell nomenclature, we can look at a provider as an adapter that gives us access to a particular data store. For instance, once you buy a compatible Universal Serial Bus (USB) cable and plug one end into a portable hard drive and the other into a USB port on your computer, you have access to all the resources on that external disk drive.

Likewise, Windows PowerShell ships with the following default PSProviders, as they're called:

```
PS C:\> Get-PSProvider | Select-Object -Property name, drives

Name                                  Drives
----                                  ------
Alias                                 {Alias}
Environment                           {Env}
FileSystem                            {C, E, D}
```

```
Function                        {Function}
Registry                        {HKLM, HKCU}
Variable                        {Variable}
WSMan                           {WSMan}
```

The WSMan provider appears in the **Get-PSProvider** output only if you've enabled PowerShell remoting; you'll learn how to do that later on in the book. Also, you may wonder why I used the Select-Object clause; after all, the output only has three properties.

My answer, quite honestly, is that I want to expose only the properties that directly relate to what we're learning. Why not take advantage of filtering whenever possible?

Functions Provided by a Provider

The PSProvider makes a particular data store available to you, the PowerShell user. For example, the Alias provider stores all the aliases that are defined on the local system.

The Environment provider encompasses all environment variables, the FileSystem provider opens up the file system to us, and so forth.

Although we have this collection of seven built-in PowerShell providers, that doesn't mean that these are all there are—not by a long shot.

Some Windows features and external applications bring along new PSProviders; two that come to mind are the Active Directory Domain Services (AD DS) server feature and the SQL Server relational database management system (RDBMS).

In fact, take a look at this screenshot that shows **Get-PSProvider** output on a Windows Server 2012 domain controller that also hosts a SQL Server 2012 instance:

```
PS C:\> Get-PSProvider

Name                Capabilities                          Drives
----                ------------                          ------
Alias               ShouldProcess                         {Alias}
Environment         ShouldProcess                         {Env}
FileSystem          Filter, ShouldProcess, Credentials    {C, A, D, Z}
Function            ShouldProcess                         {Function}
Registry            ShouldProcess, Transactions           {HKLM, HKCU}
Variable            ShouldProcess                         {Variable}
SqlServer           Credentials                           {SQLSERVER}
ActiveDirectory     Include, Exclude, Filter, Shoul...    {AD}
```

In the previous output, notice the **Capabilities** property. As it happens, different PSProviders offer different, well, capabilities. To wit:

▸ **ShouldProcess:** The provider supports the –**Confirm** and –**WhatIf** parameters.

▸ **Credentials:** The provider supports the use alternate credentials at runtime.

▸ **Transactions:** The provider supports atomic transactions, where one or more PowerShell statements succeed or fail together.

▸ **Filter, Include, Exclude:** The provider enables you to granularly manipulate the provider's content.

As you might think, the SQL Server PSProvider allows us to tap into any database in the local SQL Server instance (assuming that our user account has permissions, of course). The same goes for the Active Directory PSProvider.

What's important to understand is that PSProviders aren't directly accessible to us. Instead, PSProviders are used through a related technology known as the PSDrive.

Introduction to Default PSDrives

You probably noticed the Drives property in the **Get-PSProvider** output. This data represents the entry point into that particular data store. We can use either the **Set-Location** cmdlet or its more common **cd** alias to switch our context from the default provider (FileSystem) to, say, the Variable PSProvider. Check out this partial output from my Windows 8.1 system:

```
PS C:\> Set-Location Variable:
PS Variable:\> dir

Name                          Value
----                          -----
$                             Variable:
?                             True
^                             Set-Location
args                          {}
buffer                        80,5000
ConfirmPreference             High
console                       System.Management.Automation.Internal.Host.In...
ConsoleFileName
DebugPreference               SilentlyContinue
Error                         {The term 'dird' is not recognized as the nam...
ErrorActionPreference         Continue
ErrorView                     NormalView
ExecutionContext              System.Management.Automation.EngineIntrinsics
false                         False
FormatEnumerationLimit        4
HOME                          C:\Users\Tim
Host                          System.Management.Automation.Internal.Host.In...
```

```
input                   System.Collections.ArrayList+ArrayListEnumera...
LASTEXITCODE            0
MaximumAliasCount       4096
```

We don't need to concern ourselves specifically with what these variables mean; we have plenty of time for that when we delve into Windows PowerShell scripting later on in the book. For now, I just want you to get comfortable with navigating among the different providers.

We can use **Get-PSDrive** to obtain a listing of available PSDrives on our computer:

```
PS C:\> Get-PSDrive

Name          Used (GB)   Free (GB) Provider     Root
----          ---------   --------- --------     ----
Alias                               Alias
C               123.37      109.17 FileSystem   C:\
Cert                                Certificate  \
D                                   FileSystem   D:\
E               334.51     1528.48 FileSystem   E:\
Env                                 Environment
Function                            Function
HKCU                                Registry     HKEY_CURRENT_USER
HKLM                                Registry     HKEY_LOCAL_MACHINE
Variable                            Variable
WSMan                               WSMan
```

You'll observe that some PSProviders (namely FileSystem and Registry) offer more than one PSDrive.

A Familiar Navigation System

Notice that we specify a colon (:) when we change context to a PSDrive. Remember that the concept of drives is intentional with all its metaphorical baggage. In other words, we browse PSDrives using the standard Cmd.exe navigation commands we've always used.

Dir, you'll recall, is just an alias for **Get-ChildItem**. Linux aficionados can use **ls** if they want. In point of fact, check out the following partial output where we get a list of all system aliases (alii?) while working in the context of the Variable PSDrive:

```
PS Variable:\> ls alias:

CommandType     Name
-----------     ----
Alias           % -> ForEach-Object
Alias           ? -> Where-Object
Alias           ac -> Add-Content
Alias           asnp -> Add-PSSnapin
Alias           cat -> Get-Content
```

```
Alias            cd -> Set-Location
Alias            chdir -> Set-Location
Alias            clc -> Clear-Content
Alias            clear -> Clear-Host
Alias            clhy -> Clear-History
Alias            cli -> Clear-Item
Alias            clp -> Clear-ItemProperty
Alias            cls -> Clear-Host
```

Thus, if we want to return our focus to the file system, no problem; just use **cd** or **Set-Location** to switch to that PSDrive:

```
PS Variable:\>cd c:
```

TIP

Some PowerShell users employ the **sl** alias for **Set-Location**, by the way. So many options to choose from!

The FileSystem provider is a bit different from some of the other PSProviders inasmuch as it includes a separate PSDrive for each mounted volume on your system. We'll delve more into that point in a moment.

```
PS Variable:\> cd c:
PS C:\> dir


    Directory: C:\


Mode               LastWriteTime      Length Name
----               -------------      ------ ----
d----        4/22/2014    7:57 PM            Intel
d----        8/22/2013   10:22 AM            PerfLogs
d-r--       10/13/2014    1:03 PM            Program Files
d-r--       10/13/2014    1:10 PM            Program Files (x86)
d-r--        4/30/2014    1:18 PM            Sandbox
d----        7/21/2014   11:08 AM            savedhelp
d----        9/29/2014   11:49 AM            temp
d-r--         9/2/2014    8:36 AM            Users
d----       10/13/2014   12:23 PM            Windows
```

What's an Item?

Thus far, you see that these PSDrives were designed to give you the comfort of navigating different data stores in a familiar way by using Linux- or Windows-like shell commands (actually aliases to PowerShell cmdlets, as you know).

Once you start delving into PSDrives, you'll come across the word *item* all the time in cmdlet listings:

```
PS C:\> Get-Command -Noun *item* | Where-Object {$_.CommandType -eq "cmdlet"}

CommandType      Name                              Source
-----------      ----                              ------
Cmdlet           Clear-Item                        Microsoft...
Cmdlet           Clear-ItemProperty                Microsoft...
Cmdlet           Copy-Item                         Microsoft...
Cmdlet           Copy-ItemProperty                 Microsoft...
Cmdlet           Get-ChildItem                     Microsoft...
Cmdlet           Get-ControlPanelItem              Microsoft...
Cmdlet           Get-Item                          Microsoft...
Cmdlet           Get-ItemProperty                  Microsoft...
Cmdlet           Get-ItemPropertyValue             Microsoft...
Cmdlet           Invoke-Item                       Microsoft...
Cmdlet           Move-Item                         Microsoft...
Cmdlet           Move-ItemProperty                 Microsoft...
Cmdlet           New-Item                          Microsoft...
Cmdlet           New-ItemProperty                  Microsoft...
Cmdlet           Remove-Item                       Microsoft...
Cmdlet           Remove-ItemProperty               Microsoft...
Cmdlet           Rename-Item                       Microsoft...
Cmdlet           Rename-ItemProperty               Microsoft...
Cmdlet           Set-Item                          Microsoft...
Cmdlet           Set-ItemProperty                  Microsoft...
Cmdlet           Show-ControlPanelItem             Microsoft...
```

In PSProvider nomenclature, everything is an "item," whether we are talking about a variable, a directory, a file, or a Registry value. Once again, the PowerShell team strives to give us a standardized, unified interface for working with different data stores.

NOTE

Help! I'm in Alias Overload

In this hour, I've tried (perhaps to the point of overkill) to stress that we can access and use these PSDrives by using aliases that map to well-loved shell commands (**dir**, **ls**, **cd**, **type**, **cat**, and the like).

However, for the duration of this hour, I'll instead use the underlying commands instead of the aliases, with some exception. I need you to never forget that when you use aliases that "look and feel" like their Linux or DOS counterparts, you are actually running PowerShell commands under the hood.

Okay, then. I'm confident that you have a basic understanding of what PSProviders and PSDrives are. It's now time to learn how to leverage these data stores to accomplish meaningful work with Windows PowerShell. We'll start with the FileSystem provider, the use of which should already be familiar to you.

Using the FileSystem Provider

We'll start with the FileSystem provider because, frankly, you are connected to this provider by default every time you start a Windows PowerShell session.

To start, let's view all the PSDrives that are associated with your system's FileSystem PSProvider. Remember that your output may not match mine:

```
PS C:\> Get-PSDrive -PSProvider FileSystem

Name          Used (GB)     Free (GB) Provider      Root
----          ---------     --------- --------      ----
C               124.49        108.05 FileSystem    C:\
D                            FileSystem    D:\
E               334.51       1528.47 FileSystem    E:\
```

On my Windows 8.1 computer, I have three PSDrives that (not coincidentally) map to the three volumes that are attached to the system.

Under the hood, those three mount points (C:, D:, and E:) actually correspond to functions. Look at the following partial output:

```
PS C:\> Set-Location Function:
PS Function:\> Get-ChildItem

CommandType     Name
-----------     ----
Function        A:
Function        B:
Function        C:
Function        cd..
Function        cd\
Function        Clear-Host
Function        D:
Function        E:
```

Pretty cool, isn't it? In the name of improving your efficiency with the shell, you can also make use of the –Path parameter of Get-ChildItem to recast the previous example:

```
Get-ChildItem -Path Function:
```

By now you are well aware that the PowerShell team uses function definitions and other "smoke and mirror" techniques to make PowerShell as intuitive as possible for users.

One more thing: you need to understand that although PSProviders all do the same basic thing (exposing different datastores as if they are filesystems), each PSProvider has its own capability. The FileSystem provider, for instance, has –File and –Directory parameters that aren't supported by, say, the Function: provider.

Long story short, you'll need to experiment as you work with different PSProviders to see what's possible in each respective context.

Working with Get-ChildItem

We use **Get-ChildItem** to enumerate the contents of a FileSystem path:

```
PS C:\> Get-ChildItem


    Directory: C:\


Mode                LastWriteTime     Length  Name
----                -------------     ------  ----
d----        4/22/2014    7:57 PM             Intel
d----        8/22/2013   10:22 AM             PerfLogs
d-r--       10/13/2014    1:03 PM             Program Files
d-r--       10/14/2014    4:06 PM             Program Files (x86)
d-r--        9/2/2014     8:36 AM             Users
d----       10/13/2014   12:23 PM             Windows
-a---        4/23/2014    9:42 PM       1024  .rnd
-a---        7/23/2014   11:28 AM          0  CaptivateLog.log
-a---        7/14/2014   12:52 PM         27  testscript.ps1
-a---        7/23/2014   10:50 AM      16214  verb.txt
-a---        10/3/2014   12:05 PM       5638  x.txt
```

The **Get-ChildItem** command is quite flexible. Why not examine the object's properties and methods?

```
Get-ChildItem | Get-Member
```

If you run the preceding command on a file system location that contains both directories and files (as my C: drive contains), two objects are returned: **DirectoryInfo** objects for directories, and **FileInfo** objects for files.

Here's another example: By now you understand how to do filtering with **Where-Object** and comparison operators. Let's retrieve all objects in my C: drive that have the name **prog** in them:

```
PS C:\> Get-ChildItem *prog*


    Directory: C:\
```

```
Mode                LastWriteTime     Length Name
----                -------------     ------ ----
d-r--       10/13/2014   1:03 PM             Program Files
d-r--       10/14/2014   4:06 PM             Program Files (x86)
```

Wow. That syntax behaves exactly like Cmd.exe, doesn't it? However, you and I both know that we're dealing with positional parameters here. Let's examine the help file:

```
Get-Help Get-ChildItem -Full
```

And here is the syntax for the first parameter set:

```
Get-ChildItem [[-Path] <String[]>] [[-Filter] <String>] [-Exclude <String[]>]
[-Force ] [-Include <String[]>] [-Name ] [-Recurse ] [-UseTransaction
<SwitchParameter>] [<CommonParameters>]
```

We see that **–Path** is the first parameter:

```
-Path <String[]>
    Specifies a path to one or more locations. Wildcards are permitted. The
    default location is the current directory (.).

    Required?                    false
    Position?                    1
    Default value                Current directory
    Accept pipeline input?       true (ByValue, ByPropertyName)
    Accept wildcard characters?  true
```

Notice that although this parameter exists in the first position, it is technically optional. By default, **Get-ChildItem** returns a listing of objects within the current working directory. However, you can pass a path to the command with no problem:

```
Get-ChildItem -Path D:\projects\march
```

Next we have the **–Filter** parameter:

```
-Filter <String>
    Specifies a filter in the provider's format or language. The value of this
    parameter qualifies the Path parameter. The syntax of the filter,
    including the use of wildcards, depends on the provider. Filters are more
    efficient than other parameters, because the provider applies them when
    retrieving the objects, rather than having Windows PowerShell filter the
    objects after they are retrieved.

    Required?                    false
    Position?                    2
    Default value
    Accept pipeline input?       false
    Accept wildcard characters?  true
```

The most important thing to take from the **–Filter** parameter is that it does, as we've seen in practice, accept wildcards as input.

Obviously, there is more than one way to get the job done in PowerShell. Look here:

```
PS C:\> Get-ChildItem | Where-Object { $_.Name -like "*prog*" }


    Directory: C:\


Mode                LastWriteTime     Length Name
----                -------------     ------ ----
d-r--         10/13/2014    1:03 PM          Program Files
d-r--         10/14/2014    4:06 PM          Program Files (x86)
```

It all depends on what you're most comfortable with.

Let me turn you loose on a Try It Yourself exercise so you can delve into creating, modifying, and deleting file system objects by using Windows PowerShell.

▼ TRY IT YOURSELF

Using the FileSystem Provider

In this exercise, you'll use the FileSystem provider to create and modify directories and files. Don't worry; we won't operate on any of your existing content.

Prepare for this exercise by starting an elevated PowerShell session. It's useful to see a graphical depiction of the directory/file hierarchy you'll build, so look at Figure 8.1 for guidance. Let's get started.

1. We'll begin by setting our current working directory to the root of drive C:

   ```
   Set-Location C:\
   ```

2. As previously mentioned in passing, all file system objects, whether they be directory of file, are items. So, we use **New-Item** to build out our directories:

   ```
   PS C:\> New-Item -Name "practice" -Type Directory


       Directory: C:\


   Mode                LastWriteTime     Length Name
   ----                -------------     ------ ----
   d----         10/15/2014   10:25 AM          practice
   ```

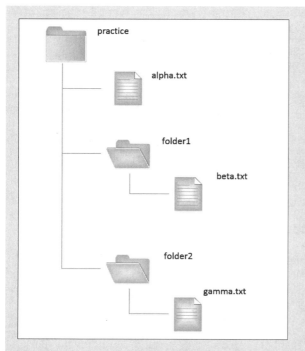

FIGURE 8.1
The file system hierarchy we're building.

TIP

You technically aren't required to use quotation marks to enclose your object names, but I suggest doing so as a matter of practice.

We can use the **–Path** parameter to create the other two folders without changing our current working directory:

```
New-Item -Path "C:\practice" -Name "folder1" -Type Directory
New-Item -Path "C:\practice" -Name "folder2" -Type Directory
```

3. Historically, I always use the statement **dir *.** to fetch a listing of only directories in a location. That won't work in PowerShell, sadly. Instead, we need to access the **PsisContainer** property of the **DirectoryInfo** object. By the way, **PsisContainer** can be read as "PowerShell object that is a container."

```
Set-Location c:\practice
Get-ChildItem | Where-Object {$_.psiscontainer}

    Directory: C:\practice
```

```
Mode              LastWriteTime        Length Name
----              -------------        ------ ----
d----        10/15/2014  10:27 AM             folder1
d----        10/15/2014  10:28 AM             folder2
```

Is this making sense so far? Let's shift our focus back to the root of C:

```
Set-Location C:\
```

4. We can create new, empty files by using **New-Item** as well. As you doubtless observed by now, the **–Type** parameter is the "secret sauce" that instructs PowerShell what kind of item you're seeking to create:

```
New-Item -Name "alpha.txt" -Type File
New-Item -Path "c:\practice\folder1" -Name "beta.txt" -Type File
New-Item -Path "c:\practice\folder2" -Name "gamma.txt" -Type File
```

5. Now let's add some data to one of the files and then read it back. We use **Add-Content** to, well, add new data to the file, and **Get-Content** to dump the contents to the console:

```
PS C:\> Add-Content "alpha.txt" -Value "This is some sample data."
PS C:\> Get-Content "alpha.txt"
This is some sample data.
```

6. Time to get fancy! Let's now use what we call a parenthetical expression to copy and paste the content of alpha.txt into gamma.txt:

```
PS C:\> Add-Content "C:\practice\folder2\gamma.txt" -Value (Get-Content "C:\
➥alpha.txt")
PS C:\> Get-Content -Path "C:\practice\folder2\gamma.txt"
This is some sample data.
```

7. Why don't we add some more data to alpha.txt and then pop the file open in Windows Notepad? You can see this output from my computer by examining Figure 8.2.

```
Add-Content "alpha.txt" -Value "Here is more data." | notepad alpha.txt
```

NOTE

We already know that PowerShell can launch (most) external executables, so it makes sense that we can start Notepad from within the PowerShell environment. It's also cool, to me anyway, that the **Add-Content** cmdlet helpfully appends your new data on a new line instead of running it flush into your existing text.

8. You'll finish this exercise by cleaning up your environment a bit. The **Remove-Item** command in the following example nukes the beta.txt file and forces the operation:

```
Remove-Item -Path "c:\practice\folder1\beta.txt" -Force
```

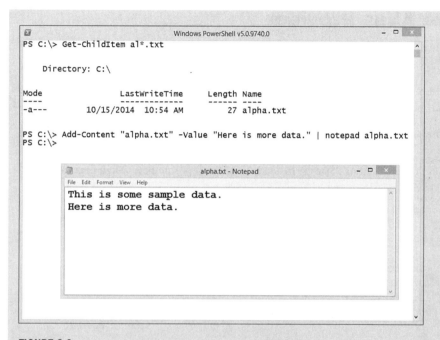

FIGURE 8.2
Who says that you need a word processor to author text files?

What about deleting directories? Make sure to **Set-Location** to the root of drive C:, and we'll delete the entire practice folder and file hierarchy. Be careful with this one! The **–Recurse** parameter is helpful because it moves through all subdirectories in the current path, but in the context of deletion, it's pretty scary.

```
Remove-Item -Path "c:\practice" -Recurse
```

NOTE

You might recall the arithmetic order of operations from grade school that states parentheses as the highest-priority operator. In Windows PowerShell, we place the expression that we want PowerShell to process first within parentheses.

For instance, what if we have a text file containing a list of server hostnames, and we want to obtain a service listing from them all by using the **–ComputerName** parameter? We can use parentheses to ensure that PowerShell retrieves the server name list before passing the data as values to **–Computername**.

```
Get-Service -Computername (Get-Content "D:\servernames.txt")
```

Using the Alias Provider

An alias is simply an alternate name for a PowerShell command or parameter. The purposes of aliases are as follows:

▶ To make PowerShell more accessible to those with shell scripting experience in Windows or other operating systems.

▶ To allow the administrator to issue PowerShell commands with less typing.

To be honest, I don't use the Alias PSDrive. Instead, I use the separate PowerShell commands that are devoted to aliases:

```
PS C:\> Get-Command -Noun alias
```

```
CommandType     Name                                               Source
-----------     ----                                               ------
Cmdlet          Export-Alias                                       Microsoft...
Cmdlet          Get-Alias                                          Microsoft...
Cmdlet          Import-Alias                                       Microsoft...
Cmdlet          New-Alias                                          Microsoft...
Cmdlet          Set-Alias                                          Microsoft...
```

We don't need to worry about creating and managing aliases using the aforementioned commands at this point; there is time for that in a later hour. For now I want to focus on using the PSProvider.

Using the Alias PSDrive

We access the contents of the Alias PSDrive as usual:

```
Set-Location Alias:
```

As an author, I need to be mindful of page count in my books. However, I want you to review the printed list of built-in aliases in Windows PowerShell v5. So, here is at least some partial output to give you a feel for what's there:

```
PS Alias:\> Get-ChildItem | Select-Object -Property name, definition
```

```
Name                                  Definition
----                                  ----------
%                                     ForEach-Object
?                                     Where-Object
ac                                    Add-Content
asnp                                  Add-PSSnapIn
cat                                   Get-Content
cd                                    Set-Location
chdir                                 Set-Location
```

Spend some time studying those aliases; you'll doubtless find some you hadn't thought of before or knew existed.

NOTE

I know that I'm preaching to the proverbial choir by saying this, but you can greatly extend your Windows PowerShell knowledge by regularly consulting the internal About documentation. Don't forget to run **Update-Help –Force** first to ensure that you have the latest and greatest information.

Here are some about help files that are relevant to this hour of training:

▶ about_Aliases

▶ about_Functions

▶ about_Providers

▶ about_Variables

Using the Registry Provider

The Windows Registry is the configuration database for Windows systems. PowerShell splits the PSDrives along the lines of the HKEY_LOCAL_MACHINE and HKEY_CURRENT_USER hives, as you can see here:

```
PS C:\> Get-PSDrive -PSProvider Registry | Select-Object –Property name, root

Name                                    Root
----                                    ----
HKCU                                    HKEY_CURRENT_USER
HKLM                                    HKEY_LOCAL_MACHINE
```

Retrieving Registry Values

Let's say that we need to view the value and associated properties that are associated with the DisablePreviewDesktop DWORD Registry value that is present in Windows 8.1 machines; this value, which disables the Aero Peek graphical user interface (GUI) feature when set to 1, exists in the following Registry path:

```
HKEY_CURRENT_USER\Software\Microsoft\Windows\CurrentVersion\Explorer\Advanced
```

To address this, let's first shift our location to the proper key within the HKCU hive:

```
Set-Location HKCU:\Software\Microsoft\Windows\CurrentVersion\Explorer\Advanced
```

Now is when things get a bit strange. Know that as consistent as Windows PowerShell is in most respects, some providers behave a bit differently from other ones.

For instance, run a **Get-ChildItem** and see what comes back. If you pop open the graphical
Registry Editor, you know darned well that the Advanced key contains many, many values of
different data types. You can try **Get-Item**, but you'll be prompted for pipeline input. (Press
Ctrl+C to break out of the input prompt.)

What we need to do is specify a value for the **–Path** positional parameter either by position or by
value. Second point: Use the dot (.) character to denote the current directory:

```
PS HKCU:\Software\Microsoft\Windows\CurrentVersion\Explorer\Advanced> get-item .


    Hive: HKEY_CURRENT_USER\Software\Microsoft\Windows\CurrentVersion\Explorer


Name                            Property
----                            --------
Advanced                        Start_SearchFiles    : 2
                                StoreAppsOnTaskbar    : 0
                                ServerAdminUI         : 0
                                Hidden                : 1
                                ShowCompColor         : 1
                                HideFileExt           : 0
                                DontPrettyPath        : 0
                                ShowInfoTip           : 1
                                HideIcons             : 0
                                MapNetDrvBtn          : 0
                                WebView               : 1
                                Filter                : 0
                                ShowSuperHidden       : 1
                                SeparateProcess       : 1
                                AutoCheckSelect       : 0
                                IconsOnly             : 0
                                ShowTypeOverlay       : 1
                                ShowStatusBar         : 1
                                ListviewAlphaSelect   : 1
                                ListviewShadow        : 1
                                TaskbarAnimations     : 0
                                StartMenuInit         : 6
                                ReindexedProfile      : 1
                                NavPaneShowAllFolders : 1
                                AlwaysShowMenus       : 1
                                HideDrivesWithNoMedia : 0
                                SharingWizardOn       : 0
                                TaskbarSizeMove       : 1
                                MMTaskbarEnabled      : 0
                                MMTaskbarMode         : 0
                                DisablePreviewDesktop : 1
                                TaskbarSmallIcons     : 0
                                TaskbarGlomLevel      : 0
                                ShellViewReentered    : 1
```

We can invoke the related **Get-ItemProperty** cmdlet to retrieve Registry key or value properties:

```
PS HKCU:\Software\Microsoft\Windows\CurrentVersion\Explorer\Advanced>
➥Get-ItemProperty -Path . -Name DisablePreviewDesktop

DisablePreviewDesktop : 1
PSPath                : Microsoft.PowerShell.Core\Registry::HKEY_CURRENT_USER\
                        software\Microsoft\Windows\CurrentVersion\Explorer\
                        Advanced
PSParentPath          : Microsoft.PowerShell.Core\Registry::HKEY_CURRENT_USER\
                        Software\Microsoft\Windows\CurrentVersion\Explorer
PSChildName           : Advanced
PSDrive               : HKCU
PSProvider            : Microsoft.PowerShell.Core\Registry
```

Editing Registry Values

As you can see from the preceding output, Aero Peek is disabled on my system. We can verify that by understanding that a value of 1 for this value means "DisablePreviewDesktop is enabled." Of course, the logic is strange, because normally I think of *enabled* as meaning "enabled" instead of "disabled." Anyway, why don't we go ahead and enable the value by using Windows PowerShell. The code is simple, little more than our previous command:

```
Set-ItemProperty -Path . -Name DisablePreviewDesktop -Value 0
```

TIP

If you try this on your system, make sure to run **Get-ItemProperty** again to verify that the change "took."

Using Extended Providers

Over the lifetime of your computer, in particular Windows Server machines, you may wind up with additional PowerShell providers. So, it's to your advantage to run **Get-PSProvider** regularly on your servers; you may be surprised at what you see.

Active Directory Provider

When you promote a Windows Server computer to be an AD DS domain controller, you'll have local access to the AD PSDrive. To make the provider available, you need to load the ActiveDirectory PowerShell module:

```
Import-Module -Name ActiveDirectory
```

What's cool about Windows PowerShell v3 and later is that modules will autoload whenever you invoke a command contained within a locally available module.

Watch me drill into my domain controller's Active Directory Directory Service:

```
PS C:\> cd AD:
PS AD:\> dir
Name             ObjectClass        DistinguishedName
----             -----------        -----------------
earthfarm        domainDNS          DC=earthfarm,DC=lan
Configuration    configuration      CN=Configuration,DC=earthfarm,DC=lan
Schema           dMD                CN=Schema,CN=Configuration,DC=earthfarm,DC=lan
DomainDnsZones   domainDNS          DC=DomainDnsZones,DC=earthfarm,DC=lan
ForestDnsZones   domainDNS          DC=ForestDnsZones,DC=earthfarm,DC=lan
```

As you know if you're an experienced AD administrator, Active Directory is divided into the domain, schema, and configuration partitions. By using the **Item** commands that we already know, we can view and edit the underlying Active Directory objects and properties.

SQL Server Provider

In SQL Server 2012, the main PowerShell module is called SQLPS:

```
Import-Module -Name sqlps
```

By using cd or **Set-Location**, we can also dive into a SQL Server instance and potentially interact with database objects as shown in the following partial output from my server:

```
PS SQLSERVER:\SQL\dc2013\default\Databases\WSS_Logging\Views> dir
Schema                       Name                            Created
------                       ----                            -------
dbo                          AccessServicesMonitoring        10/14/2014 9:40 AM
dbo                          AccessServicesResourceConsumpt  10/14/2014 9:40 AM
dbo                          AccessServicesResponseTimes     10/14/2014 9:38 AM
dbo                          AppStatistics                   10/14/2014 9:37 AM
dbo                          AppUsage                        10/14/2014 9:37 AM
dbo                          BandwidthUsage                  10/14/2014 9:37 AM
dbo                          ClientServiceActionUsage        10/14/2014 9:38 AM
dbo                          ClientServiceRequestUsage       10/14/2014 9:38 AM
dbo                          EDU_OperationStatsUsage         10/14/2014 9:37 AM
dbo                          ExportUsage                     10/14/2014 9:37 AM
```

Summary

If you've understood everything I presented so far in this book, you are already a productive PowerShell professional. Congratulations. You know that the provider system is what undergirds the PowerShell runtime environment. The truth of the matter is that you always work in the context of a provider, whether you know it or not.

In Hour 9, "Formatting, Exporting, and Converting Windows PowerShell Output," we turn our attention to formatting PowerShell output not only for onscreen display, but also for external files. As you'll learn, Windows PowerShell offers us tremendous variety in how we can present data to our boss, our colleagues, our customers, and beyond.

Q&A

Q. In this hour, you taught me all about Set-Location. What are Push-Location and Pop-Location?

A. We can use **Push-Location** to "push" the current working directory to an in-memory stack. We then can quickly return to our original location by invoking **Pop-Location**.

As you develop PowerShell scripts, you'll often use these commands (aliased to **pushd** and **popd**, respectively) to return the user to their original directory location after your script has completed execution.

Here's a quick example:

```
PS C:\> Push-Location windows
PS C:\windows> cd system32
PS C:\windows\system32> Pop-Location
PS C:\>
```

Q. Is the Environment PSDrive anything like the set command that I use in the Cmd.exe environment?

A. Yes, it's similar, but of course PowerShell gives us much more power. If you send the **set** command to PowerShell, the shell will get confused. This is because **set** is a Cmd.exe command.

By contrast, the Environment PSDrive also gives us access to all current user and system environment variables, but we have all the PowerShell goodness to go along with the data.

Q. Can I create my own PowerShell provider and drive by using Windows PowerShell?

A. I'm afraid not. To author PowerShell artifacts, including cmdlets, providers, and drives, you'll need to author them by using a .NET language such as C# or Visual Basic (VB).

Workshop

First of all, if you choose to accept this challenge, do so on a nonproduction machine just to be safe.

Using only Windows PowerShell, perform the following tasks:

- ▶ Create a new Registry key called TestKey located in the Registry path HKEY_CURRENT_USER\Environment.

- ▶ Within the TestKey key, create a new DWORD value named TestValue, and set the value to hexadecimal 0.

- ▶ Obtain a listing of all contents of the TestKey key.

- ▶ Delete both the TestKey key and the TestValue value, and confirm the modification.

Quiz

1. Which of the following statements lists all the contents of the FileSystem provider?

    a. **Get-PSProvider –PSDrive FileSystem**

    b. **Get-PSDrive –PSProvider FileSystem**

    c. **Get-Item –Path FileSystem**

2. The Alias PSProvider allows you to view, but not create, edit, or delete, alias definitions.

    a. True

    b. False

3. Which of the following PSProviders stores the value for **$host**?

    a. FileSystem

    b. Function

    c. Variable

Answers

1. The correct answer is B. This question tests your understanding of PSProviders versus PSDrives. We need to obtain a list of PSDrives that are associated with the FileSystem PSProvider, and you can use the **–PSProvider** parameter of **Get-PSDrive** to do just that.

2. The correct answer is B. You can do whatever you want to the aliases defined on our system by manipulating data in the Alias PSDrive. However, I recommend that you instead employ the dedicated alias cmdlets to perform these actions.

3. The correct answer is C. This isn't a trick question; you should be able to apply deductive reasoning to answer it correctly even though we didn't work with the Variable: drive much in this hour.

NOTE

Recall that all PowerShell variables start with a dollar sign. Going further, **$host** is a variable that stores the value of the current PowerShell host application. So, this variable and its associated data are located within the Variable: drive.

Formatting, Exporting, and Converting Windows PowerShell Output

What You'll Learn in This Hour:

▶ How the PowerShell formatting subsystem works

▶ Formatting PowerShell output

▶ Exporting PowerShell output

▶ Converting PowerShell output

The reasons behind the Windows PowerShell best practice of *filter left* are threefold:

▶ You are always in a pipeline, whether you know it or not.

▶ You waste system and potentially network resources when you push more objects through the pipeline than you need to display in output.

▶ The PowerShell formatting commands de-serialize output, which renders the data useless unless it's at the end of the pipeline.

We can now extend our Windows PowerShell mantra to "filter left, format right." By the time you finish this hour, you'll understand intimately why this best practice exists.

It's this final bullet point with which we are most concerned in the beginning of this hour of training. How does the PowerShell formatting subsystem decide whether to display pipeline output as a table or a list? How can we take control of the formatting process?

This hour also covers all the particulars of exporting and converting pipeline output so that our deliverables match our needs. Let's get to work.

How the PowerShell Formatting Subsystem Works

Let's begin this discussion by viewing the built-in PowerShell **Out** cmdlets:

```
PS C:\> Get-Command -Verb out*

CommandType     Name                                    Source
-----------     ----                                    ------
Cmdlet          Out-Default                             Microsoft...
Cmdlet          Out-File                                Microsoft...
Cmdlet          Out-GridView                            Microsoft...
Cmdlet          Out-Host                                Microsoft...
Cmdlet          Out-Null                                Microsoft...
Cmdlet          Out-Printer                             Microsoft...
Cmdlet          Out-String                              Microsoft...
```

The content we see in our PowerShell host application (which in this book has been the console host for the most part) is a result of our PowerShell code being "handed off" to the internal formatting subsystem via **Out-Default** and then, ultimately, **Out-Host**.

Let's run a common cmdlet that we've seen plenty of times:

```
PS C:\> Get-Service

Status    Name             DisplayName
------    ----             -----------
Stopped   AdobeARMservice  Adobe Acrobat Update Service
Stopped   AdobeFlashPlaye... Adobe Flash Player Update Service
Stopped   AeLookupSvc      Application Experience
Running   Agent            VPDAgent
Stopped   ALG              Application Layer Gateway Service
Stopped   AppIDSvc         Application Identity
```

It is neither coincidence nor magic that PowerShell displays only the Status, Name, and DisplayName columns in the host by default. Nor is it coincidence or otherworldly that the output shows up in a table view instead of, say, a list view.

To prove that you are in fact always in the default pipeline, run the following commands and verify that the output is identical:

```
Get-Service
Get-Service | Out-Default
Get-Service | Format-Table | Out-Host
Get-Service | Out-Host
```

These **Out** cmdlets represent the end of the pipeline; the cmdlet accepts PSObjects as input, but has utterly no outputs.

NOTE

According to the **Out-Default** help description:

The **Out-Default** cmdlet sends output to the default formatter and the default output cmdlet. This cmdlet has no effect on the formatting or output of Windows PowerShell commands. It is a placeholder that lets you write your own **Out-Default** function or cmdlet.

Digging Deeper

Okay. So at this point you know that everything you put into your PowerShell pipelines runs through **Out-Default** unless you override by specifying another **Out-** option. I also told you that PowerShell uses an internal formatting subsystem to determine which view to present your output, which properties to display, and so forth.

The "secret sauce" to the PowerShell formatting subsystem is the **Type** property, also known as the object type. Under the hood, PowerShell has a whole bunch of predefined layouts that it calls into action depending on the data type incoming through the pipeline.

Remember how we see a tabular view if we run **Get-Service** with no additional options? Let's see how PowerShell responds if we "super size" the output by adding in all properties:

```
PS C:\> Get-Service | Select-Object -Property *

Name                 : AdobeARMservice
RequiredServices     : {}
CanPauseAndContinue  : False
CanShutdown          : False
CanStop              : False
DisplayName          : Adobe Acrobat Update Service
DependentServices    : {}
MachineName          : .
ServiceName          : AdobeARMservice
ServicesDependedOn   : {}
ServiceHandle        : SafeServiceHandle
Status               : Stopped
ServiceType          : Win32OwnProcess
Site                 :
Container            :

Name                 : AdobeFlashPlayerUpdateSvc
RequiredServices     : {}
CanPauseAndContinue  : False
CanShutdown          : False
```

```
CanStop                 : False
DisplayName             : Adobe Flash Player Update Service
DependentServices       : {}
MachineName             : .
ServiceName             : AdobeFlashPlayerUpdateSvc
ServicesDependedOn      : {}
ServiceHandle           : SafeServiceHandle
Status                  : Stopped
ServiceType             : Win32OwnProcess
Site                    :
Container               :
```

Whoa! What happened? In a nutshell, PowerShell used its internal formatting rules that are associated with **ServiceController** objects. Evidently if you ask for too many columns (with "too many" being decided for you by the subsystem, although the threshold is usually five columns), PowerShell automatically switches to a list view, which makes sense from a readability standpoint.

Where Does the PowerShell Formatting Subsystem Live?

The rule files that PowerShell uses for automatic formatting can be found in the Windows PowerShell installation directory; to visit this directory directly (alliteration!), type **cd $PSHome** in your console session.

Next, run **dir *.format.ps1xml** to get a listing of the files. Parsing their contents is beyond the scope of this training, but if you're up to the challenge, have fun! Just for grins, you can see the formatting codes for **ServiceController** objects in Figure 9.1. You can also read the about_Format.sp1xml help file, which contains useful background information.

Out-GridView

When we pipe our PowerShell output to **Out-Gridview**, PowerShell displays our results in an interactive table. Try this:

```
Get-Service | Out-Gridview
```

Read the help article for **Out-Gridview**; as expected, the cmdlet accepts PSObjects and does not return any output to the pipeline by default. The two things that I love about **Out-Gridview** are as follows:

- ▶ You can perform quick sorts by clicking the column headers.

- ▶ You can perform quick filtering by clicking **Add Criteria**.

FIGURE 9.1
Here we see the view definition that governs how PowerShell displays output from ServiceController objects.

You can see this behavior in action by looking at Figure 9.2.

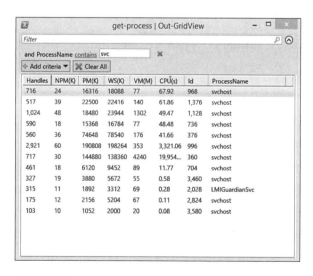

FIGURE 9.2
The Out-Gridview cmdlet puts our pipeline output in an interactive display.

Out-Gridview is a quick and convenient way to interact with PowerShell output. Just remember to put this formatting/output command at the end of your pipeline. Try this:

```
Get-Process | Select-Object -Property Name, WorkingSet, PeakWorkingSet |
➡Sort-Object -Property WorkingSet -Descending | Out-GridView
```

In the previous example we (1) retrieve all processes, (2) filter out properties we don't need in the output, (3) sort the result set, and (4) display the massaged output in an interactive table.

CAUTION

One important "gotcha" with **Out-Gridview** is that it requires that you have the Windows PowerShell Integrated Scripting Environment (ISE) installed; this isn't always the case with some Windows Server configurations.

Formatting PowerShell Output

What we're going to do now is "hijack" the built-in PowerShell formatting subsystem by replacing its **Out-Default** rules with our own. Windows PowerShell includes three core formatting commands:

▶ **Format-Table**, aliased to **ft**

▶ **Format-List**, aliased to **fl**

▶ **Format-Wide**, aliased to **fw**

Each of these formatting views has particular use cases, and we'll investigate them one command at a time.

Format-Table

By default, the **Get-PSSnapin** cmdlet returns its output in list view. Let's run the command alone, and then try piping to **Format-Table** next:

```
PS C:\> Get-PSSnapin

Name        : Microsoft.PowerShell.Core
PSVersion   : 5.0.9740.0
Description : This Windows PowerShell snap-in contains cmdlets used to manage
              components of Windows PowerShell.


PS C:\> Get-PSSnapin | Format-Table
```

```
Name                          PSVersion              Description
----                          ---------              -----------
Microsoft.PowerShell.Core     5.0.9740.0             This Windows PowerShell ...
```

Here's the deal: If the PowerShell formatting engine gives you a table by default, you don't have to worry about invoking **Format-Table** because PowerShell already does it for you. By contrast, when the result comes back as a list and you need to see a table, you have this command.

Actually, it might be useful for you to manually invoke **Format-Table** even when the **Out-Default** output is a table. The reason for this is that **Format-Table** includes some cool parameters.

For instance, the **–wrap** parameter wraps text when the default column width truncates the output:

```
PS C:\> Get-PSSnapin | Format-Table -Wrap

Name                          PSVersion              Description
----                          ---------              -----------
Microsoft.PowerShell.Core     5.0.9740.0             This Windows PowerShell
                                                     snap-in contains cmdlets
                                                     used to manage components
                                                     of Windows PowerShell.
```

Invoking the **–AutoSize** parameter of **Format-Table** can greatly improve readability when you find that the default column widths are too small. Try this:

```
PS C:\> Get-Process -Name powershell | Format-Table -Property Path,Name,Id,Company

Path                    Name                           Id Company
----                    ----                           -- -------
C:\Windows\Syste... powershell                        384 Microsoft Corpor...


PS C:\> Get-Process -Name powershell | Format-Table -Property Path,Name,Id,Company
➥-AutoSize

Path                                                   Name       Id Compan
                                                                     y
----                                                   ----       -- ------
C:\Windows\System32\WindowsPowerShell\v1.0\powershell.exe powershell 384 Mic...
```

The **–AutoSize** parameter functions in much the same way that autosizing works in Microsoft Excel. The columns are automatically adjusted to accommodate the column with the widest value. Sadly, the PowerShell console has a limited horizontal screen buffer, so in the previous example, you'll observe that we still get truncation. Every stumbling block is an opportunity, naturally, so be aware if you aren't already that you can programmatically change the console's buffers at any time.

That said, the **–AutoSize** parameter should show the full column width for at least the first properties, so I advise you to use **Select-Object** to specify the columns that you absolutely need to see first in the list.

TIP

In general, I tend to prefer **–Wrap** to **–AutoSize**, but your mileage may vary.

We use the **–property** parameter to specify the columns and their order in output. This parameter differs from **Select-Object** because **–property** doesn't actually filter out any data. Instead, it suppresses display of the columns we don't want to see, and presents the ones that we do. For example:

```
PS C:\> Get-Service | Format-Table -Property Name, DependentServices -Wrap

Name                             DependentServices
----                             -----------------
AdobeARMservice                  {}
AdobeFlashPlayerUpdateSvc        {}
AeLookupSvc                      {}
Agent                            {}
ALG                              {}
AppIDSvc                         {}
Appinfo                          {}
Apple Mobile Device              {}
AppMgmt                          {}
AppReadiness                     {}
AppXSvc                          {}
AudioEndpointBuilder             {Audiosrv}
Audiosrv                         {}
AxInstSV                         {}
BDESVC                           {}
BFE                              {WdNisSvc, WdNisDrv, SharedAccess,
                                 RemoteAccess...}
```

Finally, we can organize table output by specifying the **–GroupBy** parameter. In the following example, we'll group services by their status:

```
PS C:\> Get-Process | Sort-Object -Property BasePriority | Format-Table -GroupBy
➥BasePriority -Wrap

    BasePriority: 0
```

Handles	NPM(K)	PM(K)	WS(K)	VM(M)	CPU(s)	Id	ProcessName
-------	------	-----	-----	-----	------	--	-----------
0	0	0	4	0		0	Idle

```
   BasePriority: 4
```

Handles	NPM(K)	PM(K)	WS(K)	VM(M)	CPU(s)	Id	ProcessName
-------	------	-----	-----	-----	------	--	-----------
123	8	1596	5980	37	0.05	27296	SearchFilterHost
308	11	1872	7568	62	0.08	27580	SearchProtocolHost

```
   BasePriority: 6
```

Handles	NPM(K)	PM(K)	WS(K)	VM(M)	CPU(s)	Id	ProcessName
-------	------	-----	-----	-----	------	--	-----------
586	28	12276	3124	163	37.56	3964	SettingSyncHost
449	22	6748	1572	130	7.53	3260	AAM Updates Notifier

Format-List

The **Format-List** command is there to help us in situations when the tabular view just doesn't give us the clear details that we require. Specifically, **Format-List** formats the pipeline output as a property list in which each property shows up on a new line.

Consider the following example:

```
PS C:\> Get-Service | Format-List
```

```
Name                 : AdobeARMservice
DisplayName          : Adobe Acrobat Update Service
Status               : Stopped
DependentServices    : {}
ServicesDependedOn   : {}
CanPauseAndContinue  : False
CanShutdown          : False
CanStop              : False
ServiceType          : Win32OwnProcess

Name                 : AdobeFlashPlayerUpdateSvc
DisplayName          : Adobe Flash Player Update Service
Status               : Stopped
DependentServices    : {}
ServicesDependedOn   : {}
CanPauseAndContinue  : False
CanShutdown          : False
CanStop              : False
ServiceType          : Win32OwnProcess
```

What's so beautiful about the list format is that, although it's *a lot* of output, you can include as many properties as you want in your output and still be able to read the results. Check this out:

```
PS C:\> Get-Process | Select-Object -Property * | Format-List
```

```
__NounName                : Process
Name                      : AAM Updates Notifier
Handles                   : 449
VM                        : 136151040
WS                        : 1585152
PM                        : 6909952
NPM                       : 22272
Path                      : C:\Program Files (x86)\Common
                            Files\Adobe\OOBE\PDApp\UWA\AAM Updates
                            Notifier.exe
Company                   : Adobe Systems Incorporated
CPU                       : 7.5625
FileVersion               : 7.0.0.324
ProductVersion            : 7.0.0.324
Description               : AAM Updates Notifier Application
Product                   : AAM Updates Notifier Application
Id                        : 3260
PriorityClass             : BelowNormal
HandleCount               : 449
WorkingSet                : 1585152
PagedMemorySize           : 6909952
PrivateMemorySize         : 6909952
```

What you see in the previous output is only partial output from a single process. Wow! Hey, sometimes you need all the output information as is possible to solve a problem, right?

Like **Format-Table**, **Format-List** supports the **–property** parameter. This parameter allows us to specify the object parameters in the output and the order in which they are listed:

```
PS C:\> Get-Process | Format-List -Property Name, BasePriority, PriorityClass
```

```
Name          : AAM Updates Notifier
BasePriority  : 6
PriorityClass : BelowNormal

Name          : acrotray
BasePriority  : 8
PriorityClass : Normal

Name          : adobeconnectaddin
BasePriority  : 8
PriorityClass : Normal
```

As you discover new PowerShell commands and think about how you can use them in your work, you'll definitely want to study and actually run the examples that are included in each PowerShell command's help file. You can do so most efficiently by typing something like the following:

```
Help <cmdlet-name> -Example
```

My readers with sharp eyes will observe that I've adapted many of the examples in this hour directly from the relevant help files.

Format-Wide

The **Format-Wide** cmdlet is near and dear to me because its operation is so similar to one of the first MS-DOS commands I learned:

```
C:\>dir /w
 Volume in drive C is SYSTEM
 Volume Serial Number is B691-5B48

 Directory of C:\

.rnd                    about.txt               alpha.txt
CaptivateLog.log        file.txt                [folder1]
get.txt                 getservice.html         help.txt
[Intel]                 member.txt              [PerfLogs]
[Program Files]         [Program Files (x86)]   [Sandbox]
[savedhelp]             sdf.txt                 serv.txt
spool.txt               [temp]                  testscript.ps1
[tools]                 [Users]                 verb.txt
[Windows]               x.txt
              15 File(s)          326,237 bytes
              11 Dir(s)   106,133,311,488 bytes free

C:\>
```

If you try the **dir /w** (or even **Get-ChildItem –w**, or something similar), you'll be sorely disappointed. We use **Format-Wide** when we want to see single-item data in a multicolumn display.

For instance, let's say we just want to see all the process names we have running on our system. Do this:

```
PS C:\> Get-Process | Format-Wide

AAM Updates Notifier              acrotray
adobeconnectaddin                 AppleMobileDeviceService
ApplePhotoStreams                 APSDaemon
audiodg                           chrome
chrome                            chrome
conhost                           conhost
csrss                             csrss
dasHost                           dllhost
Dropbox                           dwm
Evernote                          EvernoteClipper
EvernoteTray                      explorer
explorer                          hkcmd
iCloudDrive                       iCloudServices
Idle                              igfxpers
iPodService                       iTunesHelper
JabraDeviceService                JabraSkypeDriver
jusched                           L4301_Solar
LMIGuardianSvc                    LogMeIn
LogMeInSystray                    lsass
```

To invoke the "classic" use of wide output in the file system, try something like this:

```
PS C:\windows\System32> Get-ChildItem | Format-Wide -Column 3

    Directory: C:\windows\System32

[0409]                [AdvancedInstallers]    [AppLocker]
[ar-SA]               [bg-BG]                 [Boot]
[Bthprops]            [catroot]               [catroot2]
[CodeIntegrity]       [Com]                   [config]
[Configuration]       [cs-CZ]                 [da-DK]
[de-DE]               [Dism]                  [downlevel]
[drivers]             [DriverStore]           [DRVSTORE]
[dsc]                 [el-GR]                 [en]
[en-GB]               [en-US]                 [es-ES]
[et-EE]               [fi-FI]                 [fr-FR]
[FxsTmp]              [GroupPolicyUsers]      [he-IL]
```

The **–column** parameter allows us to specify how many columns we want to see in the output. We also have the mutually exclusive **–AutoSize** parameter that functions the same way it does with **Format-Table**.

```
Get-Process | Select-Object -First 15 | Format-Wide -AutoSize
```

Try the preceding command both with and without **–AutoSize** and compare the output difference.

We now know what's involved in changing the output display of our pipeline data. In the next section, we turn our attention to exporting the output for nonhost display.

Exporting PowerShell Output

The format commands we spent time getting to know in this hour of training are great when we're working in a PowerShell host application like the ISE or the console host.

However, what if you are required to produce, say, a printed report of PowerShell output? What if you simply find it easier to parse a lot of data in a text editor instead of scrolling through a shell session window?

Windows PowerShell has you covered. In this section, you'll become familiar with the following export commands:

- **Out-File**
- **Out-Printer**
- **Export-Csv**
- **Export-Clixml**

We won't cover **Out-Gridview** for the following reasons:

- We already discussed this command earlier in the hour.
- The **Gridview**, as nice as it is, has no built-in capacity for printing or exporting to other formats.

Here we want to discover ways to get PowerShell output into a flexible file type.

Out-File

In the Cmd.exe and Linux command shells, you can use the redirection operator (>) to export the output to a text file. The Windows PowerShell team supports the use of the greater than symbol as a redirection operator.

TIP
_____

Note that > is *not* an alias for **Out-File**. Therefore, I strongly suggest that you invoke the honest-to-goodness **Out-File** cmdlet so that you can customize the output with parameters.

_____

In the example shown in Figure 9.3, I use the **–FilePath** parameter positionally, specifying my output as a text file named service.txt that will be saved in my current working directory.

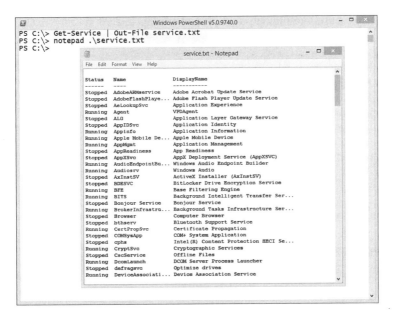

FIGURE 9.3
Piping to Out-File is a super-fast way to put your pipeline output in a nearly universal file format. However, watch out for column truncation.

By default, **Out-File** generates a Unicode-encoded text file. You can encode in ASCII instead by specifying the –**Encoding** parameter.

The main gotcha you'll see with **Out-File** is output truncation. For example, did you notice that the Name column is truncated in Figure 9.3? That's not cool.

The good news is that **Out-File** has a –**Width** parameter that accepts integer values that specify the number of characters allocated for the output file's line width. However, you may find that the output isn't what you expect. Try this:

```
Get-Service | Out-File -FilePath "C:\servicelist.txt" -Width 120 |
➥Notepad "c:\servicelist.txt"
```

Did you notice that that **Name** property remains truncated? Annoying. Check out Figure 9.4 for one workaround.

In the Figure 9.4 solution, we insert a **Format-Table –AutoSize** into the pipeline before we create our text file. Unless we do this, the Name column "arrives" at **Out-File** with the **Name** property already truncated. No amount of –**Width** futzing around can make an already truncated column untruncated.

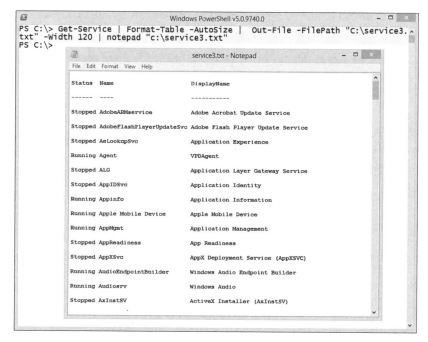

FIGURE 9.4
Adding the -AutoSize parameter to Format-Table ensures that you don't lose data due to column width truncation.

Out-Printer

The **Out-Printer** cmdlet was added in Windows PowerShell v4, and sends the pipeline output to your default printer by, well, default.

For instance, let's print out a copy of the wonderful about_Redirection help file to our default printer:

```
Get-Help about_Redirection | Out-Printer
```

But what if we want to specify that HP printer we use that's located down the hall sometimes? No problem; we can simply specify the Universal Naming Convention (UNC) network path to the printer by using the **–Name** parameter:

```
Get-Help about_Format.ps1xml |
➥Out-Printer –Name "\\printserver01\HPLaserL2-Hallway"
```

Export-CSV

As nice as it is to have a handy-dandy text file containing our PowerShell output, there arise occasions when we simply need to do more "stuff" with the exported output.

As you probably know, the comma-separated value (CSV) file format structures plain text in a rudimentary way; namely, by separating data fields with a comma character.

The advantage to CSV is that we can manipulate the data to our heart's content in any CSV-aware application. For instance, let's take the following output, export to CSV, and then open the file in Microsoft Excel. Figure 9.5 shows you a screenshot:

```
Get-Service | Export-Csv -Path "C:\services.csv"
start excel "C:\services.csv"
```

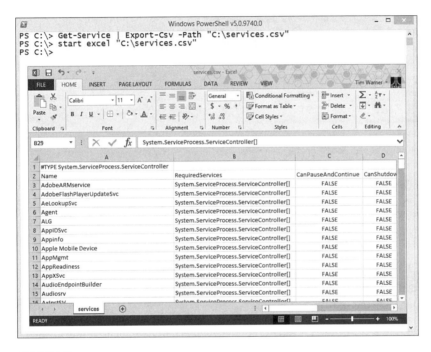

FIGURE 9.5
After you have your PowerShell output in CSV format, you can import the file into many different application types for analysis.

The previous example first creates the CSV file, starts an instance of Microsoft Excel, and then loads the CSV file. Pretty cool, isn't it?

TIP

Of course, those of you with experience with delimited file formats wonder whether we can use other delimiters besides the comma. Naturally, the answer is yes.

According to the **Export-Csv** help file, we can pass quoted character data to the **–Delimiter** parameter. Of course, the comma is the default delimiter if you don't specify one in your code.

For instance, to get a tab-delimited text file, specify **–Delimiter** "`t" in your code. By the way, that character before the lowercase *t* is the backtick character, also called the grave accent.

While we're on the subject of PowerShell and CSV file support, why don't we get a run of all the commands that reference CSV:

```
PS C:\> Get-Command -Noun *csv*

CommandType       Name                                Source
-----------       ----                                ------
Function          Get-PcsvDevice                      PcsvDevice
Function          Restart-PcsvDevice                  PcsvDevice
Function          Set-PcsvDeviceBootConfiguration     PcsvDevice
Function          Start-PcsvDevice                    PcsvDevice
Function          Stop-PcsvDevice                     PcsvDevice
Cmdlet            ConvertFrom-Csv                      Microsoft...
Cmdlet            ConvertTo-Csv                        Microsoft...
Cmdlet            Export-Csv                           Microsoft...
Cmdlet            Import-Csv                           Microsoft...
```

We'll address the **Convert** cmdlets in the upcoming section, but I want to remind you that we can use **Import-Csv** to ingest an incoming CSV file.

What may be surprising to you is that **Import-Csv** takes simple string data as an input (which is fully expected), but outputs objects. Look at this partial output as proof:

```
PS C:\> Import-Csv -Path services.csv | Get-Member

    TypeName: CSV:System.ServiceProcess.ServiceController

Name                  MemberType     Definition
----                  ----------     ----------
Equals                Method         bool Equals(System.Object obj)
GetHashCode           Method         int GetHashCode()
GetType               Method         type GetType()
ToString              Method         string ToString()
CanPauseAndContinue NoteProperty System.String CanPauseAndContinue=False
```

Wow! That's some powerful stuff right there.

Export-Clixml

Ah, the Extensible Markup Language (XML). Although raw XML code somewhat resembles Hypertext Markup Language (HTML), its purpose is totally different. XML actually has more in common with CSV, come to think of it.

In a nutshell, XML is a data description markup language. Instead of describing how data should be presented, which HTML does, XML seeks to define the meaning of your data. It's a wonderful format because, like CSV, exported XML data can be imported by almost any line of business application.

For instance, you can export XML from PowerShell and re-import the file by using PowerShell on another computer. Alternatively, you can transfer data between database systems using only XML.

True enough, you can use the **ConvertTo-Xml** cmdlet if you need to convert PowerShell output to industry standard XML format. However, **Export-Clixml** is a little bit different.

I like to describe **Export-Clixml** as a way to export PowerShell pipeline data, in all its three-dimensional object-oriented glory, in a format that PowerShell recognizes internally.

For instance, suppose that you needed to analyze a process list from computerA on your administrative workstation, named computerB. First you generate the PowerShell-based XML file:

```
Get-Process | Export-Clixml -Path computerAproc.xml
```

It will take a bit longer to generate the XML file than it did to create a CSV because the XML format attempts to represent all the pipeline data, preserving all aspects of it.

You can then use the corresponding **Import-Clixml** cmdlet to ingest the file on computerB:

```
PS C:\> Import-Clixml -Path .\processes.xml | Get-Member


   TypeName: Deserialized.System.Diagnostics.Process

Name                MemberType    Definition
----                ----------    ----------
GetType             Method        type GetType()
ToString            Method        string ToString(), string ToString(s...
Company             NoteProperty  System.String Company=Adobe Systems ...
CPU                 NoteProperty  System.Double CPU=7.609375
Description         NoteProperty  System.String Description=AAM Update...
FileVersion         NoteProperty  System.String FileVersion=7.0.0.324
```

Look at the preceding partial output: The **Import-Clixml** cmdlet takes string data as input and "spits out" deserialized process objects. Of course, although the output looks just like a live run of **Get-Process**, it's crucial that we remind ourselves that the imported process list represents a point-in-time snapshot of running processes from computerA.

NOTE
_____

Those of you in my readership who know a thing or two about XML won't be happy about the **Export-Clixml** formatting because it isn't as "pretty" as traditional XML.

This disparity speaks to what I've been saying; namely, **Export-Clixml** is used to save PowerShell output as objects that can be fully deserialized back into PowerShell.

For standards-based XML files, use **ConvertTo-Xml**. (We discuss this cmdlet in a little while.)

We'll now enter the final phase of this chock-full hour of training, in which we consider how to convert PowerShell output to other file types.

Converting PowerShell Output

Okay, I'll bet you $20 to a boxful of stale jelly donuts that the question on your mind is this: "What's the difference between **Export-Csv** and **ConvertTo-Csv**?"

Great question, actually. Let's answer the question by practicing:

```
$export = Get-Process | Export-Csv -Path export.csv
$convert = Get-Process | ConvertTo-Csv
$export | Get-Member
$convert | Get-Member
```

So, what did you discover? C'mon, flex your Windows PowerShell muscles. When I ran the previous four lines of code, I discovered the following:

▶ **Export-Csv** dumps you out of the pipeline; all you get is a lousy CSV file.

▶ **ConvertTo-Csv** returns a list of string objects and keeps you in the pipeline.

The take-home message here is that you should use **Export-Csv** if you actually need a CSV text file right then and there, and you should use **ConvertTo-Csv** if you have additional PowerShell work you need to do on the converted data.

ConvertTo Options

Why don't we have a look at all the ConvertTo cmdlets that are included in Windows PowerShell:

```
PS C:\> Get-Command -Verb ConvertTo*

CommandType     Name                                      Source
-----------     ----                                      ------
Cmdlet          ConvertTo-Csv                             Microsoft...
Cmdlet          ConvertTo-Html                            Microsoft...
Cmdlet          ConvertTo-Json                            Microsoft...
Cmdlet          ConvertTo-SecureString                    Microsoft...
Cmdlet          ConvertTo-TpmOwnerAuth                    TrustedPl...
Cmdlet          ConvertTo-Xml                             Microsoft...
```

As mentioned previously, XML is a nearly universal data description format, and we should use **Export-Clixml** when we want to export and import XML from within PowerShell, or between PowerShell and other applications.

ConvertTo-Xml is great when we need to keep the XML data in the pipeline for further processing. However, its usage is confusing at first.

For example, suppose that we want to save the contents of C:\Windows\System32 as an XML file. We would do something like this:

```
PS C:\> Get-ChildItem "c:\windows\system32" | ConvertTo-Xml

xml                                    Objects
---                                    -------
version="1.0"                          Objects
```

What the heck? Where's our XML file? Well, the help file says that **ConvertTo-Xml** outputs an **XmlDocument** object, but it says we need to leverage the **Save()** method to get that done. Recall that a method refers to a predefined action that a PowerShell object can perform. Figure 9.6 shows you the results of the following code on my computer.

```
$xml = Get-ChildItem "C:\Windows\System32" | ConvertTo-Xml
$xml.Save("C:\contents.xml")
notepad "C:\contents.xml"
```

Lastly, you may wonder how we can generate HTML reports for web display. I hope you're thinking about this properly, namely something like this: "Hmm. I know that the **Convert** command is going to output a series of strings that conform to HTML. However, I'll probably need to add another element in my pipeline to get an honest-to-goodness HTML file."

Correctamundo! Check out the following code, which nabs all running services, converts the object data to HTML, and then generates the HTML file. Figure 9.7 shows you the output graphically.

```
Get-Service | Where-Object {$_.Status -eq "Running"} |
➥Select-Object -Property DisplayName, DependentServices |
➥ConvertTo-Html | Out-File services.html
start iexplore "c:\services.html"
```

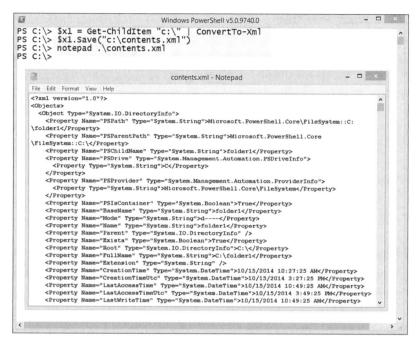

FIGURE 9.6
We use ConvertTo-Xml to generate industry-standard XML data and documents.

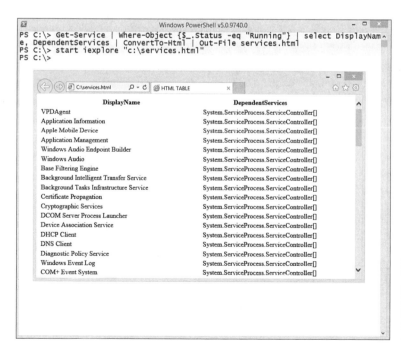

FIGURE 9.7
We can leverage our mastery of the Windows PowerShell pipeline to craft W3C-standard HTML files from PowerShell output.

How to Make HTML Output Prettier

Have you ever created a website? Nowadays the trend in web design is the notion of semantic development, where we do all our page layout in (X)HTML, our styling with Cascading Style Sheets (CSS), and data display and manipulation with XML.

You can indeed "pretty up" your PowerShell HTML output by attaching a CSS file to your output file. To get started with that, simply specify a relative or absolute path to your CSS by invoking the **CssUri** parameter:

```
Get-Service | ConvertTo-HTML –CssUri "styles.css"
```

Windows PowerShell will automatically add a **<link>** tag in the **<head>** portion of the HTML document that references the external stylesheet.

Your Final Exam

Let's apply everything we've learned over the course of this hour by completing the following Try It Yourself exercise.

▼ TRY IT YOURSELF

Exporting and Converting Windows PowerShell Output

In this Try It Yourself exercise, you'll gain some valuable experience in outputting PowerShell pipeline data into various formats. To get started, create a folder on your C: drive called **practice** and fire up an elevated Windows PowerShell console host session.

Specifically, in this scenario you're asked to enumerate the processes that are configured to start automatically every time the computer boots. You'll limit your Registry investigations to the HKEY_LOCAL_MACHINE hive, however.

1. Let's start by switching to the Registry PSDrive and browse to the Registry key that stores autostart processes.

   ```
   cd HKLM:
   cd \Software\Microsoft\Windows\CurrentVersion\Run
   ```

2. Run a directory listing. (Remember that **Get-ChildItem** doesn't work with the Registry provider.) What view does PowerShell select for you by default?

   ```
   Get-ItemProperty –Path .
   ```

   You should find that PowerShell displays the data in **Format-List** view by default. This makes the output pretty easy to look at, honestly.

3. Let's look at the Registry output as a table instead:

```
Get-ItemProperty -Path . | Format-Table
```

Blech! Most of the time, the PowerShell formatting subsystem chooses the most appropriate view.

4. Man, the Registry provider is weird. You'll notice a bunch of PS* metadata objects in your results. Let's filter out the PS items by naming only the startup items that exist in the key and storing them in a variable. (Note that the following output is specific to my Windows 8.1 computer.)

```
PS HKLM:\software\microsoft\Windows\CurrentVersion\Run> $startup =
➥Get-ItemProperty -Path . | Select-Object HotKeysCmds, IgfxTray, "LogMeIn
➥GUI", Persistence

PS HKLM:\software\microsoft\Windows\CurrentVersion\Run> $startup | Format-List

HotKeysCmds : "C:\Windows\system32\hkcmd.exe"
IgfxTray    : "C:\Windows\system32\igfxtray.exe"
LogMeIn GUI : "C:\Program Files (x86)\LogMeIn\x64\LogMeInSystray.exe"
Persistence : "C:\Windows\system32\igfxpers.exe"
```

5. We'll finish with a flourish by exporting the output as a CSV for later analysis in another application:

```
$startup | Export-Csv -Path "c:\practice\startupitems.csv"
```

Make sure that you open up the CSV file and verify that its contents match your expectations.

Summary

There you have it! Now you can not only build a PowerShell pipeline that returns exactly the data you need to do your job, but now you know how to format it, export it, and convert it as well. Trust me, aliases like **ft** and **fl** will become a natural part of your PowerShell vocabulary before too long.

That said, you need to remember always that automation and administrator convenience lay at the heart of Windows PowerShell. It's all and good being able to log on to a computer locally to perform our PowerShell-based administration, but how can you, for instance, establish a remote PowerShell session?

Is it possible to run PowerShell commands or even scripts on multiple computers simultaneously? You know me well enough by now that the vast majority of my rhetorical questions can be answered in the affirmative.

The next two hours dive deeply into the waters of PowerShell remoting.

Q&A

Q. I still don't get it. Why are their Export, Import, ConvertTo, and ConvertFrom cmdlets for CSV and XML? Doesn't that overcomplicate things?

A. It doesn't have to complicate things. Think of it this way: The **Export** and **Import** commands generate files on disk—period. If you want CSV, you have **Export-CSV**. If you want XML, you have **Export-Clixml**.

By contrast, if you simply need to represent the object data as CSV or XML in the pipeline, you should use **ConvertTo**. However, you saw in this hour that you can pipe **ConvertTo** output to **Out-File** to generate a file on disk if you need to.

Q. When I browsed the Convert command I saw ConvertTo-Json and ConvertFrom-Json. What the heck is that all about?

A. JavaScript Object Notation (JSON, pronounced *JAY-sahn*) is a lightweight alternative to XML. JSON performs the same function as XML; namely, accurately representing structured data in a format that can easily be passed over the network and between systems. JSON is used a lot in web development.

Q. How can I generate a PDF from PowerShell pipeline input?

A. Doing this is easy if you have Adobe Acrobat Professional installed on your computer. Acrobat Pro includes the Adobe PDF virtual printer, so you can produce a Portable Document Format (PDF) file quite easily:

```
Get-Service | Out-Printer -Name "Adobe PDF"
```

Workshop

Using your new-found PowerShell-Fu (like Kung-fu, but applied to PowerShell development), generate an HTML report that has all columns visible (no truncation) and meets the following specifications:

▶ Displays the first 50 entries from the System event log on your computer, sorted by time in descending order.

▶ Output should include these properties in this order: **EntryType**, **Time**, **Source**, **Message**.

▶ Output should be grouped by **EntryType**.

Quiz

1. Will the following PowerShell statement work as expected?

```
Get-EventLog -LogName System | Out-Gridview | Sort-Object -Property Time -Desc
```

   a. Yes

   b. No

2. Will the following PowerShell statement work as expected?

```
PS C:\> Get-EventLog -LogName System | Sort-Object -Property Time |
ConvertTo-HTML | Out-File -FilePath "c:\system-events.html"
```

   a. Yes

   b. No

3. How can we quickly determine the inputs and outputs of a given PowerShell command?

   a. Pipe to **Get-Member**

   b. Pipe to **Select-Object**

   c. Consult the help file

   d. Add the **–WhatIf** parameter

Answers

1. The correct answer is B. The reason this PowerShell "one liner" won't work is that **Out-Gridview** doesn't return any objects to feed into **Sort-Object**. Remember that the **Out-** commands terminate the pipeline. However, if you switch the **Sort-Object** and **Out-Gridview** positions, the code will run just fine.

2. The correct answer is A. Remember that the **ConvertTo** cmdlets return objects to the pipeline, so we can easily pipe to **Out-File** to generate the HTML file from the output.

3. The correct answer is C. Of these choices, only consulting the help file gives us a concise summary of the input and output data types for a given PowerShell command.

Implementing One-to-One Windows PowerShell Remoting

What You'll Learn in This Hour:

What You'll Learn in This Hour:

- ▶ Understanding classic Windows PowerShell remote access
- ▶ Introducing "true" PowerShell remoting
- ▶ Enabling Windows PowerShell remoting
- ▶ Creating a Windows PowerShell remote session
- ▶ Sending scripts over the network

In my career as a Windows systems administrator, I've found that the more work I can do from the comfort of my administrative workstation, the better. Through the wonders of Remote Desktop Protocol (RDP), I'm able to establish full-fidelity Windows Desktop sessions with all my servers to accomplish any administrative task I'm asked to perform.

However, as nice as RDP connections are, they involve a lot of network overhead. Why not establish a remote Windows PowerShell session instead?

The goal of this hour is to get you up to speed with how remoting works in Windows PowerShell. Here we'll constrain our discussion to single-host (also called one-to-one) remote management. In Hour 11, "Implementing One-to-Many Windows PowerShell Remoting," we'll step into the big leagues and learn to run remote PowerShell commands on multiple computers simultaneously in what's called the "fan-out" remoting scenario.

Are you excited? I hope so! Let's get to work.

Understanding Classic Windows PowerShell Remote Access

You may be aware by now that several Windows PowerShell commands include a –**ComputerName** parameter that accepts either a single host name or a comma-separated list of computer names. Try this (to save space, I give you only partial output from my computer):

```
PS C:\> Get-Command -CommandType Cmdlet -ParameterName ComputerName |
➥Select-Object -Property name

Name
----
Add-Computer
Clear-EventLog
Connect-PSSession
Enter-PSSession
Get-EventLog
Get-HotFix
Get-Process
Get-PSSession
Get-Service
Get-WmiObject
Invoke-Command
```

What you may not know and that I'm happy to tell you is that while the **–ComputerName**
parameter does allow you to send PowerShell commands to remote hosts and receive their output on your local system, this technique isn't "PowerShell remoting" in the current sense of the
term.

What do I mean? Simply this: The **–ComputerName** parameter, with a few exceptions that we'll
discuss shortly, was programmed by the Windows PowerShell team separately for each command that supports it. So, there is no shell-wide, universal remoting architecture at play yet.

Here are some other challenges with **–ComputerName** from a network manager's viewpoint:

▶ The **–ComputerName** parameter uses proprietary, legacy network protocols such as
Distributed Component Object Model (DCOM) and Remote Procedure Calls (RPCs).

▶ Those legacy protocols connect on random TCP and UDP ports, making this type of remote
access problematic on firewalled networks.

▶ The remote commands you send to multiple computers are processed serially, one host at
a time, instead of in parallel like modern PowerShell remoting does.

So, Should I Avoid the –ComputerName Parameter?

Don't get me wrong. Although I'm about to show you a much more efficient way to perform
Windows PowerShell remote management, there is no doubt that in some one-to-one remoting
scenarios, use of the **–ComputerName** parameter is simply more direct. For instance, let me grab
a quick list of all services on my remote server named server01:

```
Get-Service -ComputerName server01
```

When you learn about the **Invoke-Command** cmdlet later in this hour, you'll probably gravitate toward the –**ComputerName** parameter for many "in and out" or "quick and dirty" remoting tasks. However, this legacy remote access method will work only if you've addressed the Windows Firewall issue.

As a tease for what you'll learn in the next hour on one-to-many PowerShell remoting, the –**ComputerName** remote access method breaks down sometimes when you try to hit multiple hosts. Check this out:

```
PS C:\> Get-Service -ComputerName mem1, dc1

Status   Name              DisplayName
------   ----              -----------
Stopped  AeLookupSvc       Application Experience
Stopped  AeLookupSvc       Application Experience
Stopped  ALG               Application Layer Gateway Service
Stopped  ALG               Application Layer Gateway Service
```

Yikes! How do you know which host corresponds to which service name? Thus lies one of the "fatal flaws" of the legacy PowerShell remote access method. More on that in Hour 11.

TIP

Incidentally, if you examine the members of the preceding pipeline, you'll discover a **MachineName** property. This can fill the bill in many cases.

Introducing "True" PowerShell Remoting

Beginning in Windows PowerShell v2, Microsoft added "true" remote management capability to Windows PowerShell. Instead of employing custom code on a per-cmdlet basis, we have a single, unified remote access method that works across the entire shell.

Even better, Windows PowerShell remoting eschews the proprietary DCOM and RPC protocols in favor of the industry standard Web Services-Management (WS-Man) protocol, which communicates over HTTP(S) and uses only 1-2 communications ports. Awesome.

Take a look at Figure 10.1, and I'll walk you through how Windows PowerShell remoting works in a nutshell:

▶ Any commands you send from your computer are executed on the remote hosts.

▶ The data transmitted across your network consists of deserialized XML content.

▶ The output that is returned from the remote systems is reconstituted back into full-fidelity object data.

▶ The remote output represents a point-in-time snapshot of the remote systems.

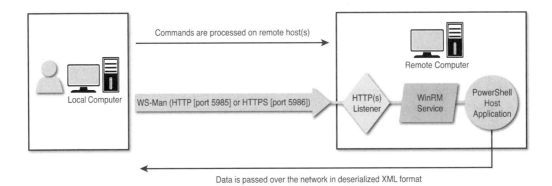

FIGURE 10.1
How Windows PowerShell remoting works.

This final bullet point bears a couple more sentences of explanation. Let's say that you send **Get-Process** to another computer on your network. The process list you see on your local system represents the process list on the remote box at the point in time that the remote host executed your command. It's not real-time data, but it's pretty close.

So far, you know how to execute PowerShell on remote systems by specifying the **–ComputerName** parameter. I'm sure you are champing at the proverbial bit to learn what's involved in conducting "true" PowerShell remoting.

Well, step one is to make sure that remoting is enabled on any remote Windows computer with which you want to interact.

WS-Man and WinRM

As stated earlier, Windows PowerShell remoting employs the industry standard WS-Man proto-col. This is great news because only two communications ports are required for remoting to work: TCP port 5985 for unencrypted HTTP, and TCP port 5986 for encrypted HTTPS.

Any local-area network (LAN) worth its salt allows HTTP/HTTPS traffic; if you do use Windows Firewall, you'll have to allow only incoming traffic on one (or both) of the WS-Man ports and you're all set.

Windows Remote Management (WinRM) is the underlying Windows service that controls the behavior of the WS-Man protocol. Therefore, enabling PowerShell remote management involves a few key tasks:

▶ Start the WinRM service.

▶ Configure the WinRM service to autostart at boot.

- ▶ Create an HTTP or HTTPS listener.

- ▶ Enable the appropriate Windows Firewall exceptions.

I have great news for you before you scratch your head and say, "How in the world do I do all that stuff?" You can instruct Windows PowerShell to perform all of the remoting setup tasks with a single PowerShell cmdlet, as discussed next.

Enabling Windows PowerShell Remoting

Microsoft has gradually leveraged the WinRM service in its server and client operating systems for a few years now, so Windows PowerShell isn't the only consumer of this service. Some of you might remember the old command-line statement:

```
Winrm -quickconfig
```

NOTE

Astute PowerShell students may be familiar, at least by name, with the **Set-WSManQuickConfig** cmdlet. If you read the help file for this cmdlet, it appears to fulfill all the requirements for enabling PowerShell remoting.

However, you should still use **Enable-PSRemoting** instead because in addition to actually invoking **Set-WSManQuickConfig, Enable-PSRemoting** also makes important session configuration adjustments in order to tightly bind Windows PowerShell to WS-Man and WinRM.

There is no need to bother with the WinRM.exe command line tool because the **Enable-PSRemoting** cmdlet performs all the actions that WinRM **–quickconfig** does, and also makes some PowerShell-specific system tweaks.

Method 1: Enabling Remoting with Windows PowerShell

The **Enable-PSRemoting** cmdlet was introduced in Windows PowerShell v4. PowerShell remoting is enabled by default in Windows Server 2012 R2, but you'll need to enable remoting on all Windows client systems and servers running previous versions of Windows Server.

Make sure that you're running an administrative PowerShell session and run the following command:

```
Enable-PSRemoting
```

Ah, what happened? If you did this on a client computer, you probably saw the error shown in Figure 10.2.

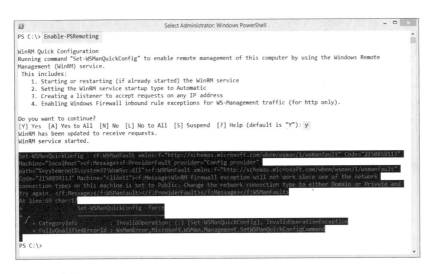

FIGURE 10.2
How Windows PowerShell remoting works.

The first couple lines of red PowerShell error text usually tell you exactly what the problem is. As it happens, enabling PSRemoting will fail if one or more of your network adapters is associated with the "Public" location profile. This is a problem you'll only see on Windows client operating systems.

Of course, this security feature exists by design; after all, you don't necessarily want someone on your hotel's Wi-Fi network attempting PowerShell remote connections on your corporate laptop.

The solution to the Public network adapter problem involves a choice: one option involves your forcing the enablement of PSRemoting by adding the **–SkipNetworkProfileCheck** parameter, as shown in Figure 10.3.

In addition to or instead of **-SkipNetworkProfileCheck**, you can use **–Force** to automatically confirm all the prompts that you see in Figure 10.3.

```
Enable-PSRemoting -Force
```

NOTE

Your other choice to resolve the Public network adapter SNAFU is to reassign the network card to use another location profile. I do not spend time in this book covering those steps, but if you need the procedure, check out the article "Setting Network Location to Private" at the Windows PowerShell Blog: http://is.gd/S2o0tP.

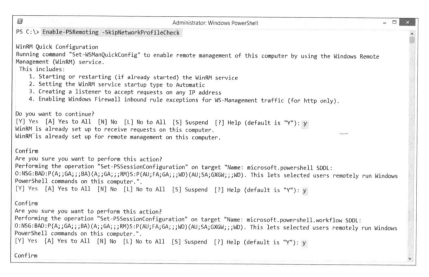

FIGURE 10.3
You can use parameters to force-enable PowerShell remoting.

Method 2: Enabling Remoting with Group Policy

If you have only a few Windows computers on which you'll manage with PowerShell remoting, the **Enable-PSRemoting** cmdlet is all you need. However, for IT pros who need to enable remoting on entire racks full of server machines, running one-off cmdlets is out of the question.

The good news is that we can use Group Policy in Active Directory Domain Services (AD DS) environments to enable PSRemoting.

If you're a domain administrator, fire up the Group Policy Management Console (GPMC), and create or edit a Group Policy Object (GPO), enabling the following policies:

▶ **Allow remote server management through WinRM**, located in the Group Policy path Computer Configuration\Administrative Templates\Windows Components\Windows Remote Management (WinRM)\WinRM service. Set the filter to *; this enables the WinRM service.

▶ **WinRM service**, located in the path Computer Configuration\Preferences\Control Panel Settings\Services. Configure the service to autostart.

▶ **Windows Firewall**, located in the path Computer Configuration\Policies\Administrative Templates\Network\Network Connections\Windows Firewall\Domain Profile. Define an inbound port exception for TCP 5985 or 5986, depending on whether you're using HTTP or HTTPS. To do this, you'll modify the Windows Firewall: Allow Local Port Exceptions and Windows Firewall: Define Inbound Port Exceptions policies.

It's kind of a bummer that you need to separately configure WinRM and Windows Firewall separately like this, but it's all we have at the moment for enterprise enablement of Windows PowerShell remoting.

Sadly, with the GPO method we're still missing the session configuration tweaks made by **Enable-PSRemoting**. For more information about how to work around this limitation, see the internal help file about_Remote_Troubleshooting.

Now that we have PowerShell remoting enabled on at least one remote host, let's turn our attention to how to actually make an honest-to-goodness remote connection. Turns out there are at least two ways—are you surprised?

Method 3: Enabling Remoting in a Workgroup

In an Active Directory forest, internal trust relationships and the mutual authentication used by the Kerberos authentication protocol means that we don't have to worry about swapping digital certificates or its equivalent to enable PowerShell remoting.

However, in a workgroup environment, where every system is a proverbial island unto itself, trust is a very real issue. Unless you solve this problem, you won't be able to do PowerShell remoting in a workgroup.

NOTE

In this book, we do not go the route of creating and exchanging digital certificates; if you need to know how this works, consult this excellent post at the Ramblings on Windows Development blog: http://is.gd/IclbZv.

Instead, we'll assume that in a workgroup environment we're concerned more with making the technology work than in ensuring top security.

What we need to do is populate the TrustedHosts lists in our source computer with the computer names of any remote hosts to which we want to connect. You heard me correctly; we configure trusted hosts on the connecting side, not the connected side.

We can view the current status of our workgroup computer's TrustedHosts list by accessing the WS-Man PSDrive:

```
Get-Item WSMan:\localhost\Client\TrustedHosts
```

The list should be empty by default, of course. We then can add a computer name to which we want to connect by using **Set-Item**:

```
Set-Item WSMan:\localhost\Client\TrustedHosts –Value client3
```

We have lots of flexibility in how we populate the TrustedHosts list. For instance, we can add the following:

▶ A comma-separated list of computer names (client3, client4, client5)

▶ A wildcard match on a domain name (*.contoso.local)

▶ A global wildcard (*) to add all remote hosts that are enabled for Windows PowerShell remoting

CAUTION

Of course, the last option is nice from a convenience standpoint, but not so wise from a security perspective.

In my experience, adding new computers to the TrustedHosts list is wonky. There seems to be no way as of Windows PowerShell v5 to add multiple individual computer names to the TrustedHosts list. When you add a second entry individually, it overwrites the entry that is currently stored.

The workaround I suggest is to use the **–Force** and **–Concatenate** switches to append a new computer name to the list:

```
PS C:\>Set-Item WSMan:\localhost\Client\TrustedHosts Client2 -Force -Concatenate
PS C:\>Get-Item WSMan:\localhost\Client\TrustedHosts

   WSManConfig: Microsoft.WSMan.Management\WSMan::localhost\Client

Type              Name            SourceOfValue      Value
----              ----            -------------      -----
System.String     TrustedHosts                       client3,client2
```

Now that you have your target remote computer in your local machine's TrustedHosts list, you can use **Enter-PSSession** as usual to make a remote Windows PowerShell console session. We actually haven't covered how to do that yet, so please continue reading!

Creating a Windows PowerShell Remote Session

We use the **Enter-PSSession** and **Exit-PSSession** cmdlets to establish a remote interactive session with a trusted host. In terms of authentication, you connect in the security context of your current credentials. Therefore, if you are a domain administrator, you'll have those same privileges on the remote computer.

For instance, let me establish a remote session from my Windows Server 2012 R2-based server named MEM1 to my Server 2012 R2 domain controller named DC1 without explicitly specifying credentials. You can see the workflow in Figure 10.4.

```
                        Administrator: Windows PowerShell                    _ □ X
PS C:\> hostname
mem1
PS C:\> Enter-PSSession -ComputerName dc1
[dc1]: PS C:\Users\Administrator\Documents> hostname
dc1
[dc1]: PS C:\Users\Administrator\Documents> get-eventlog -LogName System -Newest 3

   Index Time          EntryType    Source           InstanceID Message
   ----- ----          ---------    ------           ---------- -------
    3619 Oct 30 09:20  Information  Service Control M...  1073748860 The AppX Deployment Service...
    3618 Oct 30 09:20  Information  Service Control M...  1073748860 The Windows Store Service (...
    3617 Oct 30 09:20  Information  Service Control M...  1073748860 The Windows Store Service (...


[dc1]: PS C:\Users\Administrator\Documents> Exit-PSSession
PS C:\>
```

FIGURE 10.4
Windows PowerShell remoting allows us interactive command-line access to a trusted remote computer.

Let me summarize the actions I performed in the Figure 10.4 screenshot:

▶ Retrieved the local computer's hostname

▶ Made the PowerShell remoting session with DC1 under my current credentials

▶ Retrieved the hostname to verify we're remotely connected and obtained the newest three entries from that system's System Event log

▶ Disconnected the session

Of course, the second run of hostname wasn't necessary because Windows PowerShell displays the hostname of the remote system in the command prompt.

Remember that for all intents and purposes, we are "present" on the remote system. Therefore, we can perform any action, no matter how invasive, up to the limit of our user credential.

This means, too, that we have access to all PowerShell modules that are available on the remote system.

```
[dc1]: PS C:\>Get-Module -ListAvailable
```

When you're ready to disconnect, you can use **Exit-PSSession** or the alias **exit**. If you happen to close the PowerShell session window instead of formally exiting, don't worry about it; PowerShell will automatically close the connection for you.

Tweaking PowerShell Session Parameters

As much as possible, you want to be a conscientious Windows PowerShell administrator and not leave remoting sessions open unless you actually need them. As of Windows PowerShell v3, you can actually disconnect a remote session and let any remote PowerShell that you have running continue. To do this, use **Disconnect-PSSession** instead of **Exit-PSSession**.

While we're on the subject, you should spend some time browsing the WSMan: PSDrive to see what PowerShell session configuration parameters are available. You'll find that you can customize stuff like the maximum number of remote sessions allowed, session timeout values, and so forth. Group Policy in Windows Server 2012 R2 allows you to set these same session parameters at potentially a domain or forest Active Directory scope.

Taking Control of Remote Sessions

We must always keep in mind the Windows PowerShell mantra that "everything is an object." This truism applies to remote sessions as well. As long as you have the system resources to support it, you can have several remoting sessions going on at once. To create a persistent remoting session, use the **New-PSSession** cmdlet. Of course, there is a matching **Get-PSSession** that is useful for retrieving session metadata.

```
PS C:\> New-PSSession -ComputerName dc1

 Id Name           ComputerName    State       ConfigurationName        Availability
 -- ----           ------------    -----       -----------------        ------------
  3 Session3       dc1             Opened      Microsoft.PowerShell     Available
```

Notice that the session has an ID value, a friendly name, and is currently in Opened status. Let's connect to that session now:

```
Enter-PSSession -Name "Session3"
```

We'll then exit the session and verify that the session is gone:

```
Exit-PSSession
Get-PSSession
```

Wait, what? You should find if you try this yourself that the connection still exists. These created remoting sessions are persistent little buggers, aren't they?

We can nuke the session by leveraging the handy dandy **Remove-PSSession** cmdlet:

```
Remove-PSSession -Name "Session3"
```

Using Variables and Alternate Credentials

As a convenient shorthand, you can store Windows PowerShell remote sessions in a variable for easier access:

```
$dc1 = New-PSSession -ComputerName dc1 -Credential domain\administrator
```

Notice that we can specify alternate credentials by specifying the **–Credential** parameter and your username in either domain\username or computer\username format. As you can see in Figure 10.5, Windows PowerShell securely captures your password in a modal dialog box. This is a great relief that we never have to pass passwords in plain text.

FIGURE 10.5
Many Windows PowerShell commands support authentication with alternate credentials, and passwords are captured securely.

I want you to parse the following output because it proves that the entire remote session with dc1 has been captured in my variable **$dc1**. By examining the members of **$dc1** we observe that the session is defined as a **PSSession** object with accompanying methods and properties.

```
PS C:\> $dc1

Id Name          ComputerName    State    ConfigurationName     Availability
-- ----          ------------    -----    -----------------     ------------
 5 Session5      dc1             Opened   Microsoft.PowerShell     Available

PS C:\> $dc1 | Get-Member

   TypeName: System.Management.Automation.Runspaces.PSSession
```

```
Name                        MemberType    Definition
----                        ----------    ----------
Equals                      Method        bool Equals(System.Object obj)
GetHashCode                 Method        int GetHashCode()
GetType                     Method        type GetType()
ToString                    Method        string ToString()
ApplicationPrivateData Property           psprimitivedictionary ApplicationPrivateData
                                          {get;}
Availability                Property      System.Management.Automation.Runspaces.
                                          RunspaceAvailabilit...
ComputerName                Property      string ComputerName {get;}
ConfigurationName           Property      string ConfigurationName {get;}
Id                          Property      int Id {get;}
InstanceId                  Property      guid InstanceId {get;}
Name                        Property      string Name {get;set;}
Runspace                    Property      runspace Runspace {get;}
DisconnectedOn              ScriptProperty System.Object DisconnectedOn {get=$this.
                                          Runspace.Disconnec...
ExpiresOn                   ScriptProperty System.Object ExpiresOn {get=$this.Runspace.
                                          ExpiresOn;}
IdleTimeout                 ScriptProperty System.Object IdleTimeout {get=$this.
                                          Runspace.ConnectionIn...
OutputBufferingMode         ScriptProperty System.Object OutputBufferingMode {get=$this.
                                          Runspace.Conn...
State                       ScriptProperty System.Object State {get=$this.Runspace.
                                          RunspaceStateInfo....
```

The object nature of the captured session means that we can manipulate the session by using the so-called dot notation favored by object-oriented programmers.

For instance, try the following commands out in your own environment and see the data that's returned:

```
$dc1.id
$dc1.Name
$dc1.ExpiresOn
```

Sadly, we don't have methods available to us to disconnect/remove the session. Instead, we can make use of the good old pipeline:

```
$dc1 | Remove-PSSession
```

By now you understand exactly why the preceding statement works: The **$dc1** variable is a **PSSession** object, and the **–Session** parameter of **Remove-PSSession**, which is a required positional parameter, accepts **PSSession** objects. Therefore, the pipeline components fit together hand in glove.

Okay. I think you understand how one-to-one remoting with session objects works. We'll next consider how to send one or more Windows PowerShell commands to a remote host without the overhead of a persistent connection session.

Sending Scripts over the Network

If you simply need to send a single Windows PowerShell statement to a remote host, you may be best off by leveraging the –**ComputerName** parameter:

```
PS C:\> Get-Process -Name svchost -ComputerName dc1

Handles  NPM(K)    PM(K)      WS(K) VM(M)   CPU(s)     Id ProcessName
-------  ------    -----      ----- -----   ------     -- -----------
    379      34     9120      12284    64              620 svchost
    353      14     3160       9776    48              624 svchost
    369      16     2872       6776    28              668 svchost
    458      17    12068      14116    60              816 svchost
   1493      52    18968      34628   207              840 svchost
    961      31     9276      18004   100              872 svchost
```

However, if you have a pipeline full of PowerShell to transmit, or even an entire .ps1 script file, you should consider using **Invoke-Command**.

The **Invoke-Command** cmdlet is extremely powerful because it leverages WS-Man/WinRM-based remoting, and can target one or more remote hosts simultaneously.

The two parameters that you'll use most of the time with **Invoke-Command** are –**ComputerName** and –**Scriptblock**. Don't be fooled by the use of "computername"; we're dealing with contemporary Windows PowerShell remoting here:

```
Invoke-Command –ComputerName dc1 –ScriptBlock {Get-WMIObject –Class Win32_process |
➡Where-Object {$_.threadcount –gt 8}}
```

TIP

Notice the curly braces ({}); this syntax denotes an expression in Windows PowerShell. The previous example is a bit gnarly because we have two expressions: the **ScriptBlock** itself and the **Where-Object** one.

By the way, what we're doing in the previous example is asking our remote host to return a list of all processes with a CPU thread count that is greater than eight. We'll deal with Windows Management Instrumentation (WMI) in all its glory later on in this book.

We also can combine persistent remote sessions with **Invoke-Command**. Watch this:

```
$dcone = New-PSSession -ComputerName dc1
Invoke-Command -ScriptBlock {Get-Module -ListAvailable} -Session $dcone
```

In Hour 11, when you learn how to perform one-to-many remoting, this syntax will come back to haunt you in a good way. Imagine targeting dozens of computers simultaneously with your Windows PowerShell statements and scripts!

Using Invoke-Command with Windows PowerShell Scripts

You'll learn in Hour 19, "Introduction to Windows PowerShell Scripting," how to author your very own Windows PowerShell .ps1 script files. For now, what you should know is that you need to (temporarily) modify the script execution policy on the remote machine before you can send over a script for remote execution.

Take a look at the following partial output, and I'll walk you through it:

```
PS C:\> Enter-PSSession -ComputerName dc1
[dc1]: PS C:\Users\Administrator\Documents> Set-ExecutionPolicy -ExecutionPolicy
➡Unrestricted
[dc1]: PS C:\Users\Administrator\Documents> Exit-PSSession
PS C:\> Invoke-Command -ComputerName dc1 -FilePath "C:\myscript.ps1"

Status    Name               DisplayName                          PSComputerName
------    ----               -----------                          --------------
Stopped   AeLookupSvc        Application Experience               dc1
Stopped   ALG                Application Layer Gateway Service     dc1
Stopped   AppIDSvc           Application Identity                  dc1
Stopped   Appinfo            Application Information               dc1
Stopped   AppMgmt            Application Management                dc1
```

First I establish an interactive remote session with dc1 to relax the script execution policy. Second, I disconnect and run **Invoke-Command**, specifying the fully qualified path to my .ps1 script file by using the **–FilePath** parameter.

I want to finish this hour by giving you a chance to practice what you've learned.

▼ TRY IT YOURSELF

Working with Windows PowerShell Remote Access and Remoting

In this Try It Yourself exercise, you'll have the opportunity to experiment with both the "old school" remote access methods and "true" Windows PowerShell remoting.

To complete these steps, you need two computers that are joined to an Active Directory domain and enabled for Windows PowerShell remoting. Although we won't undertake any destructive actions, be careful if you attempt these steps on a production network.

This exercise assumes that you're working from a Windows Server 2012 R2 member server named MEM1 and that you want to perform remote operations on a Windows Server 2012 R2 domain controller named DC1. Of course, you'll substitute hostname values for your own computers' hostnames. Let's begin:

1. We begin by verifying that DC1, our remote host, is open for business. Instead of ping, we can leverage the **Test-Connection** Windows PowerShell cmdlet:

   ```
   Test-Connection dc1
   ```

2. Let's obtain the BIOS version from our remote host. Are we using WS-Man remoting here or no? How can you tell?

   ```
   Get-WMIObject -ComputerName dc1 -Class Win32_BIOS
   ```

3. Next, we'll look at the error messages from the remote system's System log, formatted as a list for easier reading.

   ```
   Invoke-Command -ComputerName dc1 -ScriptBlock {Get-EventLog -LogName System |
   ➥Where-Object {$_.EntryType -eq "Error"} | Format-List}
   ```

4. If we're going to be working with DC1 for a while, why not store the remote session persistently in a variable?

   ```
   $remote = New-PSSession -ComputerName dc1
   ```

   Make sure to verify that the remote session is active and in an opened state:

   ```
   $remote
   ```

5. Now it's time to enter that session and execute a remote command directly from the context of the remote computer:

   ```
   Enter-PSSession -Session $remote
   Get-Process | Where-Object {$_.Status -eq "Running"} |
   ➥Export-Csv -Path \\mem1\c$\dc1-runningservices.csv
   ```

   Do you see what we've done? We captured the running services on DC1, created a CSV report, and placed it on our local computer's C: drive. Awesome.

6. We can now verify that the file exists and scan its contents:

```
Exit-PSSession
Notepad "c:\runningservices.csv"
```

7. Let's imagine that you need to disconnect the remote session from your local computer and you plan to resume the session from yet another computer. First, make a note of the session name:

```
Get-PSSession
```

Second, we'll disconnect:

```
Get-PSSession -Name "SessionName" | Disconnect-PSSession
```

8. Then, from the same or another computer in the same domain, we can actually pick up the session again.

Run **Get-PSSession** to get the session name for the disconnected session, and then pick up where you left off:

```
Enter-PSSession -Name "SessionName"
```

9. When you're finished with the session, destroy the remote session entirely:

```
Get-PSSession -Name "SessionName" | Remove-PSSession
```

Summary

At this point, you should be comfortable with using the **–ComputerName** parameter of selected Windows PowerShell commands to make old-school remote access calls to other systems.

You also understand to a good degree of depth how we can (1) interact directly on remote systems with the PSSession cmdlets and (2) send Windows PowerShell commands or entire script files to a remote system.

Hour 11 builds on what you learned here by applying Windows PowerShell remoting to several target systems.

Q&A

Q. Is there a way to tell in advance whether a particular remote system is enabled for Windows PowerShell remoting?

A. Sadly, no. You could always try an Enter-PSSession and determine whether you get in, but if you can't, there are many reasons why the connection may fail besides disabled remoting. Windows PowerShell expert Lee Holmes wrote a nifty PowerShell script, however, that addresses this issue exactly. Check out his Test-PSRemoting script at Lee's blog at http://is.gd/nsD1iX.

Q. Is it possible to chain together Windows PowerShell remoting sessions?

A. Yes, you actually can "chain" remoting sessions, although it's generally considered a bad practice due to increased complexity and network overhead. By *chaining*, I mean establishing a **PSSession** with a remote host, and then issuing **Enter-PSSession** from within that remote host to connect to yet another machine.

There is one good use case that I can think of for PowerShell session chaining. You might not be able to connect to a particular machine directly due to network policy. So, you could establish a session with a computer that can connect to the target machine, and nest the second remoting session inside the first one.

Q. Can you access other PSProviders on a remote computer by using session-based remoting?

A. You have to remember that when you enter a remote PSSession with another host, you are effectively sitting at the local keyboard of that machine. This means you have access to all installed modules, PSProviders, and other assets that are available on that box.

Workshop

Using your ever-growing Windows PowerShell skill set, do some Internet research (or scan later hours in this book) to craft a Windows PowerShell script named lastbootup.ps1. The script should contain the following code:

```
Get-WMIObject -Class Win32_OperatingSystem -ComputerName localhost |
➡Select-Object -Property CSName,@{n="Last Booted";
➡e={[Management.ManagementDateTimeConverter]::ToDateTime($_.LastBootUpTime)}}
```

In the preceding example, make sure to break the first line at the pipe, and make sure that the **Select-Object** statement runs on a single line.

What the script does is query the local host's WMI repository to fetch the last boot time. We need to do some datetime conversions by making a direct call to the .NET Framework because the default WMI datetime format is unreadable.

Next, send the script to a remote host on your network. Of course, that remote host will need to be in the same Active Directory domain as you are, or in the same workgroup with remoting enabled, et cetera and so forth.

Quiz

1. Which of the following Windows PowerShell commands retrieves a list of cmdlets that are directly related to persistent sessions?

   a. gcm *session*

   b. gc –verb *psssession*

   c. gc *pssession*

   d. gcm –noun *pssession*

2. The **Disconnect-PSSession** command removes the Windows PowerShell remote session.

   a. True

   b. False

3. In your experience, will the following command run or produce an error, assuming that the remote computer dc1 is online and configured for Windows PowerShell remoting?

   ```
   Invoke-Command –ComputerName dc1 –Command { "c:\windows" | gci }
   ```

   a. Yes

   b. No

Answers

1. The correct answer is D. If you use **gcm**, the alias for **Get-Command** with the wildcard parameter **–noun *pssession*** matches only those Windows PowerShell commands with a noun that includes the string **pssession**.

2. The correct answer is B. The **Disconnect-PSSession** is great for when we want to detach from the remote connection and re-connect to it at a later time, or even from another system. We use the **Remove-PSSession** command to destroy persistent remoting connections.

3. The correct answer is A. You probably need to try this out yourself to demonstrate that the code is correct, but it most assuredly is. For grins, I added some stuff to that Windows PowerShell one-liner intended to throw you off:

   ▶ You can actually use **–Command** instead of **–Scriptblock**; for some Windows PowerShell administrators, the alias is easier to remember.

▶ The padded space in my expression doesn't effect the operation of the scriptblock. Some PowerShell administrators add a space before and after their expression and the curly braces to enhance script readability.

▶ The alias **gci** can be used as a substitute of **Get-ChildItem**.

▶ Although I would normally write the command as **gci** "**c:\windows**", you can write it the other way around because **Get-ChildItem** expects string data (plain text) as input.

Implementing One-to-Many Windows PowerShell Remoting

What You'll Learn in This Hour:

▶ One-to-many remote access in the classic scenario

▶ One-to-many remoting with persistent sessions

▶ Managing session configurations

▶ One-to-many remoting with the Windows PowerShell ISE

▶ Passing input to remote commands

Imagine if your boss asked you to verify the operating system hotfix status of all 25 servers in your organization. How can you accomplish this task without RDP'ing to each box, one at a time, and copying/pasting screenshots or raw text data into, say, an Excel spreadsheet?

You don't want to concern yourself with such busywork, believe me. Instead, you can employ Windows PowerShell to hit all 25 servers at once, gathering the hotfix data, sending the results back to your administrative workstation, and even aggregating the results into a CSV or HTML report. That's true power, my friend.

In this hour we use many of the same commands you learned in Hour 10, "Implementing One-to-One Windows PowerShell Remoting." However, the key difference here is that we are now concerned with one-to-many remoting instead of the one-to-one variety. We have much to do. Let's get to work.

One-to-Many Remote Access in the Classic Scenario

Remember that the –**ComputerName** parameter that is programmed into selected Windows PowerShell commands is coded separately for each command. Therefore, you really need to read the help file for a given command to see whether –**ComputerName** accepts only single computer names or a comma-separated array. For example, check this out:

```
PS C:\> Get-Help Get-WmiObject -Parameter ComputerName

-ComputerName <String[]>
    Specifies the target computer for the management operation. Enter a fully
    qualified domain name, a NetBIOS name, or an IP address. When the remote
    computer is in a different domain than the local computer, the fully qualified
    domain name is required.

    The default is the local computer. To specify the local computer, such as in a
    list of computer names, use "localhost", the local computer name, or a dot (.).

    This parameter does not rely on Windows PowerShell remoting, which uses
    WS-Management. You can use the ComputerName parameter of Get-WmiObject even if
    your computer is not configured to run WS-Management remote commands.

    Required?                      false
    Position?                      named
    Default value
    Accept pipeline input?         false
    Accept wildcard characters?    false
```

The **–ComputerName** parameter of **Get-WMIObject** is pretty standard fare; we can specify any kind of string object, including a comma-separated list of computer names:

```
Get-WMIObject -ComputerName mem1, mem2 -Class Win32_BIOS
```

Or we can take a file containing a one-column listing of any number of computer names, extract its context, and feed the string as an array to the **–ComputerName** parameter:

```
Get-WMIObject -ComputerName (Get-Content "c:\servernames.txt") -Class Win32_BIOS
```

You can run the following Windows PowerShell statement to retrieve the commands that have the **–ComputerName** parameter but don't have the **–Session** parameter. This is a great way to differentiate "classic" remote access commands from the ones that support contemporary Windows PowerShell remoting:

```
Get-Command | Where-Object { $_.Parameters.Keys -contains "ComputerName" -and
➥$_.Parameters.Keys -NotContains "Session" }
```

Weaknesses with the Classic One-to-Many Model

We must recall that because "classic" Windows PowerShell remote access relies on older, proprietary network protocols like DCOM and RPC, you won't have the efficiency available that you have with contemporary PowerShell remoting.

TIP

Remember that when you use the **–ComputerName** parameter to target more than one host, each remote host is contacted one at a time and not in parallel.

That said, you can do some cool stuff. Let me describe what's happening in the following mini-script:

```
$comp = "dc1", "mem1", "mem2"
$data = Get-WmiObject -Class Win32_OperatingSystem -ComputerName $comp
$data | select @{Name="Host"; Expression={$_.PSComputerName}}, Caption, Version,
➥BuildNumber | Format-Table -AutoSize

PSComputerName Caption                                             Version  BuildNumber
-------------- -------                                             -------  -----------
DC1            Microsoft Windows Server 2012 R2 Datacenter 6.3.9600 9600
MEM1           Microsoft Windows Server 2012 R2 Datacenter 6.3.9600 9600
MEM2           Microsoft Windows Server 2012 R2 Datacenter 6.3.9600 9600
```

Before we analyze the code in depth, I want to say a few words about the PSComputerName property. This incredibly useful property was introduced in Windows PowerShell v3 and is actually an alias to the __SERVER property. Note that neither WS-Man remoting nor PSComputerName are available in Windows PowerShell v2, so you should either update the PowerShell version on those machines or content yourself with WMI-based remoting. Now, back to our regularly scheduled programming.

In the first line, we define a variable named **$comp** that contains an array of server hostnames. In the second line, we create a second variable, named **$data**, that uses classic remote access to retrieve operating system metadata for all three computers by using WMI.

TIP

I also created a hash table to create a custom column name. Specifically, I did this to name the column Host instead of PSComputerName. Hash tables are a neat trick that you should take advantage of wherever possible.

Formally defined, a hash table is a collection of key/value pairs. In my experience, hash tables constitute a "Swiss Army Knife" that's useful in any context when you have more complex data relationships that you need to store in a single object.

In the third line, we construct a display pipeline that (1) selects only four output columns and (2) formats the table such that the columns display all data contained therein.

Now, in my little three-server network in my office, I retrieved the results of the previous command nearly instantaneously. However, if I needed to pull OS metadata from, say, 300 machines, then I had better go for a long walk while the command processes.

One-to-Many Remoting with Persistent Sessions

For the remainder of this hour, we concern ourselves with "true" Windows PowerShell remoting methods. Specifically, we begin by delving deeper into persistent remote session objects.

Let's say that we needed to check the contents of the Run Registry key on two of your Windows Server 2012 member servers:

```
HKEY_LOCAL_MACHINE\SOFTWARE\Microsoft\Windows\CurrentVersion\Run
```

We'll begin by creating a variable to hold our two remote servers and verifying that the object was successfully created:

```
$s = New-PSSession -ComputerName mem1, mem2
PS C:\> $s
```

Id	Name	ComputerName	State	ConfigurationName	Availability
2	Session2	mem2	Opened	Microsoft.PowerShell	Available
1	Session1	mem1	Opened	Microsoft.PowerShell	Available

Next we'll invoke the... well, **Invoke-Command** command (like my wordplay?) to enumerate the contents of the Run Registry key. As you know by now, we generally can't use **Get-ChildItem** to retrieve values from the Windows Registry PSProviders. Instead, we use **Get-ItemProperty**:

```
Invoke-Command -Session $s -ScriptBlock {Get-ItemProperty -Path
➥"HKLM:\SOFTWARE\Microsoft\Windows\CurrentVersion\Run"}
```

Watch Out for Line Continuation

As we proceed deeper and deeper into the forest of Windows PowerShell mastery, some of our commands will wrap to multiple lines (such is one of the pitfalls of the printed book format).

If you run one of my code examples and don't get the expected results, be careful of line continuation. You can break a single Windows PowerShell statement across multiple lines only at either the pipe (|) or by using a grave accent (`). Unless you use one of these methods, PowerShell will raise an error because it thinks the wrapped lines are supposed to be separate statements.

You'll find that Windows PowerShell remoting session output includes the **PSComputerName** property by default, which makes it simple to figure out which output came from which remote computer.

Working with Disconnected Sessions

I can't emphasize enough how powerful the disconnected sessions feature is in Windows PowerShell v3 and later. For this illustration, I borrow a scenario from the **Disconnect-PSSession** help.

Suppose that you created a persistent remote session to three servers named DC1, DC2, and DC3 to do some work:

```
$s = New-PSSession -ComputerName dc1,dc2,dc3 -Name ITTask -Credential domain\tech
Enter-PSSession -Session $s
```

NOTE

Notice that we use the **–name** optional parameter to give our session a friendly name.

In your remote work on DC1 you receive strange errors that leave you scratching your head. You call your boss, who instructs you to disconnect the session so that she can log in to the session from her workstation:

```
Exit-PSSession
Get-PSSession -Name ITTask | Disconnect-PSSession
```

Now our boss can run **Get-PSSession** to view the disconnected session metadata, and then connect to it:

```
Get-PSSession -ComputerName dc1,dc2,dc3 -Name ITTask
$admin = Connect-PSSession -ComputerName DC1 -Name ITTask -Credential domain\
➥administrator
Enter-PSSession -Session $admin
```

I slipped in a new command on you. **Connect-PSSession** is used to resume a disconnected session. So, you see in summary that we can disconnect and resume sessions in much that same way that you can park calls in a Voice over IP (VoIP) telephony network.

Managing Session Configurations

In Windows PowerShell remoting, we can send PowerShell commands or script files to up to 32 remote computers simultaneously by default. Remember that this is parallel processing, too; those 32 machines are all remotely executing your code at the same time. Powerful!

NOTE

Keep in mind that the source computer in this one-to-many scenario reserves memory and a session for every one of those remote connections.

If you have a beefy administrative workstation and need to bump up the maximum number of remote targets, you can add the **–ThrottleLimit** parameter to your **Invoke-Command** statement.

For instance, let's suppose that you have a text file with 75 computers that you need to feed into the pipeline. Moreover, you need to send the PowerShell script config.ps1 to every one of the remote boxes:

```
$fanout = New-PSSession -ComputerName (Get-Content "C:\scripts\computers.txt")
Invoke-Command -Session $fanout -FilePath "c:\scripts\config.ps1" -ThrottleLimit 75
```

This means that the config.ps1 will be processed in parallel by 75 computers simultaneously. If, for instance, there were 100 computers in the queue, more computers would be added to the 75-member parallel processing "team" as sessions completed their work.

The Importance of Unhiding Extensions

You may use Windows Explore to create a new PowerShell script file named myscript.ps1 only to discover that Windows PowerShell doesn't recognize the file as a PowerShell script.

As you probably know, Windows (even in the server OS) hides extensions for known file types by default. As PowerShell scripters, we need to see our extensions at all time.

Although you feasibly could disable the default extension-hiding behavior by using Windows PowerShell and the Registry provider, it's probably easiest to use either the Folder Options Control Panel item (see Figure 11.1) or Group Policy.

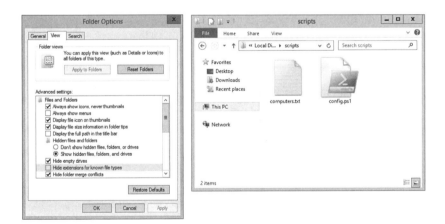

FIGURE 11.1
We need to show file extensions on any Windows computer that we plan to use for Windows PowerShell scripting.

Creating a Constrained Endpoint

Recall in our initial description of Windows PowerShell remoting that the enablement of such involves not only starting the WinRM server, defining Windows Firewall exceptions, and creating and HTTP or HTTPS listener, but also the creation of a connection endpoint.

As it happens, you can define custom configuration endpoints to constrain, or limit, the stuff that particular remote users can do. You can also use a custom session configuration file to set up the environment to your liking (automatically loading custom Windows PowerShell modules, for instance).

NOTE

This is a big deal because traditional profile scripts do not run in Windows PowerShell remote sessions.

Let's imagine that we want to create a custom session configuration to allow our help desk staff to run Get commands on our domain controller, but no other Windows PowerShell commands.

The first thing we need to do is to create a new PowerShell session configuration file. Of course, there's an app...er...cmdlet for that:

```
New-PSSessionConfigurationFile -Path "c:\scripts\GetCommandsOnly.pssc"
➥-VisibleCmdlets Get-*
```

We then register the new session configuration with the local system. You'll be prompted for confirmation and informed that the action restarts the WinRM service.

```
Register-PSSessionConfiguration -Name GetOnly -Path "c:\scripts\GetCommandsOnly.pssc"
```

You can add a startup script to your custom session configuration:

```
Set-PSSessionConfiguration -Name GetOnly -StartupScript "c:\scripts\get-startup.ps1"
```

Remote users need Execute permission on the session configuration in order for it to work. Fortunately, we can use the **–ShowSecurityDescriptorUI** switch to accomplish that goal. Figure 11.2 shows the user interface (UI).

```
Set-PSSessionConfiguration -Name GetOnly -ShowSecurityDescriptorUI
```

To retrieve a list of the built-in session configurations along with any that you created, run the following statement:

```
Get-PSSessionConfiguration | Format-List -Property Name, Permission
```

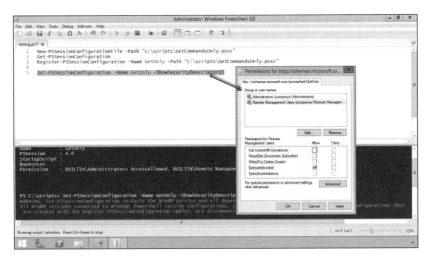

FIGURE 11.2
You may need to make permissions changes to a custom configuration in order to make it behave as expected.

The trick to constrained endpoints is taking pains to ensure that, in this example, our help desk staff connect to the target computer with the correct session configuration. (I'll leave it to you to figure out how best to implement this practice.)

```
$s = New-PSSession -ComputerName DC1 -ConfigurationName GetOnly
```

One-to-Many Remoting with the Windows PowerShell ISE

I feel as if we've sort of neglected the Windows PowerShell Integrated Scripting Environment, or ISE. It's a powerful tool for authoring Windows PowerShell scripts, but it's also a nifty learning/command discovery tool.

I like to start the ISE from within my administrative Windows PowerShell console session:

```
ise
```

That was easy, wasn't it?

Creating a Remote Session Tab

Once you have the ISE open, you can start a new remoting session in any of three ways:

▶ Click the **New Remote PowerShell Tab** button from the ISE toolbar, as shown in Figure 11.3.

▶ Click **File > New Remote PowerShell Tab** from the menu system.

▶ Press **Ctrl+Shift+R**.

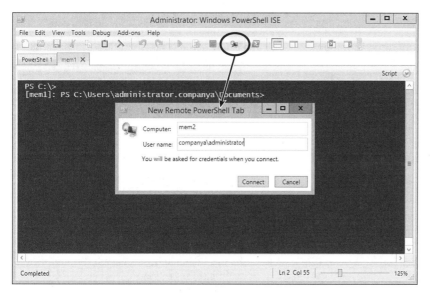

FIGURE 11.3
The Windows PowerShell ISE can host multiple remote sessions; notice that remote session tabs are shaded differently from local sessions.

In any event, you'll be prompted to specify the hostname of the computer to which you want to remotely connect. Of course, you can specify alternate credentials if you need to do that.

TRY IT YOURSELF ▼

One-to-Many Remoting with the Windows PowerShell ISE

In this Try It Yourself exercise, you'll not only boost your experience with one-to-many remoting, but you'll also gain some comfort with the ISE interface.

In this example, I'm running Windows ISE on my DC1 server and making remote connections to my two member servers, MEM1 and MEM2. If you are fortunate enough to have a practice lab set up with three virtual machines (VMs), you can follow these steps to see remoting in action yourself:

1. First of all, make sure you've started ISE with administrative credentials. (Hint: If the title bar doesn't say Administrator, you're not in an elevated session.)

2. If the Commands add-on is displayed, which it usually is by default, click its close button to remove it.

3. Click **File > New Remote PowerShell Tab** and establish an administrative session on another computer in your environment.

4. Once you see the shaded remote tab, click the **Show Script Pane Top** button to place a blank .ps1 script pane above the "live" console session below.

5. Now we're cooking with gas! The goal of the script we're about to create is to generate a text-based report that lists the Windows roles and features that are currently installed on the local system.

   To get started, create a folder named scripts in the root of your local server's C: drive. We'll use this folder as a central repository for reports generated on remote machines.

   Add the following lines to your new script file; make sure that you're doing this in the remote tab!

   ```
   Import-Module -Name ServerManager
   Get-WindowsFeature | Where-Object {$_.Installed -eq "True"}
   ```

   If you're running Windows PowerShell v3 or later, you technically don't need the **Import-Module** statement. However, I included it for educational purposes.

6. Now let's modify that **Get-WindowsFeature** pipeline to generate a concise list of installed roles and features on the remote computer:

   ```
   Get-WindowsFeature | Where-Object {$_.Installed -eq "True"}| Format-List
   ➡-Property Name, DisplayName, Subfeatures -Expand Both
   ```

   Incidentally, I threw in the **-Expand Both** parameter and value to ensure that the subfeature hash table displayed all of its contents instead of truncating like it normally does.

7. We're almost finished with our script. Let's make the pipeline even longer by making the output **filename** pick up the hostname of the local computer and copying the file to the scripts folder on our dc1 server. I'm just going to give you the entire script here at once:

   ```
   Import-Module -Name ServerManager
   $hostname = Hostname
   Get-WindowsFeature | Where-Object {$_.Installed -eq "True"} | Sort-Object
   ➡-Property Name | Format-List -Property Name, DisplayName, Subfeatures
   ➡-Expand Both | Out-File "c:\$hostname.txt"
   Copy-Item -Path "c:\$hostname.txt" -Destination "\\dc1\c$\scripts"
   ```

TIP
If you receive an "Access is denied" error when performing the file copy, you may need to adjust any NTFS or shared folder permissions as necessary and retry. You might need to close and reopen the remote session in order to refresh the security account token associated with the session as well.

8. Before you close the remote tab, click **File > Save As** to save your new script file. Put it in your local system's scripts folder (you should see the report from the remote machine in here as well), and name it **remote-features.ps1**.

9. Close the remote tab. Remember, you should be at your source computer—in my case, the dc1 box.

10. From the local session, either in the ISE or from a PowerShell console session, use one-to-many remoting to blast the script at any other remoting-enabled hosts in your network:

```
$computers = New-PSSession -ComputerName dc1, mem2
Invoke-Command -Session $computers -FilePath "c:\scripts\remote-features.ps1"
```

If you receive errors, closely scrutinize the first few lines of the error message and debug accordingly. Welcome to the wild and wooly world of administrative scripting.

Passing Input to Remote Commands

A core principle of any automation or scripting language is to modularize your code as much as possible by parameterizing your function calls. Wait! One more time in English, please.

Here's the deal: Imagine we need to craft a PowerShell script that gathers the most recent entries from a particular Event log. Some days we might want to pull from the Application log, and other days we may need to retrieve entries from the Security log. We also want to perform this action on multiple computers simultaneously by using PowerShell remoting.

Fire up an ISE session, save your script file, and let's get this done. We'll begin by defining two variables to hold an Event log name and value for the number of newest entries to see:

```
$log = "Application"
$newest = 5
```

What I've provided are simply default values; we can change their values as much as we want to later. Next, we'll use **Invoke-Command** with the **param()** function and the **–ArgumentList** parameter to make our code highly dynamic.

Don't get freaked out by the following pipeline; I'll explain each section in detail:

```
Invoke-Command -ComputerName dc1,mem1,mem2 -ScriptBlock { param($logname,$entries)
➡Get-EventLog -LogName $logname -Newest $entries } -ArgumentList $log,$newest
```

Our goal is to modularize two **Get-EventLog** parameters: **–LogName** and **–Newest**. To do this, we prepend the **param()** function to our scriptblock. In this example, **$logname** corresponds to the **–LogName** parameter value, and **$entries** corresponds to the **–Newest** parameter value.

To actually pass arguments into the script block, we call –**ArgumentList**, specifying the two variables we originally created. Now the way this works is extraordinarily low-tech: it's all in the order of the variables.

Because **$logname** occurs first in the **param()** function, it receives as input the value of **$log**. Likewise, because **$entries** is second in the **param()** function, it receives its value from the **$newest** variable argument.

In Windows PowerShell, the **PSComputerName** property is always returned in the output by default, so we'll be able to quickly differentiate which output came from which remote computer.

From now on, we can simply change the values for **$log** and **$newest** and re-run the **Invoke-Command** statement to obtain entries of different lengths from different logs. That's good automation.

A Bit on Implicit Remoting

As we wrap up our two-hour miniseries on Windows PowerShell remoting, it occurs to me that you should be aware of a useful feature of the shell called *implicit remoting*. This isn't exactly a one-to-many remoting scenario, but it's good information. That's my story, and I'm sticking to it.

Implicit remoting allows you to load modules on the local computer that aren't available locally. For instance, you could load up the Active Directory module on a member server or administrative workstation. Yes, we have the Remote Server Administration Tools (RSAT), but here we seek a low-overhead solution.

Importing a Module from a Remote Computer

One requirement for implicit remoting is that you have an open session with the target system. This is easily accomplished, as you now well know:

```
$s = New-PSSession -ComputerName dc1
```

Next, we'll instruct PowerShell to load the Active Directory module into our current remote session:

```
Invoke-Command -Session $s -ScriptBlock { Import-Module -Name ActiveDirectory }
```

Note that while the Active Directory module is in memory on the remote system, we haven't yet made those cmdlets available on our local box. Here comes the good stuff:

```
PS C:\>Import-PSSession -Session $s -Module ActiveDirectory -Prefix ACD
```

ModuleType	Version	Name	ExportedCommands
Script	1.0	tmp_40db02f5.ayz	{Add-ACDADCentralAccess...

The previous statement imports all commands from the remote Active Directory module and prepends them with the prefix ACD. I just made up the ACD prefix off the top of my head; your goal is to think up a prefix that (1) is easy to remember and (2) isn't likely to conflict with any other prefixes in use on your local system.

Essentially, you have access to the imported commands, which you can use in a local PowerShell session. However, under the hood, the commands actually execute on the remote system.

For instance, you can retrieve a list of the local/remote commands:

```
Get-Command -Noun ACD*
```

This technique is called implicit remoting because you execute locally imported cmdlets and use them as such, when under the covers the commands execute remotely.

Also don't forget to destroy the remote session (and any imported modules) when you're finished working:

```
$s | Remove-PSSession
```

Summary

I'm pleased because you now know how to apply your Windows PowerShell expertise on not only your local computer but literally any number of remote systems. Congratulations on picking up some really valuable job skills.

Have you ever wondered, "Wouldn't it be so convenient to get a Windows PowerShell session from my smartphone or tablet?" Yeah, so have I. Well, if you have at least one Windows Server 2012 R2 computer in your network, you can stand up a PowerShell Web Access gateway and securely perform PowerShell remoting from potentially anywhere in the world and from potentially any kind of network-enabled device.

Q&A

Q. Why is it that I can only see properties and not methods of output returned by remote computers?

A. Remember that data you receive from remote computers with PowerShell is deserialized XML; therefore, you are essentially seeing a read-only snapshot of that data, and will have only properties available to you (technically they are a few methods, but these aren't useful in most cases). Witness:

```
PS C:\> Invoke-Command -ComputerName dc1 -ScriptBlock { Get-WmiObject -Class
➥Win32_Process | Select-Object -Property Name, { $_.GetOwner().User } } |
➥Get-Member
```

```
   TypeName: Deserialized.Selected.System.Management.ManagementObject

Name                    MemberType      Definition
----                    ----------      ----------
Equals                  Method          bool Equals(System.Object obj)
GetHashCode             Method          int GetHashCode()
GetType                 Method          type GetType()
ToString                Method          string ToString()
 $_.GetOwner().User     NoteProperty     $_.GetOwner().User =null
Name                    NoteProperty    System.String Name=System Idle Process
PSComputerName          NoteProperty    System.String PSComputerName=dc1
PSShowComputerName      NoteProperty    System.Boolean PSShowComputerName=True
RunspaceId              NoteProperty    System.Guid RunspaceId=e725fad3-6010-4936-
                                        b8f2-a2e803073a03
```

Do you notice the deserialized object data type? One way around this is to be more selective in the data you pull from the remote system and do your selection and other operations locally:

```
PS C:\> Invoke-Command -ComputerName dc1 -ScriptBlock { Get-WmiObject -Class
➥Win32_Process} | Select Name, { $_.GetOwner().User }  | Get-Member

   TypeName: Selected.System.Management.Automation.PSCustomObject

Name                    MemberType      Definition
----                    ----------      ----------
Equals                  Method          bool Equals(System.Object obj)
GetHashCode             Method          int GetHashCode()
GetType                 Method          type GetType()
ToString                Method          string ToString()
 $_.GetOwner().User     NoteProperty     $_.GetOwner().User =null
Name                    NoteProperty    System.String Name=System Idle Process
```

Of course, if you need the remote data to have "full fidelity," you shouldn't serialize or deserialize anything, but instead establish an interactive session with the remote computer and operate directly on that system.

Q. **I need to do workgroup-based PowerShell remoting, but I'm uncomfortable with the lack of security offered by the TrustedHosts list. How tough is it to set up HTTPS authentication?**

A. It's a fair amount of work and potentially expensive, especially if you need to purchase a Secure Sockets Layer (SSL) digital certificate from a public certificate authority (CA).

Actually setting up the HTTPS listener involves, somewhat surprisingly, no PowerShell, but a lot of Winrm.exe and work in the Certificates Microsoft Management Console (MMC) snap-in.

NOTE

For further information on setting up HTTPS authentication for Windows PowerShell remoting in a nondomain environment, check out Don Jones's wonderful (free) eBook *Secrets of Windows PowerShell Remoting* at http://is.gd/7u8gWo. In the book, Don describes how to obtain and install SSL certificates in exhaustive detail.

Q. Is session data passed over a remote Windows PowerShell connection encrypted?

A. In an Active Directory domain environment, Kerberos provides for mutual authentication and never transmits the user's passwords in any form. The session (payload) data is also encrypted by using HTTP-Kerberos, so that's good news.

In a nondomain environment, though, we're not using Kerberos, so unless you have installed SSL certificates or are using Internet Protocol Security (IPsec), your session data will traverse the network connection in plain text.

Workshop

Use Windows PowerShell remoting to obtain a list of the top 10 processes on each of your other systems, sorted by CPU utilization in descending order. Figure out a way to combine all the remote data into an HTML report.

Download the MakeCert.exe command-line tool from the Windows Software Development Kit (SDK, located at http://is.gd/XDaH3s). Figure out how to create self-signed digital certificates and bind them to the listeners on two non-domain-joined computers. Next, configure remoting between the two computers to use SSL encryption.

Quiz

1. In an Active Directory domain environment, the following Windows PowerShell statement will run as expected:

```
Invoke-Command -ComputerName 192.168.1.2, 192.168.1.23 -ScriptBlock
➥{Get-Process - Select-Object -First 10}
```

    a. True

    b. False

2. You can use the _____ PSDrive to view and edit Windows PowerShell session configuration properties.

    a. Alias

    b. WSMan

    c. Registry

    d. Environment

3. Which of the following commands completely destroys a stored Windows PowerShell remoting session?

    a. Exit-PSSession

    b. Remove-PSSession

    c. Disconnect-PSSession

    d. Destroy-PSSession

Answers

1. The correct answer is B. In a domain environment, Kerberos is the default authentication protocol. As it happens, Kerberos does not accept IP addresses, but only DNS hostnames. Keep this fact in mind throughout your Windows PowerShell remoting endeavors.

2. The correct answer is B. You probably applied simple reason to arrive at the right answer. Windows PowerShell session configuration data is intimately tied to the WSMan-based endpoint created when you ran **Enable-PSRemoting**. So, we can probe the WSMan PSDrive to get to those values.

3. The correct answer is B. Exiting a remote PowerShell session leaves the persistent session open. Disconnecting the session "hangs up" the connection but allows it to be resumed later on the local computer or even a remote machine. We use **Remove-PSSession** to completely destroy a remoting session.

HOUR 12
Deploying Windows PowerShell Web Access

What You'll Learn in This Hour:

▶ Introducing Windows PowerShell Web Access

▶ Setting up the Windows PowerShell Web Access gateway

▶ Testing the Windows PowerShell Web Access gateway user experience

▶ Managing the gateway

Imagine the following: You and your family are on vacation at some sunny, paradise-like resort. You were so firmly committed to enjoying yourself during this vacation that you brought only your iPad and not your company-issued laptop.

So anyway, there you are, lounging on a deck chair with your iPad, when you receive an urgent phone call from the company CEO. Turns out that your corporate Exchange Server just went down, and the users are in an uproar.

As it happens, you have a Windows PowerShell script tucked away in the file system of the Exchange Server that you know will solve the problem. How in the world can you get a remote Windows PowerShell prompt from your iPad, for heaven's sake?

I have great news for you: Window Server 2012 and Windows Server 2012 R2 include a brand-new feature called Windows PowerShell Web Access (PSWA) that does indeed give you remote PowerShell capability from just about any Internet-connected device under the sun.

By the conclusion of this hour, you'll fully understand how to implement PSWA and use it while at the same time maintaining maximum network security.

Introducing Windows PowerShell Web Access

The PSWA gateway is sometimes called "PowerShell through a keyhole" because with it you can tightly control (1) which domain users can access the gateway and (2) which remote systems the authenticated users are allowed to connect to.

The great beauty of PSWA is the freedom that it affords. Specifically, the only web browser requirements to access the gateway are that the browser must be able to do the following:

- ▶ Communicate with HTTPS

- ▶ Accept HTTP cookies

- ▶ Run JavaScript

Thus, we have no requirements on runtimes like .NET, Java, Silverlight, or Flash. No dedicated app is required to use the gateway, either. We could feasibly run remote PowerShell from the "comfort" of our Android smartphone.

You can tell your company's security administrators that we secure PSWA in the same way that we secure, say Outlook Web Access (OWA) to the outside world.

Take a look at Figure 12.1 and I'll walk you through the high-level overview of the technology.

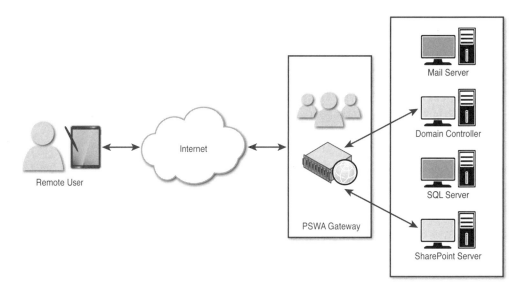

FIGURE 12.1
Schematic diagram of Windows PSWA gateway.

Beginning from the left side of Figure 12.1, we see an Active Directory administrator making a secure HTTPS connection over the Internet to the PSWA gateway. Specifically, the PSWA gateway is an Internet Information Services (IIS) web application. Of course, to make the gateway

Internet-accessible means that you must place the gateway on a screened subnet that is protected by a firewall; those particular configuration details are beyond the scope of this book.

Nevertheless, the IIS server communicates with your internet Active Directory domain controllers to authenticate the remote user. Next, PSWA authorization rules grant selected user/group accounts remote PowerShell access to pre-specified hosts on the internal network.

Do you see how constrained the authentication and authorization are? Hence the phrase "Windows PowerShell through a keyhole."

I think you can also see why PSWA is called a *gateway*; the feature provides users the ability to pass through the gateway to the target machines that they need to administer remotely.

Setting Up the Windows PSWA Gateway

Standing up a PSWA gateway requires three discrete configuration steps:

- ▶ Installing the Windows PSWA feature
- ▶ Configuring the gateway
- ▶ Defining authorization rules

Installing the PSWA Feature

In Windows Server 2012 R2, we could always use the Server Manager GUI tool to add the PSWA feature. However, this is a Windows PowerShell book, so there's no way we are going to rely on the graphical user interface (GUI) when we can flex our Windows PowerShell muscles.

First, let's list the feature itself from an elevated Windows PowerShell console session:

```
PS C:\> Get-WindowsFeature -Name *powershellweb* | Format-List -Property Name,
➡DisplayName, Description

Name        : WindowsPowerShellWebAccess
DisplayName : Windows PowerShell Web Access
Description : Windows PowerShell Web Access lets a server act as a web gateway,
through which an organization's users can manage remote computers by running
WindowsPowerShell sessions in a web browser. After Windows PowerShell Web Access is
installed, an administrator completes the gateway configuration in the Web Server
(IIS) management console.
```

Second, we'll install the feature:

```
PS C:\> Install-WindowsFeature -Name WindowsPowerShellWebAccess
➥-IncludeAllSubFeature -IncludeManagementTools


Success Restart Needed Exit Code     Feature Result
------- -------------- ---------     --------------
True    No             Success       {Windows PowerShell Web Access}
```

It's easy to leave out the **–IncludeManagementTools** switch and then wonder where the role or feature's administrative interface went. This step will activate the IIS web server if you don't already have the role installed on the local box.

The feature installation also gives you a new Windows PowerShell module called, appropriately enough, powershellwebaccess. Let's see what commands are contained therein:

```
PS C:\> Import-Module –Name PowerShellWebAccess
PS C:\> Get-Command -Module PowerShellWebAccess


CommandType      Name                          ModuleName
-----------      ----                          ----------
Function         Install-PswaWebApplication    powershellwebaccess
Function         Uninstall-PswaWebApplication  powershellwebaccess
Cmdlet           Add-PswaAuthorizationRule     powershellwebaccess
Cmdlet           Get-PswaAuthorizationRule     powershellwebaccess
Cmdlet           Remove-PswaAuthorizationRule  powershellwebaccess
Cmdlet           Test-PswaAuthorizationRule    powershellwebaccess
```

The module is pretty small because there isn't a heck of a lot to managing the gateway. In the next phase, we'll install the gateway itself, and then create authorization rules.

Configuring the Gateway

We use the **Install-PSWAWebApplication** function to actually create the PowerShell Web Access website. Unless you specify otherwise, the gateway takes over the IIS default website and packs the bits into a virtual directory named pswa.

To get a quick view of the function's parameters, invoke the command window:

```
Show-Command Install-PSWAWebApplicaton
```

As shown in Figure 12.2, we have the following optional parameters:

▶ **Confirm:** Prompts you for confirmation before performing the function's actions

▶ **UseTestCertificate:** Uses a self-signed digital certificate for authentication and encryption (good for testing environments, but definitely not for production)

▶ **WebApplicationName:** Virtual directory name; defaults to pswa

▶ **WebSiteName:** Friendly name of the IIS website; defaults to Default Web Site

▶ **WhatIf:** Tests what would happen if the command executes, but doesn't actually execute anything

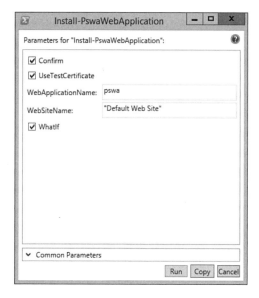

FIGURE 12.2
The Show Command window can serve as a helpful tutor in learning command parameters.

If you leave out the –UseTestCertificate parameter, you'll need to install an SSL certificate from your company's PKI or from a public CA because the PSWA gateway only uses HTTPS for connections. Obviously, this method is preferred anyway for security reasons.

Using Your Own SSL Certificate

The problem with binding a self-signed SSL to your PSWA website (or any production website, for that matter) is that no other computer on earth will trust that certificate because it hasn't been signed by a trusted certification authority (CA).

One solution is to request a Secure Sockets Layer (SSL) certificate from your organization's public key infrastructure (PKI); Active Directory Certificate Services (AD CS) is certainly up to the task. Even then, the certificates may be trusted by all computers within your organization, but out of the box there is no trust from any Internet-based hosts.

A costly solution is to purchase an SSL certificate from a public CA like GoDaddy, Entrust, or Thawte. In any event, you can bind the digital certificate to your IIS website either by using the Internet Information Services (IIS) Manager tool or by using the **New-WebBinding** PowerShell cmdlet.

In my environment, I already bound an SSL certificate to the default web site on my PSWA host, so I'll just run the function with all defaults:

```
PS C:\> Install-PswaWebApplication
Creating application pool pswa_pool...

Name                    State        Applications
----                    -----        ------------
pswa_pool               Started

Creating web application pswa...

Path            : /pswa
ApplicationPool : pswa_pool
EnabledProtocols : http
PhysicalPath    : C:\Windows\Web\PowerShellWebAccess\wwwroot
```

Do you see what happened?

TIP

You should open the IIS Manager MMC console to verify the creation of the new application pool and virtual directory on the target website.

At this point, you can fire up a web browser and point it to the PSWA gateway. For instance, my gateway is found at http://mem1.earthfarm.lan/pswa, and Figure 12.3 shows you the logon screen.

In Figure 12.3, notice the red Certificate Error warning in the address bar. You'll see this bar if you use a self-signed certificate.

Although we can view the logon screen, we won't get into a remote PowerShell connection no matter how hard we try. This is because we haven't created any authorization rules yet; let's take care of that crucial detail right now.

Defining Authorization Rules

Before you run **Add-PSWAAuthorizationRule** to actually define a rule, you need to perform two core Active Directory-related actions and one PowerShell action:

▶ Create one or more global groups for authorized PSWA target computers.

▶ Create one or more Windows PowerShell session configuration files to customize the PowerShell session environment for PSWA users.

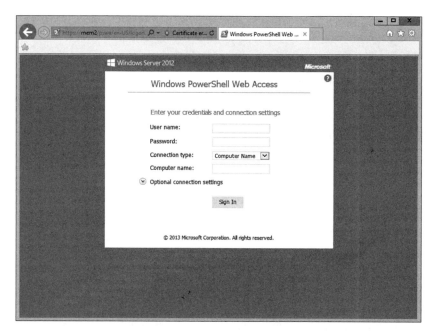

FIGURE 12.3
The Windows PSWA logon page.

You can be as relaxed or as controlling as you want to be when defining these authorization rules and session configurations. In my lab environment, I chose to do the following:

- Use the Domain Admins built-in global group to contain my PSWA users.

- Create a global group called InfServers that contains the servers that I want to allow participating with PSWA.

- Use the default Windows.PowerShell session configuration because I don't want to constrain administrators' ability to run commands on the remote servers.

Now, on to the authorization rule definition:

```
Add-PSWAAuthorizationRule -ComputerGroupName domain\InfServers -UserGroupName
➥"domain\Domain Admins" -ConfigurationName Microsoft.PowerShell
```

To verify that the rule "took," we can run the following statement:

```
PS C:\> Get-PswaAuthorizationRule
```

Id	RuleName	User	Destination	ConfigurationName
--	--------	----	-----------	-----------------
0	Rule 0	companya\domain admins	companya\infservers	Microsoft.PowerShell

I made a minor mistake inasmuch as I forgot to give the authorization rule a friendly name by specifying the –RuleName parameter. Here's the breakdown of the major parameters for your reference in any event:

- ► **ComputerGroupName:** This is the Active Directory group that specifies the servers that PSWA remote users are allowed to connect to. If you look at the **Add-PSWAAuthorizationRule** help, you'll see that you can use other parameter sets if you need to specify individual computers by name.

- ► **UserGroupName:** Again, you can leverage another parameter set with the **–UserName** parameter if you need to specify individual users instead of entire AD groups.

- ► **ConfigurationName:** This, of course, is the PowerShell session configuration that will be loaded when a PSWA user is authenticated and connects to an allowed remote target.

For test environments, you can use the following wildcard syntax to create a fully wide-open PSWA authorization rule:

```
Add-PSWAAuthorizationRule –Username * -ComputerName * -ConfigurationName *
```

Obviously, you wouldn't dream of writing an authorization rule like that in a production environment.

NOTE

In IT security, we draw a clear line of delineation between authentication and authorization. Specifically, authentication refers to validating a user's credentials. With PSWA, IIS and Active Directory handle the task.

Once a user is authenticated by the identity provider, his or her account may be authorized to access network resources up to any preconfigured permission limits. With PSWA, your authorization rules determine what your authenticated users can do on which remote systems.

Testing the Windows PSWA User Experience

Now the time has come to test out the PSWA gateway. Fire up a web browser and connect to your PSWA server address; you'll see at least some of the interface shown in Figure 12.4.

You'll always need to supply the following four parameters to succeed in your remote session:

- ► **User name:** Specify your username in the format domain\username.

- ► **Password:** Self-explanatory, I think.

- ► **Connection type:** The choices are Computer Name or Connection URI; the most common choice is the former.

▸ **Computer name:** Note that there is no browse option; you need to know the hostname of your target server.

FIGURE 12.4
The Windows PSWA logon page gives remote administrators a lot of flexibility in terms of how their session operates.

If you expand Optional connection settings, you'll see additional parameters you can leverage to customize your session:

▸ **Destination computer credentials:** This option allows you to authenticate to the gateway with your previously given credentials, but run the remote PowerShell session under another identity.

▸ **Configuration name:** Again, there is no browse option. You need to know the name of the session configuration you need, or you'll see the default choice, Microsoft.PowerShell, populated by default.

▸ **Authentication type:** Choices are Basic, Negotiate, CredSSP, Digest, or Kerberos.

▸ **Use SSL:** You'll want to specify Yes here unless you have a compelling reason not to do so (troubleshooting, for instance).

▶ **Port number:** Although your initial connection to the gateway happens on the standard HTTPS port (TCP port 443), remember that we're also using Windows PowerShell remoting, which uses TCP 5985 by default.

▶ **Application name:** Leave this option alone; it specifies WS-Man remoting.

If your user account isn't authorized by the gateway, you'll see the error message shown in Figure 12.5.

FIGURE 12.5
You'll see this error message if your user account isn't authorized to use the gateway.

If your user account does match your authorization rule, you are shuttled to the target computer you specified and you'll see the interface shown in Figure 12.6.

Running Remote Windows PowerShell in a Web Browser

Take a look at the PSWA interface in Figure 12.6 and I'll walk you through the controls at the bottom of the screen.

▶ **Submit:** You can press **Enter** or click this button to execute your current PowerShell statement.

▶ **Cancel:** This button breaks out of the currently executing PowerShell code in the same way that the Ctrl+C shortcut works in an interactive session.

▶ **Tab Complete:** Use this button to autocomplete your code.

► **History:** Click these buttons to cycle backward and forward through the command history buffer.

► **Save:** Disconnects the current session such that you or another user can resume it later.

► **Exit:** Closes and removes the remote PowerShell session.

FIGURE 12.6
Here we are, running Windows Powershell from a Web browser console session. Cool!

Remember that you're actually logged onto the remote system; therefore, any **Out-** or **Export-** output you save to say, the C: drive will be visible in the file system on that computer and not on your remote machine.

Disconnecting and Reconnecting Sessions

By closing your PSWA session by clicking Save instead of Exit, you'll save that session on that remote box until the session timeout specified in your session configuration file.

If you attempt a connection to the same target server before the session timeout expires, you'll see the dialog box shown in Figure 12.7.

FIGURE 12.7
The Windows PSWA gateway makes beautiful use of the disconnected sessions feature.

TIP

As discussed in the about_remote_disconnected_sessions conceptual help file, we can specify how long disconnected sessions remain active on a system in several ways.

We can modify the value of the WSMan setting IdleTimeout. We can also run **New-PSSessionOption** from within PSWA, specifying a value for the **–IdleTimeout** parameter.

Come to think of it, you could also include the **PSSession** idle timeout value you need in your session configuration file. Who'd have thought?

You also saw in Figure 12.7 that rather than resume a previously disconnected session, you can choose to create a brand-new session.

Here's something interesting: let's imagine that the current authorization rule allows your user account access to two servers, MEM1 and MEM1. You use the PSWA gateway to obtain a PowerShell command prompt on MEM1. Do you think you can now remote to MEM2?

As you can see in Figure 12.8, PSWA will not allow you to "chain" remoting sessions by default, even if your user account is otherwise authorized to connect to that second system directly through the gateway. Oh well, we tried! You can work around the well-known "second hop" authentication problem, but that's way beyond the scope of this introductory book.

FIGURE 12.8
Busted! PSWA won't let you try to access another computer from your browser-based session, even if you are allowed PSWA access through the authorization rule.

Managing the Gateway

Okay. So you're probably wondering what's required for your PSWA gateway in terms of ongoing maintenance. For that, we'll mark a blissful return to Windows PowerShell rather than a browser instance.

Let's say that Maurice, one of your domain users, complains to you that he can't get access to the target server named MEM1. We can start by checking the status of our PSWA authorization rules:

```
PS C:\> Get-PswaAuthorizationRule
```

Id	RuleName	User	Destination	ConfigurationName
--	--------	----	-----------	-----------------
0	Rule 0	companya\domain admins	companya\infservers	Microsoft.PowerShell
1	Rule 1	companya\maurice	companya\mem2	Microsoft.PowerShell

Okay. We see that Maurice's user account is allowed access to MEM2, but since his account isn't a member of Domain Admins, he isn't authorized to connect to members of the infservers global group, which I happen to know includes MEM2.

I'll take care of adding Maurice's user account to Domain Admins; all we have left to do is to remove authorization rule 1:

```
Remove-PswaAuthorizationRule -Id 1
```

To verify Maurice's access, let's use **Test-PswaAuthorizationRule**:

```
Test-PswaAuthorizationRule -ComputerName MEM2 -UserName "companya\maurice"
```

If you get nothing back, that means the user's account isn't picked up by any authorization rule. If there is a match, you'll see the **Get-PswaAuthorizationRule** output that matches the user.

Finally, if your security needs dictate that you remove the entire PSWA instance, you can issue a command similar to the following (here I assume you installed the gateway using default values and with the test certificate):

```
Uninstall-PswaWebApplication -DeleteTestCertificate
```

Now let's close this hour by giving you some practice time with the technology. Before you start that Try It Yourself exercise, be forewarned that you'll need to have a test pod already configured to follow my steps in order. Specifically, my test lab looks like this:

- ▶ Virtual machine (VM) named DC1 that is configured as an Active Directory domain controller and a PSWA gateway
- ▶ Two additional VMs on the same logical network that will represent allowed and disallowed PSWA targets

With that disclaimer out of the way, let's get to work.

▼ TRY IT YOURSELF

Locking Down Your Windows PSWA Gateway

Your task in this scenario is to give Raymond Bond, your help desk employee, remote access to a single Windows Server host named MEM2. An additional constraint here is that Raymond should have only the ability to issue **Get** commands during his remote PowerShell sessions with MEM2.

To prepare for this exercise, create a standard Active Directory user named **Raymond Bond** and set up a PSWA gateway with default values.

1. We'll begin by logging on locally to our domain controller/PSWA gateway, firing up an elevated PowerShell console session, and defining a new session configuration file:

   ```
   New-PSSessionConfigurationFile -Path "C:\GetSession.pssc" -VisibleCmdlets
   ➥Get-* -SessionType RestrictedRemoteServer
   ```

2. Our next move, of course, is to register the **GetSession** session configuration file with the gateway host:

   ```
   Register-PSSessionConfiguration -Path "C:\GetSession.pssc" -Name "GetSession"
   ➥-Force
   ```

3. Whoops. We need to change the security descriptor on our GetSession configuration to give Raymond Read and Execute permissions:

   ```
   Set-PSSessionConfiguration -Name GetSession -ShowSecurityDescriptorUI
   ```

4. Let's now create our new PSWA authorization rule:

```
Add-PswaAuthorizationRule -ComputerName mem2.companya.pri -UserName
➥"companya\rbond" -ConfigurationName "GetSession" -RuleName "HelpDesk"
```

5. Open a web browser on the gateway and browse to the Windows PSWA login page. Specify Raymond's username and the name of the target computer. (I have MEM2, but of course you'll substitute values that match your environment.)

   Did he get access to MEM2? No? Why?

6. The problem here is that the default PSWA connection binds to the Microsoft.PowerShell session configuration, which Raymond has no access to. Therefore, we need to go back to the login page, expand the optional connection settings, and change the configuration name to **GetSession**.

   Bingo! You should be in like Flynn (whatever that means... perhaps I should Google that right now).

7. Issue some standard **Get** commands such as **Get-Service**, **Get-Process**, and **Get-ChildItem**. Do these commands work okay? They should because Raymond uses a session configuration that permits **Get** commands.

   Incidentally, if we forgot to specify the **RestrictedRemoteServer** session type in our **GetSession** configuration file, even **Get** commands would fail because, you'll recall, PowerShell commands always terminate by default with **Out-Default**. That isn't a **Get** command, so...

8. Now try issuing non-**Get** commands such as **Test-Connection**, **Set-Date**, or **New-Alias**. You should find that these operations fail.

9. To finish up, log out and try to connect Raymond to your other server. You should find that this action fails as well.

10. If you receive errors or see unexpected behavior, remember to research the help files and review your settings for your authorization rules and PowerShell session configurations, especially their permissions.

Summary

I think we've accomplished something significant in this hour of training. You learned how to run remote Windows PowerShell sessions from your smartphone. Personally, I find it a bit ironic and definitely humorous that I can do PowerShell administration from my Apple iPad, which is capable of rendering no Silverlight or Flash content. In my opinion, Windows PSWA gateway is a great response to the vendor-infighting and incompatibilities that we systems administrators have to deal with every day.

In the next hour, we give Windows PowerShell some additional work to do. By using the job subsystem, we can give Windows PowerShell the ability to multitask.

Q&A

Q. I don't have the money to purchase a public SSL certificate, and I don't have the time to deploy AD CS. Can I use a self-signed certificate with PSWA in a production domain?

A. You can do that, but the administrative overhead is unnecessary. By using a self-signed certificate, all your users will see repeated certificate errors when they connect to the gateway. You could use Group Policy to propagate the certificate to your users' computer certificate stores, but that isn't a good idea on general principle.

In sum, because the number of people using the PSWA gateway probably isn't going to be significant, you can get away with using a self-signed certification in production if it's your only option. The session data will, in fact, be encrypted with SSL/TLS.

Q. I use an iPad to access our company's PSWA gateway, and I don't seem to have a Tab key. I miss my PowerShell tab completion.

A. Don't worry. Look at the bottom control bar once you're in a PSWA PowerShell session. Do you see the Tab Complete button? Click that when you want to autocomplete a command, parameter, or enumeration value. Done and done!

Workshop

In your test lab environment, deploy a Windows PSWA gateway that uses an SSL certificate issued by your very own AD CS certification authority. (Yes, I'm trying to get you immersed in other aspects of Windows system administrator as an added bonus.)

Next, secure the gateway by implementing session configuration files and authorization rules.

Finally, use Windows PSWA to get a list of the currently running service on the local machine, but send the results in CSV format to another server on your network.

Quiz

1. The Windows PSWA gateway works on most any web browser as long as the browser supports _____.

   a. Java

   b. JavaScript

   c. XML

   d. CSS

2. What is the net effect of the following authorization rule?

```
Add-PswaAuthorizationRule * * *
```

   a. No users are allowed to any target host.

   b. Some users are allowed access to any target host, but only if a session configuration file is present.

   c. No users are allowed access to some hosts, regardless of the presence or absence of a session configuration file.

   d. Any user is allowed to any target host.

3. You can install the PSWA gateway on an IIS website other than the default web site.

   a. True

   b. False

Answers

1. The correct answer is B. The low system requirements are one of the gateway's greatest strengths. As long as your web browser can connect via HTTPS, accept browser cookies, and can process JavaScript code, you should be able to conduct remote PowerShell sessions through that gateway.

2. The correct answer is D. By passing in asterisks to the **Add-PswaAuthorizationRule** cmdlet, we supply wide-open wildcard values to the **–Username**, **-ComputerName**, and **–ConfigurationName** parameters. This configuration is easy to perform and works well in a lab, but you never, ever want to define an authorization rule like this on a production network.

3. The correct answer is A. By specifying the **–WebApplicationName** and **–WebSiteName** parameters, you can indeed host a PSWA gateway instance on an IIS server that may, for example, already allocate the default web site to another application.

HOUR 13
Multitasking Windows PowerShell

What You'll Learn in This Hour:

- ▶ Investigating the PowerShell job architecture
- ▶ Controlling job behavior
- ▶ Understanding parent and child jobs
- ▶ Introducing the **–AsJob** parameter
- ▶ Scheduling jobs
- ▶ Reviewing what we've learned

You may have noticed in your Windows PowerShell practice thus far that you temporarily lose control over your session when you execute one or more commands. This behavior is by design; you give the shell a set of instructions, and it goes about its business until it's finished, after which you get your prompt back.

Wouldn't it be nice to send commands to PowerShell to process in the background? Think of how this would enhance your productivity! You send a script to the shell, get your prompt back, and then you're free to, say, send another script to the shell.

Of course, you could spawn multiple Windows PowerShell sessions to do this, but as it turns out, this approach is unnecessary.

Windows PowerShell includes a built-in job architecture that enables us to get PowerShell truly multitasking. By the end of this hour, you'll understand all about how the jobs system works.

Investigating the PowerShell Job Architecture

The UNIX/Linux operating system family has long had the ability to send shell commands to the background for "behind the scenes" processing. Thanks to the Windows PowerShell team, we now also have this ability.

Let's begin by seeing what job-related cmdlets are available to us:

```
PS C:\> Get-Command -Noun Job

CommandType      Name
-----------      ----
Cmdlet           Debug-Job
Cmdlet           Get-Job
Cmdlet           Receive-Job
Cmdlet           Remove-Job
Cmdlet           Resume-Job
Cmdlet           Start-Job
Cmdlet           Stop-Job
Cmdlet           Suspend-Job
Cmdlet           Wait-Job
```

By now, you should be familiar enough with the common PowerShell verbs so as to have a grasp of what you can do with these job cmdlets.

Starting a Background Job

Windows PowerShell is a bit quirky in spots, I'm sure you'd agree with me. This statement applies to how these PowerShell background jobs run under the hood. You'll see this in Technicolor when I tell you about parent and child jobs later in this hour.

For now, let's create a new job that searches our E: drive for all Adobe Acrobat PDF files:

```
$gci = Start-Job -ScriptBlock { Get-ChildItem -Path "E:\" -Filter *.pdf -Recurse }
```

First of all, I invite you to try that **Get-ChildItem** command without using a job; you'll find that your PowerShell session locks up for an uncomfortably long time. However, when you submit a job, you can immediately resume your work in the shell.

Second, notice that I saved the job to a variable. This is a habit that you should adopt concerning jobs. In my experience it's much easier to work with jobs if you store the job object in an easy-to-remember, brief variable name.

Checking Job Status

Now, let me walk you through how we can check on job status and comprehend the output:

```
PS C:\> Get-Job

Id     Name       PSJobTypeName   State     HasMoreData    Location
--     ----       -------------   -----     -----------    --------
2      Job2       BackgroundJob   Running   True           localhost
```

Of course, **Get-Job** run with no parameters retrieves all existent jobs on the local system. If we know the name, ID, or variable name of a job, we can leverage that in the following ways:

```
Get-Job -Id 2
Get-Job -Name Job2
$gci | Get-Job
```

Incidentally, notice in that output that Windows PowerShell automatically assigns incrementing names to your jobs. In addition to or instead of using a variable, you can specify a friendly name:

```
PS C:\> $gs = Start-Job -Name "Antimalware" -Scriptblock {Get-Service |
➥Where-Object { $_.Name -like "*malware*"} | Stop-Service}
PS C:\> $gs
```

```
Id    Name          PSJobTypeName   State      HasMoreData    Location
--    ----          -------------   -----      -----------    --------
4     Antimalware   BackgroundJob   Completed  False          localhost
```

Understanding Job Status Output

Okay, enough with the fun and games. We need to understand what each of those output fields means. Let's get to it:

- ▶ **Id:** Unique identifier

- ▶ **Name:** Optional friendly name

- ▶ **PSJobTypeName:** System-defined job type

- ▶ **State:** Current status

- ▶ **HasMoreData:** Absence or presence of output being held in session RAM

- ▶ **Location:** Where the job is running

I want to draw your attention to the **HasMoreData** property. If this property returns Boolean true, that means that PowerShell is holding the job results in RAM for you and you haven't yet seen it.

Retrieving Job Data

Let's return to the original example:

```
PS C:\> $gci = Start-Job -ScriptBlock {Get-ChildItem -Path "E:\" -Filter *.pdf
PS C:\> Get-Job
```

Id	Name	PSJobTypeName	State	HasMoreData	Location
--	----	-------------	-----	-----------	--------
2	Job2	BackgroundJob	Running	True	localhost

You can view the output of a job, even one that is still running, by using **Receive-Job**:

```
Receive-Job -Id 2
```

Again, you can use the name, ID, or variable name, depending on your preference.

The gotcha with **Receive-Job** is that unless you specify the –**Keep** parameter, viewing completed job output dumps it all from memory. I'm not kidding. To test this, wait until your PDF search job completes, and then run a **Receive-Job** on it. Look here:

```
PS C:\> Get-Job
```

Id	Name	PSJobTypeName	State	HasMoreData	Location
--	----	-------------	-----	-----------	--------
2	Job2	BackgroundJob	Completed	True	localhost

```
PS C:\> Receive-Job -Name "Job2"

#output omitted to save space

PS C:\> Get-Job
```

Id	Name	PSJobTypeName	State	HasMoreData	Location
--	----	-------------	-----	-----------	--------
2	Job2	BackgroundJob	Completed	False	localhost

```
PS C:\> Receive-Job -Id 2
PS C:\>
```

Ouch! That hurts. Notice that PowerShell changes the **HasMoreData** property value to **False** once it's dumped the job results from memory. By contrast, whenever we do either of the following (other command variants are possible, naturally):

```
Receive-Job -Id 2 -Keep
Get-Job -Id 2 | Receive-Job -Keep
```

we can retrieve the job results as many times as we want to, and PowerShell will keep the job and the output in memory until the session is closed or we remove the job. By the way, you know that the job data is being retained in memory whenever you see the **HasMoreData** job property is set to **True**.

TIP

Get into the habit of using the **–Keep** parameter whenever you use **Receive-Job**. Remember that we use Windows PowerShell to make our work faster and more convenient; we never want to create unnecessary and excess work for ourselves or others.

I want you to know that **Start-Job** accepts entire PowerShell scripts as input. The **–FilePath** parameter is excellent when you have a long-running script that you don't want to tie up your current session. Here's an example of its usage:

```
Start-Job -Name TaskScript -FilePath "C:\scripts\pstasklist.ps1"
```

Controlling Job Behavior

At this point you know how to define a job, fetch its status, and receive its output. In the next sections, we'll learn how to stop, resume, and delete jobs.

Stopping a Job

Okay, let's put a couple jobs into the queue and fetch their status:

```
PS C:\> $txt = Start-Job -ScriptBlock {Get-ChildItem -Path "C:\" -Filter *.txt
➡-Recurse}
PS C:\> $png = Start-Job -ScriptBlock {Get-ChildItem -Path "C:\" -Filter *.png
➡-Recurse}
PS C:\> Get-Job
```

Id	Name	PSJobTypeName	State	HasMoreData	Location
--	----	-------------	-----	-----------	--------
2	Job2	BackgroundJob	Running	True	localhost
4	Job4	BackgroundJob	Running	True	localhost

You probably noticed that the system-generated ID values don't increment exactly by one. For instance, my first job has ID 2, and the second job has ID 4. What's the deal? Don't worry; we'll discuss parent and child jobs soon enough.

More immediately, however, we have the problem that these two resource-intensive jobs are running concurrently and potentially slowing down our system. Let's stop the first job:

```
Stop-Job -Id 2
```

There. If you run another **Get-Job**, you'll observe that this first job now shows a state of Stopped. The **True** value for **HasMoreData** means that we can retrieve the job results as usual. Of course, the job results will contain the data from the start of the job until the moment you stopped it.

Alternatively, we can supply a comma-separated list of **ID** or **Name** values to **Stop-Job**:

```
Stop-Job -Id 2,4
```

Resuming a Stopped Job

I'm sorry to say that once a PowerShell background job is stopped, you can't simply pipe it to **Start-Job**, however logical that approach may seem to you.

As proof, let's fetch the methods for a stopped job on my test system:

```
PS C:\> Get-Job -id 2 | Get-Member -MemberType Method


    TypeName: System.Management.Automation.PSRemotingJob

Name                 MemberType Definition
----                 ---------- ----------
Dispose              Method     void Dispose(), void IDisposable.Dispose()
Equals               Method     bool Equals(System.Object obj)
GetHashCode          Method     int GetHashCode()
GetType              Method     type GetType()
LoadJobStreams       Method     void LoadJobStreams()
StopJob              Method     void StopJob()
ToString             Method     string ToString()
UnloadJobStreams     Method     void UnloadJobStreams()
```

CAUTION

Notice that we have a **StopJob()** method but nothing to restart it. Therefore, the takeaway here is don't stop a job unless you actually want to stop it permanently.

Stopped and completed jobs remain in the **Get-Job** queue until either the session is closed or you manually purge the queue.

If you need to pause a job for later resumption, you should use the **Suspend-Job** and **Resume-Job** cmdlets, respectively. However, those cmdlets are intended for Windows PowerShell workflow jobs, and we haven't arrived at workflows yet. Stay tuned for that content!

Deleting Jobs from the Queue

If you need to "nuke" jobs from the queue, we bring **Remove-Job** into action. Here are three examples of its usage. (You should know the proverbial drill by now.)

```
Remove-Job -Id 6
Remove-Job -Name MyJob
$job | Remove-Job
Remove-Job -State Failed
```

This last example is interesting. The **-State** property exists in most of the **Job**-related cmdlets. Here's a comprehensive listing of the **-State** enumeration:

- ▶ NotStarted

- ▶ Running

- ▶ Completed

- ▶ Failed

- ▶ Stopped

- ▶ Blocked

- ▶ Suspended

- ▶ Disconnected

- ▶ Suspending

- ▶ Stopping

If you need to swing the so-called heavy hammer, you can run either of the following commands to remove every job in the queue, regardless of its status:

```
Get-Job | Remove-Job
Remove-Job *
```

Understanding Parent and Child Jobs

I alluded earlier to the fact that the jobs that accrue over time in your current session do not necessarily follow an ordinal (1, 2, 3, and so on) pattern. Instead, you're likely to see jumps like the following:

```
PS C:\> Get-Job

Id    Name          PSJobTypeName   State       HasMoreData   Location
--    ----          -------------   -----       -----------   --------
12    test          BackgroundJob   Completed   True          localhost


PS C:\> Start-Job -ScriptBlock {Get-EventLog -LogName System}

Id    Name          PSJobTypeName   State       HasMoreData   Location
--    ----          -------------   -----       -----------   --------
14    Job14         BackgroundJob   Running     True          localhost
```

Your first thought when you view the previous output is probably "Hey, what happened to job ID 13?"

That's actually a good question. Let's investigate.

Teasing Apart Parent and Child Jobs

In Windows PowerShell, any job you submit to the shell is assigned the next available Id number; this entry is always a parent job. A parent job can be considered the named "container" for the job object; each parent job has at least one child job that actually undertakes the work.

For example, if you were to send a PowerShell job to 20 remote computers, you would see 1 parent job and 20 child jobs, one for each remote system.

In our current example, we can leverage the –**IncludeChildJob** parameter of **Get-Job** to see what happened to elusive job ID 13:

```
PS C:\> Get-Job -Id 12 -IncludeChildJob

Id    Name     PSJobTypeName   State       HasMoreData   Location
--    ----     -------------   -----       -----------   --------
12    test     BackgroundJob   Completed   True          localhost
13    Job13                    Completed   True          localhost
```

Aha! Now we see what's going on, correct? The good news is that you can (in general) avoid interacting with child jobs directly in most circumstances. In other words, querying the parent job provides a summation of all its children's activities, status, and so forth.

Nevertheless, you may run into situations (especially with remoting jobs) where one or more child jobs mail return a Failed State and you need to query the child jobs directly. To do this, we apply the same consistent syntax we've used all along:

```
PS C:\> Get-Job -IncludeChildJob

Id    Name     PSJobTypeName   State       HasMoreData   Location
--    ----     -------------   -----       -----------   --------
12    test     BackgroundJob   Completed   True          localhost
13    Job13                    Completed   True          localhost
14    Job14    BackgroundJob   Completed   True          localhost
15    Job15                    Completed   True          localhost


PS C:\> Receive-Job -Id 15 -Keep

   Index Time          EntryType    Source             InstanceID Message
   ----- ----          ---------    ------             ---------- -------
   50845 Nov 07 12:00  Information  EventLog           2147489661 The sys...
   50844 Nov 07 11:28  Information  mbamchameleon      1073803264 Failed ...
   50843 Nov 07 11:28  Information  mbamchameleon      1073803264 Failed ...
```

This probably goes without saying, but I'll say it just for the record: When you run **Get-Job** with the –**IncludeChildJob** parameter, the parent jobs are the ones with a value for the **PSJobType** property, and the child jobs are the ones with a blank value for that property. Just saying.

Introducing the –AsJob Parameter

With "classic" WMI-based PowerShell remoting, we look for PowerShell commands that include the **–ComputerName** parameter. Sadly or not, there exists no such parameter with **Start-Job**:

```
PS C:\> Get-Help Start-Job -Parameter * | Select-Object -Property Name

Name
----
ArgumentList
Authentication
Credential
FilePath
InitializationScript
InputObject
LiteralPath
Name
PSVersion
RunAs32
ScriptBlock
DefinitionName
DefinitionPath
Type
```

No problem! Some Windows PowerShell commands, whether remoting-aware or not, can be "crammed" into job objects by the inclusion of the **–AsJob** parameter. Let's investigate job-compatible commands on my Windows 8.1 system running Windows PowerShell v5 preview:

```
PS C:\> Get-Command * -CommandType cmdlet -ParameterName AsJob |
➥Select-Object-Property Name

Name
----
Get-WmiObject
Invoke-Command
Invoke-WmiMethod
Remove-WmiObject
Restart-Computer
Set-WmiInstance
Stop-Computer
Test-Connection
```

Let me give you a simple example of how we can leverage the **–AsJob** parameter in-line with one of the previously given cmdlets:

```
PS C:\> $bios = Get-WmiObject -Class Win32_BIOS -AsJob
PS C:\> $bios | Get-Job
```

Id	Name	PSJobTypeName	State	HasMoreData	Location
16	Job16	WmiJob	Completed	True	localhost

Using the **–AsJob** parameter creates garden-variety job objects just like **Start-Job** does. You interact with the jobs here in the same way as we've grown accustomed to over the course of this hour of training.

Sending Remote Jobs

You've doubtless noticed our old friend **Invoke-Command** in that previous command list. Cool! Why don't we undertake some WSMan remoting goodness with a couple computers on our network?

NOTE

For those of you who haven't read all of my previous hours (and why wouldn't you?), you should understand that you'll need to enable Windows PowerShell remoting on any target systems in your network environment before any remote jobs will work as expected. We discuss remoting to a great depth in Hours 10, "Implementing One-to-One Windows PowerShell Remoting," and 11, "Implementing One-to-Many Windows PowerShell Remoting."

```
PS C:\> $metadata = Invoke-Command -ComputerName localhost,mem2,dc1 -ScriptBlock
➥{Get-WmiObject -Class Win32_OperatingSystem} -AsJob
PS C:\> $metadata
```

Id	Name	PSJobTypeName	State	HasMoreData	Location
18	Job18	RemoteJob	Failed	True	localho...

Yikes! Why did my remote job blow up? Take a moment if you would to observe the PSJobTypeName (RemoteJob) and the job state (Failed). Dang!

Well, in this case the parent job task isn't giving us enough information to troubleshoot the failure. Let's dip into the child jobs:

```
PS C:\> Get-Job -id 18 -IncludeChildJob
```

Id	Name	PSJobTypeName	State	HasMoreData	Location
18	Job18	RemoteJob	Failed	False	localho...
19	Job19		Completed	False	localhost
20	Job20		Failed	False	mem2
21	Job21		Failed	False	dc1

Okay. So we see that PowerShell created a separate child job ID for each computer I targeted in my **$metadata** job object. You can verify that by scanning the **Location** property values. We also observe that the only job that completed was the task on my local computer.

You know what we need to do next, right? We need to receive the contents of a failed job. Let's do that now:

```
PS C:\> Receive-Job -Id 20 -Keep
[mem2] Connecting to remote server mem2 failed with the following error
message : The WinRM client cannot process the request. If the authentication
scheme is different from Kerberos, or if the client computer is not joined to
a domain, then HTTPS transport must be used or the destination machine must be
added to the TrustedHosts configuration setting. Use winrm.cmd to configure
TrustedHosts. Note that computers in the TrustedHosts list might not be
authenticated. You can get more information about that by running the
following command: winrm help config. For more information, see the
about_Remote_Troubleshooting Help topic.
    + CategoryInfo          : OpenError: (mem2:String) [], PSRemotingTransport
    Exception
    + FullyQualifiedErrorId : ServerNotTrusted,PSSessionStateBroken
```

Okie-dokie. If you've hung in with me throughout this book, you can easily determine what the problem is: My local host is part of a workgroup, and the dc1 and mem2 remote computers are members of an Active Directory domain.

Therefore, I'll have to populate my local computer's TrustedHosts list with those remote computer names before my remote commands will work:

```
Set-Item WSMan:\localhost\Client\TrustedHosts —Value dc1,mem2
```

Now, as the drama coach says to the student: "One more time—with feeling!"

```
PS C:\> $metadata2 = Invoke-Command -ComputerName localhost,mem2,dc1 -ScriptBlock
➡{Get-WmiObject -Class Win32_OperatingSystem} -AsJob
```

This time, the results should be a bit friendlier.

By the way, you can name these "inline" jobs; simply specify the **–jobname** parameter, as follows:

```
PS C:\>Invoke-Command -ComputerName (Get-Content -Path "c:\servers.txt")
➡-Command { Get-Process } -AsJob -JobName "RemoteJob"
```

Scheduling Jobs

Windows PowerShell jobs come in three basic varieties:

- **Traditional" background jobs** represent what we've dealt with exclusively thus far.

- **Scheduled jobs** are what we're gearing up to learn now.

- **Workflow jobs** will be covered later on in this book.

The PowerShell team added scheduled jobs to the feature list in Windows PowerShell v3. The idea here is to create a programmatic equivalent of the Windows Task Scheduler. In point of fact, scheduled PowerShell jobs are indeed registered with the Windows Task Scheduler service.

Workflow jobs are what I term "PowerShell jobs on steroids." These jobs can do some pretty powerful things, such as survive system restarts and respond to other events.

With no further ado, let's dive into the technology and see what's what.

Creating an On-Demand Scheduled Job

As it happens, the cmdlets we use to define and manage scheduled PowerShell jobs are contained in a different dynamic link library (DLL) from the "regular" background jobs. Look here:

```
PS C:\> Get-Command *scheduledjob* | Select-Object -Property Name
Name
----
Disable-ScheduledJob
Enable-ScheduledJob
Get-ScheduledJob
Get-ScheduledJobOption
New-ScheduledJobOption
Register-ScheduledJob
Set-ScheduledJob
Set-ScheduledJobOption
Unregister-ScheduledJob
```

Not surprisingly, we use **Register-ScheduledJob** to, well, register a new Windows PowerShell job on the local computer:

```
PS C:\> Register-ScheduledJob -Name ArchivePS1
➡-ScriptBlock {ls $home\*.ps1 -Recurse | Copy-Item -Destination "e:\archive"}

Id      Name            JobTriggers     Command
--      ----            -----------     -------
1       ArchivePS1      0               ls $home\*.ps1 -Recurse | Copy-It...
```

Here are some notes regarding the previous command and output:

▶ Because I didn't add a trigger condition for this job, it won't run automatically at any time. You can see the 0 value for the **JobTriggers** property.

▶ I'm using **ls**, a UNIX-friendly alias for **dir** (which is, in turn, an alias for **Get-ChildItem**). I just want to make sure you haven't forgotten about the common aliases.

▶ **$home** refers to the currently logged on user's home directory.

▶ The scriptblock searches the user's home folder for *.ps1 script files and copies them to an archive location.

Now, if you're following along at home, I want you to close your Windows PowerShell session window. Yes, I mean it. Start a brand-new PowerShell console session and run **Get-ScheduledJob** like I did:

```
PS C:\> Get-ScheduledJob

Id          Name          JobTriggers     Command
--          ----          -----------     -------
1           ArchivePS1    0               ls $home\*.ps1 -Recurse | Copy-It...
```

Whoa! Isn't that cool? These scheduled jobs aren't session-specific like ordinary background jobs are. If you open the Windows Task Scheduler tool on you computer and browse the task library to the following location,

```
Task Scheduler Library\Microsoft\Windows\PowerShell\ScheduledJobs
```

you will indeed see a new object representing your new scheduled job. Figure 13.1 shows the interface.

Because Windows PowerShell creates the scheduled job as an XML-based Task Scheduler task, there is nothing to prevent you from adding triggers and other parameters to the task directly with Windows Task Scheduler.

However, you're here to learn Windows PowerShell, so we'll consequently constrain ourselves to managing these scheduled tasks programmatically.

By the way, you can always manually trigger a scheduled job simply by invoking **Start-Job** as usual. You just need to know the name or ID of the scheduled job and you're golden:

```
PS C:\> $s = Get-ScheduledJob -Id 1
PS C:\> $s.StartJob()

Id      Name          PSJobTypeName      State      HasMoreData      Location
--      ----          -------------      -----      -----------      --------
2       ArchivePS1    PSScheduledJob     Running    True             localhost
```

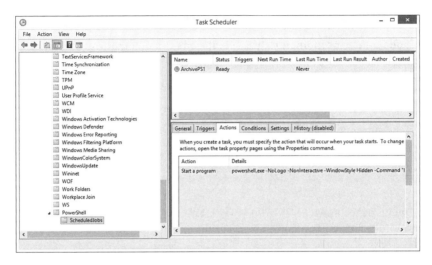

FIGURE 13.1
Windows PowerShell scheduled jobs appear in the Windows Task Scheduler utility.

In the preceding example, we obtained a reference to our scheduled job object and then invoked the object's **StartJob()** method to kick it off. Do you remember how to view the properties and methods that are attached to an object?

Adding Triggers to Scheduled Jobs

If we try to receive data from our sample ArchivePS1 job, we should expect no output because this particular job has no trigger. Unless, of course, you performed an "on-demand" run of the job as I did in the previous section.

A trigger is nothing more than an event that, when the trigger's condition evaluates to Boolean True, serves to start a scheduled task.

Let's create a trigger that specifies a condition of "every morning at 3 a.m.":

```
$trigger = New-JobTrigger -Daily -At "3 AM"
```

Let me tell you: We don't have the time or space to give the scheduled PowerShell jobs engine due justice. What I can tell you is that it is required reading for you to read the following conceptual help files:

- ▶ about_Scheduled_Jobs
- ▶ about_Scheduled_Jobs_Advanced
- ▶ about_Scheduled_Jobs_Basics
- ▶ about_Scheduled_Jobs_Troubleshooting

For now, let's just go with our simple **$trigger** example. We can now plug in our trigger variable into **Register-ScheduledJob** as follows:

```
PS C:\> Register-ScheduledJob -Name NightlyReboot -ScriptBlock {Restart-Computer
➥-Force} -Trigger $trigger

Id          Name            JobTriggers     Command
--          ----            -----------     -------
1           NightlyReboot   1               Restart-Computer -Force
```

You can get even fancier by creating named option collections with the **New-ScheduledJobOption** cmdlet. Check this out:

```
$runadmin = New-ScheduledJobOption -RunElevated
```

The previous example creates an ultra-simple job option variable that specifies that the scheduled job should run with elevated credentials. Review the help file for **New-ScheduledJobOption** to learn what else is possible here.

Now we'll create yet another job, this time highly customized:

```
Register-ScheduledJob -Name InventoryScript -Trigger $trigger -ScheduledJobOption
➥$runadmin -MaxResultCount 20 -ScriptBlock {Invoke-Command -ComputerName SRV1
➥-FilePath "c:\scripts\inventory.ps1"}
```

As ginormous as the previous PowerShell one-liner is, you should understand just about all of it by this point. You'll notice that I snuck in a parameter called **–MaxResultCount**. You'll learn about that one in the next section.

Pulling Data from PowerShell Scheduled Jobs

I told you already that we don't have to worry about using **–Keep** when we invoke **Receive-Job** because scheduled job data is stored persistently on disk.

NOTE

Recall that you need to remember to add **–Keep** to your data retrieval with background jobs because that **HasMoreData** property stores the data only until the job is removed or session is deleted.

By contrast, because Windows PowerShell scheduled jobs are stored on disk rather than in memory, you can retrieve data from a scheduled job at any time without **–Keep** and still maintain access to the output.

Another cool fact is that Windows PowerShell stores result objects each time the job triggers. Thus, if a daily PowerShell job runs for seven days, then you'll have (at least) seven result sets to parse.

On my system, I manually ran the ArchivePS1 scheduled job we created earlier. Once PowerShell has data to show us, we can query for it:

```
PS C:\> Get-Job -Name ArchivePS1
```

```
Id    Name          PSJobTypeName   State       HasMoreData   Location
--    ----          -------------   -----       -----------   --------
2     ArchivePS1    PSScheduledJob  Completed   False         localhost
5     ArchivePS1    PSScheduledJob  Completed   False         localhost
```

This particular example actually doesn't have any onscreen output because we ran a directory listing and copied a bunch of files. However, we use **Receive-Job** as usual to pull the output from a scheduled job:

```
Receive-Job –Id 2
```

Know that we can use the **–MaxResultCount** parameter of **Register-ScheduledJob** to override the default value of 32 results. You may want to pare back the number of result sets stored by a scheduled task if you're concerned about disk space on your computer.

Reviewing What We've Learned

The only thing left to do in this action-packed hour is to give you a chance to solidify your understanding of the Windows PowerShell job system. To that end, here's a Try It Yourself exercise for you to work through.

▼ TRY IT YOURSELF

Creating a Scheduled PowerShell Job

In this scenario, you'll create a scheduled Windows PowerShell job that gathers the 10 most recent error messages from the local host's System event log. We'll have the job occur every Monday, Wednesday, and Friday evening at 7 p.m.

1. You can, and probably should, run the following commands to delete all the background and scheduled jobs from our local system:

```
Get-Job | Remove-Job
Unregister-ScheduledJob *
```

   You can also run the aforementioned commands after you complete this exercise to reset your local system to prehour defaults.

2. It's time to define our trigger. Remember that our trigger condition is Mon-Wed-Fri at 7 p.m. You'll see that we make use of some new parameters of the **New-JobTrigger** cmdlet, and that we specify time in 24-hour format to avoid ambiguity:

```
$trig = New-JobTrigger -Weekly -DaysOfWeek Monday, Wednesday, Friday -At
➥"19:00" -WeeksInterval 1
```

3. Now we'll create a set of scheduled job options that (1) hides the job from the Windows Task Scheduler interface; and (2) ensures that the system has been idle for at least 10 minutes in order to activate the trigger:

```
$opt = New-ScheduledJobOption -HideInTaskScheduler -IdleDuration 00:15:00
```

4. Next, let's define the scheduled job:

```
PS C:\> Register-ScheduledJob -Name NightlyErrors -ScriptBlock {Get-EventLog
➥-LogName system -EntryType Error | Select-Object -First 10 -Property
➥TimeGenerated,EventID, message | Format-List} -ScheduledJobOption $opt
```

5. Nuts! We forgot to add our trigger object! No problem; there's a cmdlet for that. We can retroactively add options or triggers to an existing scheduled job.

First, we pull the **NightlyErrors** job into our session:

```
PS C:\> Get-Scheduledjob -Name NightlyErrors
```

```
Id          Name            JobTriggers       Command
--          ----            -----------       -------
4           NightlyErrors   0                 get-eventlog -LogName system-Ent...
```

Second, we can use the pipeline and **Set-ScheduledJob** to modify the existing job definition, adding in the **$trig** trigger object as a parameter value:

```
PS C:\> Get-ScheduledJob -Name NightlyErrors | Set-ScheduledJob -Trigger $trig
PS C:\> Get-Scheduledjob -Name NightlyErrors
```

```
Id          Name            JobTriggers       Command
--          ----            -----------       -------
4           NightlyErrors   1                 get-eventlog -LogName system-Ent...
```

Sweet! Looks pretty good thus far.

6. Let's pack our new **NightlyErrors** job into a variable and then force-run it once or twice:

```
$ne = Get-ScheduledJob -Name NightlyErrors
$ne.StartJob()
```

7. Just for grins, I want you to inspect the members of our scheduled job object in order to familiarize yourself with what's possible with this object:

```
$ne | Get-Member
```

8. Now that we know our scheduled job has result data, we can retrieve child job metadata and ultimately the output itself:

```
PS C:\> Get-Job -Name NightlyErrors -IncludeChildJob

Id      Name           PSJobTypeName      State        HasMoreData      Location
--      ----           -------------      -----        -----------      --------
8       NightlyErrors  PSScheduledJob     Completed    True             localhost
10      Job10                             Completed    True             localhost

PS C:\> Receive-Job -Id 8

TimeGenerated : 11/7/2014 1:18:13 PM
EventID       : 7001
Message       : The Computer Browser service depends on the Server service
                which failed to start because of the following error:
                %%1058

TimeGenerated : 11/7/2014 1:18:13 PM
EventID       : 7001
Message       : The Computer Browser service depends on the Server service
                which failed to start because of the following error:
                %%1058
```

When you're finished, don't forget to remove your new job object (unless you really want to use it, that is). For instance, you could try the following one-liner to remove all jobs with a **HasMoreData** value of **False**:

```
Get-Job | Where-Object { -not $_.HasMoreData } | Remove-Job
```

Summary

You now understand how to get Windows PowerShell multitasking and how to free up your session prompt whenever you need it. There's a lot to the Windows PowerShell job subsystem, that's for sure.

The good news for you is that we'll get more practice with jobs in Hour 14, "Harnessing Windows PowerShell Workflow." We'll become acquainted with Windows PowerShell workflow, which is a way to create long-running, durable jobs that can survive restarts, power outages, or just about anything else that might happen to Windows-based systems. Feel the power!

Q&A

Q. I noticed a cmdlet called Enable-ScheduledJob. Does this mean that I need to manually enable any scheduled PowerShell jobs that I create?

A. The **Enable-ScheduledJob** cmdlet is used to reenable a scheduled job that has been disabled with **Disable-ScheduledJob**. Read those help files; they contain the answers to questions you and I haven't even thought of yet!

Q. Why in the world does Receive-Job dump the job results from memory by default? I can't remember to type –Keep every time!

A. I asked Don Jones, noted Windows PowerShell MVP, and his reply was that the default behavior is consistent with the Windows PowerShell philosophy of conserving as many system resources as possible. So, the **Receive-Job** default behavior is meant to save you valuable hard disk space.

Q. Is there a way for me to set the –Keep switch parameter set to $True by default to ensure I never lose job results data?

A. Yes, there is a way, actually. All you need to do is run the following statement during your session or add the line to your Windows PowerShell profile script:

```
$PSDefaultParameterValues.Add("Receive-Job:Keep",$True)
```

Workshop

1. Create a one-time, on-demand job that generates a report of all the Microsoft Word (.doc or .docx) files on your hard drive. Create a CSV report that sorts the files alphabetically by filename.

2. Create a scheduled job that synchronizes your computer's clock with time.windows.com every four hours.

Quiz

1. What is the result of the following Windows PowerShell statement:

```
Get-Help * -Parameter AsJob | Format-Wide Name –Column 3
```

   a. Retrieves the runtime status of the three most recent jobs

   b. Retrieves the help files for all job-related cmdlets

   c. Retrieves a list of commands that have the ability to run as a job

   d. Retrieves help files as a job and outputs them in a three-column wide display

2. The Windows job queue is not self-cleaning.

   a. True

   b. False

3. Which of the following statements is true concerning Windows PowerShell jobs?

   a. The **HasMoreData** property is **True** if job results data is being held in memory.

   b. The **State** property is **True** if job results data is being held in memory.

   c. When you run **Get-Job**, all results data is purged from memory unless you specify the –**Keep** switch.

   d. Receive-Job is used to fetch job results data only from background jobs.

Answers

1. The correct answer is C. All we're doing here is querying the help file index for commands that contain the –**AsJob** parameter. The **Format-Wide** statement simply brings back the output in a three-column wide display.

2. The correct answer is A. Remember that, at least within a session, we must manually remove any jobs that we don't need anymore from the queue.

3. The correct answer is A. This question tests your ability to comprehend the output from **Get-Job**. Recall that the **HasMoreData** property registers **True** if job data is being held in RAM. Remember, too, that unless you specify the –**Keep** parameter (or if you make a scheduled job), the data is purged from memory after you receive it once.

HOUR 14
Harnessing Windows PowerShell Workflow

What You'll Learn in This Hour:

- ▶ Understanding how PowerShell workflow operates
- ▶ Writing your first Windows PowerShell workflows
- ▶ Running a workflow as a job
- ▶ Understanding workflow activities
- ▶ Tying everything together

I think I've done a pretty good job so far (even if I do say so myself) of introducing you gradually to the Windows PowerShell language and environment. We started off with the bare rudiments, and if you understand everything we've done to this point, you now have a solid footing in Windows PowerShell.

That said, we're going to depart from that paradigm a bit in this lesson. Some Windows PowerShell MVPs have told me that workflow has no place in an entry-level Windows PowerShell book; other PowerShell professionals, including myself, disagree. I chose to include this subject anyway for the following reasons:

- ▶ I have faith in your abilities and desire to learn Windows PowerShell at a deeper level.

- ▶ The scripting we do in this chapter serves as a "boot camp" introduction to that subject, which we'll treat formally later on in this book.

- ▶ If you found real-world business value in Windows PowerShell remoting, I think you'll be deeply impressed with what you can do with Windows PowerShell workflow.

Now that we've covered the preliminaries, let's get to work.

Understanding How PowerShell Workflow Operates

In Microsoft nomenclature, a *workflow* is a named set of programmed steps that accomplish some business process. As it happens, Microsoft developed a workflow "engine" based on the .NET Framework called Windows Workflow Foundation, or WF.

Software developers can build WF-based workflows by using a variety of tools. However, for our purposes, we're concerned only with the Windows PowerShell entry point for WF.

NOTE

Microsoft originally abbreviated Windows Workflow Foundation WWF, until they were sued by the World Wildlife Fund, who owns the trademark on that name. Whoops! Hence, Microsoft now encourages us to refer to their workflow engine simply as WF.

Attributes of a Windows PowerShell Workflow

If you've played around with writing reusable Windows PowerShell scripts, you probably wonder what workflow brings to the table that can't be accomplished with a "bread and butter" .ps1 script file.

Here's the deal: Windows PowerShell workflow is optimized for durable, long-running business processes. We're talking about PowerShell code that can survive system restarts, power outages, and other interruptions. PowerShell workflows can be paused and resumed at a later time, picking up precisely where they left off. That's some powerful stuff, for sure.

The host (computer) that runs the workflow must have at least Windows PowerShell v3 installed and also be enabled for WSMan-based remoting. The target computers that will receive and process workflow activities should have at least Windows PowerShell v2 installed. Surprisingly, you can actually run Windows Management Instrumentation (WMI) workflow activities on target systems that do not even have Windows PowerShell installed. This isn't magic, though: you run the workflow activities on the local host and then query the target.

Taking Care of Preliminaries

Before we go any further in Windows PowerShell workflow, I need to make sure that you are comfortable with creating PowerShell script files by using the Windows PowerShell integrated scripting environment (ISE). While we're at it, to really comprehend workflow, you need to know what a function is.

To that point, we'll accomplish both goals by the following Try It Yourself exercise.

Writing a Simple Windows PowerShell Script File

In this Try It Yourself exercise, you create a stored script named MyFunction.ps1 that contains a simple function definition. By the end of this exercise you'll know how to create, save, and run PowerShell script files.

1. Start an administrative Windows PowerShell console session, and then open the Windows PowerShell ISE by typing **ise** and then pressing **Enter.**

2. When the ISE appears, close the Commands add-in if you have that visible. Next, click **File > New** to create a new, blank script file. Quickly thereafter, click **File > Save As** to save the file in the root of C: drive under the name **myscript.ps1**.

3. You need to relax your system's script execution policy temporarily so that you can run scripts as much as you need to. Run the following command in the ISE console pane:

```
Set-ExecutionPolicy -ExecutionPolicy Unrestricted
```

   When you're finished working in this chapter, you can reset your execution policy to whatever it was originally. (Remember that **Get-ExecutionPolicy** gives you the current policy.)

4. We're going to write a simple function that takes two numbers, adds them together, and displays the result in the console. A function is nothing more than a named code block that we can run as many times as we need to later.

   The Windows PowerShell ISE includes a nifty snippets feature that makes it easier to remember code syntax. Assuming that you have your script pane on top and your console pane on the bottom (as shown in Figure 14.1), right-click the top (script) pane and select **Start Snippets** from the shortcut menu.

FIGURE 14.1
Crafting a simple Windows PowerShell script by using the ISE.

In the drop-down menu, scroll down and then double-click **Function** to add its snippet to the script pane. You can see this snippet code in lines 1–4 in Figure 14.1.

5. Edit the snippet text to match what you see in lines 7–11 in Figure 14.1. We are creating a function named **adder** that accepts two parameters; the parameters are stored in the variables **$n1** and **$2**.

   Notice that we place the "meat" of the function inside curly braces, {}. In line 9, we store the sum of the two variables inside a third variable named, logically enough, **$sum**.

   Finally, we use **Write-Host** to give the user the addition results in the host application.

6. Now press **Enter** a couple times and create the **adder2** function shown in lines 14–22 in Figure 14.1. Here I want to show you that we can take greater control over the parameters fed to a function by including a **Param()** block to the function body.

   In lines 17 and 18, we perform some low-level data validation by specifying the integer data type for the **$num1** and **$num2** variables. The rest of **adder2** behaves exactly like the original **adder** function. Note that you can also write functions that take no parameters.

7. Save your work and now switch to a separate PowerShell console session window. Set your location to the root of drive C:

```
Set-Location C:\
```

Next, run **Import-Module** to bring your two new functions into memory. Congratulations; you just built your first Windows PowerShell module:

```
Import-Module .\myscript.ps1
```

8. To finish, call each function the same way, by specifying the function name and two integers to be passed in as arguments. For instance, try this:

```
Adder 2 2
Adder2 44.44 65.66
```

You can see example output by inspecting the console pane in Figure 14.1.

Writing Your First Windows PowerShell Workflow

Suppose that you need to find a quick way to determine which of your Active Directory domain's computers are online. Let's simplify the scenario by assuming that you've disabled Windows Firewall within your network perimeter.

Why don't you write a workflow that pings every single computer within the domain?

NOTE

In my lab environment, I'll author and run the workflow on my Windows Server 2012 R2 domain controller.

The Nonworkflow Method

Let's start by retrieving a list of all domain-joined computers:

```
PS C:\> $computers = Get-ADComputer -Filter * | Select-Object -Property DNSHostName

DNSHostName
-----------
dc1.companya.pri
mem1.companya.pri
mem2.companya.pri
```

We'll continue by leveraging the cool cmdlet **Test-Connection** to send 2 ICMP Echo Request messages to each domain computer. We stored the computer list in a variable for a reason, as you'll see later:

```
Foreach ($computer in $computers) {Test-Connection -ComputerName $computer -Count 2
➥-ErrorAction SilentlyContinue
```

Okay, I added some stuff you haven't seen before. The **Foreach** keyword is an iterator; this means that we can feed each computer object contained in the **$computers** variable to an expression, one object at a time. For **Test-Connection**, the **–Count** parameter determines how many ping messages we send, and the **–ErrorAction SilentlyContinue** clause tells PowerShell to continue through the **$computers** list if an error condition is tripped, suppressing the error message. The Continue error action shows you the error message. Isn't it nice to always have options?

The previous two script lines work well enough, but the process is slow because

▶ You don't get your prompt back until the entire process is completed.

▶ Each computer needs to finish its processing before the next computer is contacted.

By combining Windows PowerShell workflow with parallelism and potentially jobs, we can rapidly speed up long-running processes like this. Let me show you how that works now.

Defining the Workflow

The reason why I threw you into the proverbial deep end of the pool earlier by having you create a simple function is because Windows PowerShell workflows look and behave much like ordinary script functions.

One thing to keep in mind is that workflows don't support positional parameters. This shouldn't pose a problem for us because I recommended to you quite a bit thus far to use named parameters for explicitness' sake.

TIP
___

Best practice guidance from Microsoft actually recommends that we name our functions and workflows with the same verb-noun syntax that standard commands use.

To that point, fire up the ISE and create the following workflow in a new script file:

```
Workflow Test-WFComputers {
    Param(
        [string[]]$Computers
    )
    Foreach -parallel ($computer in $Computers) {
        Test-Connection -ComputerName $computer -Count 1 -ErrorAction
SilentlyContinue
    }
}
```

The entire script is shown in Figure 14.2; let me explain what's going on:

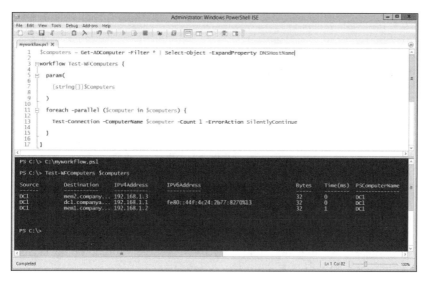

FIGURE 14.2
Our workflow sample script.

- ▶ **Line 1**: Here you populate the $computers variable with the array of domain-joined computers.

- ▶ **Line 3**: You define a workflow with the workflow keyword; you can add parameters and the body exactly the same way that you do for functions.

- ▶ **Line 7**: Here you define a single array-type parameter to hold the list of computer names. You could bring in a CSV file too, if you want. Flexibility is key here.

- ▶ **Console pane**: Notice that once you load the workflow definition into memory, you can call it the same way you can for Windows PowerShell functions.

Running a Workflow as a Job

I want to revisit the powerful PowerShell jobs architecture that we learned about in the previous chapter. First, let's fire up a new script file in the Windows PowerShell ISE and define a parallel script workflow that grabs the newest five entries from the local computer's System, Security, and Application event logs:

```
Workflow Get-EventLogData
{
Parallel
    {
        Get-EventLog -LogName System -Newest 5
        Get-EventLog -LogName Security -Newest 5
        Get-EventLog -LogName Application -Newest 5
    }
}
```

After we load the workflow into memory (which we can do, you'll recall, by either running the workflow definition within the ISE or using **Import-Module** to feed the definition into your current session), we can add the **–AsJob** parameter to define the workflow run as a job:

```
PS C:\>Get-EventLogData –AsJob –JobName eventz
```

Id	Name	PSJobTypeName	State	HasMoreData	Location
--	----	-------------	-----	-----------	--------
12	eventz	PSWorkflowJob	NotStarted	True	localhost

Of course, we can use **Receive-Job** with the **–Keep** parameter to fetch the job results. The long story short is that besides the job type name change (notice that workflow jobs show up as **PSWorkflowJob** objects), there is no difference in daily operation between traditional background jobs and workflow jobs as shown in Figure 14.3.

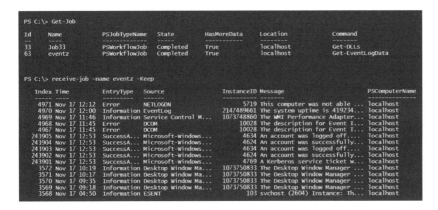

FIGURE 14.3
Workflow jobs behave the same as any other Windows PowerShell job.

Refactoring the Script for Multiple Targets

Let's combine what we've learned thus far. Here we'll refactor (which is a fancy programmer term for *edit*) our **Get-EventLogData** workflow to include all domain computers. It's amazing to me how fast these parallel workflows are.

Here's the definition for our new **Get-WFEventLogData** parallel workflow:

```
$computers = Get-ADComputer -Filter * | Select-Object -ExpandProperty DNSHostName

workflow Get-WFEventLogData {
  param(
    [string[]]$computers
  )

  foreach -parallel ($computer in $computers) {
        Get-EventLog -LogName System -Newest 5 -PSComputerName $computer
        Get-EventLog -LogName Security -Newest 5 -PSComputerName $computer
        Get-EventLog -LogName Application -Newest 5 -PSComputerName $computer
  }
}
```

We then can combine parallel workflow, Windows PowerShell remoting, and the jobs engine in a truly magestic way:

```
Get-WFEventLogData $computers -AsJob -JobName DomainELs
Receive-Job -Name DomainELs -Keep
```

When you run **Receive-Job**, take special note of the **PSComputerName** property; this is how you'll differentiate the output from the different remote target computers.

NOTE

When you create a workflow in Windows PowerShell, the script code is converted into Extensible Application Markup Language (XAML, pronounced ZAM-mel) and passed to the WF engine running on your machine.

Thus, you can look at PowerShell workflow as an administrator-friendly front-end to the WF. Typically, programmers use Visual Studio to author WF workflows directly in XAML. Aren't you glad that you don't have to worry about that complexity? I am.

Understanding Workflow Activities

The **Parallel** and **Foreach –parallel** constructions that we've used heavily in this chapter are examples of workflow activities. As it happens, Windows PowerShell workflow supports a number of different activities:

▶ **CheckPoint-Workflow**: Saves the state of a running workflow

▶ **Suspend-Workflow, Resume-Workflow**: Temporarily stops or resumes a running workflow, respectively

▶ **Sequence**: A block of sequential statements within a workflow script

Checkpointing a Workflow

When you think of Windows PowerShell workflow, I want you to think of a long-running task or sequence of tasks that can be fully managed and is durable in terms of surviving system restarts and so forth.

You can place checkpoints in your workflow definition to save the state of the workflow at that point. This persistent data is saved in the user profile hierarchy on the computer that is hosting the workflow session.

You need to be judicious in your placement of checkpoints in your workflow jobs because they incur a performance and system resource cost. Essentially, think during your workflow authoring, "Where is a logical save point where I would want to flush the data to disk so that I can resume from that point later if I want to?"

It's also important that we ask, "How do I use checkpoints?" That's a good question. The purpose of checkpoints is that if our workflow bombs out partway through (due to an unexpected power outage, for instance), we can "restart" the workflow by running it again. However, we aren't actually restarting the workflow from scratch, but from the most recent checkpoint in the script. Got it?

The easiest way to include checkpointing in a workflow is to specify the **$PSPersist** common parameter. For instance, take the following sample workflow that gathers TCP/IP configuration information:

```
Workflow Get-IPConfig
{
    Get-NetAdapter
    Get-NetIPAddress
}
```

We add the common parameter when we call the workflow from the PowerShell command line. (Remember to add the workflow to your session first.)

```
PS C:\> Get-IPConfig -PSPersist $true
```

Or we can run the workflow against an array of computer objects:

```
PS C:\> Get-IPConfig -PSComputerName mem1, mem2, dc1 -PSPersist $true
```

You'll notice that your workflow takes a bit longer to run than if you hadn't used the **–PSPersist** parameter; that's to be expected because checkpointing incurs overhead.

You can also "granularlize" the use of **–PSPersist** by adding the parameter in-line with your workflow code.

The following example takes a checkpoint after each **Get-** statement in the simple **Get-IPConfig** workflow:

```
Workflow Get-IPConfig
{
    Get-NetAdapter -PSPersist $true
    Get-NetIPAddress -PSPersist $true
}
```

Yet another way to add checkpoints to our workflow activities is to add the **Checkpoint-Workflow** cmdlet:

```
Workflow Get-IPConfig
{
    Get-NetAdapter
    Get-NetIPAddress
    Checkpoint-Workflow
    Get-WMIObject -Win32_NetworkAdapterConfiguration
}
```

In the previous example, we add a checkpoint after the second action completes, but before the third one starts.

NOTE

In my experience with Windows PowerShell, I've seen administrators attempt to leverage PowerShell workflows to automate system configuration. For instance, you might author a workflow that renames a computer, joins it to an Active Directory domain, and then installs some roles or features.

While you technically can implement workflow for this purpose, I think Desired State Configuration (DSC) is a better fit for this type of configuration. You'll learn all about DSC a bit later on in the book.

In the meantime, I suggest that you consider workflow a method for gaining full control over long-running scripting tasks rather than a "one-stop" system configuration solution.

Suspending and Resuming a Workflow

We now understand that checkpoints make a workflow more durable and efficient, at least from a time perspective. Did you know that you can also manually suspend and resume a PowerShell workflow? Yes, you can. You can actually start and suspend the workflow on one computer, and then resume it from another computer! Cool stuff.

Let's use this simple workflow that generates a comprehensive directly listings of all dynamic link library (.dll) and device driver (*.sys) files in the current system's C:\Windows\System32 directory path:

```
workflow Get-DLLs
{
    Get-ChildItem -Path "C:\Windows\System32" -Filter *.dll -Recurse -ErrorAction
➥SilentlyContinue | Select-Object PSComputerName, Name, Length | Sort-Object Name

    Get-ChildItem -Path "C:\Windows\System32" -Filter *.sys -Recurse -ErrorAction
➥SilentlyContinue | Select-Object PSComputerName, Name, Length | Sort-Object Name
}
```

Now this is admittedly an artificial example, but I wanted to use a workflow that will, in fact, take a long time to complete if we target multiple hosts:

```
Get-DLLs -PSComputerName dc1,mem1,mem2
```

You better go get a cup of coffee while you wait for this workflow to complete. One option if, for instance, you need to add some "breathing room" in the script is to add **Suspend-Workflow** in between the **Get-ChildItem** statements:

```
workflow Get-DLLs
{
    Get-ChildItem -Path "C:\Windows\System32" -Filter *.dll -Recurse -ErrorAction
➥SilentlyContinue | Select-Object PSComputerName, Name, Length | Sort-Object Name

Suspend-Workflow

    Get-ChildItem -Path "C:\Windows\System32" -Filter *.sys -Recurse -ErrorAction
➥SilentlyContinue | Select-Object PSComputerName, Name, Length | Sort-Object Name
}
```

Let's load the workflow definition into our session. In the ISE, that's as easy as running the workflow script, calling the *workflow*, and then running **Get-Job** to see what's what:

```
PS C:\> Get-DLLs -PSComputerName dc1,mem1,mem2
PS C:\> Get-Job
PS C:\>Get-Job
Id    Name    PSJobTypeName       State        HasMoreData    Location
--    ----    -------------       -----        -----------    --------
33    Job33   PSWorkflowJob       Suspended    True           localhost
```

Did you see what happened? Even though I didn't define that run of **Get-DLLs** as a job, you'll observe in the **Get-Job** output that PowerShell created a **PSWorkflowJob** and listed its state as **Suspended**.

You'll recall when we studied jobs that the **Suspend-Workflow** and **Resume-Workflow** commands are constrained for use with workflow. Well, here we are, friend.

Now here's where the magic happens. We can now shut off our computer, go home, come back the next day, and resume the workflow where it was suspended.

TIP

By the way, PowerShell indeed makes a checkpoint when it suspends the workflow. This should make sense to you because we need a persistent workflow state from which to resume later.

First, we must manually load the **PSWorkflow** module in our new session:

```
Import-Module PSWorkflow
```

If we run **Get-Job**, we'll see the same job listing as we saw earlier. To resume, we'll call **Resume-Job** along with the job ID or name:

```
PS C:\>Resume-Job -Id 3
Id    Name   PSJobTypeName     State      HasMoreData   Location
--    ----   -------------     -----      -----------   --------
3     Job33  PSWorkflowJob     Running    True          localhost
```

Because workflow jobs behave the same as ordinary background or scheduled jobs, we can use **Receive-Job**, **Remove-Job**, and the other job cmdlets to interact with our suspended/resumed workflow job.

Adding a Sequence to a Workflow

The **Sequence** activity specifies a block of, well, sequential statements that run within a parallel script block. Consider the following example:

```
Workflow Get-Feats
{
    Parallel
    {
        InlineScript {Get-WindowsFeature -Name *DNS*}
        InlineScript {Get-WmiObject Win32_NetworkAdapterConfiguration}
            Sequence
            {
                $PSVersionTable.PSVersion
                $env:ComputerName
            }
    }
}
```

This workflow simply gathers the DNS server installation status, network interface card setup, PowerShell version, and hostname of target server systems. However, the code is more interesting than that, so let me walk you through it in more detail:

▶ **Line 3**: As stated, we have to put our **Sequence** statements inside of a **Parallel** block.

▶ **Lines 5–6**: **InlineScript** is how we can run ad hoc script blocks inside of a workflow.

▶ **Line 7**: The **Sequence** code fires before anything else in the script, and it does so in the specified order. Therefore, you use **Sequence** when you have tasks that must complete first and in order.

Tying Everything Together

It seems to me that having you run one more Try It Yourself exercise is just what the proverbial doctor ordered in terms of helping you solidify these admittedly complex topics in your mind.

Completing the following exercise requires at least two computers joined to the same domain. On dc1, which is my workflow "originating" computer, I'll author a workflow that does the following:

▶ Renames a computer

▶ Reboots the machine

▶ Resumes the workflow automatically after restart

▶ Reports on the computer name change

▶ Reports on the system's disk configuration

▼ TRY IT YOURSELF

Using Workflow to Rename and Restart a Remote Computer

In this Try It Yourself exercise, you'll write a workflow that renames and reboots a remote domain-joined system. After the reboot, you'll have the workflow generate a couple simple reports.

1. Fire up an elevated Windows PowerShell ISE session and create a new script in the root of the C: drive titled **renamebox.ps1**.

2. Author the workflow; you can see the code in Figure 14.4. In line 4 of the script, we create a string input parameter that represents the new computer name.

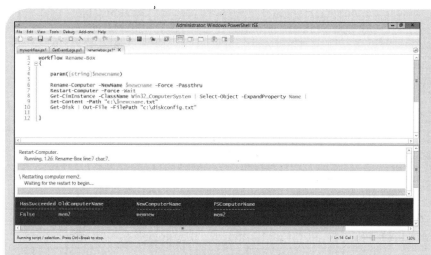

FIGURE 14.4
Running a workflow in the ISE gives us valuable feedback on the running state.

In line 6, we use **Rename-Computer** to perform the rename.

In line 7, we use **Restart-Computer** with the **–Wait** switch; this parameter is crucial to the workflow operation because it instructs the workflow quite literally to wait until the target system or systems have come back from their reboot before continuing the workflow.

In lines 9 and 10, we simply create a couple text file reports that give us the new system name and some metadata concerning hard disk configuration.

3. When you've finished typing the workflow, press **F5** in the ISE to load the **Rename-Box** workflow definition into session memory.

4. You can now invoke the workflow. Here you'll add domain administrator credentials to make sure that you don't get a pesky "Access Denied" error:

```
Rename-Box -newcname memnew -PSComputerName mem2 -PSCredential companya\
➥administrator
```

Summary

You have every right to feel a bit overwhelmed at this point. Not only did we broaden and deepen our understanding of PowerShell jobs, but we also covered the complex topic of workflow and gave you a "jump into the deep end of the pool" quick-start on PowerShell scripting.

The good news is that we'll formally treat PowerShell scripting later in the book, so you'll have an opportunity to fill in conceptual blanks and gain more valuable practice.

In the meantime, though, I'm sure you noticed that we have used the **Get-WMIObject** cmdlet a lot in the book thus far. I hope that you've been wondering, "What is this WMI stuff used for?" because the next chapter serves as your "boots on the ground" introduction not only to Windows Management Instrumentation (WMI) and Common Information Model (CIM) but also your introduction to and use of regular expressions.

Q&A

Q. Am I allowed to use any Windows PowerShell cmdlet in a workflow?

A. I'm glad you asked that question, because there are in fact several native PowerShell commands that are not usable in workflow. These cmdlets are shown in Table 14.1.

TABLE 14.1   Windows PowerShell Cmdlets that are Disallowed in Workflow

Add-History	Invoke-History
Add-PSSnapin	New-Alias
Clear-History	New-Variable
Clear-Variable	Out-GridView
Complete-Transaction	Remove-PSBreakPoint
Debug-Process	Remove-PSSnapin
Disable-PSBreakPoint	Remove-Variable
Enable-PSBreakPoint	Set-Alias
Enter-PSSession	Set-PSBreakPoint
Exit-PSSession	Set-PSDebug
Export-Alias	Set-StrictMode
Export-Console	Set-TraceMode
Get-Alias	Set-Variable
Get-History	Start-Transaction
Get-PSBreakPoint	Start-Transcript
Get-PSCallStack	Stop-Transcript
Get-PSSnapin	Trace-Command
Get-Transaction	Undo-Transaction
Get-Variable	Use-Transaction
Import-Alias	Write-Host

The reason why those cmdlets are disallowed should make sense to you if you remember that PowerShell workflows are meant to run to completion with no user intervention. Most of the disallowed cmdlets require some sort of "nurse maiding" for them to do their work. To be sure, authoring PowerShell workflows forces you to think ahead and creatively author scripts that are self-running and self-correcting. This is easier said than done in most cases.

Q. You used the **InlineScript** statement a bit in this chapter, but you never formally introduced it. What is this construct used for?

A. We add **InlineScript** blocks to our workflow when we need to add PowerShell code that is normally disallowed in a Windows PowerShell workflow. You can even define and use variables within an **InlineScript** code block.

Q. Can I author PowerShell workflows from my Windows 8.1 administrative workstation? I'm concerned because my workflow may reference server-only commands such as Get-WindowsFeature.

A. Not to worry; you are eminently free to craft and run workflows from your administrative workstation that runs a Windows client operating system. Remember that you'll be targeting your server workflows *at servers*, and PowerShell remoting and the workflow engine take care of the rest.

Workshop

I'd like you to revisit the Try It Yourself exercise "Using Workflow to Rename and Restart a Remote Computer," extending it in the following ways:

▶ Create a simple text file that contains a list of computer names in your test network.

▶ Create a second text file that contains the new names for the aforementioned systems.

▶ Edit the workflow such that you feed it both text files as input. Your goal is for the workflow to rename and reboot multiple computers. Make sure that you use PowerShell workflow's parallel execution capability.

Quiz

1. The "look and feel" of PowerShell workflows closely resembles that of PowerShell _____.

    a. cmdlets

    b. aliases

    c. functions

    d. providers

2. Which of the following cmdlets is used to initiate execution of a suspended Windows PowerShell workflow job?

   a. **Resume-Job**

   b. **Restart-Job**

   c. **Receive-Job**

   d. **Get-Job**

3. Which of the following is used to load the workflow script myscript.ps1, which contains a workflow named **Set-SysConfig**, into your current session?

   a. .\Set-SysConfig

   b. .\myscript.ps1

   c. **Get-Command –CommandType workflow**

   d. start myscript.ps1 Set-SysConfig

Answers

1. The correct answer is C. As you'll learn about at great depth later in this book, functions are named code blocks that can be reused and tweaked to the administrator's heart's content. Windows Powershell workflows use a very function-like syntax and runtime behavior.

2. The correct answer is A. Windows PowerShell workflow jobs can be suspended, which checkpoints their state to disk. Later, an administrator can load up the **PSWorkflow** module and issue **Resume-Job** to resume the workflow at its last checkpoint.

3. The correct answer is B. This is a tricky question, but it's important for me to ask to ensure you understand what's going on. We can "dot source" the workflow script file to bring the enclosed **Set-SysConfig** workflow into memory.

   After we've loaded the workflow script, we can then call **Set-SysConfig** as we would any other cmdlet.

Introducing WMI and CIM

What You'll Learn in This Hour:

▶ Defining WMI and CIM
▶ Getting comfortable with WMI
▶ Using Windows PowerShell WMI commands
▶ Using Windows PowerShell CIM commands

When we discussed Windows PowerShell remote-access technologies earlier in the book, I may have given Windows Management Instrumentation (WMI) a bad rap. After all, I "dissed" the specification's reliance on firewall-unfriendly remoting protocols such as Remote Procedure Calls (RPCs) and the Distributed Component Object Model (DCOM), not to mention the fact that WMI remote access processes on multiple remote computers in series rather than in parallel.

Despite these limitations, however, WMI is actually a powerful and useful standard—certainly a required skill for any self-respecting Windows PowerShell administrator.

So, the good news is that you can access just about any aspect of a Windows system's hardware and software subsystems with WMI. The bad news (besides the remote-access stuff) is that WMI has a steep learning curve because the technology has never been properly made user friendly.

Aren't you excited to learn how to use WMI via Windows PowerShell? Well, I'm looking forward to teaching you, so let's dive right in and get to work.

Defining WMI and CIM

From the "You gotta learn to crawl before you learn how to walk" files, let's begin our consideration of WMI by first defining what the heck the acronym means from a practical perspective.

Windows Management Instrumentation (WMI) is Microsoft's proprietary implementation of a "vendor-neutral" standard called the Common Information Model (CIM, pronounced SIM). The CIM standard, in turn, defines a standardized interface to describe computer system hardware and software. Microsoft developed WMI instead of accessing the CIM classes originally because CIM was a young technology. Nowadays, since CIM has matured, Microsoft sees its utility and embraces it fully.

Do you remember Simple Network Management Protocol (SNMP)? Well, we can consider WMI and CIM as a successor to that standard. The idea is that we can use a SQL-like database query syntax to query a system's configuration in a way that isn't, at least on paper, tied to any particular vendor's proprietary standards.

NOTE

CIM and its related systems management standard, Web-Based Enterprise Management (WBEM) are, well, managed by a consortium of technology vendors called the Distributed Management Task Force (DMTF), of which Microsoft is proudly a member. Learn more about the DMTF by visiting their Web site at http://dmtf.org.

By the way, we've seen quite a few acronyms in this hour thus far, haven't we?

Where Does WMI Exist?

As it happens, all Windows server and client operating systems since 2000 or so have a built-in database of WMI information called, appropriately enough, the *WMI repository*.

In a moment, we'll tour the repository, so I want to warn you up front: It's kind of a mess. You'll see references to both WMI and CIM throughout the repository, and later on in this hour, you'll be exposed to both WMI and CIM cmdlets.

NOTE

The thing to remember through all this is that, for our purposes, WMI and CIM are the same thing. Specifically in Windows PowerShell, the CIM cmdlets are essentially updated "wrappers" around older WMI calls.

The WMI "database" actually consists of all contents of the directory C:\Windows\System32\ WBEM; if you go in there, prepare to see a thorny thicket of different file types. Specifically, the WMI repository proper resides in the WBEM\Repository subdirectory, but that's beyond our scope or interest in this book.

The marquee file type in WMI is the Managed Object Format (MOF) file, which we'll deal with in great detail later in the book when we learn how to use Desired State Configuration (DSC; yes, again with the acronyms).

In the meantime, I show you some of the contents of a WMI MOF file in Figure 15.1.

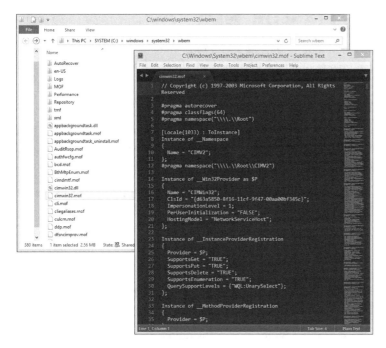

FIGURE 15.1
The WMI/CIM repository exists under the \Windows\System32\WBEM path, and object definitions are written in the MOF file format.

NOTE

In the CIM standard, we describe all elements of a managed IT environment in plain-text files written in the Managed Object Format, or MOF (pronounced MOFF). If you've ever seen XML syntax, you'll be pretty much at home when reading MOF files.

Even with Windows PowerShell DSC, we ordinarily don't have to worry about interacting with MOF files directly. Instead, we use WMI/CIM browser utilities, write queries using the Windows Query Language (WQL), or run WMI/CIM PowerShell cmdlets.

That said, you do need to gain a certain level of comfortability with the MOF file type if you plan to implement DSC on Windows PowerShell v4- or v5-based systems.

Enough with the background theory; you probably want to actually see your Windows computer's WMI repository in action. That's what we cover next.

Getting Comfortable with WMI

As your instructor, I feel that it is mandatory that we spend some time familiarizing ourselves with WMI itself before we begin investigating the WMI-related Windows PowerShell cmdlets.

A Quick Primer of WMI Terminology

If you can stay awake long enough to make it through the Distributed Management Task Force's (DMTF) CIM specification literature (available here for those who are interested: http://www.dmtf.org/standards/cim), you'll learn that the CIM repository consists of the following elements:

▶ **Schema.** This refers to the overall WMI repository on a Windows computer. Specifically, the schema is a collection of namespaces and is defined directly by the DMTF.

▶ **Namespace.** This term describes a particular subtree of the CIM/WMI schema. The most common namespace in Windows management is ROOT\CIMv2.

▶ **Class.** Each namespace contains a number of related classes, or object blueprints. For instance, the root\MicrosoftDNS namespace contains a class called MicrosoftDNS_AType, which defines the structure and content of DNS host (A) records.

▶ **Instance.** If your computer contains data for a class, the data objects themselves are called instances (for instance, a Windows DNS server should have multiple instances of the **MicrosoftDNS_AType** class corresponding to every A record in its zone(s).

▶ **Property.** You should already know what a property is; this is a granular attribute of a class instance (**IPAddress** is a representative property of the **MicrosoftDNS_AType** class instance).

▶ **Method.** You know this already. That said, WMI/CIM contains scant few methods; mostly you'll find yourself retrieving property values.

Now let's turn our attention to some of the more common tools with which we investigate the WMI/CIM schema.

WMI Browser Tools

Windows itself includes a command-line WMI client called WMIC; run the following statement from an elevated Windows PowerShell console session to retrieve the syntax:

```
Wmic /?
```

That's all I'm going to say about WMIC because as far as command-line tools go, we're all about Windows PowerShell. One of the biggest frustrations that many Windows systems administrators have with WMI (myself certainly included) is how inconsistent Microsoft's support of the technology is.

NOTE

Microsoft offers a set of WMI administrative tools as a free download (http://bit.ly/1xNcgb6). However, I find the two browser-based WMI/CIM explorer tools almost completely unusable on Windows 7 or Windows 8 systems.

As you can see in Figure 15.2, you need to (at the least) press **F12** to invoke the Internet Explorer developer dashboard and then set the browser compatibility level to IE 7. Even still, I found the WMI and CIM object browsers to behave clunkily under recent versions of Internet Explorer.

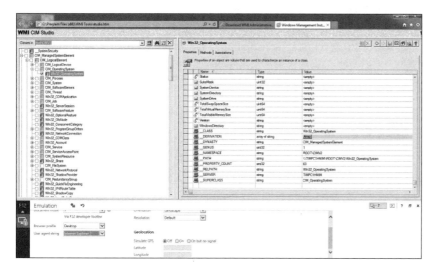

FIGURE 15.2
If you can get it to load on your system, the Microsoft WMI administrative tools include a couple browser-based WMI/CIM object explorers.

NOTE

"So enough complaining, Tim. What WMI browser tool *do* you recommend?" you might wonder. Fair enough. If you want to pay for an enterprise-class WMI tool, check out WMI Explorer 2014 from Sapien Technologies (http://www.sapien.com/software/wmiexplorer).

If, however, you seek a freeware solution, look no further than the WMI Explorer 2.0 tool from Codeplex.com (https://wmie.codeplex.com/). Besides the "price," this WMI Explorer is stable, works well, and because it's an open source project, you can actually peek at the source code if you're curious about the tool's under-the-hood plumbing.

Why don't we undertake a Try It Yourself exercise to give you some hands-on time with the CodePlex-based WMI Explorer?

▼ TRY IT YOURSELF

Exploring WMI Classes and Instances

In this Try It Yourself exercise, you'll use the free WMI Explorer from CodePlex (https://wmie.codeplex.com/) to gain some fundamental familiarity with browsing your computer's WMI repository.

Specifically, we'll investigate the Win32_LogicalDisk instance(s) on your system to view metadata concerning your computer's installed hard disk or disks.

The WMI Explorer tool downloads as a ZIP archive; extract the WMIExplorer.exe tool from the ZIP to a suitable location on your computer's hard drive to begin.

1. Because so much of WMI/CIM requires administrative privileges, start WMI Explorer by right-clicking its icon and selecting **Run as Administrator** from the shortcut menu.

2. To connect to your local system, simply click **Connect**, as shown in annotation A in Figure 15.3.

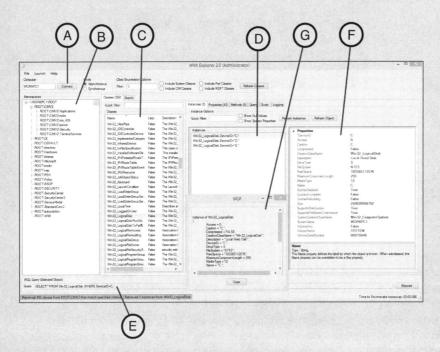

FIGURE 15.3
The WMI Explorer 2.0 from CodePlex.com is a perfectly suitable WMI/CIM browser. And you can't beat the price! (free)

3. I've found that right-clicking gives me the best experience with this tool. In the Namespaces pane, right-click **ROOT\CIMV2** (annotation B) and select **Enumerate Classes** from the shortcut menu. You'll see the Classes pane (annotation C) fill up with class names.

4. Scroll the ROOT\CIMV2 classes until you find Win32_LogicalDisk. Next, right-click that class and select **Enumerate Instances** from the context menu.

   By the way, another approach to find the class you need is to type **logicaldisk** into the Quick Filter text box and press **Enter**.

   Just accept **Win32** as one of the many quirks of WMI/CIM; the classes use the Win32 prefix even though your computer is 64-bit in all likelihood.

5. The Win32_LogicalDisk class lists instances (in this case, formatted volumes present on your system) in the Instances pane (annotation D). Simply left-click one of your volumes to view its properties in the Properties pane (annotation F).

6. WMI supports a SQL-like query language that Microsoft calls WMI Query Language, or WQL. WMI Explorer helpfully provides the query syntax in a separate pane (annotation E). This query help can prove extraordinarily helpful when, for instance, you want to attach a WMI filter to an Active Directory Group Policy Object (GPO).

7. Spend some time examining the properties that WMI provides regarding your system's logical disks. You can see stuff like the file system type, free space, quota information, and so forth. I want you to appreciate how much potentially useful data you can pull from the WMI repository.

8. For grins, right-click one of your instances and select **Show MOF** from the shortcut menu. As you can see in annotation G in Figure 15.3, WMI Explorer shows you the underlying Managed Object Format (MOF) definition for that instance. This definition may prove useful to you when you architect MOF files for use with Windows PowerShell DSC.

Some Useful WMI Classes

At this point, you should have a better idea of how the WMI repository works from a practical perspective. In my experience, the biggest challenge to retrieving system configuration data via WMI is figuring out which class contains the information you require.

To that point, let me provide you with a handy quick reference of some of the most useful and most popular WMI classes. In addition to the class name, I give you some of the cool data you can pull from the class:

- ▶ **Win32_BIOS**: BIOS make, model, and version number

- ▶ **Win32_PhysicalMemory**: Everything you wanted to know about your system's hardware RAM sticks

- ▶ **Win32_DesktopMonitor**: Display resolution

- ▶ **Win32_NetworkAdapter**: Network interface card (NIC) statistics

- ▶ **Win32_OperatingSystem**: Everything you wanted to know about the Windows OS version installed on the target system

- ▶ **Win32_StartupCommand**: List of autostart software

- ▶ **Win32_Process**: Running processes

- ▶ **Win32_Service**: Installed system services

- ▶ **Win32_Product**: Installed software

Okay, now that we've covered WMI/CIM, you're fully prepared to learn how we can leverage our Windows PowerShell skills to query the WMI repository on one or more target systems.

Using Windows PowerShell WMI Commands

Let's dive right in by enumerating the core WMI Windows PowerShell cmdlets:

```
PS C:\> Get-Command -Noun *wmi* | Select-Object -Property Name

Name
----
Get-WmiObject
Invoke-WmiMethod
Register-WmiEvent
Remove-WmiObject
Set-WmiInstance
```

Of these five commands, the two we're most concerned with are **Get-WMIObject** and **Invoke-WMIMethod**.

Using Get-WMIObject

As stated previously, you're pretty much out of luck using **Get-WMIObject** unless you know the class name that you're looking for. Given that you know the class name, you can use standard Windows PowerShell pipeline syntax to go from there.

If you really want to list all the classes contained within a given namespace, simply use the optional **–Namespace** parameter:

```
Get-WMIObject –Namespace "root\cimv2" -List
```

Let's begin our WMI investigations by viewing all the process names on the local system:

```
Get-WMIObject –Class Win32_Process | Select-Object -Property processname
```

Now we can drill into a specific running process:

```
Get-WMIObject –Query "SELECT * FROM win32_Process WHERE Name='WMIExplorer.exe'"
```

Because the results of a WMI call are so verbose, you'll observe that the PowerShell formatting subsystem displays all the properties in a list view.

You know, **Get-WMIObject** binds to the root\CIMv2 by default, so that's why we don't have to explicitly give a **–namespace** parameter. For that matter, the **–class** parameter is positional. Thus, we can use the **gwmi** alias with the **–class** positional parameter to retrieve system BIOS information with very little typing:

```
PS C:\> gwmi win32_bios

SMBIOSBIOSVersion : A10
Manufacturer      : Dell Inc.
Name              : Default System BIOS
SerialNumber      : 6GZKHS1
Version           : DELL   - 6222004
```

Dipping Our Toes into WQL

If you've used WMI in other contexts, then you may already have familiarity with Windows Query Language (WQL). This SQL-like syntax enables us to query WMI classes by using what looks, feels, and behaves like standard database access language syntax.

For example, we can use the **–query** parameter of **Get-WMIObject** here to list specific information concerning the logical disk instances on our local system:

```
PS C:\> Get-WMIObject -Query "SELECT * FROM win32_logicaldisk" |
➥Select-Object –Property drivetype, freespace, size | Format-Table -AutoSize

drivetype      freespace          size
---------      ---------          ----
        3   103254388736   249690058752
        5
        3  1640549728256  2000364236800
```

NOTE

You know how I taught you to use Tab completion wherever possible in Windows PowerShell? Ordinarily, Tab completion allows you to quickly type cmdlet names, parameter names, and even parameter values.

Yeah, well, that stuff doesn't work with WMI. You're on your own in terms of typing namespaces, classes, instances, and properties. As I've said, WMI is a strange beast. It's a shame, too, because so many products use WMI and its data is so useful to us as Windows systems administrators.

The other occasion where WQL comes into play is with the **–filter** parameter of **Get-WMIObject**.

For instance, what if we want to list disks on our system that have more than 1 TB of free space? We could do the following:

```
PS C:\> Get-WmiObject -Class win32_logicaldisk -Filter
➥"freespace > 1000000000000"

DeviceID     : E:
DriveType    : 3
ProviderName :
FreeSpace    : 1640549728256
Size         : 2000364236800
VolumeName   : BACKUP1
```

TIP
_____

It is important to note that WQL uses its own expression syntax. For instance, WQL uses **>** and **<** instead of **–gt** and **–lt**, respectively.

Also, the wildcard operator **%** is used instead of *.

_____

Check out the following example which retrieves all services that include the string SQL:

```
Get-WMIObject -Query "SELECT * FROM Win32_Service WHERE name LIKE '%sql%'"
```

Sigh. Inconsistency abounds! Yes, we can use the * wildcard in our WQL **SELECT**, but the **WHERE** clause uses %. Moreover, the inner **LIKE** expression is delimited by single quotes. Remember that when we invoke the **–query** or **–filter** parameters of **Get-WMIObject**, we're switching gears to WQL syntax instead of PowerShell syntax.

NOTE
_____

If you're interested in learning more about WQL specifically, check out this nifty article called "WMI Query Language by Example" from the Code Project: http://www.codeproject.com/Articles/46390/WMI-Query-Language-by-Example.

_____

Querying the WMI Repository Remotely

The good news is that the **Get-WMIObject** cmdlet supports remote access through the **–ComputerName** parameter. So, we can pull potentially vast amounts of system configuration data from multiple computers in our network.

The bad news is that WMI uses the legacy Distributed Component Object Model (DCOM) and Remote Procedure Call (RPC) protocols, which use random connection ports and are decidedly firewall unfriendly. Also, the remote-access process is sequential rather than parallel, leading to some potentially long waits for results.

Combining Background Jobs with Remote WMI Calls

I suggest that you create background jobs to manage remote WMI calls. This gives you your PowerShell prompt back so that you can continue issuing commands and getting done what you need to get done.

The following example creates a background job called RemoteWMI that queries three computers for their physical memory-related metadata:

```
PS C:\> Start-Job -Name RemoteWMI -ScriptBlock {Get-WmiObject -ComputerName
➡localhost,mem1,mem2 -Query "SELECT * FROM Win32_PhysicalMemory" | Select-Object
➡-Property PSComputername, Description, DeviceLocator, FormFactor, MemoryType,
➡Capacity}

Id  Name        PSJobTypeName   State    HasMoreData  Location  Command
--  ----        -------------   -----    -----------  --------  -------
11  RemoteWM    BackgroundJob   Running  True         localhost Get-WmiObject -Compute...
```

Isn't that cool? By combining the jobs architecture with remote WMI calls, we can compensate for the performance issues of WMI remote access.

As you know, we can use **Receive-Job** to fetch the query results:

```
PS C:\> Receive-Job -name RemoteWMI -keep

PSComputerName: DC1
Description   : Physical Memory
DeviceLocator : RAM slot #0
FormFactor    : 8
MemoryType    : 2
Capacity      : 4294967296
RunspaceId    : 7611ae06-a1bd-49cc-ba92-0fbc7ebfc231

PSComputerName: MEM1
Description   : Physical Memory
DeviceLocator : RAM slot #0
FormFactor    : 8
MemoryType    : 2
Capacity      : 4294967296
RunspaceId    : 7611ae06-a1bd-49cc-ba92-0fbc7ebfc231

PSComputerName: MEM2
Description   : Physical Memory
```

```
DeviceLocator : RAM slot #0
FormFactor    : 8
MemoryType    : 2
Capacity      : 4294967296
RunspaceId    : 7611ae06-a1bd-49cc-ba92-0fbc7ebfc231
```

Calling WMI Methods

Once you gain initial familiarity WMI namespaces, classes, instances, and properties, you'll probably start wondering what actions you can actually perform on WMI objects.

I hate to continue being the bearer of bad news for you, but there exist scant few methods in the WMI/CIM repository. Two notable exceptions are the **Reboot** and **Shutdown** methods of the **Win32_OperatingSystem** class, as shown in Figure 15.4.

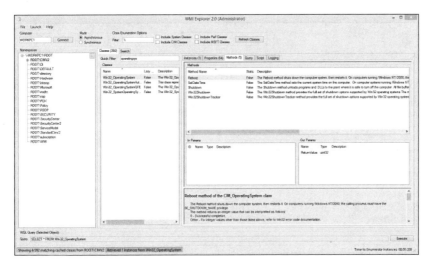

FIGURE 15.4
WMI has historically been used by Windows systems administrators to reboot or shut down local or remote computers.

As you can see in Figure 15.4, after you've selected a namespace and class, you can use the WMI Explorer navigation tabs to browse between properties and methods.

As you probably suspected, we use **Invoke-WMIMethod** to, well, invoke a WMI method call on local/remote machines. In the following example, I reboot my MEM2 member server computer from my administrative computer:

```
Get-WMIObject –Class win32_operatingsystem –Computername mem2 |
➡Invoke-WMIMethod –Name Reboot
```

Boom! In my lab, MEM2 immediately rebooted with no questions asked. If you are running Windows 8.1 or Windows Server 2012, you can use **Restart-Computer** or **Stop-Computer** to reboot or shut down a local or remote computer, respectively. Under the covers, those cmdlets are nothing more than "wrappers" for WMI calls.

Using Windows PowerShell CIM Commands

Technically, Microsoft has deprecated the WMI cmdlets in favor of their CIM counterparts. Here, let's see what we're working with in Windows PowerShell v5:

```
PS C:\> gcm -noun *cim* | select name

Name
----
Get-CimAssociatedInstance
Get-CimClass
Get-CimInstance
Get-CimSession
Invoke-CimMethod
New-CimInstance
New-CimSession
New-CimSessionOption
Register-CimIndicationEvent
Remove-CimInstance
Remove-CimSession
Set-CimInstance
```

As you can see, we have **Get-CIMInstance** and **Invoke-CIMMethod**, which directly correlate to the **Get-WMIObject** and **Invoke-WMIObject** cmdlets, respectively.

What's the Deal with CIM Cmdlets?

What I enjoy about the new CIM cmdlets is that they give us the very same access to the WMI/CIM repository as the WMI cmdlets do, but we also can take advantage of the latest and greatest advances in remoting technology.

That is to say, the CIM cmdlets use the vendor-neutral Web Services for Management (WS-Man) protocol; this makes the CIM cmdlets potentially useable on non-Windows systems and also makes for a much more firewall-friendly remoting environment.

Recall, too, that WS-Man/WinRM cmdlets can contact up to 25 remote computers at a time in parallel by default. We have some excellent performance at our disposal now.

I'm going to turn you loose on one more Try It Yourself exercise to get you familiar with the CIM cmdlets. In my test lab, I have a three-node Active Directory domain. However, you can certainly get by with only two systems.

▼ TRY IT YOURSELF

Using the PowerShell CIM Commands

In this exercise, you'll apply what you now know about WMI, CIM, and PowerShell remoting to gain some experience with the new PowerShell CIM cmdlets.

In my lab, I'm running all commands from my DC1 Windows Server 2012 R2 domain controller. I also have two Windows Server 2012 R2 member servers named MEM1 and MEM2. Let's get to work:

1. Let's start out in the proverbial shallow end of the pool by retrieving OS information from the local system:

   ```
   Get-CimInstance -ClassName win32_operatingsystem
   ```

   Now, notice that **Get-CIMInstance** uses **–ClassName** instead of **–Class** as its parameter name. The cool thing, though, is that you can still use **–Class** and have the cmdlet succeed.

2. Next, we'll run the same query, this time against MEM1 and MEM2 as well:

   ```
   Invoke-Command -Computername localhost,MEM1,MEM2 -ScriptBlock
   ➥{ =Get-CIMInstance -ClassName Win32_OperatingSystem }
   ```

3. The CIM cmdlets make it easier to discover classes, by the way. To that end, let's enumerate all the root\CIMv2 classes that include the keyword *disk*:

   ```
   Get-CIMClass -ClassName *disk*
   ```

   An unexpected surprise I found when using the new CIM cmdlets is that Tab completion works as expected! Try it out for yourself by pressing **Tab** after you add the **–ClassName** parameter.

4. We'll finish this exercise with a small example of how you can leverage CIM cmdlets to actually modify system configuration. Here you'll add a simple comment to the **Comment:** property of your system's Microsoft XPS Document Writer default printer.

   To start, let's create a reference to the XPS virtual printer:

   ```
   $xpsprinter = Get-CIMInstance -ClassName Win32_Printer -Filter "Name =
   ➥'Microsoft XPS Document Writer'"
   ```

5. You can view the properties by piping our new variable to **Get-Member** as usual. Note that many of these properties are read-only, and that finding writable CIM instance properties can be challenging:

   ```
   $xpsprinter | Get-Member -MemberType Properties
   ```

6. Now let's modify the **Comment:** property text by using traditional dot notation:

   ```
   $xpsprinter.Comment = "This comment is courtesy of Windows PowerShell."
   ```

7. The previous line of code won't actually commit until we "seal" it by invoking the **Set-CimInstance** cmdlet, like so:

```
Set-CIMInstance -InputObject $xpsprinter
```

8. Cool. Before we open the XPS Document Writer graphical user interface (GUI), let's verify the change by using only Windows PowerShell:

```
$p = Get-Printer -Name "Microsoft XPS Document Writer"
$p.Comment
```

Did you see the new comment text? Great. Now open the Print Management Microsoft Management Console (MMC) from the PowerShell console:

```
Printmanagement.msc
```

9. In the Print Management console, open All Printers, right-click the **Microsoft XPS Document Writer**, and select **Properties** from the shortcut menu. Observe your newly changed Comment property, shown in Figure 15.5.

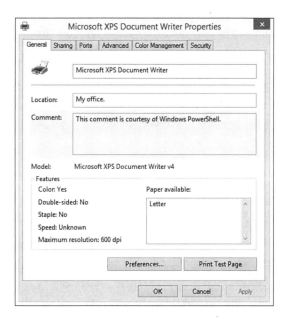

FIGURE 15.5
We can make changes to writable properties by leveraging Windows PowerShell and CIM.

NOTE

At one time, Microsoft attempted to compete against the ubiquitous Adobe Portable Document Format (PDF) file format with their own XML-based format called XML Paper Specification, or XPS.

The XPS Document Writer is a print-to-file virtual printer that allows you to convert document files into XPS format. The XPS Document Writer behaves the very same way as the Adobe PDF virtual printer behaves in Adobe Acrobat Professional. To be honest with you, I've never found the XPS format to be anything more than a proprietary, faux-vendor-neutral annoyance. However, I recognize that "your mileage may vary," as the saying goes.

Summary

If you've ever used Microsoft enterprise products like System Center, Lync Server, SharePoint Server, or Exchange Server, you're actually using a lot of WMI/CIM. This hour of training was important for you because you now have a Windows PowerShell-based entry point into the truly wild and wooly world of Windows Management Instrumentation. Use your newfound powers wisely!

In Hour 16, "Searching and Filtering with Regular Expressions," we turn our attention to regular expressions. RegEx, as the technology is called, enables you to perform much more granular pattern matching than you've seen thus far with the * and % operators. Stay tuned for more fun and learning.

Q&A

Q. One of my friends gave me this cool PowerShell one-liner to retrieve Windows desktop settings for a particular domain account:

```
Get-WMIObject -Class Win32_Desktop -Filter "name='COMPANYA\\Administrator'"
```

What is the purpose of the double backslashes here? I find that confusing.

A. Do you remember when I said that PowerShell and WMI/WQL have different syntax rules? Here's a good example: In WMI/WQL, the backslash (\) is an escape character. Therefore, to get WMI to recognize that backslash separating domain name and username literally, we must first escape it. For reference, Windows PowerShell itself uses the backtick (`) as an escape character.

Q. I'm logged on to my administrative workstation using standard user credentials. How can I make WMI calls on remote machines using administrative credentials?

A. The WMI and CIM commands both support the **–Credential** parameter. However, the parameter works for remote access scenarios only. That is, you cannot specify alternate creds for
a local WMI call. Here's an example of making a remote WMI call by using domain administrator credentials:

```
Invoke-Command –Computername MEM1,MEM2 –ScriptBlock { Get-CIMInstance
➥-ClassName Win32_logicaldisk -Credential "companya\administrator" }
```

Q. **Given the spotty or nonexistent nature of WMI/CIM documentation within Windows itself,
where should I go to learn more about the WMI classes, instances, properties and methods?**

A. Great question. I suggest that you open your favorite search engine (mine is Google) and
run a search. Dollars to donuts, the first search result will point you to a page in the
Microsoft Developer Network (MSDN) online libraries. For instance, suppose that I want
details on the **Win32_LogicalDisk** class. First I'll run a Google power search:

```
WMI "win32_logicaldisk"
```

Next, I'll read the associated MSDN article, some of which I show in Figure 15.6.

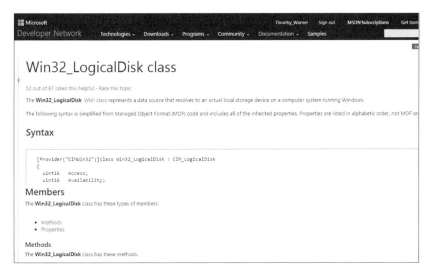

FIGURE 15.6
Although we are likely not developers, the MSDN site is the best documentation source for Microsoft WMI/
CIM classes.

Workshop

If you have only a single system available to you, use your knowledge of WMI and Windows Powershell to receive all TCP/IP client information you can from a Powershell session. I'm talking about data like IP address, DNS server addresses, link speed, and so forth.

If you are fortunate enough to have multiple computers available to you, retrieve the same information from all systems. Be sure that the return data allows you to differentiate which data came from which remote computer.

Finally, take your aggregated return data and generate a nice CSV file that you can import into Excel and turn into a beautiful report.

Quiz

1. The CIM cmdlets access a different data corpus than WMI.

    a. True

    b. False

2. As you add roles and services to your Windows Server computer, you'll have additional WMI namespaces from which to retrieve data.

    a. True

    b. False

3. WMI instance properties contain a qualifier that lists their writability.

    a. True

    b. False

Answers

1. The correct answer is B. Please understand this: Regardless of whether we use WMI or CIM cmdlets, there is one and only one WMI repository on our Windows-based system. We can actually look at the PowerShell CIM commands as more administrator-friendly "wrappers" around WMI calls.

2. The correct answer is B. You'll find that the WMI namespaces may be different on your different server and client systems depending upon what capabilities are installed on that box. For instance, you'll find DNS and Active Directory namespaces on domain controllers.

    That said, just because you have a namespace available to you doesn't mean that your system has populated class instances. For example, the Root\CIMV2 namespace has a class named Win32_TapeDrive, but I would be hard-pressed to believe that most of your systems have connected tape drives available.

3. The correct answer is A. I admit that my asking you this question was a bit unfair because we didn't discuss qualifiers in this hour. However, I want to make sure that you don't move beyond this hour without understanding the concept of qualifiers.

In a nutshell, a qualifier is a type of subproperty. Consider, for instance, the following code snippet and partial output:

```
PS C:\> $class = Get-CimClass -ClassName win32_printer
PS C:\> $class.CimClassProperties

Name               : Caption
Value              :
CimType            : String
Flags              : Property, ReadOnly, NullValue
Qualifiers         : {MaxLen, read}
ReferenceClassName :

Name               : ShareName
Value              :
CimType            : String
Flags              : Property, NullValue
Qualifiers         : {Description, MappingStrings, read, write}
```

Notice that the **Qualifiers** property of the **Caption** class property is read-only, whereas the **ShareName** class property is writable. So, you can write yourself some PowerShell in short order to retrieve instance properties that are either read-only or writable, depending on your business needs.

HOUR 16

Searching and Filtering with Regular Expressions

What You'll Learn in This Hour:

▸ Revisiting the wildcard operators

▸ Understanding Regular expressions

▸ Using the **–Match** parameter

▸ Using **Select-String**

▸ Using the RegEx type accelerator

Let's say that you desperately need to find a specific PowerShell function that you wrote two years ago, but you have no earthly idea in which PowerShell script file the function resides. Or perhaps your company needs to attain industry compliance, part of which requires that you identify all Excel files throughout your organization that contain personally identifiable information such as Social Security numbers or credit card numbers.

What's a busy Windows systems administrator to do? In this case, our old standby wildcard characters (* and ?) won't cut the mustard.

Well, we can combine Windows PowerShell code with regular expression syntax to get the aforementioned jobs done in no time. No doubt about it: RegEx is a huge topic, and certainly is comprehensive enough to warrant its own book.

My goal in this hour of training is to give you the most important and powerful regular expression integration points with Windows PowerShell to add to your scripting and automation toolbox. Let's begin.

Revisiting the Wildcard Operators

The asterisk (*) wildcard operator has been with us since the earliest days of MS-DOS. The asterisk is also used in regular expressions, although its meaning is different. Nonetheless, I use the asterisk all the time in my Windows PowerShell console code.

Fire up an elevated Windows PowerShell console session and let's work through a number of examples.

Traditional Wildcard Search Syntax

The asterisk wildcard is used to match on any one or more characters. For instance, you may want to examine the commands contained within the Windows Server 2012 R2 DNS Server module. Is the module name DNS, DNSServer, or something else?

At any rate, we can rest assured that the module includes at least the string DNS in it, so let's try this:

```
Get-Command -Module *dns*
```

TIP

I like to both prepend and append an asterisk to catch matches that occur both before/after the static string. Another spot where I use the asterisk is when I'm searching directories for a particular file type.

In the following example, I obtain a listing of all .ps1 script files that exist in my home folder hierarchy. (Remember that the tilde, ~, is a shortcut representation of your user account's home folder.)

```
PS C:\> Get-ChildItem -Path ~ -Recurse -Filter *.ps1
    Directory: C:\Users\Tim\Desktop

Mode              LastWriteTime        Length Name
----              -------------        ------ ----
-a----            12/3/2014   3:43 PM    1201 70-413-Session02.ps1


    Directory: C:\Users\Tim\Documents\WindowsPowerShell

Mode              LastWriteTime        Length Name
----              -------------        ------ ----
-a----            11/24/2014  8:36 AM     876 Microsoft.PowerShell_profile.ps1
```

Next I'll search my E: drive for Microsoft Excel .xls and .xlsx files that end in the string **report**:

```
PS C:\> Get-ChildItem -Path E: *report.xl*

    Directory: E:\

Mode              LastWriteTime        Length Name
----              -------------        ------ ----
-a----            12/5/2014  10:42 AM       0 janreport.xls
-a----            12/5/2014  10:42 AM       0 march-report.xlsx
```

Do you see how the asterisk works? It's a simple substitution matching operator. We also have the question mark (?), which is used to match on a single character. For example, the statement

```
C:\> dir log?.txt
```

matches log1.txt and log9.txt, but would not match log22.txt because the question mark matches only a single character before the .txt part.

One more example: Watch as I use the question mark wildcard to fetch report files from 2000–2009:

```
PS C:\> Get-ChildItem -Path "C:\reports" -Filter 200?.xls?

    Directory: C:\reports

Mode                LastWriteTime         Length Name
----                -------------         ------ ----
-a----        12/5/2014  10:43 AM           2048 2002.xls
-a----        12/5/2014  10:43 AM           4096 2006.xlsx
```

NOTE

Incidentally, I have another file in my C:\Reports directory called 2010.xls that wasn't picked up in the earlier search, as expected.

Yes, I've also been playing around with using the formal **Get-ChildItem** cmdlet and its alias, **gci**, to keep your skills sharp. Note also that I sometimes supply the **–Path** and **–Filter** positional parameters by name, and sometimes I pass only the value. By now you should understand exactly how cmdlets work in the pipeline.

I like to describe regular expressions as "wildcards on steroids" because they are so much more powerful and flexible than the time-worn * and ? wildcard operators.

Okay, enough review with the traditional string search wildcards. As I said, regular expression syntax embraces both the asterisk and the wildcard, but their meaning is different. This introduces the question: How does PowerShell know whether you're using regular expressions or not? Let's answer that question right now.

Understanding Regular Expressions

At this point, we're both comfortable with a *string* being defined as a sequence of alphanumeric/nonalphanumeric characters, correct? Good. Regular expressions, which are also called *RegExes* (yes, that's the plural form), are nothing more than special text strings that describe a search pattern.

It's true that the format of regular expressions takes some getting used to if you aren't already a computer programmer. Regular expression syntax is implemented directly in the Linux/UNIX/OS X command-line shells and is a component of any mainline programming language in use today.

To that point, we must remember that Windows PowerShell has the .NET Framework at its core. Correspondingly, we can leverage the .NET Framework's implementation of regular expression syntax in our Windows PowerShell code.

History of Stephen Cole Kleene

The American mathematician Stephen Cole Kleene invented regular expressions in 1956; so, this search/filtering syntax has been around since the earliest days of computer programming.

In point of fact, the asterisk (*) wildcard is officially called the Kleene star, named after Dr. Kleene himself. Let's actually learn our first bit of RegEx syntax by learning how the * is used with RegEx.

To pick up our earlier question, you're wondering how PowerShell knows that you're invoking regular expression syntax when you need to do a pattern match on a string.

Where to Use Regular Expressions in PowerShell

In my work with Windows PowerShell, I use regular expressions in the following contexts:

▶ When I'm using the **–match** parameter in a **Where-Object** expression

▶ When I'm using the **Select-String** cmdlet to search file content for matches

▶ When I use RegEx objects in my PowerShell scripts

As you've come to expect, you'll learn how to use regular expressions in all three aforementioned contexts.

Setting Up Our Test Environment

Let's now take the next step and learn some of the most common RegEx operators through practical examples. Our first order of business is to choose a folder containing myriad file types for our regular expression searching pleasure.

As a case study, we'll use a folder I created in the root of my C: drive called docs that contains a bunch of "dummy" content:

```
PS C:\> dir c:\docs

    Directory: C:\docs

Mode            LastWriteTime        Length Name
```

```
----                 -------------         ------- ----
-a----      12/4/2014   12:48 PM           0 1234-sales-data-2334.txt
-a----      12/4/2014   11:40 AM          19 creditcard.txt
-a----     12/12/2014    9:58 AM           0 log1.txt
-a----     12/12/2014    9:58 AM           0 log22.txt
-a----     12/12/2014    9:58 AM           0 log9.txt
-a----      12/4/2014   11:47 AM           0 logfile23.txt
-a----      12/4/2014   11:47 AM           0 logfile29.txt
-a----      12/4/2014   11:47 AM           0 logfile41.txt
-a----      12/4/2014   11:41 AM           0 myletter.doc
-a----      12/4/2014   11:47 AM           0 mymodule.ps1m
-a----      12/4/2014   11:40 AM           0 myscript.ps1
-a----      12/4/2014   12:05 PM          64 phone.txt
-a----      12/4/2014   11:40 AM          11 pii.txt
-a----      12/4/2014   12:48 PM           0 statusreport3234.xlsx
-a----      12/4/2014   11:40 AM           0 timescript.ps1
-a----      12/4/2014   11:42 AM           0 webpage1 - Copy.html
-a----      12/4/2014   11:42 AM           0 webpage1.html
-a----      12/4/2014   11:31 AM     1659462 WindowsUpdate.log
-a----      12/4/2014   11:41 AM           0 worddoc2013.docx
```

Sharp-eyed readers will observe the file size on most of the previously listed files. All I did was use **New-Item** to generate empty files with the appropriate extension, like so:

```
New-Item -Type file -Name "bogusfile.docx"
```

I encourage you to create a C:\docs folder just like I did so that you can work through these examples with me.

Using the –Match Parameter

The **–match** parameter is supported in only one cmdlet in Windows PowerShell:

```
PS C:\> Get-Command -ParameterName match | Select-Object -Property Name

Name
----
Where-Object
```

By the way, you can leverage these .NET-based regular expression rules no matter which PowerShell version you're running. I'm relieved as your instructor to finally show you a PowerShell feature that isn't at least in some way version dependent.

Besides using **–match** in a **Where-Object** expression, you can also send string comparison statements to Windows PowerShell directly. For example, try the following examples and think about why each evalues either to Boolean True or False. I numbered the lines to make the expressions easier to identify:

```
(1) Set-Location -Path C:\docs
(2) "nowhere" -match "where"
(3) "gingerbreadman" -match "bread"
(4) "cookie" -match "cake"
(5) "tim" -notmatch "tim"
(6) "Tim" -cmatch "tim"
```

Here's the rationale:

▶ **Example 1**: Here we're simply shifting our focus to the C:\docs directory so that we don't have to specify a –**Path** when we use formal expressions later on in the hour.

▶ **Example 2**: True because RegEx finds *where* inside the source string regardless of its position by default.

▶ **Example 3**: True for the same reason as example 2.

▶ **Example 4**: False because there exists no matching *cake* string within *cookie*.

▶ **Example 5**: False because –**notmatch** evaluates to True only if the compared strings do indeed match. (Tricky, eh?)

▶ **Example 6**: False because both –**cmatch** and –**cnotmatch** work with case sensitivity.

We observed in the previous examples that regular expression matches "float" throughout the source string. That works fine in some cases, but what if you needed to match a string only from the beginning of the string? Or the end? Hang on; we're getting there.

Windows PowerShell includes a built-in automatic variable named **$matches** that is helpful when you're troubleshooting regular expressions. For instance, try the following:

```
PS C:\docs> "myfaveexpression" -match "fave"
True
PS C:\docs> $Matches

Name                    Value
----                    -----
0                       fave
```

Using RegEx Anchors and Ranges

In the .NET/PowerShell RegEx implementation, we can use the caret (^) and dollar sign ($) characters to "anchor" our match to the beginning or the end of a string, respectively.

In our C:\docs example folder, for instance, let's say we wanted to see only those files that begin with *log*:

```
PS C:\docs> Get-ChildItem | Where-Object { $_.name -match "^log" }

    Directory: C:\docs

Mode                LastWriteTime         Length Name
----                -------------         ------ ----
-a----        12/12/2014     9:58 AM           0 log1.txt
-a----        12/12/2014     9:58 AM           0 log22.txt
-a----        12/12/2014     9:58 AM           0 log9.txt
-a----         12/4/2014    11:47 AM           0 logfile23.txt
-a----         12/4/2014    11:47 AM           0 logfile29.txt
-a----         12/4/2014    11:47 AM           0 logfile41.txt
```

Perhaps this isn't the strongest example because we can do the same thing with the old-fashioned wildcard in a much more simple way:

```
Dir log*.txt
```

TIP

I'm not here to mediate an argument for or against RegEx. Instead I advise you to use your best judgment. If the old-school * or ? wildcards don't give you enough power in your **Where-Object** expression, know that you can invoke the **–Match** parameter in your expression.

As we did previously, let's do some direct evaluations to give us a feel for how anchors work in string comparisons:

```
(1) "8675309jenny" –match "^jenny"
(2) "8675309jenny –match "$jenny"
(3) "tim" –match "t[iou]m"
(4) "tim" –match "t[^ewi]m"
```

Here's the rationale:

▶ **Example 1**: False because the RegEx looks for *jenny* only at the beginning of the string.

▶ **Example 2**: True because *jenny* appears at the end of the string.

▶ **Example 3**: True because the letter between *t* and *m* is *i*, which falls within the range specified.

▶ **Example 4**: False because the caret here matches only when the characters enclosed within brackets are not contained in the source string. (Tricky, I know.)

TIP

Because the $ and ^ anchors can be somewhat inflexible, it's a good idea to broaden their use with ranges, which I showed you in examples 3 and 4 above.

One of the coolest applications of the range RegEx is when you want the flexibility of a wildcard while at the same time constraining the degree of wildness, if that makes sense. To wit, check this out:

```
PS C:\docs> "Warner TPS Report 21" -match "^[a-z]"
True
PS C:\docs> $matches
```

```
Name                      Value
----                      -----
0                         W
```

If you're thinking, "Yeah, that's cool, but what if I needed to do a range or wildcard match at the beginning *and* the end of a string?" you're on the right track. Let's take the next step in our learning together, okay?

Using RegEx Qualifiers

Qualifiers are where we start to "step on" what you already know about the asterisk and question mark operators.

In RegEx notation, the period (.) matches any single character. In other words, the period is to RegEx as the question mark is to traditional Windows command-line wildcard syntax.

In RegEx, the asterisk (*) matches zero or more instances of the preceding character. The question mark (?) matches zero or one instance of the preceding character class, which we'll learn about in the next section.

Finally, we use the backslash (\) in RegEx as an escape character. The backslash will be one of your most frequently accessed RegEx tools because we Windows systems administrators deal with the backslash all the time in other contexts, such as Universal Naming Convention (UNC) paths, Windows NT-style usernames, and so forth.

We need escape characters when we want PowerShell to interpret the following character differently from its literal meaning. For instance, if we wanted to match a UNC path like \\server\ share, we'd need to (at the least) escape each backslash with the RegEx escape character:

```
\\server\share -match "^\\\\"
```

Run the following list of examples in your PowerShell session and think about why PowerShell evaluates each to True or False. Remember also that you can echo the contents of **$matches** to see exactly on which characters PowerShell made the match.

```
(1) "domain\username" -match "[a-z]*\\[a-z]*"
(2) "tim.warner" -match "tim\.warner"
(3) "username" -match "^user$"
(4) "bat" -match "b.t"
(5) "The Titanic" -cmatch "Tit..ic"
```

Here are the answers:

▶ **Example 1**: True because we asked for a letter before the backslash, we escaped the backslash, and then asked for a letter after the backslash. (Check out the **$matches** result to see what PowerShell did.)

▶ **Example 2**: True because we're escaping the period character. If we didn't do this, RegEx would apply a different meaning to the period character.

▶ **Example 3**: False. Even though we match on *user* in the front of the string, the dollar sign here matches *user* on the end as well.

▶ **Example 4**: True because the RegEx use of the dot or period is to match on zero or one characters.

▶ **Example 5**: True because we're performing a case-sensitive match on two characters that occur between two fragments of the word *Titanic*.

Single or Double Quotes?

Earlier in this book, I told you that you can surround string data in PowerShell by using either single quotation marks or double quotes. That's true. However, you now understand enough PowerShell to take your understanding to the next level.

In PowerShell, double-quoted strings translate variables into their underlying value. By contrast, single-quoted strings leave the variable as is. For instance:

```
PS C:\docs> $w = "world"
PS C:\docs> Write-Host "Hello $w"
Hello world
PS C:\docs> Write-Host 'Hello $w'
Hello $w
PS C:\docs>
```

I wanted to tell you this now because we use quotes all the time in our RegEx expressions, and you'll eventually begin integrating variable declarations into your scripts more and more. One of my goals as your instructor is to prevent your being unpleasantly surprised by Windows PowerShell behavior.

Using RegEx Character Classes

So far, we've seen some RegEx "wildcard" action, as well as how we can broaden the scope of our RegEx filtering with sets (such as [aeiou]) and ranges (such as [a–z], [0–9], and so on).

Personally, I'm grateful for character classes, which take the form of a backslash (escape character) and a letter, which substitute for more complex match types.

Following is a rogue's gallery of my favorite RegEx character classes:

▶ **\w**: Matches any alphanumeric character

▶ **\W**: Matches any nonalphanumeric character

▶ **\s**: Matches any whitespace

▶ **\S**: Matches any non-whitespace

▶ **\d**: Matches any digit

▶ **\D**: Matches any non-digit

TIP

Note that some of these character classes are case sensitive. If you're a longtime Windows systems administrator like me, this takes a bit of getting used to.

You can also use curly braces, {}, to specify match counts. This method is especially convenient when used with the digit (\d) character class. For instance, the following expression evaluates to True because PowerShell matches on at least two digits, but no more than four:

```
"4567" -match "\d{2,4}"
```

Once again, I want to run you through an obstacle course of examples for you to try on your computer:

```
(1)  "quepublishing.com" -match "\w"
(2)  "quepublishing.com" -match "\w*"
(3)  "192.168.128.14" -match "\d{1,3}\.\d{1,3}\.\d{1,3}\.\d{1,3}"
```

▶ **Example 1**: This is true, but if you look at the **$matches** contents, you'll note that PowerShell matched only on the *q*. Believe me when I tell you that using RegExes requires a lot of troubleshooting to make sure you don't get unexpected/erroneous results.

▶ **Example 2**: True, and now we're cooking with gas because the match is on the entire string instead of only the first character.

▶ **Example 3**: True because we are matching on one to three digits, a literal period, and so on for the four octets that comprise an IPv4 address.

Example 3 bears some further investigation. When you saw the True result, you probably thought, "Oh cool. Now I know the RegEx formula to match on IP addresses."

Not so fast. Remember that valid IPv4 address octets run from 0 to 255. Therefore, both of the following bogus IP address still evaluate to True:

```
"256.0.300.132" -match "\d{1,3}\.\d{1,3}\.\d{1,3}\.\d{1,3}"
"blah10.0.0.1" -match "\d{1,3}\.\d{1,3}\.\d{1,3}\.\d{1,3}"
```

What's going on here? Well, we can approach a fix to this problem by using anchor characters. Let's try the following:

```
"blah10.0.0.1" -match "^\d{1,3}\.\d{1,3}\.\d{1,3}\.\d{1,3}$"
```

The preceding expression evaluates to False, of course. However, notice that we could still compare numbers that aren't legal for IPv4 addresses.

NOTE

Keep in mind that there is no business logic in regular expressions. Instead, all it does is do string comparison and pattern matching. It's up to us as systems administrators to build failsafe mechanisms into our expressions to ensure that only valid data is captured.

I'll leave the IPv4 address validation for your challenge at the end of this hour.

NOTE

Although book publishers ordinarily don't advocate authors pointing readers to their competition, you truly should be aware of *Mastering Regular Expressions* by Jeffrey Friedl (http://amzn.to/1xaU7CI) and published by O'Reilly Media. Many Windows PowerShell experts use this as their "go to" RegEx reference.

PowerShell itself includes the about_Regular_Expressions conceptual help article, which is super helpful. In terms of online RegEx reference, many experts point to Regular-Expressions.info, but I find its content overly dense. Because PowerShell uses the .NET implementation of RegEx, Microsoft itself has a nice Regular Expression Reference site at http://msdn.microsoft.com/library/az24scfc. aspx. What great RegEx resources have you discovered in your travels?

At this point, given enough practice, you should be able to use regular expressions to filter files (or any object, really) by using the **–match** parameter of the **Where-Object** cmdlet.

For instance, the following PowerShell two-liner retrieves all dynamic link library (DLL) files located in your System32 folder that begin with *f* and whose filename contains exactly five characters:

```
$regex = '^f(.{5})\.dll$'
Get-ChildItem –Path c:\windows\system32\*.dll | Where-Object { $_.Name -match
➥$regex }
```

By way of review, we stored the RegEx string in a variable named, appropriately enough, **$regex**, and popped that variable in our **–match** paramter clause. Done and done! Once you get the basics of RegEx filtering down, the biggest time sink will be figuring out exactly what you're looking to match on.

Using Select-String

We covered the **–match** parameter pretty thoroughly, haven't we? You may be wondering, though, how we can perform matches inside of files. After all, as a Windows systems administrator you may need to locate personally identifiable data (PII) in a stack of text files on your HR department file server.

To that end, we have the built-in **Select-String** cmdlet, which does nothing else but find text in strings and files.

The two main parameters in **Select-String** are **–pattern**, which represents your RegEx expression, and **–path**, which points PowerShell to a particular file location.

A Practical Select-String Example

Consider the C:\docs example folder we created together at the beginning of the hour:

```
PS C:\docs> Get-ChildItem


    Directory: C:\docs


Mode                LastWriteTime         Length Name
----                -------------         ------ ----
-a----        12/4/2014   12:48 PM              0 1234-sales-data-2334.txt
-a----        12/4/2014   11:40 AM             19 creditcard.txt
-a----       12/12/2014    9:58 AM              0 log1.txt
-a----       12/12/2014    9:58 AM              0 log22.txt
-a----       12/12/2014    9:58 AM              0 log9.txt
-a----        12/4/2014   11:47 AM              0 logfile23.txt
-a----        12/4/2014   11:47 AM              0 logfile29.txt
-a----        12/4/2014   11:47 AM              0 logfile41.txt
-a----        12/4/2014   11:41 AM              0 myletter.doc
-a----        12/4/2014   11:47 AM              0 mymodule.ps1m
-a----        12/4/2014   11:40 AM              0 myscript.ps1
-a----        12/4/2014   12:05 PM             64 phone.txt
-a----        12/4/2014   11:40 AM             11 pii.txt
-a----        12/4/2014   12:48 PM              0 statusreport3234.xlsx
-a----        12/4/2014   11:40 AM              0 timescript.ps1
-a----        12/4/2014   11:42 AM              0 webpage1 - Copy.html
-a----        12/4/2014   11:42 AM              0 webpage1.html
-a----        12/4/2014   11:31 AM        1659462 WindowsUpdate.log
-a----        12/4/2014   11:41 AM              0 worddoc2013.docx
```

I wrote my name in two random files in that directory. Let's try to figure out which ones:

```
PS C:\> Select-String -Path "c:\docs\*.*" -Pattern "warner"

docs\log9.txt:3:Timothy Warner
docs\logfile41.txt:13:Tim Warner was here. blah blah
```

There! We have our answer. Notice that **Select-String** helpfully gives us the context of each match it found.

Hey, it's time for a Try It Yourself exercise. This will give us some good, real-world experience with using RegEx and **Select-String**.

Locating PII by Using Regular Expressions and Select-String

In this Try It Yourself exercise, you'll use **Select-String** and your newfound regular expression syntax knowledge to locate fake personally identifiable data in the C:\docs sample folder.

To get started, let's limit ourselves to the text files in that folder. Pick out three text files, and add one of the following types of PII-like data to them:

▶ Social Security number: 123-45-6789
▶ Telephone number: 123-555-1212
▶ Email address: jane.user@fakemail.com

1. Let's start with Social Security number, and let me start off by cutting to the chase: I use RegExBuddy ($39.95; http://www.regexbuddy.com) because this nifty graphical user interface (GUI) RegEx utility makes it easy to look up RegEx expressions for useful data like SSNs. In fact, Figure 16.1 shows you the RegExBuddy interface.

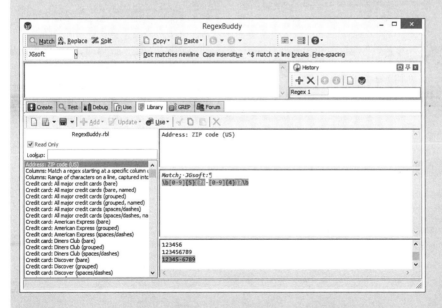

FIGURE 16.1
RegExBuddy makes it a snap to look up practical RegEx expressions to match stuff like credit card numbers, Social Security numbers, and ZIP codes.

If you have RegExBuddy (you can download a free trial version), open the program and navigate to the Library tab. In the Lookup field, type **social security number**. Voilà!

2. We should test that our Social Security number RegEx pattern works:

```
PS C:\> "132-32-3232" -match "\b[0-9]{3}-[0-9]{2}-[0-9]{4}\b"
True
PS C:\> "132-323-3232" -match "\b[0-9]{3}-[0-9]{2}-[0-9]{4}\b"
False
```

TIP
_____
Remember that we can only scratch the surface of RegEx in a single book chapter.
_____

In the previous code example, the **\b** character class looks for word boundaries. Placing a **\b** before and after the pattern ensures that the SSN occurs in isolation and is not run up flush against other string data.

3. Let's now run **Select-String** to get our matches:

```
PS C:\> Select-String -Path "c:\docs\*.*" -Pattern "\b[0-9]{3}-[0-9]{2}-[0-9]
➥{4}\b"

docs\log9.txt:8:social security number: 123-45-6789
docs\pii.txt:1:132-23-4224
```

4. Good so far. Turning to RegExBuddy again, I found a candidate RegEx expression to location telephone numbers in any of the standard North American formats. Here's the **Select-String** for that. While we're at it, we'll pipe the results to a text file so we can save the results. All hail the Windows PowerShell pipeline!

```
PS C:\> Select-String -Pattern "^[0-9]\d{2}-\d{3}-\d{4}" -Path "c:\docs\*.*"

docs\phone.txt:2:607-445-8885
docs\phone.txt:6:123-555-1212
```

By the way, if you don't want to use RegExBuddy, there are certainly free online alternatives. Check out RegExLib.com sometime and browse their comprehensive expression list.

5. To wrap this up, let's look for email addresses contained in at least one file in our C:\docs folder. Once again, I found a doozy of an expression in RegExBuddy:

```
PS C:\> Select-String -Path "c:\docs\*.*" -Pattern "\b[A-Z0-9._%+-]+@[A-Z0-9.
➥-]+\.[A-Z]{2,4}\b"

docs\pii.txt:3:Email address: jane.user@fakemail.com
```

That particular RegEx expression we're using is flexible. You should find that the following strings all evaluate to True:

```
Tim.warner234@fakemailaddress.com
Joe_user_234a@anotherfakeone.com
```

Using the RegEx Type Accelerator

The .NET Framework itself contains a class called **System.Text.RegularExpressions.Regex** that we can use to store RegEx expressions. Now earlier in the hour we did something like this:

```
$regex1 = "\b[A-Z0-9._%+-]+@[A-Z0-9.-]+\.[A-Z]{2,4}\b"
```

This is a nice shorthand for adding a RegEx expression to, for instance, the **–match** parameter. However, if we run that **$regex1** variable into **Get-Member**, we see that it's just a plain old garden-variety string. We can't do much with simple System.string objects in this context.

In PowerShell, we're concerned with "three-dimensional" objects with properties and methods. If the .NET Framework gives us RegEx objects, let's use those where we can, eh?

Check this out: We can use the PowerShell RegEx type accelerator to create RegEx objects directly. Here's the syntax:

```
PS C:\> [regex]$regex2 = "\b[A-Z0-9._%+-]+@[A-Z0-9.-]+\.[A-Z]{2,4}\b"
PS C:\> $regex2 | Get-Member

    TypeName: System.Text.RegularExpressions.Regex
```

If you recall, the RegEx expression we're using here is one that can match and simultaneously validate email addresses. To perform a match by using a RegEx object, we can invoke the object's native **match()** method, like so:

```
$email = tim@email.com
$regex2.match($email)
```

Summary

My head hurts. How are you doing? This was a truly "heavy" hour, and in my opinion, a subject matter that can and will drive math-phobic systems administrators away from learning Windows PowerShell.

It need not be like that, however. I've given you the basic "hows and whys" of using regular expressions in PowerShell, and I've provided you with some excellent resources to turn to when you're stuck.

I cannot stress this point enough: Don't spin your cognitive wheels trying to re-create a RegEx expression that a hundred people have already done in front of you, and perhaps better. Use your resources and apply the expressions intelligently to solve your business goals.

In Hour 17, "Managing Software with Windows PowerShell OneGet," we'll turn our attention to something completely different; namely, how to install and maintain software from the command line by using the **OneGet** package manager manager (no, that isn't a typo).

Q&A

Q. We've done quite a bit of RegEx-powered searching here, but is it possible to use PowerShell to replace text?

A. But of course! One way to replace string text is to feed text into the **–replace** operator:

```
PS C:\> "Susan Harter" -replace "Harter","Warner"
Susan Warner
```

That's a super simple example, but you can add a RegEx expression, with character classes, quantifiers and everything, to your **–replace** operator to get more granular in your replace work.

If you liked what we did in this hour with constructing RegEx objects, you should be aware that RegEx objects have a **replace**() method as well. Check it out on your own.

Q. How compatible are regular expressions in different programming languages?

A. I like to draw a comparison between cross-language RegEx with the Structured Query Language (SQL) database access language. With SQL, you find that most relational database management system vendors adhere to *most* of the SQL standards, but they tend to sprinkle in some vendor-specific tweaks to the language.

Likewise, you'll find that PowerShell's RegEx implementation follows pretty closely to what you'll find in other programming languages. Remember always, though, that if you find a good reference for .NET RegEx, hang on to it because all of that syntax applies completely to Windows PowerShell.

Speaking of reference, Wikipedia has a nice data table called "Comparison of regular expression engines" that you might want to examine: https://en.wikipedia.org/wiki/Comparison_of_regular_expression_engines.

Q. Is it more efficient to use Get-ChildItem and the pipeline when I'm using Select-String to find string matches?

A. Excellent question. You know that you're "getting" Windows PowerShell when you start wondering whether one method is faster than another, system resource utilization-wise.

Indeed, if you're going to, say, parse an entire folder filled with *.log files, you should use the **–Filter** parameter with **Get-ChildItem** first before invoking **Select-String**. Here's an example:

```
Get-ChildItem -Path "C:\LogFiles" -Filter *.log -Recurse | Select-String
➥-Pattern "Mozilla"
```

Workshop

In this hour, you learned how to write a regular expression to capture string data that may represent IPv4 addresses in the form 192.168.1.1.

For your challenge, research how you can use a RegEx to validate that a given string capture is a valid IPv4 address. The following strings should evaluate to True:

```
0.0.0.0
172.16.32.34
```

The following strings should evaluate to False:

```
10.0.1.256
10.0.1.1 (that's an "O" in the address!)
```

Quiz

1. How does PowerShell evaluate the following RegEx statement, and does it validate a UNC path correctly?

   ```
   "66\\ServerXYZ\Share1" -match "\\\\\w+\\\w+"
   ```

   a. True, and yes, it does.

   b. True, but no, it doesn't.

   c. False, and yes, it does.

   d. False, but no, it doesn't.

2. How does PowerShell evaluate the following RegEx expression?

   ```
   "Error XBCSE" -match "X[BCD]SE"
   ```

   a. True

   b. False

3. Why does the following RegEx expression evaluate to False?

   ```
   "domain1\twarner" -match "\*twarner"
   ```

   a. We need to remove the asterisk.

   b. We need to escape the backslash.

   c. We need to use single quotes instead of double quotes.

Answers

1. The correct answer is B. The RegEx expression does indeed validate the string, but it doesn't work to validate UNC paths, which take the form of \\servername\sharename.

   The \w+ notation matches any alphanumeric character, and the + matches one or more instances of any alphanumeric character.

   We can fix the problem by using a RegEx anchor like this:

   ```
   PS C:\> "66\\ServerXYZ\Share1" -match "^\\\\\w+\\\w+"


   False
   ```

2. The correct answer is B. Remember that when we use a set like [**BCD**] or [**459**] we're matching on a single character. So, in other words, the entire [] set looks only for one character. The following RegEx expression would evaluate to True:

   ```
   "Error XBCSE" -match "X[BCD]CSE"
   ```

3. The correct answer is B. In PowerShell we use the backtick (`) as an escape character, but we use the backslash to do the same thing in RegEx syntax.

   Here the asterisk looks for one or more occurrences of the previous character. In this expression, we want to match on the backslash literal, followed by the string *twarner*. Let's try the expression again, this time escaping the backslash so that PowerShell interprets the character literally:

   ```
   "domain1\twarner" -match "\\*twarner"
   ```

Managing Software with Windows PowerShell OneGet

What You'll Learn in This Hour:

- ▶ Understanding IT-related terminology
- ▶ Preparing your environment
- ▶ Browsing package repositories
- ▶ Installing software from the command line
- ▶ Managing providers and packages
- ▶ Hosting a private **OneGet** respository

Several years ago, I worked as a systems administrator for a research center in a large university. Several of the infrastructure servers ran Red Hat Linux, so I got my first experience with installing and maintaining software from an entirely command-line environment.

It was quite an adventure, let me tell you, especially for someone accustomed to performing "Click-click-next" installs in Windows. At that time, package managers like yum, rpm, and apt were in their infancy, so nine times out of ten a software installation would fail midway through because I was missing some software component dependency or another.

To be sure, Linux command-line software installation has come a long way. Nowadays, package managers resolve dependencies automatically, and can even be configured to update themselves with no administrator intervention.

Thanks to Windows PowerShell v5 and the **OneGet** module, we Windows systems administrators finally have command-line (read: potential for automated) software installation and maintenance available to us.

By the time you finish this hour, you'll understand how to use **OneGet** to download, install, update, and remove software on local/remote computers. One important word of warning, however: As I write this book, Windows PowerShell v5 is in "Technical Preview" mode, which means that the code is prerelease and highly volatile.

Therefore, it's a good bet that by the time you're studying this book, some of the **OneGet** particulars may have changed a bit. The good news is that I focus on the "bigger picture" here, so you should be able to adapt easily to however **OneGet** looks in its final release form.

Shall we begin?

Understanding IT-Related Terminology

Like most IT-related concepts, our first task is to understand the underlying terminology.

Package

A *package* is a named collection of files and dependent objects that comprise a software application. The specifics of how a package is created depends on the package manager and the willingness of the person creating the package to adopt standards to ensure a good user experience with the package.

Package Manager

A *package manager*, proper, is a tool that enables us, the system administrators, to manage software packages on our computer. For instance, on Debian Linux systems, we use the Advanced Package Tool (APT) to discover, install, maintain, and uninstall software, all from the Terminal prompt.

In the Windows .NET world, **NuGet** (http://nuget.org, and pronounced like *nougat*) is a solution-level package creation and management system that is used by Windows PowerShell **OneGet**. The phrase *solution level* is important here because, in general, only software developers work with **NuGet** directly to develop software and portable software packages. In PowerShell, we can look at **NuGet** as an underlying package management "engine" that supports all the other package providers we have installed on our system.

Going further, in the Windows PowerShell world, **NuGet** takes the roles of both package creation tool and package manager. Yes, the terminology here is slippery and difficult for just about everyone to understand at first.

NOTE

The Windows PowerShell team promotes **Chocolatey** (http://chocolatey.org) as your "go to" package manager with Windows PowerShell v5 **OneGet**. Understand that because I write this book while Windows PowerShell v5 is in a preview state, this situation is subject to change.

Repository

A *repository* for our purposes is an online location that aggregates software packages and makes them available for free download by users. As I said, Microsoft puts a lot of trust into the **Chocolatey** repository, so that's what we'll use throughout this hour.

Keep in mind, though, that command-line software management is built not only on much open-source software but also on community spirit. The **Chocolatey** repository is a community-maintained software repo. Therefore, you have to be willing to trust that the software you download from the Chocolatey Gallery hasn't been maliciously tampered with. We'll talk more about this important issue later.

NOTE

The Linux community has a long and colorful history of using wordplay when naming products. We find that this open source tradition carries forward into the Windows PowerShell **OneGet** framework.

Specifically, **NuGet** is a wordplay on the confectionary nougat. As you probably know, chocolate often accompanies nougat in candy, so we have the hand-in-glove, tongue-in-cheek wordplay **Chocolatey NuGet**, or "Chocolaty nougat." Clever, eh?

OneGet

OneGet, which was originally called **PowerShellGet**, is the Windows PowerShell module that enables us administrators to interact with these package managers and software repositories.

OneGet isn't a package manager, per se, but rather a package management aggregator. Over time, we'll be able to add all sorts of different package providers and repositories such as Cygwin and PyPi.

Assuming you have Windows PowerShell v5 installed, you can get a list of the core **OneGet** commands in the usual fashion:

```
PS C:\>Get-Command -Module OneGet | Format-Table -AutoSize

CommandType Name                        Version Source
----------- ----                        ------- ------
Cmdlet      Find-Package                1.0.0.0 OneGet
Cmdlet      Get-Package                 1.0.0.0 OneGet
Cmdlet      Get-PackageProvider         1.0.0.0 OneGet
Cmdlet      Get-PackageSource           1.0.0.0 OneGet
Cmdlet      Install-Package             1.0.0.0 OneGet
Cmdlet      Register-PackageSource      1.0.0.0 OneGet
Cmdlet      Save-Package                1.0.0.0 OneGet
Cmdlet      Set-PackageSource           1.0.0.0 OneGet
Cmdlet      Uninstall-Package           1.0.0.0 OneGet
Cmdlet      Unregister-PackageSource    1.0.0.0 OneGet
```

You'll learn how to use all of these commands as we work through this hour of training.

NOTE

Once again, I need to remind you that I wrote this hour while Windows PowerShell v5 was still in pre-view mode. In fact, I had to revise the contents of this hour because in their most recent Windows Management Framework (WMF) 5 update, the PowerShell team renamed one of the cmdlets.

Preparing Your Environment

Although much of Windows PowerShell is backward compatible to version 2, **OneGet** has a hard dependency on Windows PowerShell v5. This means that the only Windows operating systems that support PoSH v5 (see my sidebar "About PoSH" for some background on this strange term for PowerShell) can take advantage of **OneGet**. Bummer, right?

Specifically, only Windows 8.1, Windows Server 2012 R2, and Windows 10 (Client and Server) can run Windows PowerShell v5. Again this information is provisional, but my understanding is that the PowerShell team is working furiously to make PowerShell v5 compatible with Windows 7.

About PoSH

You might have noticed that up until now I've decidedly avoided referring to Windows PowerShell as PoSH, POSH, PoSh, or any combination thereof. The origin of this abbreviation is unclear, but per-sonally I find the term cutesy and potentially misleading.

To be sure, your mileage may vary. For instance, I know some PowerShell experts who detest the **NuGet/Chocolatey** naming convention, and this doesn't bother me at all. At any rate, I wanted to mention PoSH at least once in this book for completeness' sake; you're sure to come across the term in an article or conversation, and I want to do everything I can to ensure your overall PowerShell proficiency.

If you're reading this book prior to the first official release of WMF 5, I suggest that you run a Google search for **download WMF 5.0** and download/install the latest version of the WMF that's available to you.

Retrieving Package Providers

Fasten your seatbelt and start your engine! Please start an elevated Windows PowerShell console session and run the following command to retrieve a list of built-in package providers:

```
PS C:\> Get-PackageProvider

Name                     Version    Features           DynamicOptions
----                     -------    --------           --------------
ARP                      6.4.9883.0 {}                 {IncludeWindowsIns...
msi                      6.4.9883.0 {[file-extensions,... {AdditionalArguments}
PSModule                 6.4.9883.0 {[supports-powersh... {OneGetProvider, L...
```

We can look at a package provider in much the same way that we consider PSProviders. Do you remember how, for instance, the **FileSystem** provider gives you PSDrives for each volume on your system?

In the same way, package providers open up connection to one or more corresponding package sources. First, though, let's briefly define the three built-in package providers:

▶ **ARP**: This stands for Add/Remove Programs and corresponds to the software installed and managed through the Programs and Features Control Panel item.

▶ **MSI**: This stands for Microsoft Software Installer and presumably deals with .msi and .msp installation packages that have arrived on your computer via Windows Update or System Center Configuration Manager.

▶ **PSModule**: This provider is attached directly to the **NuGet** package management framework.

Now let's look at the specific package sources that are exposed by our installed package providers:

```
PS C:\> Get-PackageSource | Format-List *

Name         : PSGallery
Location     : https://www.powershellgallery.com/api/v2/
Source       : PSGallery
ProviderName : PSModule
Provider     : Microsoft.OneGet.Implementation.PackageProvider
IsTrusted    : False
IsRegistered : True
IsValidated  : False
Details      : {[InstallationPolicy, Untrusted], [OneGetProvider, NuGet],
               [PublishLocation,
               https://go.microsoft.com/fwlink/?LinkID=397527&clcid=0x409]}

Name         : MSPSGallery
Location     : http://search.microsoft.com/default.aspx
Source       : MSPSGallery
ProviderName : PSModule
Provider     : Microsoft.OneGet.Implementation.PackageProvider
IsTrusted    : True
```

```
IsRegistered : True
IsValidated  : False
Details      : {[InstallationPolicy, Trusted], [OneGetProvider, NuGet],
               [PublishLocation,
               http://go.microsoft.com/fwlink/?LinkID=397635&clcid=0x409]}
```

Notice that both the PSGallery and MSPSGallery package sources are given to us via the **PSModule** provider. Notice also the **IsTrusted**, **IsRegistered**, and **IsValidated** properties. These are crucial properties indeed because they speak to whether our computer trusts the package content that's offered by the sources.

Alright, you are probably itching to see what actual packages are available; let's address that question next.

Browsing Package Repositories

We can run **Find-Package** with no additional arguments to perform a completely open query for available packages given our currently loaded package providers:

```
PS C:\> Find-Package

The provider 'nuget v2.8.3.6' is not installed.
'nuget' may be manually downloaded from
'https://oneget.org/nuget-anycpu-2.8.3.6.exe' and copied to 'C:\Program
Files\OneGet\ProviderAssemblies'.
Would you like OneGet to automatically download and install 'nuget' now?
[Y] Yes  [N] No  [S] Suspend  [?] Help (default is "Y"):
```

Whoa, what's going on here? The aforementioned prompt lets us know that we need to install the **NuGet** runtime environment to delve into the PSModule package provider and PSGallery and MSPSGallery sources. We'll answer **Y** to the question and proceed.

Let's rerun **Find-Package** command, adding a bit of formatting spice:

```
PS C:\> Find-Package | Select-Object -First 10 | Format-Table -AutoSize
```

Name	Version	Status	ProviderName	Source	Summary
netscan32	5.4.9	Available	Chocolatey	chocolatey	SoftPerfe...
PublicDNS	2.0	Available	Chocolatey	chocolatey	Public DN...
toad.mysql	6.3.0.642	Available	Chocolatey	chocolatey	Toad for ...
cimer	0.6	Available	Chocolatey	chocolatey	cimer
SQLMaintenanceSolution	0.6	Available	Chocolatey	chocolatey	SQL Maint...
setacl	3.6.0	Available	Chocolatey	chocolatey	
marker	0.0.6.0	Available	Chocolatey	chocolatey	Marker - ...
cruisecontrol.net	1.8.4.0	Available	Chocolatey	chocolatey	CruiseCon...
treetrim	1.0.3	Available	Chocolatey	chocolatey	Trim sour...
compareit	4.2.0	Available	Chocolatey	chocolatey	Compare I...

Again, what the heck is going on here? When and where did the **Chocolatey** package source show up? As it turns out, the installation of **NuGet** brings along **Chocolatey** for the ride automagically. Look here:

```
PS C:\> Get-PackageProvider

Name                 Version     Features           DynamicOptions
----                 -------     --------           --------------
ARP                  6.4.9883.0  {}                 {IncludeWindowsIns...
msi                  6.4.9883.0  {[file-extensions,... {AdditionalArguments}
PSModule             6.4.9883.0  {[supports-powersh... {OneGetProvider, L...
Chocolatey           2.8.3.6     {[uri-schemes, Sys... {SkipDependencies,...
NuGet                2.8.3.6     {[supports-powersh... {Destination, Skip...
```

Hmm. So now we have two new package providers: **NuGet** and **Chocolatey**. Let's review our package sources again:

```
PS C:\> Get-PackageSource

Name              ProviderName    IsTrusted  IsRegistered IsValidated
----              ------------    ---------  ------------ -----------
PSGallery         PSModule        False      True         False
MSPSGallery       PSModule        True       True         False
chocolatey        Chocolatey      False      True         False
```

Notice that although PowerShell loaded and registered the **Chocolatey** repository, it did not set the **IsTrusted** flag to True.

NOTE

In terms of your approach to PowerShell **OneGet**, you have two choices: You can either trust that the software packages contained within a given repository are trustworthy, or you can create your own private repository.

Each method has its respective advantages and disadvantages. I think the general "word on the street" is that because Microsoft is invested in the **Chocolatey** project, they take a greater degree of responsibility in ensuring the integrity of all of its repository software. As with everything else in technology, you need to counterbalance higher security with higher administrator convenience.

Of course, we can use **OneGet** cmdlet parameters to constrain our package search to a particular repository. To wit:

```
Name                           Version  Status     ProviderName Source
----                           -------  ------     ------------ ------
xFirefox                       1.0.0    Available  PSModule     https://www.pow...
xPSDesiredStateConfiguration   3.0.3.3  Available  PSModule     https://www.pow...
xWebAdministration             1.3.2.2  Available  PSModule     https://www.pow...
xChrome                        1.0.0    Available  PSModule     https://www.pow...
xJea                           0.2.16.2 Available  PSModule     https://www.pow...
```

```
xDatabase                   1.1.2    Available PSModule     https://www.pow...
PSReadline                  1.0.0.12 Available PSModule     https://www.pow...
xOneGet                     1.0.0    Available PSModule     https://www.pow...
PowerShellCookbook          1.3.1    Available PSModule     https://www.pow...
IEFavorites                 1.1      Available PSModule     https://www.pow...
```

Remember that the PSModule provider gives us PowerShell-related packages. Specifically, do you see the packages in the previous code run that start with *x*? Those are resource packages intended for use with Windows PowerShell Desired State Configuration (DSC). Therefore, of necessity, we'll revisit **OneGet** in Hour 18, "Desired State Configuration Basics," when we formally treat how to use DSC.

Using Find-Package

As I said earlier, though, we want to focus predominantly upon the **Chocolatey** package feed. If you have an idea of which software package you're interested in, simply pass the value with the **–Name** parameter:

```
PS C:\> Find-Package -Name winrar


Name       Version      Status        ProviderName      Source       Summary
----       -------      ------        ------------      ------       -------
winrar     5.11         Available     Chocolatey        chocolatey   WinRAR...
```

In the preceding code listing, I searched for the WinRAR file archive utility. Not surprisingly, given how popular WinRAR is among Windows power users, **Chocolatey** does indeed store a WinRAR package.

What is a bit surprising is to see how much closed source software, like WinRAR, that is available in the **Chocolatey** repo. My favorite open source archiver, 7-Zip, is there as well.

Anyway, PowerShell **OneGet**, working in conjunction with **Chocolatey**, gives you the most recent stable package release by default. However, you can show all package versions that are stocked by a given repository by invoking the **–Allversions** switch parameter:

```
PS C:\> Find-Package -Name winrar -AllVersions


Name       Version      Status        ProviderName      Source       Summary
----       -------      ------        ------------      ------       -------
winrar     4.11.0       Available     Chocolatey        chocolatey   WinRAR...
winrar     4.20.0       Available     Chocolatey        chocolatey   WinRAR...
winrar     5.00.0       Available     Chocolatey        chocolatey   WinRAR...
winrar     5.00.0-be... Available     Chocolatey        chocolatey   WinRAR...
winrar     5.01         Available     Chocolatey        chocolatey   WinRAR...
winrar     5.01.2014... Available     Chocolatey        chocolatey   WinRAR...
winrar     5.01.2014... Available     Chocolatey        chocolatey   WinRAR...
winrar     5.10         Available     Chocolatey        chocolatey   WinRAR...
```

Using Out-GridView

You'll probably prefer to get a more easy-to-read report of available software packages. One quick, though no-printable, option is to use **Out-Gridview**. On your computer, try the following commands. Be aware that instructing PowerShell to browse entire software repositories takes some time, so be patient:

```
Find-Package –ProviderName PSModule | Sort-Object –Property Name | Out-GridView
Find-Package –ProviderName NuGet | Sort-Object –Property Name | Out-GridView
Find-Package –ProviderName Chocolatey | Sort-Object –Property Name | Out-GridView
```

Figure 17.1 shows you my **Chocolatey** package output in gridview.

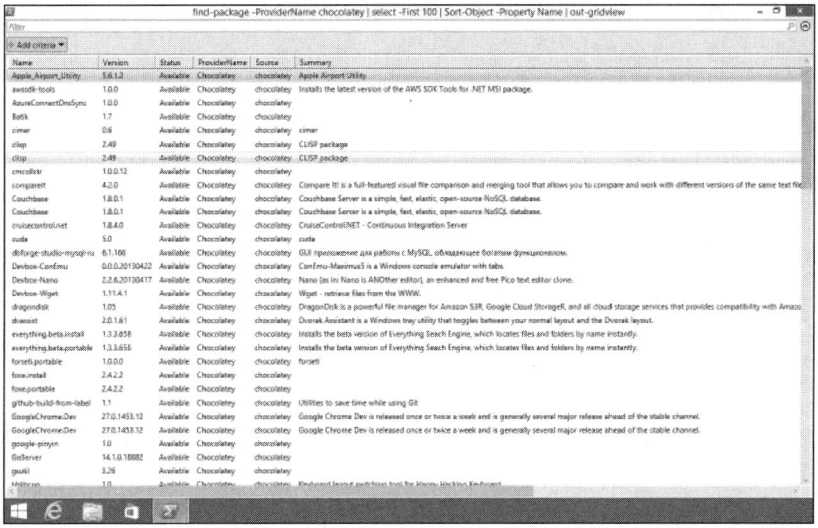

FIGURE 17.1
The gridview PowerShell output presents available package content in a (somewhat) interactive way.

Where's the Documentation?

One of the downsides of the open source world is that documentation can sometimes be missing or incomplete because some developers are more cognizant than others as to their importance.

You'll observe, for example, that the **Summary** property is at times complete, at times schematic, and more often than not missing from your **Find-Package** output. I hope that at least the Microsoft-owned and **Chocolatey** repositories will have completely documented packages someday.

Even within the **OneGet** module, the help files are skeletal at best, as shown in Figure 17.2.

FIGURE 17.2
The Find-Package help file as of WMF 5.0 Preview November 2014 is skeletal at best. Even after running Update-Help, I saw not much beyond these dense, incompletely defined parameter sets.

Installing Software from the Command Line

Having identified a piece of software that interests us, let's turn our attention to the **OneGet** cmdlet **Install-Package** and some of its more useful parameters.

At least initially, I recommend that you run **Install-Package** with the **–Verbose** switch so that you can get detailed feedback as to the package's download and installation status. Let's go ahead and install 7-Zip on our testing computer:

```
Install-Package –Name winrar -Verbose
```

When you use the **–Verbose** switch, you see a lot of yellow text. Take a look at Figure 17.3, which shows output during my install of 7-Zip (I installed WinRAR earlier). I'll walk you through the annotation callouts:

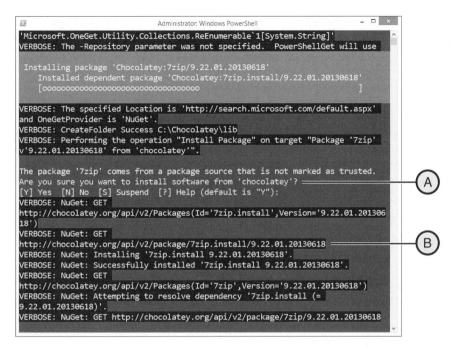

FIGURE 17.3
Installing software via Windows PowerShell means that we have the potential to bypass poorly written GUI installation routines and automate software installation for your users.

▶ **A:** If your package source isn't trusted, you'll receive this extra confirmation prompt. Later in this hour, I teach you how to mark a repository as trusted, which suppresses this prompt.

▶ **B:** Pay attention to (a) where PowerShell fetches the installation package from and (b) where PowerShell installs the software on your local computer. As we'll discuss in just a moment, the lack of standardization here is a problematic aspect of **Chocolatey** and **OneGet** in general.

Where Was the Software Installed?

If you're like me, you are accustomed to Windows software setting C:\Program Files or C:\Program Files (x86) as the default installation locations, depending on whether the software is 64-bit or 32-bit.

Sadly and infuriatingly, you won't find that level of consistency in the **OneGet** world. Remember that it is the individual or group who builds the software package who determines where the software gets installed on your computer's hard disk.

For example, let's investigate the WinRAR archiver that we just installed. We can run **Get-Package** to verify its installation:

```
PS C:\> Get-Package -Name winrar | Format-Table -AutoSize

Name                   Version Status    ProviderName Source
----                   ------- ------    ------------ ------
winrar                 5.11    Installed Chocolatey   C:\Chocolatey\lib\winrar...
WinRAR 5.11 (64-bit)   5.11.0  Installed ARP
```

Sigh. You're probably wondering what this output means. The **Source** parameter seems to tell us that WinRAR was installed in the C:\Chocolatey directory, which in itself is a deal-breaker for many IT shops that rely on Windows protection of the C:\Program Files directory and User Account Control (UAC).

Second, you'll see that WinRAR is associated not only with **Chocolatey** but the **ARP** package provider. All this means is that we can see WinRAR in the Programs and Features Control Panel.

Are you observing a general theme with **OneGet** so far? The technology seems best-suited toward two classes of PowerShell user:

- ▶ **The tinkerer**: These are people who aren't afraid to experiment and troubleshoot Windows, and like the idea of installing and managing software in an automated way.

- ▶ **Windows systems admins**: There are admins who can't install System Center Configuration Manager for one reason or another, and they like the idea of using **OneGet** to automate software installation when, say, they build user operating system images.

In other words, I can't envision the typical end-user enjoying **OneGet** very much.

Before you get too freaked out, let's check out our Start screen or Start menu and verify that the program is indeed installed. You can see that this is true for my Windows 8.1 system by looking at Figurer 17.4.

Figure 17.4 also shows us a couple more things regarding our newly installed software package:

- ▶ If we right-click the **Start** menu icon and select **Show File Location** from the shortcut menu, we see that WinRAR uses the standard, UAC-friendly C:\Program Files installation directory.

- ▶ If you're wondering how I got a Start menu on my Windows 8.1 system, let me tell you that I use either Classic Shell (http://classicshell.net) or Stardock Start8 (http://www.star-dock.com/products/start8/) on all my Windows 8.1 boxes.

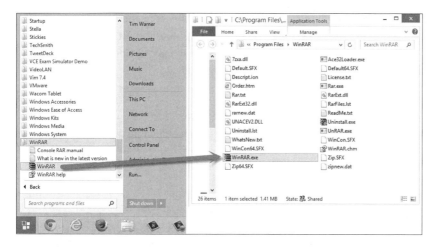

FIGURE 17.4
Some Chocolatey packages install software in the traditional location, and some don't. Make sure to experiment on a test computer first.

Installing an Application from a Subdirectory

Now let's try installing PuTTY, the free Telnet/Secure Shell client:

```
Get-Package -Name putty | Install-Package
```

Now check out Figure 17.5. Note that the PuTTY **Chocolatey** package stores the executables in a subdirectory of C:\Chocolatey, period. Wow.

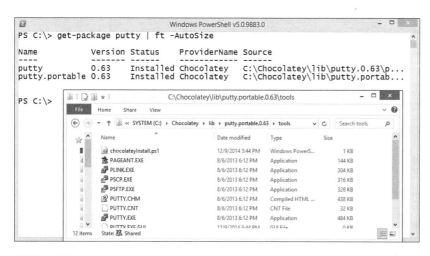

FIGURE 17.5
Wasn't it Emerson who said, "A foolish consistency is the hobgoblin of little minds"? With Chocolatey packages, we have to acccpt a certain level of inconsistency.

If you're playing along at home, you'll also see that WinRAR appears in the Programs and Features Control Panel item, but PuTTY doesn't. The same for the presence or absence of Start menu/Start screen icons. Once again, the mechanics of each package at **Chocolatey** are left up to the packager (also called the *chocolatier*, if you can believe it).

TIP

Be aware that you may have to add C:\Chocolatey to your system's search path to launch those installed software applications from the command line.

▼ TRY IT YOURSELF

Installing Software with OneGet

In this Try It Yourself exercise, I'll give you a chance to get your "sea legs" in finding, installing, and running packages from the different default package sources. If at all possible, perform these experiments on a test system. In my test lab, I have a Windows 8.1 virtual machine for which I created a pre-**OneGet** snapshot. Whenever I need to reset my environment, I simply restore the snapshot. Easy peasy.

1. Honestly, the vast majority of the packages in the PSModule provider repository are developer or PowerShell DSC related. Nonetheless, why not browse the repo's feed?

   ```
   Find-Package -ProviderName psmodule | Out-GridView
   ```

2. Now let's do the same thing, this time focusing on *all* packages:

   ```
   Find-Package -ProviderName chocolatey | Out-GridView
   ```

   Remember that you can do an **Out-File** to export the package feed to a text file, or **Export-CSV** to get the data in an Excel-friendly CSV format.

3. Just for grins, why don't we see how many packages are available via **Chocolatey**?

   ```
   Find-Package -ProviderName chocolatey | Measure-Object
   ```

   Frankly, you can get a more reader-friendly (and more informative) description of packages by browsing the **Chocolatey** package gallery at http://chocolatey.org/packages. Figure 17.6 shows you the front page.

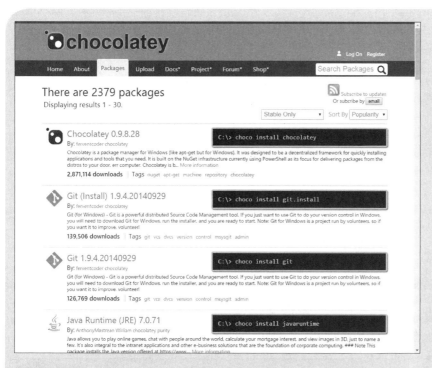

FIGURE 17.6
The Chocolatey package gallery website makes it a snap to browse the most popular and stable packages.

4. You should see that the **Chocolatey** engine itself is the most popular, if not one of the most popular, packages. Because **OneGet** in the WMF 5 Preview is so wonky and unpredictable, let's go ahead and install the **Chocolatey** package manager itself so you can "kick the tires" and see how it works when **Chocolatey** is used outside of **OneGet**.

5. Switch back to your elevated PowerShell console session and leverage the pipeline to find and install the **Chocolatey** package manager:

```
Get-Package -Name Chocolatey | Install-Package -Verbose
```

6. Good deal. Now let's use the **choco** client to install the uber-cool Sysinternals tools:

```
Choco install sysinternals
```

You should find that the **choco** client behaves very similarly to what we've been doing with **OneGet**. What's better with the **choco** client, in my humble opinion, is that **choco** gives you much more valuable metadata as it installs.

For instance, you should have noticed in the **choco** output that the Sysinternals command-line tools were installed to C:\Tools\sysinternals. The package/choco should also have told you that you might need to add the path to your **PATH** environment variable. Convenient!

7. Let's verify that the Sysinternals freeware tools suite has in fact been installed:

```
PS C:\> cd C:\tools\sysinternals
PS C:\tools\sysinternals> dir *.exe


    Directory: C:\tools\sysinternals


Mode                LastWriteTime         Length Name
----                -------------         ------ ----
-a----        4/28/2014    3:44 PM        380608 accesschk.exe
-a----        11/1/2006    2:06 PM        174968 AccessEnum.exe
-a----       11/14/2012   11:22 AM        479832 ADExplorer.exe
-a----       11/20/2007    1:25 PM       1049640 ADInsight.exe
-a----        11/1/2006    2:05 PM        150328 adrestore.exe
-a----        2/22/2011    3:18 PM        148856 Autologon.exe
-a----        9/11/2014    9:57 AM        593080 autoruns.exe
```

Sweet! If you've never used the Sysinternals tools yet, you're in for a treat. My favorites are as follows:

▶ **Bginfo:** Displays computer metadata as desktop wallpaper

▶ **Autoruns:** Shows you all the autostart processes (great for identifying malware)

▶ **Process Explorer:** A souped-up version of Windows Task Manager

▶ **Contig:** A command-line defrag tool that's great for compacting Microsoft Outlook email archives

Managing Providers and Packages

Recall that **OneGet** by default does not "trust" the **Chocolatey** repository. All this means from a practical perspective is that you receive an extra confirmation prompt when you attempt to install a package from **Chocolatey**.

Let's go ahead and use **Register-PackageSource** to trust **Chocolatey**:

```
Register-PackageSource –Name chocolatey –Location http://chocolatey.org/api/v2
➥-ProviderName chocolatey -Trusted -Verbose
```

You should now see that **Chocolatey** is trusted, validated, and registered on your local system:

```
PS C:\> Get-PackageSource

Name                    ProviderName   IsTrusted  IsRegistered IsValidated
----                    ------------   ---------  ------------ -----
chocolatey              Chocolatey     True       True         True
PSGallery               PSModule       False      True         False
MSPSGallery             PSModule       True       True         False
```

Upgrading Installed Packages

Do you remember what the most popular PowerShell verb is? That's correct: **Get**. To that point, let's use **Get-Package** to retrieve a list of installed packages:

```
PS C:\> Get-Package | Format-Table -AutoSize

Name                                                   Version
----                                                   -------
VMware Tools                                           9.6.2.1688356
Microsoft Visual C++ 2008 Redistributable - x64 9.0.30729.6161 9.0.30729.6161
Microsoft Visual C++ 2008 Redistributable - x86 9.0.30729.6161 9.0.30729.6161
Microsoft Visual C++ 2008 Redistributable - x86 9.0.30729.4148 9.0.30729.4148
Microsoft Silverlight                                  5.1.30514.0
7zip                                                   9.22.01.20130618
7zip.install                                           9.22.01.20130618
chocolatey                                             0.9.8.28
eagle                                                  7.1.0
putty                                                  0.63
putty.portable                                         0.63
sysinternals                                           2014.09.11
tweetdeck                                              1.3
winrar                                                 5.11
xActiveDirectory                                       2.1
```

"Gee, Tim, you installed multiple versions of the C++ 2008 redistributable via **OneGet**?" Ah, no, I didn't. Let's look at the same ouput without the **–AutoSize** business:

```
PS C:\> Get-Package

Name        Version     Status     ProviderName    Source       Summary
----        -------     ------     ------------    ------       -------
VMware...   9.6.2.168...Installed  msi             C:\Users\Trai...
Micros...   9.0.30729...Installed  msi             c:\0cb7fd8a45...
Micros...   9.0.30729...Installed  msi             c:\518e76f3cc...
Micros...   9.0.30729...Installed  msi             c:\27ec1fb40f...
```

```
Micros... 5.1.30514.0  Installed    msi          c:\5886070e61...
7zip      9.22.01.2... Installed    Chocolatey   C:\Chocolatey... 7-Zip ...
7zip.i... 9.22.01.2... Installed    Chocolatey   C:\Chocolatey... 7-Zip ...
chocol... 0.9.8.28     Installed    Chocolatey   C:\Chocolatey... Chocol...
eagle     7.1.0        Installed    Chocolatey   C:\Chocolatey... The EA...
putty     0.63         Installed    Chocolatey   C:\Chocolatey... PuTTY ...
putty.... 0.63         Installed    Chocolatey   C:\Chocolatey... PuTTY ...
sysint... 2014.09.11   Installed    Chocolatey   C:\Chocolatey... Sysint...
tweetdeck 1.3          Installed    Chocolatey   C:\Chocolatey... tweetdeck
winrar    5.11         Installed    Chocolatey   C:\Chocolatey... WinRAR...
xActiv... 2.1          Installed    PSModule     https://www.p... Module...
```

Look at the **ProviderName** property. I'm not sure if this is a prerelease bug or if **OneGet** is behaving as designed, but I'm getting some "bleedthrough" from the MSI provider for apps that I installed outside of PowerShell and **OneGet**. Oh well.

NOTE

As of this writing, the **OneGet** module does not include an **Upgrade-** cmdlet. Your best bet is to periodically query the latest versions of your target applications from the repositories, and simply run **Install-Package –Force** to overwrite the old version.

TIP

Caveat: I've seen some **Chocolatey** packages that are nothing more than batch files that invoke the application's graphical user interface (GUI) installer. So, you may be able to upgrade the app from the app's UI. Be mindful that simply downloading and installing an updated program version from the vendor itself may or may not patch your **Chocolatey**-based installation because, as you've seen a lot this hour, **Chocolatey** packages often install the program files outside of the traditional locations.

The **Chocolatey** package manager itself can be used in conjunction with the **ChocolateyGUI** package to make package upgrades and uninstallations easier. First install the GUI either by using **OneGet** or the **Chocolatey** command-line tool if you want to go that route:

```
Find-Package -Name chocolateygui | Install-Package
Choco install chocolateygui
```

Now you can find the ChocolateyGUI icon in the Start menu/Start screen, fire up the application, and enjoy the GUI (gooey?) chocolatey goodness! Yes, I'm a goofball. Figure 17.7 shows the **ChocolateyGUI** interface.

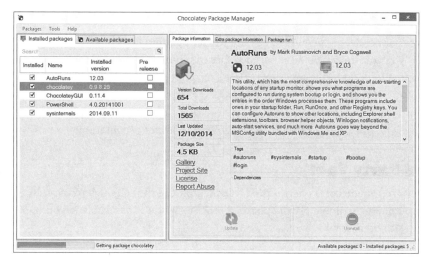

FIGURE 17.7
ChocolateyGUI is a graphical front-end to the Chocolatey package management system. Notice that we can perform package updates or uninstalls with a simple button click.

Removing Packages

The **OneGet** module includes **Uninstall-Package**, which we can leverage to remove any installed package:

```
Uninstall-Package -Name TweetDeck
```

As you can see in Figure 17.8, some "chocolatiers" simply rely on the vendor's own uninstallation routine in some cases. For instance, in Figure 17.8, you can see that I can perform an uninstallation of **ChocolateyGUI** directly by running the GUI uninstaller from the Start menu. To each his or her own.

Hosting a Private OneGet Repository

Our final subject concerns the idea of hosting your own private package repository. Perhaps your company finds it unacceptable to trust public repositories such as **Chocolatey**. Or maybe your developers inform you that they can create packages themselves that install software according to IT department policy.

As of this writing, you can deploy your own private **OneGet** repo in two ways. A detailed treatment of these is far beyond the scope of this book. Nevertheless, I want to get you pointed in the proper direction at any rate.

Using a File Share

Assuming that you or your colleagues can leverage the **NuGet** building tools directly to build .nupkg package files, you can simply pop the package files into a network shared folder and run **Register-PackageSource** to point to the repository. Here's a sample command:

```
Register-PackageSource -ProviderName chocolatey myrepo -Location \\server\share
```

In this way, you can create one or more ad hoc software repositories for use internally.

Using a Third-Party Tool

The inedo company (http://inedo.com) offers a product called ProGet that enables you to host a potentially highly available, scalable private package repository that is accessible to you and your team by using a standard web browser.

ProGet free is community supported and intended for use by small teams. Inedo's ProGet Enterprise, which costs $395/year per server as of this writing, provides scalability and high availability and is targeted for larger teams that work in different sites.

NOTE

Some readers who are familiar with Ninite (https://ninite.com/) may think, "What value does **OneGet** and **Chocolatey** have over Ninite?" That's a fair question, and I have an answer.

If you're not familiar, Ninite is a free service from which you can automatically install software packages on your system. However, the chief differences that make **OneGet** a better solution are (a) with Ninite you're limited to a single, privately owned repository while PowerShell allows you to aggregate multiple repos, and (b) with Ninite you have no visibility into package behavior; whereas with **OneGet/NuGet** you can build and deploy your own software packages from scratch.

Summary

If this hour felt somewhat tentative, your intuition is correct. After all, the **OneGet** package management solution hasn't been formally released to the public as of the publication of this book. Nevertheless, I've given you a thorough grounding in the technology such that you can easily adapt as the Windows Powershell team continues to broaden and deepen **OneGet**'s capabilities.

In Hour 18, we examine another of the "big ticket" enterprise PowerShell features: Desired State Configuration, or DSC. As I stated earlier, OneGet is the easiest way to download and install DSC resources, so the next chapter's content gives you some much-appreciated practice with package management. Until then!

Q&A

Q. How can I figure out exactly where and how Chocolatey installed a package that I installed by using the Install-Package OneGet command?

A. You'll find that the vast majority of **Chocolatey** packages downloaded through **OneGet** are contained in one or more subdirectories of C:\Chocolatey.

Specifically, you should find a ChocolateyInstall.ps1 script file nested beneath C:\Chocolatey\lib for each installed software package. Right-click that **.ps1** file and open it in your favorite text editor or the PowerShell ISE.

Within that script file you'll find the installation instructions as dictated by the person who packaged the app in the first place. Some chocolatiers rely on the application's native GUI routine, whereas others take a truly command-line approach.

Q. Why should I care about command-line software installation? What's wrong with the software vendor's GUI installation routine?

A. I find that some GUI installers are better than others. For instance, it's infuriating to me that Oracle includes third-party software along with its own Java Runtime Environment installer.

When you run packaged software from the command line, we can bypass those extra annoyances that tend to ride herd with GUI installers. Also, remember that anything we can do from the command line can be automated, resulting in a more efficient software experience. This proves especially helpful when your work centers in whole or in part on deploying software to users' computers.

Q. That Chocolatey client looks much more mature than OneGet. How do I find packages with choco?

A. That's easy to do. Let's say we needed the PuTTY SSH client and we wanted to install via **choco**. We would issue the following command:

```
PS C:\> choco list putty
jivkok.tools 1.1.0.7
kellyelton.devenvironment 1.0.0.10
kitty.portable 0.63.2.1
putty 0.63
putty.install 0.63
putty.portable 0.63
putty-d2ddw 2013.08.07
PuttyTray 0.63.021
```

Frankly, the **choco** output is formatted as nicely as **OneGet** does it. For instance, what you're seeing here aren't just package names, but package names and their corresponding version numbers *in two separate columns*. Not too obvious, to me, anyway.

Now let's imagine that we wanted to install Putty, 7-Zip, and Notepad++ simultaneously. We can do that in two lines of PowerShell:

```
$apps = @("putty", "7zip", "notepadplusplus")
$apps | foreach { chocolatey install $_. }
```

Workshop

For this hour's challenge exercise, perform the following three tasks that demonstrate your **OneGet** skills:

1. Pick out three useful packages by browsing the **Chocolatey** repository either online or directly through PowerShell.

2. Create a PowerShell .ps1 script file that installs the three packages. It's true that we don't cover PowerShell scripting until a bit later in this book, but I have confidence in your basic PowerShell skills and ability to research answers.

3. Test the PowerShell script by running it on a computer that does not contain the packages. Note that you might have to temporarily relax the script execution policy of your computer, like so:

   ```
   Set-ExecutionPolicy -ExecutionPolicy Unrestricted -Scope Process
   ```

4. Use **OneGet** to uninstall one of the three apps that you installed.

Quiz

1. Package repositories that you add to **OneGet** are trusted by default.

   a. True

   b. False

2. _____ is a solution-level package management tool that is aimed for use by software developers and package creators.

   a. NuGet

   b. OneGet

   c. Chocolatey

   d. apt-get

3. **OneGet** can be considered a package provider aggregator.

   a. True

   b. False

Answers

1. The correct answer is B. Trust is a big issue with downloadable software, of course. Although Microsoft appears to trust **Chocolatey** fully, that doesn't compel you to do so. You need to manually trust package providers in order for your computer to trust them.

2. The correct answer is A. **NuGet** is the system-level package manager that serves as the "engine" of **OneGet**. **OneGet** is the PowerShell module that gives us our core package management commands. **Chocolatey** is both a package manager, package browser, and software repository.

3. The correct answer is A. This is absolutely a true statement; **OneGet** is indeed a platform into which you can plug in package providers and associated software repositories from multiple sources.

Desired State Configuration Basics

What You'll Learn in This Hour:

▶ Historical background of DSC

▶ Basic tenets of DSC

▶ DSC authoring environment

▶ Configuring the DSC environment

▶ Writing your first configuration script

▶ A word on DSC push configuration

Desired State Configuration, also called DSC, is the marquee feature in Windows PowerShell v4 and later. Imagine being able to send configuration instructions to your servers such that, with no tedious mouse clicking on your part, the target servers simply (to quote Jean-Luc Picard from *Star Trek: The Next Generation*) "Make it so."

I'm not kidding, either. In this hour, you'll learn precisely what DSC is and how it works, and you'll see its value proposition with your own eyes. Many of my IT professional colleagues whisper that DSC may very well spell the future standard for Windows server configuration and administration. Let's make it so!

Historical Background of DSC

Windows PowerShell Principal Architect Jeffrey Snover wrote *The Monad Manifesto* in 2002, and in so doing outlined what he saw as the chief capabilities of a new command-line automation language for Windows.

Amazingly, Snover and his team at Microsoft realized every major point in that document. Specifically, with the Manifesto's fourth point, Monad Management Models, they describe the basic elements that the team ultimately delivered in Windows PowerShell v4.

DSC is a Windows PowerShell-based system configuration platform. Here's the scenario: You and/or your colleagues spend valuable hours manually configuring your Windows servers; I'm talking about tasks such as the following:

▶ Installing and configuring roles and features

▶ Installing and configuring other system software and services

▶ Deploying and maintaining file shares

▶ Managing Registry settings and environment variables

The preceding list barely scratches the surface of the myriad configuration events that must be performed on each server for that machine to be considered compliant by your organization.

However, if you have any degree of Windows systems administration experience, you know that "configuration drift" is a sad fact of life. Joe Administrator makes one setting, and then a week later Jane Administrator undoes said setting.

The configuration drift problem is all fun and games until questions of service level agreements (SLAs), licensure requirements, and industry/governmental regulations come knocking at your door, metaphorically speaking.

Long story short: DSC fills a need for us Windows server administrators, now more than ever before.

Competitive Landscape

Remember that Jeffrey Snover and the Windows PowerShell team are almost all longstanding experts in UNIX/Linux administration and systems programming. This fact should be patently obvious when you compare, say, the day-to-day operation of the Bash shell with how the Windows PowerShell command-line environment behaves.

To that point, there's no denying the fact that Snover & Co. took a leaf from the competition's playbooks with regard to this automated systems configuration framework "thing." Specifically, two market leaders in the systems configuration/automation space are also (partially) open source projects:

▶ Chef (http://www.chef.io)

▶ Puppet (http://puppetlabs.com)

Don't get too bent out of shape, though: Not only are Chef and Puppet compatible with Windows, but Microsoft Azure offers either configuration product as an option for their hosted virtual machines. Figure 18.1 shows a representative screenshot of Puppet.

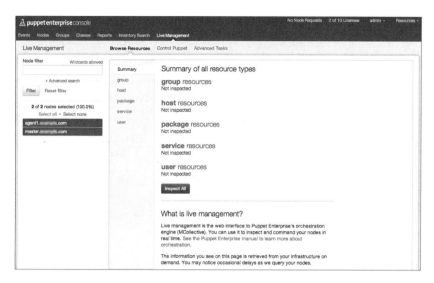

FIGURE 18.1
Puppet has a browser-based management console that makes it equally simple to autoconfigure Windows/
Linux servers.

Going further yet, we'll learn shortly that DSC can actually be extended to support the autoconfiguration and remediation of Linux/UNIX boxes in addition to Windows machines. It's a "New Microsoft," to be sure.

Finally, as cool as Puppet and Chef are as cross-platform configuration management products, they cost money to license for most business scenarios. By contrast, Windows PowerShell comes to you "free" with the cost of a Windows Server license.

One final note before we delve into DSC: Although it's possible to leverage DSC for desktop OS configuration, I'm cleaving to the most common DSC use case: server configuration. After all, most of our compliance requirements focus on how we've set up our infrastructure server computers as opposed to our users' desktop PCs.

Basic Tenets of DSC

To begin, you should understand that most DSC configuration involves using Windows PowerShell and the vendor-neutral Managed Object Format (MOF) in a declarative fashion. In programming, declarative code does not spell out exactly how the computer should complete a task. Instead, the code essentially tells the computer to "make it so" however it sees fit.

Structured Query Language (SQL) is a good example of a declarative data access language. When you run a complex **SELECT** statement, for instance, you leave it to the database itself to determine the system of index/row lookups it uses to satisfy the query results.

Likewise, in DSC, we start by describing how we'd like our servers to look in a standard Windows PowerShell configuration script. Take a look at Figure 18.2, and I'll explain how DSC works step by step.

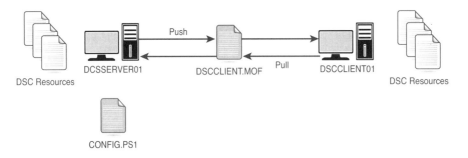

FIGURE 18.2
Windows PowerShell DSC architectural overview.

DSC Authoring Environment

As you saw in Figure 18.2, DSCSERVER01 represents our DSC authoring environment. It is on this box, which must be equipped with at least Windows Management Framework v4 or later, that we construct our configuration script.

The configuration script is a bread-and-butter Windows PowerShell file that contains the configuration instructions for one or several target systems. The configuration script is compiled into the vendor-neutral MOF and then transferred to the target systems for ingestion.

DSC Production Environment

A component of Windows Management Framework (WMF) 5 called the Local Configuration Manager (LCM) running on the target system is what receives the MOF and applies its configuration settings to the box.

DSC supports two modes for getting the MOF configuration file to the target computer. In the push model, we use the **Start-DSCConfiguration** cmdlet to initiate the MOF push.

In the pull model, the client computer polls an Internet Information Services (IIS) website running on your DSC deployment server and requests any MOF files that are specified for it.

In terms of query intervals, target nodes query the pull server every 30 minutes by default. In the push architecture, nodes reevaluate their MOF file settings every 15 minutes by default if the configuration file had autocorrection enabled. As with anything else in Windows PowerShell, you can edit those query defaults.

Finally, as you observed in Figure 18.2, something called "DSC resources" exist on both the authoring and production servers. We can consider DSC resources to be specialized Windows PowerShell modules that actually form the imperative "engine" that nodes use through their LCM to apply their desired state configurations.

Differences Between DSC and Group Policy

Some Windows systems administrators wonder, "What's the difference between DSC and Group Policy?" One difference is that DSC permanently "tattoos" the configuration settings of target nodes. You'll recall that once a Group Policy Object (GPO) no longer applies to a machine, those settings can revert to their pre-GPO values.

Another difference is that a single node can have only a single MOF file defining a particular configuration (installing and configuring IIS, for instance). By contrast, we can link multiple GPOs to each of the various Active Directory levels (site, domain, organizational unit, and local computer). Finally, GPOs grant management access principally to the computer's registry, while DSC MOF resources can "touch" any computer subsystem that's accessible by PowerShell and, by extension, the .NET Framework.

The bottom line is that DSC won't necessarily replace GPOs for systems configuration. Remember the focus with DSC, at least at this point, is to declaratively configure our servers such that "configuration drift" and deviation from compliance is no longer an issue for us.

Before we can test out DSC, we need to first prepare our environment.

Configuring the DSC Environment

Don't even think about testing, much less deploying, DSC unless all of the following are true:

▶ All participating computers have WMF 4.0 or later installed.

▶ All participating servers have Windows PowerShell remoting enabled.

▶ All Windows Server 2012 R2 and Windows 8.1 nodes have hotfix KB2883200 installed.

You can leverage Windows PowerShell to verify if that required hotfix has been applied to your system:

```
PS C:\> Get-HotFix -Id KB2883200

Source          Description     HotFixID       InstalledBy         InstalledOn
------          -----------     --------       -----------         -----------
DSCSERVER01     Update          KB2883200      COMPANY\trainer     9/30/2013
12:00:00AM
```

Windows PowerShell remoting is required because the deployment of DSC MOF files uses Web Services-Management / Windows Remote Management (WS-Man/WinRM).

A New Microsoft

In past years, Microsoft took a highly proprietary approach to how their own products interoperated (or didn't) with those of other vendors, especially open source community projects.

Jeffrey Snover went to great lengths to establish Microsoft corporate buy-in for interoperability, and this argument has paid huge dividends with cross-platform capabilities such as WS-Man, Windows Management Instrumentation / Common Information Model (WMI/CIM), and the MOF format. The idea that today we can use DSC to configure Linux computer was utterly inconceivable not too long ago.

You also need to enable the DSC bits on all participating nodes. (*Nodes* is a more descriptive term than *server* because technically DSC can be used in both server and desktop Windows versions.) From an elevated Windows PowerShell console prompt on a Windows Server box, you can run the following:

```
Install-WindowsFeature
```

Of course, we can also use Server Manager (on servers) or Windows Features (on clients) to enable DSC, as shown in Figure 18.3.

FIGURE 18.3
Here we enable Windows PowerShell DSC in Windows Server 2012 R2 (top) and in Windows 8.1 (bottom).

Loading Up DSC Resources

As of this writing, Microsoft gives us 12 in-box resources in WMF v4. These resources and their uses are as follows:

- ▶ **Archive**: Zipping and unzipping archives

- ▶ **Environment**: Managing environment variables

- ▶ **Group**: Managing local groups

- ▶ **Log**: Writes messages to the Microsoft-Windows-DSC/Analytic event log

- ▶ **Package**: Installs .msi or Setup.exe software

- ▶ **Registry**: Managing the computer and user Registry hives

- ▶ **Script**: Excellent as a "catchall" resource when you can't get what you need from an existing DSC resource

▶ **File**: Managing files and folders

▶ **WindowsProcess**: Controlling process objects

▶ **WindowsFeature**: Managing server roles and features

▶ **Service**: Controlling service objects

▶ **User**: Managing local users

If you run the following command:

```
Get-DSCResource | Select-Object { $_.parentpath }
```

you'll see that your built-in DSC resource folders are placed deep in the Windows\system32 hierarchy:

```
C:\Windows\System32\WindowsPowerShell\v1.0\Modules\<modulename>
```

That's all well and good, but when you need to install your own modules, you should place them in this path:

```
C:\Program Files\WindowsPowerShell\Modules
```

Specifically, you should place the unzipped resource folder directly inside Modules. For instance, in Figure 18.4, I show you where I placed the **xActiveDirectory** experimental module that I downloaded to my server via **OneGet**.

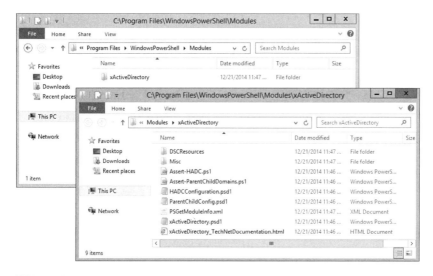

FIGURE 18.4
Here we see where to place additional DSC resources on a node's file system. Notice that a DSC resource looks and "feels" an awful lot like a traditional Windows PowerShell script module.

If your nodes are equipped with PowerShell v5 preview (which they shouldn't unless v5 has been finalized as of your reading this), I suggest you look for DSC resources by querying the repositories:

```
Get-Package -Name x*
```

The *x* prefix is used to denote prerelease or eXperimental resource packages. Therefore, you use them in production at your own risk.

DSC Resource Waves

Aside from **OneGet** repos, your best bet for discovering useful DSC resources are the DSC Resource Kit "waves" that are regularly released by the Windows PowerShell team. Each wave brings new resources to the table that allow you greater administrative control over more and more products. Sometimes you'll find that a newer wave release includes updated resources that supersede previously released versions. (The *x* in *experimental* is taken very seriously by the PowerShell community.)

Sadly, the DSC resource kit waves aren't presented in a strictly linear fashion, which can make it tricky figuring out what's what. To help you along, I'll pass on the links for the nine wave announcements that are extant as of this writing:

▶ **DSC ResKit Wave 1**: http://bit.ly/1wAZpXb

▶ **DSC ResKit Wave 2**: http://bit.ly/1wAZr15

▶ **DSC ResKit Wave 3**: http://bit.ly/1wAZpX0

▶ **DSC ResKit Wave 4**: http://bit.ly/1wAZolQ

▶ **DSC ResKit Wave 5**: http://bit.ly/1wAZmuq

▶ **DSC ResKit Wave 6**: http://bit.ly/1wAZnOU

▶ **DSC ResKit Wave 7**: http://bit.ly/1wAZnhQ

▶ **DSC ResKit Wave 8**: http://bit.ly/1wAZieb

▶ **DSC ResKit Wave 9**: http://bit.ly/1wAZnyi

Again, you simply download the resources, unzip them into the proper directory, and run **Get-DSCResource** to verify that they show up. Recall also that you need to install the resources on all participating nodes.

Writing Your First Configuration Script

Okay, it's time to start building out our DSC infrastructure, the first step of which is authoring our configuration script. Remember that although target nodes can apply only one MOF file for a given configuration, you can apply multiple MOFs to a single host as long as you don't have conflicting configuration definitions. I'm sure that, over time, the Windows PowerShell team will make it easier for administrators to manage these manifold MOF manifests (alliteration alert).

I want you to understand before we get started that creating the MOF files via a PowerShell configuration script represents only one possibility for creating the MOFs. If, perchance, you understood MOF syntax, there's nothing stopping you from creating your own MOFs from scratch using only a text editor.

In other words, we should start to see MOF authoring tools emerge from independent software vendors (ISVs) and the community at large as we progress over time. Welcome to the world of vendor neutrality and community-driven software architectures.

More About MOF Files

Remember that the MOF is not a Microsoft proprietary format, but instead is a vendor-neutral data representation format developed by the Distributed Management Task Force, of which Microsoft is a member.

MOF is used to define both management objects in CIM/WMI, and is also closely related to Web-Based Enterprise Management (WBEM) protocols such as WS-Man.

Figure 18.5 shows you what a typical MOF file looks like. I can't stress enough that DSC is a potentially vendor-neutral technology, and the tool that you use to create the MOF doesn't have to be Windows PowerShell. I submit that we'll see graphical user interface (GUI) MOF creation utilities for DSC not too long in the future; perhaps these tools already exist by the time you're reading this book.

```
1   Configuration SampleConfig1
2   {
3       Node "dscclient01"
4       {
5           File CopyScript
6           {
7               Ensure = "Present"
8               Type = "Directory"
9               SourcePath = "\\dscserver01\scripts"
10              DestinationPath = "C:\scripts"
11          }
12
13      }
14  }
15  SampleConfig1
```

FIGURE 18.5
A MOF file can be created by using PowerShell, another utility or programming language, or from scratch. As long as the MOF uses legal syntax, the method by which you produce the file is irrelevant.

Spend a moment studying the configuration script code in Figure 18.6, and I'll walk you through each line. I strongly suggest you write your DSC configuration script in the Windows PowerShell integrated scripting environment (ISE) so that you can take advantage of IntelliSense and the easy script execution controls.

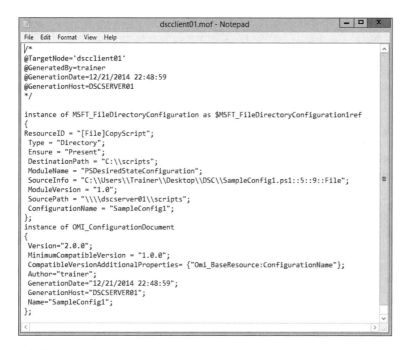

FIGURE 18.6
This DSC configuration script will produce one MOF file that is named after the specified target node.

▶ **Line 1**: We use the **Configuration** keyword in our script to denote a DSC configuration file. The configuration name is arbitrary.

▶ **Line 2**: The **Configuration** element is enclosed in top-level curly braces.

▶ **Line 3**: The **Node** keyword specifies the target node. In this first example, we're hard-coding the name of a Windows Server 2012 R2 host named dscclient01. In a later example, we'll parameterize this element with a variable so we can use one config script to target multiple nodes.

▶ **Line 4**: Indenting curly braces is optional, but an excellent practice to minimize the chance of our forgetting to close a script block and generate a runtime script failure.

▶ **Line 5**: The "meat and potatoes" of the configuration script are these subblocks. Here we specify the File DSC resource type, passing in an arbitrary name.

▶ **Line 6**: Another indented curly brace, this time enclosing the File resource script block.

▶ **Line 7**: Each DSC resource contains a number of named parameters. Like anything else in PowerShell, read the resource's online documentation to learn the acceptable values for each parameter. The **Ensure="Present"** line is ubiquitous in DSC configuration scripts, in my experience. This ensures that the policy is enforced.

▶ **Lines 8-10**: Here we plug in the details for our File DSC resource declarations. What we're doing is copying the scripts shared folder on my deployment server to a local path on the target node. As of this writing, I needed to add the source and destination node computer accounts to the shared folder's discretionary access control list (DACL) to make a UNC path work.

▶ **Lines 11–14**: Here we close up all the script blocks.

▶ **Line 15**. This is an optional line in which we call the configuration. That way we actually execute the Configuration block when we run the script in the Windows PowerShell ISE.

When you're ready, run the entire configuration script. If all goes well, you'll see output that is similar to this:

```
PS C:\Users\Trainer> C:\Users\Trainer\Desktop\DSC\SampleConfig1.ps1


    Directory: C:\Users\Trainer\SampleConfig1


Mode             LastWriteTime        Length Name
----             -------------        ------ ----
-a----           12/22/2014   8:23 AM   1736 dscclient01.mof
```

You'll note that Windows PowerShell does a couple things when you run the DSC configuration script:

▶ Creates a directory in the root of the C: drive with the same name as the .ps1 script file

▶ Creates one MOF for each node referenced in the script; the MOF files are named with the node's hostname

Customizing the Local Configuration Manager

Earlier in this hour, I told you that all DSC-enabled Windows nodes have a client component called the Local Configuration Manager (LCM) that is installed as part of WMF v4.

We can (and probably should) push a separate configuration script to our target nodes to customize the deployment parameters. First, let's run **Get-DscLocalConfigurationManager** to see what's what on my dscserver01 machine:

```
PS C:\> Get-DscLocalConfigurationManager

ActionAfterReboot               : ContinueConfiguration
AllowModuleOverWrite            : False
CertificateID                   :
ConfigurationDownloadManagers   : {}
ConfigurationID                 :
ConfigurationMode               : ApplyAndMonitor
ConfigurationModeFrequencyMins  : 15
Credential                      :
DebugMode                       : False
DownloadManagerCustomData       :
DownloadManagerName             :
LCMCompatibleVersions           : {1.0, 2.0}
LCMState                        : Ready
LCMVersion                      : 2.0
MaxPendingConfigRetryCount      :
StatusRetentionTimeInDays       : 7
PartialConfigurations           : {}
RebootNodeIfNeeded              : False
RefreshFrequencyMins            : 30
RefreshMode                     : PUSH
ReportManagers                  : {}
ResourceModuleManagers          : {}
PSComputerName                  :
```

Some of the LCM parameters are more important than others. The **ConfigurationMode** parameter tells the node what to do in terms of how it applies and refreshes DSC configurations. The
options here are as follows:

▶ **Apply**: Applies the configuration once and then doesn't check for an update or refresh
again (one-time application, in other words).

▶ **ApplyAndMonitor**: Applies the configuration and continues to validate that the node is in
compliance with the policy. If configuration drift occurs, the node does nothing.

▶ **ApplyAndAutoCorrect**: Applies the configuration, periodically checks for compliance, and
reapplies the configuration if something changes within the scope of active configurations.

Note also the **RefreshFrequencyMins** parameter. In push mode, the node checks for DSC compliance every 30 minutes. This may be far too frequent for your business needs, so let's deploy a
new set of LCM settings to our localhost and dscclient01 nodes.

Once again, take a look at our script shown in Figure 18.7, and I'll walk you through selected
parts:

```
 1  Configuration SetupLCM
 2  {
 3      param
 4      (
 5          [string[]]$NodeName = $env:computername
 6      )
 7
 8      LocalConfigurationManager
 9      {
10          ConfigurationModeFrequencyMins = 240
11          ConfigurationMode = 'ApplyAndAutoCorrect'
12          RebootNodeIfNeeded = 'True'
13          RefreshMode = 'PUSH'
14      }
15  }
16
17  SetupLCM -NodeName ("dscserver01","dscclient01")
18
```

FIGURE 18.7
By deploying an LCM configuration, we can take fine-grained control over how DSC policies are evaluated and applied by target nodes.

▶ **Lines 3–5**: These lines create an input parameter for our LCM script. Note that the **$NodeName** parameter is defined as a string array, [], which makes it a snap to target multiple nodes without having to repeat code blocks in the script file.

▶ **Line 10**: Here we specify a 4-hour refresh interval for the LCM policy refresh mode.

▶ **Line 17**: Again for convenience, we run the configuration in-line with the code, specifying two target nodes by hostname. Of course, you can import the script into your runspace by using dot sourcing. However, I like the convenience of calling the function directly in the script file. Your mileage may vary, as I've said in this book about a hundred times before.

▶   An exhaustive discussion of how to import scripts into your runspace using dot sourcing is included in Hour 19, "Introduction to Windows PowerShell Scripting."

When you run the LCM config script, you wind up with a single "meta" MOF regardless of how many nodes you target in the script. Likewise, we use a different cmdlet to apply an LCM script: **Set-DscLocalConfigurationManager**. The -**Path** parameter points to the directory that contains our LCM script:

```
Set-DscLocalConfigurationManager -Path "C:\SetupLCM"
```

Let's do a Try It Yourself exercise so that you can shore up your Windows PowerShell skills and see how DSC works with your own eyes.

Creating and Pushing a DSC Configuration

In this Try It Yourself exercise, you'll apply much of the PowerShell skills you've accrued through-out the book to apply a specific configuration to a target node.

Specifically, you'll configure a Windows Server 2012 R2 member server named dscclient01 to keep the Internet Information Services (IIS) web server installed and the default website stopped.

We'll start by using **OneGet** to download and install the **xWebAdministration** custom DSC resource module. Next we'll author our configuration script and push it to a target node. Finally, we'll verify that the configuration "took" by intentionally producing configuration drift and testing autocorrection. If you don't have WMF v5 installed on your nodes, go with v4 and simply down-load the **xWebAdministration** DSC resource package from TechNet (http://bit.ly/13VAcvz).

1. On your DSC authoring server (dscserver01 in my case), fire up an elevated PowerShell v5 session and install the **xWebAdministration** package:

```
Find-Package -Name "xWebAdministration" | Install-Package -Verbose
```

Remember that you need to run this command on all DSC nodes, which means both my authoring server as well as my dscclient01.company.pri target node.

You'll also want to verify that the DSC resource has been installed in the proper location on disk:

```
PS C:\Program Files\WindowsPowerShell\Modules> dir

    Directory: C:\Program Files\WindowsPowerShell\Modules

Mode            LastWriteTime         Length Name
----            -------------         ------ ----
d-----     12/22/2014  12:49 PM              xWebAdministration
```

2. Now open an elevated ISE instance and create a new .ps1 script file named **WebServerConfig.ps1**. Check out Figure 18.8, and I'll walk you through the most important code lines, as has become my habit:

```
1  configuration SetupIIS
2  {
3      param
4      (
5          [string[]]$NodeName = 'localhost'
6      )
7
8      Import-DscResource -Module xWebAdministration
9
10     Node $NodeName
11     {
12         # Install the IIS server role
13         WindowsFeature IIS
14         {
15             Ensure        = "Present"
16             Name          = "Web-Server"
17         }
18         # Stop the Default Web Site website
19         xWebsite DefaultSite
20         {
21             Ensure        = "Present"
22             Name          = "Default Web Site"
23             State         = "Stopped"
24             PhysicalPath  = "C:\inetpub\wwwroot"
25             DependsOn     = "[WindowsFeature]IIS"
26         }
27     }
28 }
29 SetupIIS -NodeName ("dscserver01", "dscclient01")
```

FIGURE 18.8
Our DSC configuration script ensures that IIS is installed and that the Default Web Site website is stopped.

Line 5: Once again, we parameterize the **Node** name to make the script more flexible.

Line 8: This is a bit of "smoke and mirrors." We need to run **Import-DscResource** to load our custom DSC resource into the runspace. However, this is a "dynamic keyword" and is not an honest-to-goodness PowerShell cmdlet.

Lines 13–17: Here we invoke the built-in **WindowsFeature** resource to ensure that IIS is installed on the target node.

Lines 19–25: Now we call our **xWebSite** custom DSC resource to stop the default website.

Line 25: The **DependsOn** property is helpful when a configuration setting will work only if another one is active. Logically, then, we understand that we can stop the default website only if there exists an IIS web server to begin with.

Line 29: Modify the call to the configuration to target your own machines.

3. Run your WebServerConfig.ps1 script by pressing **F5** in the integrated scripting environment (ISE) and verify that PowerShell created two MOF files in a separate directory named after the script file.

4. When you're ready, unleash the proverbial hounds and apply the new configuration by running **Start-DscConfiguration**:

```
Start-DscConfiguration -Path "C:\SetupIIS"
```

5. Because PowerShell runs DSC configuration pushes as background jobs, we can use traditional syntax to check on job status:

```
PS C:\> Receive-Job -id 7 -Keep


PSComputerName
--------------
dscclient01
dscserver01

```

Cool. No errors on my end. How has everything gone in your neck of the woods?

6. Connect to one of your target modes and see whether you can start the IIS Manager. If so, is the default website stopped? Figure 18.9 demonstrates my dscclient01 machine's compliance.

FIGURE 18.9
I'm just going to go ahead and say it: DSC rocks! Here we see the configuration applied to my dscclient01 member server.

7. Use Windows PowerShell on one of your target nodes to start the default website. Of course, this will produce configuration drift. (If you haven't configured your LCM to perform autocorrection, go back and do that now.)

```
Start-Website -Name "Default Web Site"
```

8. If you want, you can simply wait for the next DSC LCM refresh interval to test whether your server turned the default website back off. Alternatively, and perhaps more conveniently, we can force a manual update:

```
Update-DscConfiguration
```

The update will once again exist as a configuration background job. Note also that you can try **Get-DscConfigurationStatus** to review a node's current relationship to DSC.

9. Surprise! You should find that the **Update-DscConfiguration** job fails:

```
PS C:\> Receive-Job -Name Job4 -Keep
No attempt was made to get a configuration from the pull server because LCM
RefreshMode is currently set to Push.
    + CategoryInfo          : NotSpecified:
(root/Microsoft/...gurationManager:String) [], CimException
    + FullyQualifiedErrorId : MI RESULT 1
    + PSComputerName        : localhost
```

Here's the deal: DSC push mode is great for test/demo situations because it's easy to set up. However, we'll have to run **Start-DscConfiguration** again from the authoring computer to refresh this policy. It's only in a pull server scenario that nodes have the ability to refresh their policies. This makes sense because in a client refresh, we need some server from which the client can check to verify it has the correct policies applied.

A Word on DSC Push Configuration

Due to space constraints in this book, I'll simply give you the barebones, "need-to-know" information regarding setting up a DSC pull server. Let's do that in a stepwise fashion, covering the highest-level steps:

1. Download and install the **xPSDesiredStateConfiguration** custom DSC resource from the TechNet Script Center or by using **OneGet**.

2. Create and deploy your pull server configuration script. The recipe I recommend for your config script comes to us courtesy of the Windows PowerShell team directly: http://bit. ly/1ARl7pc.

3. Create and deploy an LCM configuration script. You can find an excellent example at Pwrshell.net (http://bit.ly/1ARmlAJ).

These settings are important because we change the configuration mode from push to pull and we specify the URL of the pull server's web service. We also specify how long the client waits before updating its DSC policies.

The communication between the node and the web service occurs over HTTP or HTTPS, depending on your authentication requirements. That's an important point, actually; you want to do what you can to ensure that your nodes are pulling configuration from legitimate DSC pull servers. It would be a very bad day indeed if a malicious individual stood up a bogus pull server and borked up your DSC client nodes in the absence of Secure Sockets Layer / Transport Layer Security (SSL/TLS) server authentication.

Summary

This was an awesome hour of training, wasn't it? I hope you're as stoked about DSC as I am. I don't know about you, but I can't stand manually (re)configuring servers. Declaring how a server "should" look and letting DSC take care of maintaining compliance to that configuration is plain old awesome.

In Hour 19 we'll stay within the ISE because it's finally time for us to take charge of Windows PowerShell scripting. (And here you never thought you'd be a programmer.)

Q&A

Q. I know that many PowerShell cmdlets have a -WhatIf flag that allows you to test a cmdlet before it runs. Is there a command or parameter we can use to verify that DSC is functioning on a node?

A. Yes, indeed. You'll want to run **Test-DscConfiguration -Verbose** to instruct Windows PowerShell to process all of its DSC scripts; the output returns True if all tests pass.

Q. Will you please look at my script? I ran the following two lines of code:

```
PS C:> .\LCMConfig.ps1
PS C:> SetupLCM -NodeName "dscclient01"
```

and got a bunch of red error text, as shown in Figure 18.10. What's the problem?

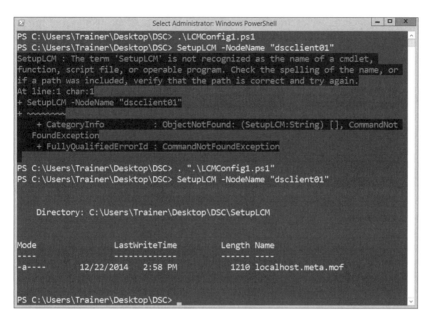

FIGURE 18.10
You need to understand the implications of "dot sourcing" your Windows PowerShell scripts.

A. The dot-slash (.\) notation simply tells PowerShell to run the present command from the current working directory and nothing more. This means that running a PowerShell script in this way runs the code contained inside the script but removes any functions, variables, and so forth from the session immediately thereafter.

Dot sourcing occurs when you type a period (.) and then type a partial or full path to a PowerShell script. (Don't forget to put quotes around the script path, including the dot slash.) The key difference with dot sourcing is that any objects defined inside the script persist in the user's current runspace. This allows us to run the DSC configuration script manually as was depicted in Figure 18.10.

Q. What is the suggested configuration refresh frequency for DSC?

A. How you configure your nodes' LCM component, and particularly the **ConfigurationFrequencyMins** property value, depends entirely on how much tolerance for configuration drift you have.

DSC network traffic is relatively low compared to, say, Group Policy. However, many Windows administrators are cool with setting refresh to 48 hours because the likelihood that a server will fall out of compliance may not be particularly high.

Workshop

Create a DSC configuration file that performs the following two tasks:

- ▶ Ensures that the Shutdown Event Tracker is enabled
- ▶ Ensures that the Google Chrome web browser is installed

The only hint I'll provide is that you need both the Registry built-in DSC resource and the xChrome custom resource to complete the configuration.

Quiz

1. You'd like to see what options are available for the **WindowsFeature** DSC resource. Which of the following commands accomplishes that goal?

   a. Get-Package

   b. Get-DscResource

   c. Get-Job

   d. Get-DscLocalConfigurationManager

2. The **UpdateDscConfiguration** cmdlet can be used only in DSC push scenarios.

   a. True

   b. False

3. A DSC authoring server running WMF 4.0 can push a configuration to a server running WMF 5.0.

   a. True

   b. False

Answers

1. The correct answer is B. Here is a run of the **WindowsFeature** DSC resource properties from my Windows Server 2012 R2 domain controller:

```
PS C:\> (Get-DscResource -Name WindowsFeature).Properties

Name                        PropertyType          IsMandatory Values
----                        ------------          ----------- ------
Name                        [string]              True {}
Credential                  [PSCredential]        False {}
DependsOn                   [string[]]            False {}
Ensure                      [string]              False {Absent, Present}
IncludeAllSubFeature        [bool]                False {}
LogPath                     [string]              False {}
Source                      [string]              False {}
```

Remember that you can run **Get-Command -module PSDesiredStateConfiguration** to retrieve a list of all DSC commands.

2. The correct answer is B. **Update-DscConfiguration** refreshes the target node only when a DSC pull server is online and available.

3. The correct answer is A. Remember that backward compatibility is a priority for the Windows PowerShell team. To use DSC, all your nodes must have the DSC bits available, which means that your Powershell version is 4 or 5 and your host operating system is Windows Server 2012/R2 or Windows 8/8.1.

Introduction to Windows PowerShell Scripting

What You'll Learn in This Hour:

- ▶ Managing execution policy
- ▶ Writing our first script: The user profile
- ▶ Writing a PowerShell function
- ▶ Adding programming logic
- ▶ Running scripts
- ▶ Pointers to master PowerShell scripting

In this hour, many of the PowerShell concepts that we've sort of taken for granted thus far have finally come home to roost, as it were. For example, at times I've had you chance the script execution policy on your system, but I haven't explained exactly what execution policy is.

Likewise, we've spent time in the integrated scripting environment (ISE), but haven't taken advantage of useful time-savers such as snippets and comment-based help.

To be sure, PowerShell scripting is a subject that is worthy of its own book. However, you'll learn enough about it in this hour of training that you'll find yourself doing stuff with Windows PowerShell that you never previously thought you could do. Are you excited? I am. Let's go.

Managing Execution Policy

Have you ever double-clicked a .ps1 PowerShell script file? If you did, you'll observe that the default association Windows has with PowerShell scripts is Windows Notepad. Try it for yourself and see.

The reason for this default file type association (which can be changed in a trivially easy fashion, so don't think that this represents bulletproof script security by any means) is to prevent a user from inadvertently running PowerShell code by attempting to open a script file for simple reading or editing.

Script Execution Options

Script execution policy is, like the .ps1 default file type association, not necessarily a security measure as it is a way to prevent accidental or unintentional script execution. Following are our execution policy options:

▶ **Restricted**: No PowerShell scripts can run, period. This is the default execution policy in Windows 8, Windows 8.1, and Windows Server 2012. I show you what happens if you try to run a PowerShell script under Restricted execution policy in Figure 19.1.

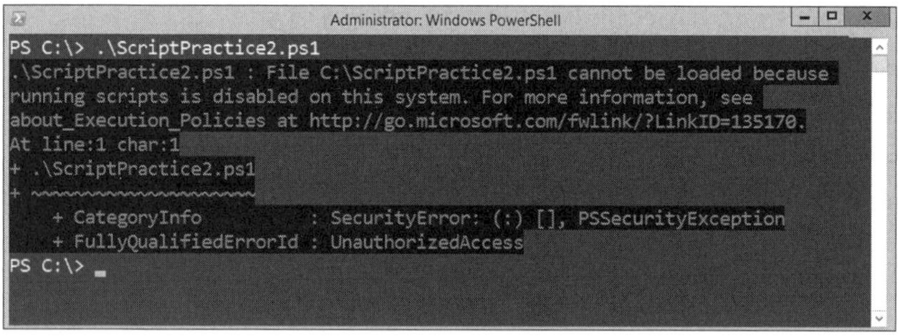

FIGURE 19.1
The Restricted script execution policy globally denies PowerShell script execution on that system.

▶ **AllSigned**: Local and remote scripts are allowed to run, provided they are signed by a trusted certificate authority.

▶ **RemoteSigned**: Local unsigned scripts can run, but remote scripts, including scripts downloaded from LAN servers or the Internet, cannot run unless they are properly signed. This is the default script execution policy in Windows Server 2012 R2.

▶ **Unrestricted**: Any scripts can run, whether local or remote, signed or unsigned.

▶ **Bypass**: Any script can run because Bypass, well, bypasses the execution policy environment. This option is good when you have PowerShell scripts nested in a larger application and you need them to be able to run successfully and quietly.

▶ **Undefined**: Effectively sets the computer's default execution policy to whatever default is relevant to the current operating system.

Viewing and Setting the Execution Policy

We use **Get-ExecutionPolicy** to retrieve the local system's script execution policy, and we use **Set-ExecutionPolicy** to set it. I show you both of these in a neat expanded view in Figure 19.2. The IntelliSense feature of the ISE is one of its biggest productivity advantages, especially when you combine IntelliSense with tab completion.

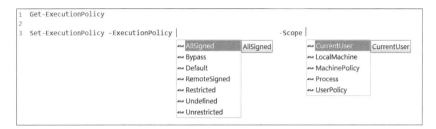

FIGURE 19.2
The Restricted script execution policy globally denies PowerShell script execution on that system.

CAUTION

I think it bears repeating that script execution policy can be changed with a simple run of **Set-ExecutionPolicy**. Even standard Windows users can run this cmdlet to disable execution policy. Therefore, this feature isn't a method for hardening your PowerShell environment. Instead, it's a way to prevent you or one of your colleagues from unintentionally damaging your network environment by running a script by accident.

A Question of Scope

You probably noticed the -**Scope** parameter of **Set-ExecutionPolicy** in Figure 19.2. Here's the deal with its options enumeration:

▶ **Process**: The execution policy change affects only the current PowerShell session. When you close the window, the policy is reset to a higher precedence scope

▶ **CurrentUser**: The policy change affects the current user. If the user logs off the system and another user logs on, the first user's execution policy is reset

▶ **LocalMachine**: The policy change affects all users of the current computer. This is the default scope if you do not override in your **Set-ExecutionPolicy** statement

Writing Our First Script: The User Profile

The profile script is a .ps1 script file that runs every time you start a new PowerShell session.

TIP

I like to use my PowerShell profile as a way to custom fit my environment for my servers. For instance, I have an **Add-PSSnapin** line in my SharePoint Server computer profile scripts to autoload the SharePoint Server 2013 cmdlets. The profile script is also a handy place to tuck your custom aliases, functions—what have you.

First, query the **$profile** automatic variable to see whether you have an active profile on the system. Although the output points to a file named Microsoft.PowerShell_profile.ps1, a quick check in your user account's Documents folder should reveal absolutely nothing. Figure 19.3 shows you the output on my dscserver01 server.

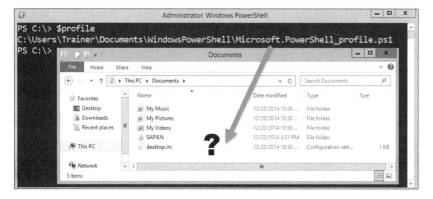

FIGURE 19.3
The $profile automatic variable is populated with a file path, but there ain't nothin' there by default in File Explorer!

Frankly, I'm being a bit dramatic with all of that. A simple run of **Test-Path $profile** returns either True or False; this is perhaps a more time-efficient way to accomplish the same goal.

Creating Our User Profile Script

Alright. Let's use the **New-Item** cmdlet along with the **$profile** automatic variable to create our profile script:

```
PS C:\> New-Item -Type File -Path $PROFILE -Force


    Directory: C:\Users\Trainer\Documents\WindowsPowerShell


Mode                LastWriteTime     Length Name
----                -------------     ------ ----
-a----      12/22/2014  10:05 PM          0 Microsoft.PowerShell_profile.ps1

PS C:\>
```

Now that the **$profile** variable actually maps to an empty file, we can run the following command to pop open the script file in good old Windows Notepad:

```
PS C:\>notepad $PROFILE
```

In Figure 19.4, you can see a very simple example of a "loaded" profile script. In it, I (a) change my directory location, (b) clear the console screen, and (c) define a custom alias.

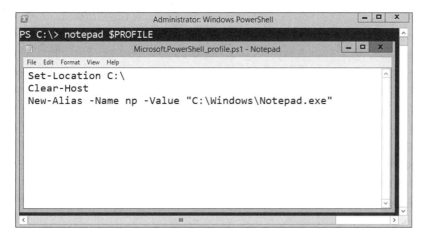

FIGURE 19.4
You can completely customize your Windows PowerShell console shell environment by populating your user profile script.

TIP

As you gain more experience with writing PowerShell functions, you'll probably want to put the most commonly used ones inside your profile script as well.

PowerShell Profile Gotchas

The first thing you need to remember about profiles is that only the remote profile is loaded (scoped at LocalMachine) when you use an **Enter-PSSession** remote session.

The paths you see in the previous code listing are likely different from your paths because I ran that command from a Vmware Workstation-based virtual machine (VM) and not a physical computer.

If you need to run a custom profile script during remote sessions, your "to do" actions involve registering to use **Register-PSSessionConfiguration**, specifying a profile script with the **-StartupScript** parameter, like so:

```
Register-PSSessionConfiguration -Name RemoteProfile -StartupScript $PSHome\
➥myprofile.ps1
```

You then make sure to invoke the new session configuration in your connection string:

```
Enter-PSSession -Computername "server01" -ConfigurationName "RemoteProfile"
```

The other "gotcha" that you should be aware of is that PowerShell actually supplies six (count 'em) different profiles. To get a feel for this, fire up the PowerShell ISE. Did the ISE respect your console profile settings? No, it did not. Look at the following output from my Windows PowerShell ISE console pane:

```
PS C:\> $profile
C:\Users\Trainer\Documents\WindowsPowerShell\Microsoft.PowerShellISE_profile.ps1

PS C:\>
```

What the heck is going on here? You should pipe **$profile** to **Get-Member** and see how many members are included in this object. For now, let's force **$profile** to give up all its secrets:

```
PS C:\> $PROFILE | Format-List -Force

AllUsersAllHosts        : C:\Windows\System32\WindowsPowerShell\v1.0\profile.ps1
AllUsersCurrentHost     : C:\Windows\System32\WindowsPowerShell\v1.0\Microsoft.
                          PowerShell_profile.ps1
CurrentUserAllHosts     : C:\Users\Trainer\Documents\WindowsPowerShell\profile.
                          ps1
CurrentUserCurrentHost  : C:\Users\Trainer\Documents\WindowsPowerShell\
                          Microsoft.PowerShell_profile.ps1
Length                  : 77

PS C:\>
```

Aha! We see that PowerShell stores "placeholders" for profiles depending on their desired scope. Therefore, if we have need to create "one profile to rule them all" on a shared server that applies the included settings to any user of a box regardless of their host application, you'd create that profile like this:

```
New-Item -Type File -Path $profile.AllUsersAllHosts -Force
```

Alternatively, you might want to create a central profile for your own use on your administrative workstation that, again, is applied no matter which host app you're using (the console, the ISE, or another utility):

```
New-Item -Type File -Path $profile.CurrentUserAllHosts -Force
```

CAUTION

One thing I'll warn you about is that troubleshooting multiple (potentially conflicting) profiles can be tricky, especially on shared server environments with multiple users and multiple hosts. My best advice to you is to keep your PowerShell profile deployment as simple as possible.

Writing a PowerShell Function

A function is a named block of code that accomplishes a particular task. Functions make your work more modular because you can write a function once and then run it as many times as you want.

In Windows PowerShell, a function works like a function from any other programming language with the exception that PowerShell functions consist of one or more Windows PowerShell statements.

Introducing Snippets

Fire up the Windows PowerShell ISE and save a new script file. Next, right-click inside the script pane and select **Start Snippets** from the shortcut menu.

Snippets are premade "stub" code blocks that are great time-savers for common PowerShell scripting tasks. Notice that in the snippets list, PowerShell offers both simple and advanced function snippets. We'll focus on the simple one in this hour.

Figure 19.5 shows our first function, called **Get-Hello**. I wrote this function by starting from the simple function snippet.

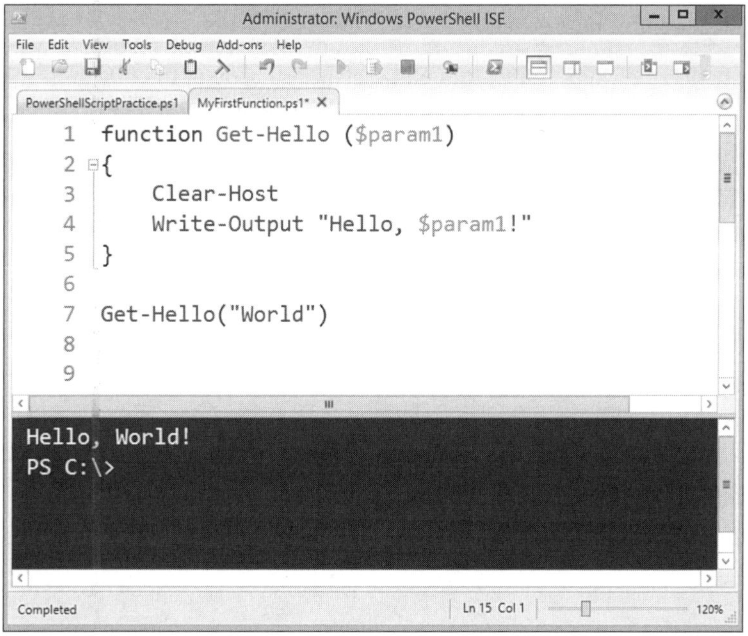

FIGURE 19.5
Our first Windows PowerShell function. This function clears the host console screen and states the obvious to any new programmer.

NOTE

Adding on to the ISE

The PowerShell team did users a solid by giving us the Windows PowerShell ISE for free with the Windows Management Framework (WMF). It's a great tool, isn't it? Well, you can make it even better in at least two ways.

First, make sure to read the help file on **New-ISESnippet**, which is the cmdlet you use to add your own custom snippets to the ISE's built-in library.

Second, within the ISE, click **Add-Ons > Open Add-On Tools Web Site** to visit the Windows PowerShell ISE Add-On Tools website. Here you can download extensions that make ISE-based scripting work even easier to perform. The ISE's extensibility is one of PowerShell's best-kept secrets; make sure that you take advantage of this power on your development workstation at the very least.

Let me walk you through each line of the function script as you cross-reference with Figure 19.5:

▶ **Line 1**: At base, we define a function by using the **function** keyword, followed by a name that (according to best practice guidance) uses the same Verb-Singular_Noun syntax that the built-in cmdlets do.

Most of the time, we add one or more parameters to a function that serve to modularize the function even more. In this simple example, we create a simple variable named **$param1**. Multiple parameters are separated by commas. Later in this hour, I show you a more flexible way to define input parameters.

▶ **Line 2**: Besides the **function** keyword, name, and parameters, the body of the function is enclosed in curly braces. Different developers place the curly braces in different ways; I like to keep the matching open and closed braces at the same indent level in order to keep track of them.

▶ **Lines 3 and 4**: You should understand this code intuitively. First we clear the console screen, and then print "Hello" concatenated to whatever text we pass to the function as the input parameter. The fact that I use double quotes for the **Write-Output** string is actually significant, as I'll explain for you in a little while.

▶ **Line 7**: This is an optional line in which we call the Get-Hello function inside the script itself. Your decision to do this is based on whether you simply want to make the function available to your PowerShell session or if you actually want to load the function and see its results immediately. Of course, the downside to hard-coding function calls like this is that, at least in this example, the user has no choice to supply a different input parameter.

TIP

Most Windows PowerShell MVPs I know cannot stand the **Write-Host** cmdlet. Why? I think their chief argument against **Write-Host** is that the output it spits out goes directly to the host application and not to the pipeline.

Remember that Windows PowerShell is an object-oriented scripting language, and we should keep data as objects throughout the entire pipeline.

As an alternative, you can use **Write-Output**, which does indeed put string objects into the pipeline. The disadvantage to **Write-Output** is that you can't do any of the fancy color formatting that you can with **Write-Host**. The best practice guidance is that you should reserve **Write-Host** to those times when you need to communicate noncritical information to your users that is not important enough to keep in the pipeline.

Functions and Quotes

Take a look at the following console code and think about what's happening under the hood:

```
PS C:\> $p = "eggs"
PS C:\> "spam and $p"
spam and eggs
PS C:\> 'spam and $p'
spam and $p
PS C:\>
```

Personally, I prefer to surround string data with double quotes because the marks are easier for my old eyes to detect. Also, PowerShell will automatically run the **ToString()** method on any enclosed variables, which results in the value's data appearing in the final string.

By contrast, using single quotes does nothing special to the variables, and the "raw" variable appears in the final string. The bottom line here is there is no "right" or "wrong" answer to the single quotes versus double quotes question. I challenge you to understand the difference so you can use them appropriately in your script code.

Adding Programming Logic

The first script we did so far is completely unexciting because it simply runs multiple cmdlets in a batch. Big deal. How about we become acquainted with some basic programming constructs that can give our PowerShell scripts more power and flexibility?

What we'll do in the next script is create something that could be genuinely useful to you in your work as a Windows systems administration.

Let's say that you allow ping traffic within your company's network, and you find yourself often pinging different servers to verify that they are online. Why not turn that tedious, repetitive task into an automation script?

You'll find the script code in Figure 19.6. I'll describe the relevant lines below:

```
 1  function Get-SystemStatus
 2  {
 3      param ([string[]]$serverList = "localhost")
 4
 5      foreach ($Server in $serverList)
 6      {
 7          If (Test-Connection -ComputerName $Server -Count 2 -Quiet)
 8          {
 9              Write-Output "$Server is up."
10          }
11          Else
12          {
13              Write-Warning "$Server is down."
14          }
15      }
16  }
```

FIGURE 19.6
Our Get-SystemStatus function accepts any number of host names as input, and provides different feedback depending upon the target's connectivity state.

▶ **Line 1**: As I said earlier, you should name your functions by using standard cmdlet syntax.

▶ **Line 3**: There's a lot going on here. First, we use the **param** keyword to formally define one or more parameters. All the parameter definitions need to be contained within a single set of parentheses. In this example, I'm declaring a string parameter named **$serverList** that accepts string array input. (That's the [] piece.) Note that I've also provided a default value; this way the function won't bomb out if someone runs **Get-SystemStatus** without the -**serverList** parameter.

▶ **Line 5**: We use the **foreach** construction to loop, or iterate, through a data collection. Recall that **$serverList** is our array of hostnames that we feed into the function; **$Server** is a newly declared value that will temporarily hold each server name that PowerShell plucks from the **$serverList** array.

▶ **Line 7**: Here we see another PowerShell scripting best practice: *Always* indent your code. Not only is your script friendlier to other users' eyes, but clearly delineated PowerShell code is infinitely easier to debug and modify later.

Anyway, in line 7, we use the **If Else** construction to perform what's known as conditional logic. The **If** statement in this function runs **Test-Connection** against each **$Server** in the **$serverName** array, sending two ICMP Echo Request messages with no user feedback.

If conditions must always ultimately evaluate to Boolean **$True** or **$False**.

▶ **Line 9**: This represents what happens when the **If** condition evaluates to **$True**.

▶ **Line 13**: This is what happens if the expression evaluates to **$False** (in other words, if the target host doesn't respond to the two ping messages). PowerShell includes a number of **Write-** cmdlets; **Write-Warning** and **Write-Error** are especially helpful when handling warning and error conditions, respectively.

▶ **Lines 14–16**: Do you see how using code indentation makes it easier to identify which closing curly brace corresponds to which opening one?

Additional ISE Niceties

Take another look at Figure 19.6, this time focusing on those strange minus sign "thingies" that appear on lines 2, 6, 8, and 12. Click one and see what happens.

One of many conveniences offered to us by a tool like the ISE is code folding, which allows you to expand and contract the different data constructs that comprise your script.

TIP
_____
I like code folding because I can reduce distraction and focus only on the data object I need to work with currently.
_____

By now, you should be familiar with the ISE IntelliSense and tab completion features. I'm profoundly colorblind, but I understand that the ISE gives script tokens different colors depending upon what kind of data the ISE detects.

For instance, you should find that cmdlets show up as one color, data types as another, variables as yet another, and so on. The color-coding makes it easy to detect stuff like misspellings, missing quotation marks, and so on.

If you want to customize the color-coding in the ISE, click **Tools > Options** and expand the Script Pane Tokens list in the Options dialog box, as shown in Figure 19.7.

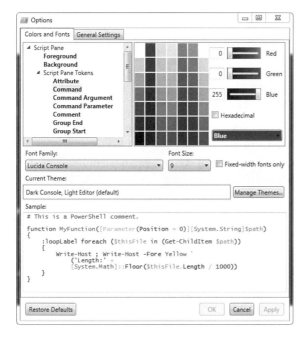

FIGURE 19.7
The Windows PowerShell ISE can be customized to suit your programmer heart's content.

Why Reinvent the Wheel?

Many Windows PowerShell experts are self-described "lazybones," which means they prefer to build their scripts by using someone else's hard work as a base.

The good news for us is that the PowerShell community is, by and large, a group of caring, giving folks, and are willing to share their code with you.

Make a habit of stopping by online PowerShell script galleries such as the PowerShell Code Repository (http://poshcode.org) or the Microsoft Script Center (http://bit.ly/1xLI6UH).

Finally, I recommend you check out the Script Browser ISE add-in (http://bit.ly/1xLIGlf). This tool enables you to browse the TechNet Script Gallery directly from within the ISE. Good stuff.

Running Scripts

It's one thing to write a good script, but it's quite another knowing how to run the darned thing. As discussed earlier, you may want to hard-code one or more function calls in the script itself. Alternatively, you may simply want to put the function into your PowerShell runspace and then call the function on your own. You can do both, too.

Our first order of business is to create a simple script. In the ISE, click **File** > **New** to create a new PowerShell script. Next, click **File** > **Save** and save the file to the root of your C: drive as **weather.ps1**.

We'll add some trivial code to prove that the script actually does something. See Figure 19.8, and I'll briefly explain what's going on.

```
weather.ps1  X
 1  function Get-Weather
 2  {
 3      $response = Read-Host -Prompt "What color is the sky right now?"
 4
 5      switch -Regex ($response)
 6      {
 7          "^[Bb]lue" { Write-Host "The sky is blue. Great!" -ForegroundColor Blue }
 8          "^[Gg]r[ae]y" { Write-Host "The sky is gray? Rain or snow. :(" -ForegroundColor DarkGray }
 9          Default {Write-Warning "Sorry, I don't recognize that color." -WarningAction Continue }
10      }
11  }
12  Get-Weather
```

FIGURE 19.8
Slowly but surely, you are building your PowerShell scripting skills. Congratulations.

▶ **Line 3**: We use **Read-Host** to capture input directly from the user. The -**Prompt** parameter reflects what the user will see at script runtime. In this case, we're storing the results in the **$response** variable.

▶ **Line 5**: The switch construction works a lot like **If/Else**, with the added benefit that switch enables us to pivot as many times as we want to. The optional -**Regex** flag allows us to evaluate the **$response** variable contents by using regular expression-based pattern matching rules.

▶ **Lines 7 and 8**: Here we take action depending upon what data is contained in the **$response** variable. In this simple example, we're providing a custom response only for two cases: the user typing the colors blue or gray.

You should recognize the regex syntax by now. We want to capture both uppercase and lowercase versions of the words, and we also want to catch users who spell gray with an e (and vice versa, of course). This is actually an important general principle of writing functions; you want to anticipate and handle all possible events that can arise during script execution.

▶ **Line 9**: The **Default** line provides a "catchall" bucket if the user simply types foo, presses Enter, and so forth. I'm using **Write-Host** here intentionally to show off its capability for color customization. The ISE will show you all options for each enumeration-loaded parameter.

▶ **Line 12**: It's okay to call the function directly from within the script while we're testing, but when you're ready to proceed, please remove this line.

We'll now turn our attention to the myriad ways in which we can run PowerShell script files. Close the ISE temporarily now and start an elevated PowerShell console session.

Running Scripts from PowerShell

Okay, let's get running! Let's focus our PowerShell session to the root of C: drive. You'll recall that this is where we stored our weather.ps1 script:

```
Set-Location C:\
```

Next, we'll want to verify that our execution policy enables us to run scripts:

```
Get-ExecutionPolicy
```

Running Scripts from Cmd.exe

Quick diversion: I want to make sure that you understand how to run a PowerShell script from Cmd. exe. Begin by opening an elevated Windows command prompt session. Next, start powershell.exe specifying the **-File** parameter:

```
C:\>powershell -file "c:\weather.ps1"
```

Because we are already in the script's directory, we could have simply specified the script name. Try running the **Get-Weather** cmdlet. Did it work?

This method of running a script loads all script contents, including functions, variables, PSDrives, and environment variables, into the current scope for use. We'll see in a moment that behavior isn't necessary matched when we run scripts from within the PowerShell environment.

We can start a PowerShell script file by using the invocation operator (&), otherwise known as the ampersand:

```
PS C:\> & .\weather.ps1
```

TIP

You should have noticed that PowerShell didn't generate an error, but didn't allow you to run the included **Get-Weather** function. You'll want to use script invocation like this when the script is called from within the source code.

The downside to using the invocation operator is that you don't get any feedback when or if things go awry with the program call. As an alternative, you can try using Invoke-Command or Invoke-Expression instead, both of which allow control over error output.

Recall also that the .\ notation represents the current working directory. We also could have done the following to load the weather.ps1 script:

```
PS C:\> & "C:\weather.ps1"
```

If you want to make all script elements persistent in your current PowerShell session, you need use dot source notation. Here's what it looks like in two path formulations:

```
PS C:\>. .\weather.ps1
PS C:\scripts\jan>. "C:\weather.ps1"
```

You type a period, add a space, and then call your script as usual. The difference, of course, is now you can run the **Get-Weather** function as often as you'd like. However, all unsaved session data goes up the flue when you close the session.

TRY IT YOURSELF ▼

Leveraging the PowerShell Community to Edit an Existing Script

In this Try It Yourself exercise, you'll load the Script Browser ISE add-on, download a good script, and edit the source code a bit so that the script better suits your needs. To complete this exercise, you need an Internet connection.

1. Start the ISE and click **Add-Ons > Open Add-On Tools Web Site**. Your default browser will open and you'll find yourself at the Windows PowerShell ISE Add-On Tools site.

2. Locate the Script Browser add-on. Download and install ScriptBrower.exe. Here's a download link if you have difficulty finding the utility: http://bit.ly/1xLIGlf. I suggest you close the ISE and reopen it after the add-on has been installed.

3. Start an elevated ISE session and verify that the Script Browser appears on the right side of the interface, as shown in Figure 19.9.

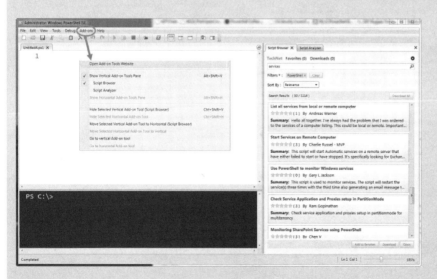

FIGURE 19.9
You'll find that browsing scripts directly from the ISE unlocks creativity and confidence with Windows PowerShell.

4. The Script Browser add-in includes scripts from many different programming languages, so we need to add a filter. Open the Filters drop-down and ensure that only PowerShell is selected. Next, run a search for services and press **Enter**.

5. Find the script called "Check for hung or stopped services" and double-click its entry in the search results.

   Spend time reading the information fields; you can even view part or all of the source code by opening the Script Snippet pane. You'll observe that you can select the source code, copy it to the Windows Clipboard, and paste it directly into the ISE script pane.

6. Click **Downloads** in the Script Browser pane, and click the **Download** button. You can then expand the Downloads pane and double-click **service_check.ps1** to pop the file into the ISE.

7. Immediately run a **File > Save as** and save a copy of the source file to the root of the C: drive, giving it a name of **service_check_modified.ps1**. This way you can keep the original file "pristine" in case you mess up and need to restore original code.

   I show you the source code for Kevin Olson's work in Figure 19.10. We're going to make some modifications to the file to suit our needs. The process of analyzing a script and tweaking it to run more effectively and efficiently is called *refactoring*.

```
service_check_modified.ps1 X
 1   #NAME: service_check.ps1
 2   #AUTHOR: Kevin Olson
 3   #DATE: 4/29/2011
 4
 5   #Machine to be monitored
 6   $Computer = "host1"
 7
 8   #Create an array of all services running
 9   $GetService = get-service -ComputerName $Computer
10
11   #Create a subset of the previous array for services you want to monitor
12   $ServiceArray = "Service1","Service2","Service3";
13
14   #Find any iWFM service that is stopped
15   foreach ($Service in $GetService)
16   {
17       foreach ($srv in $ServiceArray)
18       {
19           if ($Service.name -eq $srv)
20           {
21               #check if a service is hung ( I haven't test this, uncomment at your own risk)
22               if ($Service.status -eq "StopPending")
23               {
24               #email to notify if a service is down
25               Send-Mailmessage -to admin@domain.com -Subject "$srv is hung on $Computer" -from admin@domain.com `
26               -Body "The $srv service was found hung" -SmtpServer smtp.domain.com
27               $servicePID = (gwmi win32_Service | where { $_.Name -eq $srv}).ProcessID
28               Stop-Process $servicePID
29               Start-Service -InputObject (get-Service -ComputerName $Computer -Name $srv)
30               }
31               # check if a service is stopped
32               elseif ($Service.status -eq "Stopped")
33               {
34               #email to notify if a service is down
35               Send-Mailmessage -to admin@domain.com -Subject "$srv is stopped on $Computer" -from admin@domain.com `
36               -Body "The $srv service was found stopped" -SmtpServer smtp.domain.com
37               #automatically restart the service.
38               Start-Service -InputObject (get-Service -ComputerName $Computer -Name $srv)
39               }
40           }
41       }
42   }
43
```

FIGURE 19.10
This script is fairly well written, but we can make it much better, cleaving to PowerShell scripting best practices.

Actually, you can see the "finished" product of the script in Figure 19.11.

```
1   #NAME: service_check.ps1
2   #AUTHOR: Kevin Olson
3   #DATE: 4/29/2011
4   # Script edited by Timothy L. Warner on December 24, 2014.
5
6   function Get-ServiceInfo
7   {
8       Clear-Host
9       $Computer = Read-Host -Prompt "which computer do you want to monitor?"
10
11      $GetService = Get-Service -ComputerName $Computer
12
13      $ServiceArray = Read-Host -Prompt "Enter a single Windows service name"
14
15      foreach ($Service in $GetService)
16      {
17          foreach ($srv in $ServiceArray)
18          {
19              if ($Service.name -eq $srv)
20              {
21                  if ($Service.status -eq "StopPending")
22                  {
23                      $servicePID = (Get-WmiObject -Namespace win32_Service | Where-Object { $_.Name -eq $srv}).ProcessID
24                      write-Host "Service is hung. Restarting..." -ForegroundColor Black -BackgroundColor DarkGray
25                      Stop-Process $ServicePID
26                      Start-Service -InputObject (get-Service -ComputerName $Computer -Name $srv)
27                      Get-Service -InputObject $Service
28                  }
29                  elseif ($Service.status -eq "Stopped")
30                  {
31                      write-Host "Service is stopped. Starting..." -ForegroundColor White -BackgroundColor Red
32                      Start-Service -InputObject (Get-Service -ComputerName $Computer -Name $srv)
33                      Get-Service -InputObject $Service
34                  }
35                  elseif ($Service.Status -eq "Running")
36                  {
37                      write-Host "The service is running." -ForegroundColor Blue -BackgroundColor Cyan
38                  }
39              }
40          }
41      }
42  }
43  Stop-Service spooler
44  Get-ServiceInfo
```

FIGURE 19.11
Here is our refactored script. It's much improved from what it was, but I am confident that you can make it better yet. I'll call out the major script changes by line numbers, so keep an eye on Figures 19.10 and 19.11 as we go along.

In case you haven't put it together yet, line numbers are an absolute MUST for any decent systems programming.

In lines 1–3, we have a set of comments that provide metadata. PowerShell comments are formed by typing the octothorpe (#), followed by your documentation. Add a fourth comment to the block:

```
#Script edited by <your name> on <today's date>
```

You'll observe that the author, Kevin Olson, does a good job documenting what each part of his script does. To answer the global question "what does this script do?" I can tell you that the script detects whether one or more services on a local or remote computer are in a StopPending, or hung, state. If so, the script fires off a custom email message and attempts to start the hung service. If a monitored service is stopped, the script again generates an email message and attempts to start up the service.

In line 6, you'll see that I'm wrapping this entire script inside of a function element named **Get-ServiceInfo**. In this simple example, we won't use input parameters, but instead will ask the function caller to provide a computer name and service name interactively.

Let's have the script ask the user to supply the target computer name and service name. In Figure 19.11, lines 9 and 13, we use **Read-Host** to fetch string data from the user. At the moment, our function accepts only a single string. I'll leave it to you to refactor the function such that (a) the script uses localhost as a default computer name if the user presses Enter and (b) the user can pass more than one computer name as an array to the **$ServiceArray** variable.

The email-related code in lines 26–28 and lines 33–35 in Figure 19.10 is nice, but let's snip those lines out of the script for simplicity's sake.

Instead, look what I did in Figure 19.11, lines 19–37. Yes, that's a lot of code, but take it in parts. First, we check for a hung service (line 21); services that are hung display in a StopPending state. In this case, we tell the user that we're restarting the affected service.

In line 29, we check for a Stopped service state, and in line 35 we check for a Running state, take corrective action, and provide feedback to the user in each case.

Always think of the script caller when you write functions. We want to make the script flow as smoothly as possible, never leaving users scratching their head and asking, "What am I supposed to do next?"

In Figure 19.11, lines 43 and 44, we test the script functionality by (a) stopping an innocuous service and (b) calling the function. In the ISE, press **F5** to save and run the script. You'll be prompted for a computer name. (Use localhost if you don't have any other machines available.)

Next, supply "spooler" for the monitored service name. You should see the formatted output informing you that the service is stopped and the script is attempting a start. You'll then see the **Get-Service** feedback that confirms that the Spooler service is now running.

Of course, you can remove those test lines when you're finished testing and ready to load the script in another PowerShell session.

Some other various tweaks I made to the script include the following (all shown in Figure 19.11):

- Expanding cmdlet names and parameter names (line 23). Scripts are no place for aliases! For maximum availability and readability, always use full command and parameter names.

- Code indentation. PowerShell scripting best practice calls for three or four spaces per indent; you can customize the Tab key binding in the ISE Options dialog box.

Start an elevated PowerShell console session and load the service_check_modified.ps1 contents into the session. You do remember how to do that, correct?

Run the function a few times and experiment. Have fun.

Pointers to Master PowerShell Scripting

There's so much to learn. PowerShell functions is such a vast subject. Perhaps I'll make PowerShell script programming the subject of my next book.

In the meantime, I want to provide you with some "next step" pointers to help you self-study your way to PowerShell scripting mastery:

▶ **Scopes**: PowerShell function code can be scoped to apply its contents at various levels on local or remote systems. This is a powerful technology, and I advise you to read the about_Scopes conceptual document for more information.

▶ **Pipeline streams**: In this book, we concern ourselves primarily with the output/success pipeline stream, but did you know that PowerShell actually has four additional streams that it uses to redirect error, warning, verbose, or debug information? Ed Wilson, Microsoft's "Scripting Guy," wrote a nice blog post on PowerShell streams and redirection: http://bit.ly/1sYPYva.

▶ **Error Handling**: Many programmers swear by the Try/Catch/Finally data structure to evaluate conditions and handle any warning or error conditions that pop up. Again, I'll let the Scripting Guy tell you more about PowerShell exception handling: http://bit.ly/1sYQzND.

▶ **Comment-based help**: You should know that it's considered best practice to create comment-based help such that when users run **Get-Help** against your function, they see standard-issue documentation, including parameter descriptions and examples. Comment-based help is part of the PowerShell "advanced function" feature set; read more on this in the about_Functions_Advanced and about_Functions_Advanced_Parameters conceptual help files.

Summary

This hour was satisfying for me to write because I feel I gave you a chance to absorb some topics that we (by necessity) glossed over earlier in the book.

At this point, you should be able to browse PowerShell script galleries and have a pretty good idea what you're seeing when you parse those scripts. I hope that you have the tools you need to now begin developing your own custom scripts to automate your repetitive IT "scut" work.

In Hour 20, "Making PowerShell Code Portable with Modules," you take the content from this training hour to the next level by learning how to package your code into modules. In a way, the next hour serves as a neat bookend to this one. See you there.

Q&A

Q. When I run Get-Command -Module PSDesiredStateConfiguration, I notice that most of the commands contained within that module are classified as functions rather than cmdlets. Are these built-in functions the same as the functions we learned how to do in this hour of training?

A. Almost without exception, the built-in functions are so-called advanced functions, but yes, they are at base the same code construct you learned about in this hour.

To test this, let's investigate the **Get-DscResource** function:

```
PS C:\> (Get-Command -Name Get-DscResource).Definition
```

You'll see the function's source code spilled to your host application. Remember that all global functions that PowerShell is aware of are contained in the Function: PSDrive. Try this:

```
Get-ChildItem function:*
```

Q. I know that you pointed us to other resources to learn more about function and script scoping, but can you at least tell us the accepted best practice regarding scopes?

A. Sure. The best practice guidance from the PowerShell gurus are to avoid running your scripts in the global scope. The global scope contains assets that are available every time a PowerShell session starts on your computer. (Profile scripts run in the global scope.) You can retrieve a list of global variables thusly:

```
Get-Variable -Scope global
Get-Variable -Scope local
```

The default scope for PowerShell scripts is the script scope, which is by most accounts the right option. You can find some nice explanations and examples in the about_Scopes conceptual help file.

Q. It's clear that a (more) secure yet practical execution policy requires that my scripts be digitally signed. How can I get that done?

A. X.509 digital certificates rely upon trust, so your first question is this: Who's going to run my scripts? If the answer is "anyone in the world," you need to buy an Authenticode code-signing certificate from a public certification authority like VeriSign or GoDaddy.

If you need scripts signed for internal use only and you have an Active Directory Certificate Services (AD CS) CA available, that's another option.

For dev/test environments only, you can use self-signed certificates that are trusted by nobody besides your computer. To do this, you'll need to run Makecert.exe from the .NET Framework software development kit (SDK); this is a free download.

Next you'll run **Set-AuthenticodeSignature** to sign your PowerShell scripts with the new code-signing certificate. Note that you can't use an ordinary self-signed certificate; the certificate must exist for code signing. Sadly, the **New-SelfSignedCertificate** cmdlet cannot produce self-signed code-signing certificates as of this writing. Finally, read the about_Signing conceptual help file to round out your preliminary knowledge.

Workshop

For your challenge, create a function called **Get-Uptime** that displays how long the current or remote computer has been online. Hint: I found a solution to this problem on the PowerShell.org forums.

As a bonus challenge, sign the script with a self-signed code-signing certificate, change your execution policy to AllSigned, and test running your signed script along with some unsigned ones.

Quiz

1. Which of the following operators is used to invoke a PowerShell script from a PowerShell command line?

    a. @

    b. []

    c. &

2. Which of the following is an appropriate name for a new PowerShell function?

    a. Get-CityLocation

    b. Get-CityLocations

    c. Retrieve-CityLocation

3. All Windows PowerShell functions must include at least one input parameter.

    a. True

    b. False

Answers

1. The correct answer is C. We use the ampersand as a script invocation operator when we need to start a script from a PowerShell console session.

2. The correct answer is A. The problem with choice B is that it uses a plural noun when singular nouns are the accepted standard. The problem with choice C is that Receive is not an approved verb. Remember that you can run **Get-Verb** to retrieve a list of Microsoft-approved verbs.

3. The correct answer is B. Script functions don't have to include input parameters; they are optional.

HOUR 20
Making PowerShell Code Portable with Modules

What You'll Learn in This Hour:

- ▶ Understanding snap-ins
- ▶ Introducing PowerShell modules
- ▶ Creating our first PowerShell script module
- ▶ Using module manifests
- ▶ Adding comment-based help
- ▶ Finding modules easily

Many programmers, myself included, subscript to a development principle called DRY, or "Don't Repeat Yourself."

Let me give you an example. Let's say that I need to create 200 Active Directory user accounts along with Exchange mailboxes. If I had enough time and willingness, I could flex my Windows PowerShell muscles and power through the creation of a script that does the job.

However, why would I do that if the work has already been done (and better) by dozens of other PowerShell professionals in the community? Isn't it smarter to download a script from, say, the TechNet Script Repository or Poshcode.org?

I'll leave you to ponder that question yourself. In this hour, you learn how modules work and even how you can build your own script modules for process automation.

PowerShell modules make it easier to avoid "reinventing the wheel" and repeating tasks over and over yet again. Let's begin our module journey with a brief discussion of... snap-ins? Don't worry; all will become clear momentarily.

Understanding Snap-Ins

We'll begin by discussing snap-ins. In PowerShell, a module is simply a package that contains Windows PowerShell commands. Originally, though, Windows PowerShell v1 used a snap-in architecture for bundling and distributing code.

Here's what you need to know about PowerShell snap-ins:

▶ Snap-ins have limited functionality: In contrast to modules, which can contain just about any type of PowerShell data structure, snap-ins are restricted only to cmdlet and PSProvider definitions.

▶ Snap-ins have to be registered: Because snap-ins typically are contained in dynamic link library (DLL) files, these DLLs have to be registered on all computers on which they'll be used. By contrast, you'll see soon that PowerShell modules can be called ad hoc from any file location.

▶ Only administrators and .NET developers can make **snap-ins**: Whereas any PowerShell user can author a script module, you have to know .NET programming to write a compiled snap-in DLL. Moreover, you'll need administrative credentials to install and register snap-ins.

Defining Good Snap-Ins

You'll find that the PowerShell system cmdlets are mostly contained in snap-ins even though the module architecture has been the primary way to extend PowerShell as of version 2.0.

Don't get me wrong. Snap-ins are actually necessary in cases when (a) maximum performance is required and (b) when the cmdlets have deep dependencies in the .NET Framework and other installed components.

I've mentioned the SharePoint Server 2013 snap-in several times; this is a good example of a PowerShell interface that requires the snap-in over the module because of how interwoven SharePoint is in terms of installed and registered system components.

In any event, you can run **Get-PSSnapin** to retrieve a list of all registered snap-ins on your system:

```
PS C:\> Get-PSSnapin

Name        : Microsoft.PowerShell.Core
PSVersion   : 5.0.9883.0
Description : This Windows PowerShell snap-in contains cmdlets used to manage
              components of Windows PowerShell.
```

Adding a PSSnapin to Your Session

You kind of have to know that you need a snap-in to use them. Suppose, for instance, that we plan to use the Windows Server Migration Tools on our Windows Server 2012 R2 member server to migrate some server roles from Windows Server 2008 R2 to 2012 R2. First we install the feature:

```
PS C:\> Install-WindowsFeature Migration -IncludeAllSubFeature
➥-IncludeManagementTools
```

Next we load up the Migration Tools snap-in (the name of which I found by reading the online documentation at TechNet):

```
PS C:\> Add-PSSnapin Microsoft.Windows.ServerManager.Migration
```

Finally, we can query the commands contained in the snap-in and obtain syntax help:

```
PS C:\> Get-Command -PSSnapin Microsoft.Windows.ServerManager.Migration |
➥Select-Object -Property CommandType, Name
PS C:\> Get-Help Export-SmigServerSetting -ShowWindow
```

Other than those details, after you've loaded a snap-in's contents into your session, calling the cmdlets and accessing any providers works the same way as it does with current-generation PowerShell modules.

Automating Snap-Ins

On my SharePoint servers, I add the relevant **Add-PSSnapin** call to my profile script to ensure I have my SharePoint cmdlets every time I start a PowerShell console session. That's about the best we can do in terms of snap-in convenience. One of the cool things about modules is that, as of Windows PowerShell v3, modules autoload into your session as soon as you reference a command contained therein. More on that in a moment.

TIP

Both PowerShell snap-ins and modules support manual removal cmdlets: **Remove-PSSnapin** and **Remove-Module**, respectively.

However, I have to say that in my years of using PowerShell, I can count on one hand the number of times I've used them. Remember that the .NET Framework is excellent at cleaning up a session once you've closed it out; this is a process called (I kid you not) *garbage collection*.

Therefore, I would challenge you that making the PowerShell commands you need available to your current session is the primary point. Let the Framework take care of the thankless task of cleaning up behind you.

As is my habit as your instructor, we've flirted around with the term *module* quite a bit, but we haven't formally treated the subject. Let's address that small detail now.

Introducing PowerShell Modules

Modules became the preferred way to package PowerShell code as over version 2.0. The coolest thing to me about modules is that they are absolutely portable; no permanent system registration required. For instance, Jane can share her Foo module with Jim, Jim can place the module directory in his $PSModulePath, and PowerShell v4 autoloading takes care of the rest; Jim's free to call commands within Foo at any time.

Understanding the Module Types

Let's remember our goal here, friend: You have a library of related and useful functions contained in a script file, and you want to make it easy for you and potentially other people to run those functions in PowerShell sessions.

As mentioned previously, a PowerShell module is a package of PowerShell code. Specifically, there exist four main types of modules:

▶ **Script module**: This is a .psm1 script file that contains PowerShell code. At first blush, the only difference between a script module and a garden-variety PowerShell script is the file extension. This is the type of module we're concerned with in this hour of training.

▶ **Binary module**: This is a DLL containing a PowerShell function library. Because you need to write these with a .NET programming language, we're not concerned with binary modules.

▶ **Manifest module**: This is a script or binary module that includes a manifest file. We'll discuss these guys later in the hour because manifests make your modules "play nicer" with other users and computers.

▶ **Dynamic module**: This is a temporary, special-use module that persists only in session memory and is created with the **New-Module** cmdlet. We won't worry about this module type in this book.

Loading and Unloading Modules

In Windows PowerShell v1 and v2, finding PowerShell commands was problematic because you had to explicitly load the relevant module first by using **Import-Module**.

The PowerShell team fixed this problem as of Windows PowerShell v3. With module autoloading, the entire module is loaded into your session and all enclosed commands are available if you simply reference one of the module's commands.

For instance, suppose that you are looking for Active Directory user commands on your Windows Server 2012 R2 domain controller. First you'll list all the modules that are currently loaded into your elevated console session:

```
PS C:\> Get-Module

ModuleType Version   Name                              ExportedCommands
---------- -------   ----                              ----------------
Manifest   3.1.0.0   Microsoft.PowerShell.Management   {Add-Computer, Add...
Manifest   3.1.0.0   Microsoft.PowerShell.Utility      {Add-Member, Add-T...
```

Now you'll use **Get-Command**, run your query, and then get command help:

```
PS C:\> Get-Command -Noun *ADUser* | Select-Object -Property Name

Name
----
Get-ADUser
Get-ADUserResultantPasswordPolicy
New-ADUser
Remove-ADUser
Set-ADUser

PS C:\> Get-Help New-ADUser
```

Finally, we'll rerun **Get-Module** and verify that the **ActiveDirectory** module is now available:

```
PS C:\> Get-Module

ModuleType Version   Name                            ExportedCommands
---------- -------   ----                            ----------------
Manifest   1.0.0.0   ActiveDirectory                 {Add-ADCentralAcce...
Manifest   3.1.0.0   Microsoft.PowerShell.Management  {Add-Computer, Add...
Manifest   3.1.0.0   Microsoft.PowerShell.Utility    {Add-Member, Add-T...
```

Notice in the preceding output that the **ActiveDirectory** module and PowerShell system snap-ins both are listed as Manifest module types. You'll learn soon enough that it's best practice to include a metadata manifest with all your modules.

NOTE

Turning Off Module Autoload

Not that you would ever want to disable module autoload, it's nonetheless possible by setting the **$PSModuleAutoLoadingPreference** preference variable:

```
PS C:\> $PSModuleAutoloadingPreference="none"
```

You can read the full list of preference variables with which you can customize the environment by running **help about_preference_variables**. Remember that your changes affect only the current session; adding your custom preference overrides to your profile script to make them persistent.

Creating Your First PowerShell Script Module

I'm going to teach you how to write your own module by having us jump into the deep end of the conceptual pool. Let's begin by opening up both the integrated scripting environment (ISE) and a console session. In the console session, let's test to see whether the default custom module save location is present on the system:

```
PS C:\> Test-Path -Path $env:PSModulePath
False
```

Okay, having established that, we need to examine the contents of the **PSModulePath** environment variable:

```
PS C:\> $env:PSModulePath
C:\Users\Trainer\Documents\WindowsPowerShell\Modules;C:\Program Files\
WindowsPowerShell\Modules;C:\Windows\system32\WindowsPowerShell\v1.0\Modules\
```

If you've ever horsed around with the **Path** environment variable, **PSModulePath** works very similarly. The bottom line is that as long as your custom PowerShell modules are stored in one of the directories listed in your **PSModulePath**, PowerShell should have no difficulty autoloading them (provided that the module code itself is intact).

That having been said, current-generation Windows doesn't take too kindly to users (even administrators) placing their own files and data in protected locations like C:\Windows or C:\ Program Files. So keep that in mind, okay?

In this first example, we'll create a new custom module named **MyFirstModule**. (Give me a break; my imagination is failing me today.) Thus, we'll first create a directory in our user account's Documents folder:

```
PS C:\> New-Item -Type Directory -Path
"C:\Users\Trainer\Documents\WindowsPowerShell\Modules" -Force


    Directory: C:\Users\Trainer\Documents\WindowsPowerShell

Mode                LastWriteTime         Length Name
----                -------------         ------ ----
d-----        12/27/2014   4:39 PM                Modules
```

Note from the preceding code that we implicitly create the WindowsPowerShell directory when we specify a new subdirectory name.

Creating the Actual Module

Switch your focus to the ISE and save a new script file named **MyFirstModule.psm1** in a subfolder of the previously created \Modules folder. It's absolutely crucial that you

- ▶ Name the script module exactly as the name of its containing folder.
- ▶ Save the script as a module with the .psm1 extension.

Figure 20.1 shows both of the previous gotchas in action.

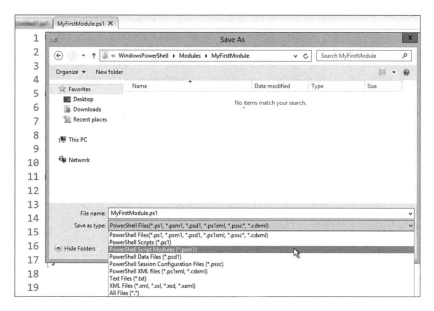

FIGURE 20.1
Saving a PowerShell script as a module.

Coolness. In this example, I've built a simple function library that you can view in Figure 20.2. I'll walk you through the relevant code lines now.

```
 1 <#
 2   # This module contains three functions for gathering WMI data.
 3 #>
 4
 5 function Get-SystemBIOS {
 6     Get-WmiObject -Class win32_bios |
 7     Select-Object -Property @{Name="Hostname";Expression= {$_.PSComputername}}, `
 8      Manufacturer, Name | Format-List
 9 }
10
11 function Retrieve-OSDetails {
12     Get-WmiObject win32_operatingsystem |
13     Select-Object -Property   @{Name="Hostname";Expression= {$_.PSComputername}}, `
14     BuildNumber, ServicePackMajorVersion, `
15     @{Name="LastBootUpTime";Expression={$_.ConverttoDateTime($_.lastbootuptime)}} |
16     Format-List
17 }
```

FIGURE 20.2
Our first script module; a collection of WMI-related functions.

▶ **Lines 1–3**: This is a comment block. You know that you can create a "one-liner" comment by using a pound sign. If you use angle brackets (<>) and pound signs, your comments can extend to multiple lines if you need.

▶ **Line 5**: This function, **Get-SystemBIOS**, makes a simple call to the **win32_bios** WMI class and formats the output as a list. Notable is the hash table in line 7 that renames the **PSComputerName** property **Hostname**.

▶ **Lines 6, 7, 12, 13, 15**: We can break PowerShell code across lines in two ways. Most PowerShell pros prefer to break at the pipe; others don't mind using the backtick (`` ` ``), which is PowerShell's default escape character. One warning if you're going to use the backtick is that there should be no space at all following the backtick; technically, you're escaping the linebreak itself, and your code will break if you add anything but a line break after the backtick.

▶ **Lines 11–16**: The second function, **Retrieve-OSDetails**, is another trivial function to fetch some OS version data. Note that the verb, **Retrieve**, is not an approved PowerShell verb as found in Get-Verb command output. That will become relevant shortly.

Running Commands Inside a Module

Now switch over to your elevated console session, and let's query the new **MyFirstModule** script module:

```
PS C:\> Get-Command -Module MyFirstModule | Select-Object -Property CommandType,
➡Name

                        CommandType Name
                        ----------- ----
                           Function Get-SystemBIOS
                           Function Retrieve-OSDetails
```

Do you feel the tingle of excitement that says, "Look, I made that!"? I hope so. Next, let's go ahead and run the two functions, one at a time:

```
PS C:\> Get-SystemBIOS

Hostname     : DSCSERVER01
Manufacturer : American Megatrends Inc.
Name         : BIOS Date: 05/23/12 17:15:53  Ver: 09.00.06

PS C:\> Retrieve-OSDetails

Hostname                 : DSCSERVER01
BuildNumber              : 9600
ServicePackMajorVersion  : 0
LastBootUpTime           : 12/27/2014 8:48:47 AM
```

Use Approved Verbs

Where's the outrage? Those of you with some experience with loading community-made modules might remember being barked at by PowerShell to the effect of "This module contains unapproved verbs! Shame on you" (or some words to that effect).

Fire up a fresh PS console session and let's manually import the **MyFirstModule** script module:

```
PS C:\> Import-Module -Name MyFirstModule
WARNING: The names of some imported commands from the module 'MyFirstModule'
include unapproved verbs that might make them less discoverable. To find the
commands with unapproved verbs, run the Import-Module command again with the
Verbose parameter. For a list of approved verbs, type Get-Verb.

PS C:\>
```

Ah, there it is. The lesson here is that if you don't want your users to see this intimidating (and verbose) message when they manually load your module, make sure that all your functions and cmdlets use approved verbs.

Using Module Manifests

The notion of adding a manifest to your PowerShell script module sounds more difficult than it actually is. Truly, manifests are a good idea because they allow you to attach valuable metadata to your module code.

Here are what I identify as the three chief purposes of the module manifest:

► Describes the contents and properties of a module.

► Defines prerequisites such as minimum PowerShell version, processor architecture, and so forth.

► Determines how module components are located and processed.

How to Build a Manifest

The actual creation of the manifest is trivial: You simply run **New-ModuleManifest** and specify the path to your module directory and the name of a .psd1 file with a matching name:

```
PS C:\> New-ModuleManifest -Path
➥"C:\Users\Trainer\Documents\WindowsPowerShell\Modules\MyFirstModule\
➥ MyFirstModule.psd1"

PS C:\>
```

It's the tweaking of the manifest contents that can be tricky. Be sure to read the help file for **New-ModuleManifest**, and check the MSDN documentation for syntax help: http://bit.ly/1BfLViN.

Figure 20.3 shows you my module manifest for **MyFirstModule**, and I highlighted a couple easy-to-understand properties.

FIGURE 20.3
Module manifests are simple text files that are stored in the same directory as their corresponding script module. The names should match between the manifest and module as well.

1. The **RootModule** property points to the location of the associated script file. We'll need to talk more about this property in a moment.

2. We use **PowerShellVersion** to constrain the module to a minimum PowerShell version. This is useful when you invoke commands and functionalities that exist only in particular PowerShell version minimums.

3. The **DotNetFrameworkVersion** property works like PowerShell version; we're specifying a base .NET version environment for the targeted module

To test things out, change the **PowerShellVersion** property to a version higher than what you're running. You'll also need to uncomment the line by removing the octothorpe (#) character. Remember you can call **$PSVersionTable** to get the local computer's PowerShell version:

```
PowerShellVersion = '6.0'
```

Yes, I understand that PowerShell v6 is in all likelihood not available as of the time you read this. However, my machine is running Windows PowerShell v5, so I want to artificially create a manifest violation.

Fire up another console session and attempt to import the **MyFirstModule** module. You should get the error shown here:

```
PS C:\> Import-Module -Name myfirstmodule
import-module : The version of Windows PowerShell on this computer is
'5.0.9883.0'. The module 'C:\Users\Trainer\Documents\WindowsPowerShell\Modules\
myfirstmodule\myfirstmodule.psd1' requires a minimum Windows PowerShell
version of '6.0' to run. Verify that you have the minimum required version of
Windows PowerShell installed, and then try again.
At line:1 char:1
+ Import-Module myfirstmodule
+ ~~~~~~~~~~~~~~~~~~~~~~~~~~~~~
    + CategoryInfo          : ResourceUnavailable: (C:\Users\Traine...irstmodu
   le.psd1:String) [Import-Module], InvalidOperationException
    + FullyQualifiedErrorId : Modules_InsufficientPowerShellVersion,Microsoft.
   PowerShell.Commands.ImportModuleCommand

PS C:\>
```

Go back and comment out the line you edited to make sure that the manifest won't block you from importing our custom module.

Troubleshooting Manifests

You might be unpleasantly surprised when you try to query your custom module for its contents:

```
PS C:\> Get-Command -Module myfirstmodule
PS C:\>
```

What in the world? Let's use **Test-Manifest** to test that our manifest file is whole, complete, and valid:

```
PS C:\> Test-ModuleManifest -Path
➡ C:\Users\Trainer\Documents\WindowsPowerShell\Modules\MyFirstModule\
➡ MyFirstModule.psd1


ModuleType Version    Name                              ExportedCommands
---------- -------    ----                              ----------------
Manifest   1.0        MyFirstModule
```

Ouch. The **ExportedCommands** property should list the module contents that should be dumped into our session.

I'll bet you $20 to a stale jelly donut that is the currently commented-out **RootModule** property in our manifest. Open up the manifest file in any text editor and edit the line to point to your module directory:

```
# Script module or binary module file associated with this manifest.
RootModule = 'C:\Users\Trainer\Documents\WindowsPowerShell\Modules\MyFirstModule'
```

Now let's see whether we can get at those commands in the module:

```
PS C:\> Get-Command -Module myfirstmodule | Select-Object -Property Name

Name
----
Get-SystemBIOS
Retrieve-OSDetails
```

Adding Comment-Based Help

I hope that if I taught you anything it's that reading the help file for any PowerShell command you need should be second nature to you. Did you ever wonder how that command-specific help is generated?

As it happens, you can add comment-based help to your scripts/functions and by using simple text-based syntax. The comment-based help template we're using for the following Try It Yourself exercise comes to us from Don Jones's excellent *TechNet Magazine* article, "Windows PowerShell: Comment Your Way to Help." You can read the article yourself at http://bit.ly/1xY6YbQ.

▼ TRY IT YOURSELF

More Practice With PowerShell Modules

In this Try It Yourself exercise, you'll create a simple module that contains one function. The wrinkle here is that you'll add comment-based help to the function to make it easier for users to learn how to use it. Let's begin:

1. You should know how to create a module file by now, so let me just give you the briefest of instructions.

   ▶ Create a PowerShell script module called **MySecondModule.psm1**.

   ▶ Create the **Modules** subdirectory inside your home folder if you haven't already done so, and create a folder named **MySecondModule**.

▸ Store the new script module file in the appropriate location and open the file in Windows PowerShell ISE

2. Take a look at Figure 20.4, and I'll walk you through the "what's what" of the function itself. (We'll do the comment-based help in a moment.)

```
1   # Syntax help from http://bit.ly/1xY6YbQ
2
3   function Get-RecentEvents {
4
5   <#
6   .SYNOPSIS
7
8   Retrieves the most recent events from any Windows event log.
9
10  .DESCRIPTION
11
12  This function performs some sorting and formatting, making it easier for the admin to see recent event log events.
13
14  .PARAMETER Log
15
16  Specifies the target Windows event log. The user needs to know the name of the log in advance.
17
18  .PARAMETER NumEntries
19
20  Specifies the number of event log entries to fetch.
21
22  .EXAMPLE
23
24  Get-RecentEvents -Log System -NumEntries 3
25
26  This example fetches the three most recent System log entries from the local computer.
27  #>
28
29      param (
30          [string]$Log,
31          [string]$NumEntries
32      )
33
34      Get-EventLog -Log $Log -Newest $NumEntries | Sort-Object -Property TimeGenerated -Descending |
35      Format-List -Property TimeGenerated, EventID, EntryType, Source, Message
36
37
38  }
39
40  # Get-RecentEvents -Log System -NumEntries 2
41
```

FIGURE 20.4
We've added comment-based help to this script module function.

Line 1: Here we provide proper attribution to Don Jones, who provided the comment-based help skeleton for us.

Line 3: We use standard Verb-Singular_Noun syntax to name our function.

Lines 29–32: Two input parameters; the first one specifies the log name, and the second one determines how many entries to fetch. Note that if we were doing an "advanced function," we could totally customize parameter behavior, specifying stuff like positional parameters, required parameters, and option enumerations.

Lines 34–35: All the **Get-RecentEvents** function does is pass two parameters to **Get-EventLog**, perform an inverse sort on the **TimeGenerated** property, and format the output as a list. No big deal, but the function itself isn't our objective here.

3. Now for the comment-based help. Don't worry about white space or lack thereof: as long as you enclose the help within multiline comment operators (<# #>), PowerShell should be able to figure out what you're trying to do.

I suggest you paste in Don's code from that *TechNet Magazine* article, and edit it to your heart's content.

4. You can make comment-based help in the top of the script file to apply to the entire thing, or you can add the comment blocks within each function.

5. Make sure to run the script in the ISE, and then, in the console pane, test the function to make sure that it behaves properly:

```
PS C:\>Get-RecentEvents -Log Application -NumEntries 10
```

6. When you finish, save your work, close the script module, and open an elevated PowerShell console session.

7. Now explicitly import the module to make sure that PowerShell finds it:

```
PS C:\> Import-Module MySecondModule
```

If you want, you can run **Get-Command –module MySecondModule** to verify that the function appears. In any event, run the **help** command to test out the comment-based help. Figure 20.5 shows my output.

```
PS C:\> Get-Help –Name Get-RecentEvents
```

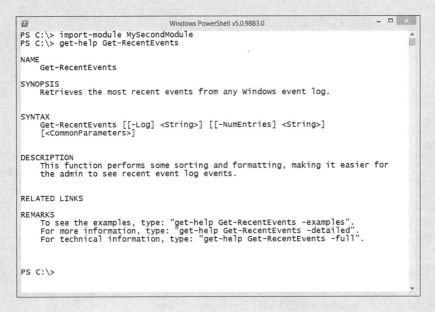

FIGURE 20.5
Notice that PowerShell itself augments your manually created help by providing a syntax description and helpful remarks.

8. Remember that you can apply what you know about using PowerShell help to your newly documented function. To wit:

```
PS C:\> Get-Help -Name Get-RecentEvents -Parameter NumEntries
PS C:\> Get-Help -Name Get-RecentEvents -Examples
```

9. Did you notice how much "extra stuff" PowerShell adds to your sparsely commented function? It's pretty awesome. To extend your learning and to see what else is possible, read the about_Comment_Based_Help and about_Functions_Advanced conceptual help files.

Finding Modules Easily

PowerShellGet is a wrapper surrounding the **OneGet** meta package manager that we learned about earlier in this book. What's awesome about **PowerShellGet** is that it makes it simpler to locate and install first- and third-party PowerShell modules.

Of course, **OneGet** and **PowerShellGet** are part of Windows PowerShell v5, so there's that limitation.

We don't have the white space to give **PowerShellGet** the coverage it deserves. However, you'll find that its usage is very similar to what you now know concerning **OneGet**.

We'll begin by querying the **PowerShellGet** module for a list of enclosed (hey!) functions:

```
PS C:\> Get-Command -Module PowerShellGet | Select-Object -Property CommandType,
➥Name

CommandType Name
----------- ----
   Function Find-Module
   Function Get-PSRepository
   Function Install-Module
   Function Publish-Module
   Function Register-PSRepository
   Function Set-PSRepository
   Function Unregister-PSRepository
   Function Update-Module
```

Next, let's generate a list of available modules:

```
PS C:\>Find-Module | Out-GridView
```

NOTE

I found that, at least as of this writing, the **PowerShellGet** public repositories contain mostly developer tools and DSC experimental resources. I hope that more public repositories will come online in the coming months. Of course, you can build your own **PowerShellGet** module repository inside your firewall if trust and security are concerns for you (and why wouldn't they be?).

I picked out a random module named **MenuShell** that makes it easy to generate console menus; let's install it:

```
PS C:\>Find-Module -Name MenuShell | Install-Module -Force
```

Once the **Install-Module** command completes successfully, you can use **Get-Command** and **Get-Help** as usual to learn how to use the module's contents. Have fun with that!

NOTE

By the way, you can browse the Microsoft PowerShell Gallery at https://msconfiggallery.cloudapp.net/ to keep abreast of **PowerShellGet** news and module availability.

Summary

Congratulations! You have swallowed and digested more Windows PowerShell in the past 20 training hours than you probably thought was possible. This hour concludes the truly "new" material in the book. In the final four training hours of this book, you'll learn how to apply and extend your PowerShell skills by applying them to practical enterprise applications that most Windows systems administrators have to work with at least periodically.

Specifically, in Hour 21, "Managing Active Directory with Windows PowerShell," you'll learn how to use Windows PowerShell to manage Active Directory.

Q&A

Q. What's the difference between PowerShell snap-ins and modules again? You said that binary modules include DLLs just like snap-ins do.

A. Here's the deal: Windows PowerShell modules are completely portable. They don't put down permanent "roots" in the Windows Registry like snap-ins do. You have to register snap-ins with the Registry; this typically requires administrator privileges.

However, all assets required by your module code exists in a single directory. This makes module code eminently portable and flexible to different environments.

Q. **How can I add a custom local or UNC path to my machine's built-in module paths?**

A. Let's say you want to add C:\Modules to your system's **PSModulePath** environment variable. First, you'll view the default module locations:

```
PS C:\> $env:PSModulePath
C:\Users\Tim\Documents\WindowsPowerShell\Modules;C:\Program Files\
WindowsPowerShell\Modules;C:\Windows\system32\WindowsPowerShell\v1.0\Modules\

PS C:\>
```

Second, you'll append the new path to your existing path. Be careful with this process because you don't accidentally want to replace the entire **PSModulePath** contents with C:\ Modules:

```
PS C:\> $env:PSModulePath + ";c:\modules"
C:\Users\Tim\Documents\WindowsPowerShell\Modules;C:\Program Files\
WindowsPowerShell\Modules;C:\Windows\system32\WindowsPowerShell\v1.0\
Modules\;c:\modules

PS C:\>
```

Note in the preceding code that we include the semicolon in the quoted string to explicitly insert that separator in our **PSModulePath**.

Q. **How can I count the number of commands contained within a module?**

A. You just pipe the **Get-Command** statement to **Measure-Object**; my default, **Measure-Object** gives you a sum:

```
Get-Command –Module Microsoft.PowerShell.Management | Measure-Object
```

If a module contains different types of commands besides just cmdlets, you can invoke the **–CommandType** parameter:

```
Get-Command –Module Microsoft.PowerShell.Management –CommandType cmdlet |
➥Measure-Object
```

Workshop

Your workshop challenge in this hour of training is a sort of "meta" exercise because you'll be abstracting your skills a bit. What the heck do I mean? Read on.

Create a new PowerShell module named **OneGetSetup** that includes two functions. The first function downloads and installs **NuGet**, enables and trusts the Chocolatey repository, and generates a report of available packages.

The second function does just the opposite; namely, resetting the **OneGet** environment to its factory defaults. Make sure to add comment-based help to your script module.

Quiz

1. Adding the **–ListAvailable** parameter to **Get-Module** tells you what?

    a. Which modules have been imported into the current session

    b. Which modules are resident on your system but not imported into your current session

    c. Which modules are available for download from the module PSGallery

2. You can import a PowerShell module no matter where it's installed on your computer.

    a. True

    b. False

3. What is the result of the following statement?

```
PS C:\>cat function:Add-CodeMember
```

    a. Concatenates the previously run function with the **Add-CodeMember** custom function

    b. Runs the **Add-CodeMember** custom function by using standard user credentials

    c. Lists the source code of the **Add-CodeMember** custom function

Answers

1. The correct answer is B. When you run **Get-Module** with no parameters, you'll see the modules whose contents are exported into your current session. The **Get-Module –ListAvailable** statement tells you which modules are available for import.

2. The correct answer is B. Windows PowerShell is easygoing as with regard to loading modules. For instance, you can manually path out to a custom module like this:

```
PS C:\>Import-Module –Name C:\modules-test\custmod1 -Verbose
```

Remember that you'll need to add your custom module storage location to your system's **PSModulePath** environment variable for module auto-load to work.

3. The correct answer is C. This can be a tough question if you don't know that **cat** is an alias for **Get-ChildItem**. If you remember that **Function:** is a **PSDrive** that stores all system and custom functions, you'll see how easy it is to "crack open" functions to view their underlying source code. Windows PowerShell is all about sharing the (source code) love.

Managing Active Directory with Windows PowerShell

What You'll Learn in This Hour:

▶ Installing Active Directory

▶ Creating common Active Directory objects

▶ Undertaking various Active Directory administration tasks

If you're a Windows systems administrator, then you definitely work with Active Directory Domain Services (AD DS) every day. When I look back at how much time I wasted in manually creating AD user accounts, group accounts, and computer accounts when I can do everything nowadays automatically with PowerShell, I shake my head sadly.

Sure, we had Visual Basic Scripting Edition (VBScript), but I always considered VBScript scripting in a production environment somewhat akin to playing with matches while standing next to a fuel pump.

In this hour, you learn how to get around Active Directory by using Windows PowerShell. After you learn these automation techniques, I bet you'll rarely use graphical AD management tools very often from now on.

Installing Active Directory

The first domain controller in an Active Directory forest is called, appropriately enough, the *forest root domain controller*, and is the security focal point of your entire forest. So, in this hour, we'll assume that you already have your forest's first domain defined. In my opinion, it's best to create the forest root domain controller the "slow way" to make sure that every single choice is made correctly at the outset.

But how can we promote a Windows Server 2012 R2 member server to a domain controller in an existing domain? Well, I'm glad you asked.

Testing for Domain Membership

Our first order of business is to ensure that our prospective domain controller is, indeed, a member of an AD domain. You can query the WMI repository for a quick answer to this question:

```
PS C:\> Get-WmiObject -Class win32_computersystem -ComputerName dscclient01 |
➥Select-Object -Property Name, Domain
```

```
Name                                        Domain
----                                        ------
DSCCLIENT01                                 company.pri
```

Now let's make sure that AD DS isn't installed on my DSCCLIENT01 box:

```
PS C:\> Get-WindowsFeature –Name AD-Domain-Services
```

```
Display Name                          Name                 Install State
------------                          ----                 -------------
[ ] Active Directory Domain Services AD-Domain-Services    Available
```

NOTE

To be perfectly blunt, if you don't know what Active Directory is, this hour might not be for you (at least not yet).

In the final four hours of training, I have the space to teach you product-specific PowerShell, but I don't have time to give you the full background information.

If you're new to Active Directory administration and you need to get your "sea legs" quickly, I recommend that you purchase and read Win*dows Server 2012 Unleashed* by my fellow Sams Publishing authors Rand Morimoto et al. (ISBN 978-0-672-33622-5; http://bit.ly/1KfbCGz). It's a big book, but will answer any question you could ever think of concerning Active Directory.

Joining a Domain

You can use **Add-Computer** on a Windows Server 2012 R2 or Windows 8.1 workgroup computer to join an Active Directory domain. Of course, you'll need to supply domain administrative credentials, or be delegated with the right to join a computer to the domain, for the process to work:

```
PS C:\>Add-Computer –Credential company\administrator –DomainName company.pri
➥-Restart
```

You can include additional parameters to your pipeline, such as –**OUPath** to designate where in AD the computer account should be created, or –**NewName** if you're renaming the computer simulataneously.

Either way, joining or unjoining a domain requires that you restart the target workstation. Speaking of which, here's how you'd unjoin a computer from an AD domain and restore it to a workgroup:

```
PS C:\>Remove-Computer -WorkgroupName "WORKGROUP" -UnjoinDomainCredential
➡"company\administrator" -LocalCredential "workstation\administrator" -Force
➡-Restart
```

Installing the Active Directory Binaries

You've already met the **Install-WindowsFeature** cmdlet before; you can also use **Add-WindowsFeature** if you're so inclined. Here we'll use the cmdlet along with a couple switch parameters to ensure we get the Active Directory PowerShell modules and Server Manager utility:

```
PS C:\> Install-WindowsFeature -Name ad-domain-services -IncludeAllSubFeature
➡-IncludeManagementTools

Success Restart Needed Exit Code    Feature Result
------- -------------- ---------    --------------
True    No             Success      {Active Directory Domain Services, Group P...
```

As you can see from this output, simply installing the AD binaries requires no restart. So, we can proceed to the actual promotion process next.

Before we do that, though, I want us to see what else is available in the **ActiveDirectory** module. Let's do a **Get-Command**:

```
PS C:\> Get-Command -Module ActiveDirectory | Format-Wide

Add-ADCentralAccessPolicyMember                    Add-ADComputerServiceAccount
Add-ADDomainControllerPasswordReplicationPolicy    Add-ADFineGrainedPasswordPolicySubject
Add-ADGroupMember                                  Add-ADPrincipalGroupMembership
Add-ADResourcePropertyListMember                   Clear-ADAccountExpiration
Clear-ADClaimTransformLink                         Disable-ADAccount
Disable-ADOptionalFeature                          Enable-ADAccount
Enable-ADOptionalFeature                           Get-ADAccountAuthorizationGroup
Get-ADAccountResultantPasswordReplicationPolicy    Get-ADAuthenticationPolicy
Get-ADAuthenticationPolicySilo                     Get-ADCentralAccessPolicy
Get-ADCentralAccessRule                            Get-ADClaimTransformPolicy
Get-ADClaimType                                    Get-ADComputer
Get-ADComputerServiceAccount                       Get-ADDCCloningExcludedApplicationList
Get-ADDefaultDomainPasswordPolicy                  Get-ADDomain
Get-ADDomainController                             Get-ADDomainControllerPasswordReplicationPol
Get-ADDomainControllerPasswordReplicationPolicyUsage   Get-ADFineGrainedPasswordPolicy
Get-ADFineGrainedPasswordPolicySubject            Get-ADForest
Get-ADGroup                                        Get-ADGroupMember
Get-ADObject                                       Get-ADOptionalFeature
Get-ADOrganizationalUnit                           Get-ADPrincipalGroupMembership
Get-ADReplicationAttributeMetadata                 Get-ADReplicationConnection
Get-ADReplicationFailure                           Get-ADReplicationPartnerMetadata
Get-ADReplicationQueueOperation                    Get-ADReplicationSite
Get-ADReplicationSiteLink                          Get-ADReplicationSiteLinkBridge
```

```
Get-ADReplicationSubnet                              Get-ADReplicationUpToDatenessVectorTable
Get-ADResourceProperty                               Get-ADResourcePropertyList
Get-ADResourcePropertyValueType                      Get-ADRootDSE
Get-ADServiceAccount                                 Get-ADTrust
Get-ADUser                                           Get-ADUserResultantPasswordPolicy
Grant-ADAuthenticationPolicySiloAccess               Install-ADServiceAccount
Move-ADDirectoryServer                               Move-ADDirectoryServerOperationMasterRole
Move-ADObject                                        New-ADAuthenticationPolicy
New-ADAuthenticationPolicySilo                       New-ADCentralAccessPolicy
New-ADCentralAccessRule                              New-ADClaimTransformPolicy
New-ADClaimType                                      New-ADComputer
New-ADDCCloneConfigFile                              New-ADFineGrainedPasswordPolicy
New-ADGroup                                          New-ADObject
New-ADOrganizationalUnit                             New-ADReplicationSite
New-ADReplicationSiteLink                            New-ADReplicationSiteLinkBridge
New-ADReplicationSubnet                              New-ADResourceProperty
New-ADResourcePropertyList                           New-ADServiceAccount
New-ADUser                                           Remove-ADAuthenticationPolicy
Remove-ADAuthenticationPolicySilo                    Remove-ADCentralAccessPolicy
Remove-ADCentralAccessPolicyMember                   Remove-ADCentralAccessRule
Remove-ADClaimTransformPolicy                        Remove-ADClaimType
Remove-ADComputer                                    Remove-ADComputerServiceAccount
Remove-ADDomainControllerPasswordReplicationPolicy   Remove-ADFineGrainedPasswordPolicy
Remove-ADFineGrainedPasswordPolicySubject            Remove-ADGroup
Remove-ADGroupMember                                 Remove-ADObject
Remove-ADOrganizationalUnit                          Remove-ADPrincipalGroupMembership
Remove-ADReplicationSite                             Remove-ADReplicationSiteLink
Remove-ADReplicationSiteLinkBridge                   Remove-ADReplicationSubnet
Remove-ADResourceProperty                            Remove-ADResourcePropertyList
Remove-ADResourcePropertyListMember                  Remove-ADServiceAccount
Remove-ADUser                                        Rename-ADObject
Reset-ADServiceAccountPassword                       Restore-ADObject
Revoke-ADAuthenticationPolicySiloAccess              Search-ADAccount
Set-ADAccountAuthenticationPolicySilo                Set-ADAccountControl
Set-ADAccountExpiration                              Set-ADAccountPassword
Set-ADAuthenticationPolicy                           Set-ADAuthenticationPolicySilo
Set-ADCentralAccessPolicy                            Set-ADCentralAccessRule
Set-ADClaimTransformLink                             Set-ADClaimTransformPolicy
Set-ADClaimType                                      Set-ADComputer
Set-ADDefaultDomainPasswordPolicy                    Set-ADDomain
Set-ADDomainMode                                     Set-ADFineGrainedPasswordPolicy
Set-ADForest                                         Set-ADForestMode
Set-ADGroup                                          Set-ADObject
Set-ADOrganizationalUnit                             Set-ADReplicationConnection
Set-ADReplicationSite                                Set-ADReplicationSiteLink
Set-ADReplicationSiteLinkBridge                      Set-ADReplicationSubnet
Set-ADResourceProperty                               Set-ADResourcePropertyList
Set-ADServiceAccount                                 Set-ADUser
```

```
Show-ADAuthenticationPolicyExpression               Sync-ADObject
Test-ADServiceAccount                               Uninstall-ADServiceAccount
Unlock-ADAccount
```

Wow! That's a lot of power, isn't it? To be sure, Active Directory is one of the most PowerShell-enabled of all Windows Server features.

TIP

Remember that the Active Directory Administrative Center (ADAC) graphical user interface (GUI) tool is actually a PowerShell host application that runs a PowerShell instance under the hood.

Promoting the Domain Controller

DCPROMO has gone the way of the dodo in Windows Server 2012. Nowadays we can promote a domain member server to domain controller either by using Server Manager or Windows PowerShell. Obviously, we'll choose the latter route.

Let's start by examining the cmdlets contained in the **ADDSDeployment** module. (Yes, I know—two entire modules devoted to Active Directory!)

```
PS C:\> Get-Command -Module ADDSDeployment | Select-Object -Property Name

Name
----
Add-ADDSReadOnlyDomainControllerAccount
Install-ADDSDomain
Install-ADDSDomainController
Install-ADDSForest
Test-ADDSDomainControllerInstallation
Test-ADDSDomainControllerUninstallation
Test-ADDSDomainInstallation
Test-ADDSForestInstallation
Test-ADDSReadOnlyDomainControllerAccountCreation
Uninstall-ADDSDomainController
```

We don't have too many cmdlets to choose from, but we'll begin with **Test-ADDSDomain ControllerInstallation** to make sure that our DSCCLIENT01 member server fulfills all the prerequisites to become a domain controller:

```
Test-ADDSDomainControllerInstallation -InstallDns -Credential (Get-Credential
➡Company\trainer) -DomainName "company.pri" | Format-List
```

In running the previous test command, you'll be prompted not only for your domain administrative password, but also the Directory Services Restore Mode (DSRM) password. If all tests pass successfully, you're ready to perform the actual promotion with the **Intall-ADDSDomainController** cmdlet:

```
Install-ADDSDomainController -InstallDns -Credential (Get-Credential
company\trainer) -DomainName "company.pri"
```

Figure 21.1 shows the promotion process from the perspective of the Windows PowerShell integrated scripting environment (ISE).

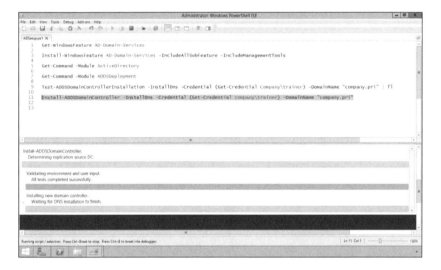

FIGURE 21.1
Promoting an AD DS domain controller by using Windows PowerShell.

To complete the promotion, you need to reboot the server. Actually, don't be surprised when the server automatically reboots, because it will do so.

Installing a New Child Domain

Sometimes a business needs to break their Active Directory forest into one or more child domains. Perhaps the reason is security related, or maybe it's political. Either way, we can create a new child domain by (1) installing **AD-Domain-Services** on a target server, and (2) running **Install-ADDSDomain**.

In the following example, we define the first domain of a child domain named child.company. pri. We also set the domain functional level to Windows Server 2008 R2:

```
PS C:\> Install-ADDSDomain -Credential (Get-Credential "company\administrator")
➥-NewDomainName "child" -ParentDomainName "company.pri" -InstallDns
➥-CreateDnsDelegation -DomainMode Win2008R2

SafeModeAdministratorPassword: ********
Confirm SafeModeAdministratorPassword: ********

The target server will be configured as a domain controller and restarted when
this operation is complete.
Do you want to continue with this operation?
[Y] Yes  [A] Yes to All  [N] No  [L] No to All  [S] Suspend  [?] Help
(default is "Y"):
```

Creating Common Active Directory Objects

After you have your domain in place, you can use Windows PowerShell to create directory service objects. For our purposes, we'll constrain our build to organizational units (OUs), domain global groups, and domain user accounts.

To be effective with PowerShell-based Active Directory, you need to understand Lightweight Directory Access Protocol (LDAP) distinguished name (DN) syntax. For instance, the DN for the Users container in the company.pri domain looks like this:

```
CN=Users,DC=Company,DC=pri
```

NOTE

In this hour, I start with the presumption that you're already familiar with basic Active Directory concepts and terminology. If you're not, I suggest that you purchase the *Active Directory Cookbook*, 4th Edition, by Brian Svidergol and Robbie Allen, published by O'Reilly (http://oreil.ly/1xCD5t6).

In that book, the authors not only give you more Active Directory PowerShell goodness than you can conceive, but also provide you with the necessary theoretical background information.

Creating Organizational Units

We use organizational units, or OUs, to, well, organize Active Directory users, groups, and computer accounts for Group Policy placement and delegated administration.

Let's create a new OU named Sales in the root of our fictional company.pri AD domain:

```
PS C:\>New-ADOrganizationalUnit "Sales" -ProtectedFromAccidentalDeletion $true
➥-Description "Sales OU"
```

The –**ProtectedFromAccidentalDeletion** parameter ensures that the new AD object cannot be accidentally deleted. We now can use **Get-ADOrganizationalUnit** to enumerate all OUs in the domain:

```
PS C:\> Get-ADOrganizationalUnit -Filter * | Select-Object -Property
➥DistinguishedName


DistinguishedName
-----------------
OU=Domain Controllers,DC=company,DC=pri
OU=Sales,DC=company,DC=pri
```

In my experience, you use the –**Filter** parameter a lot when running Active Directory PowerShell cmdlets. Your best bet is to, as I said, obtain excellent familiarity with LDAP DN syntax.

▶ It might also be helpful to review the information about regular expression syntax that we covered in Hour 16, "Searching and Filtering with Regular Expressions."

Creating Groups

Let's create a domain global group named Sales Users that we'll use to apply security to all Sales department employees in the company.pri domain:

```
PS C:\> New-ADGroup -Name "Sales Users" -SamAccountName "SalesUsers" -GroupCategory
➥Security -GroupScope Global -DisplayName "Sales Users" -Path
➥"OU=Sales,DC=Company,DC=pri"
```

Now if you run the following PowerShell one-liner, you'll see all OUs, which can get cumbersome to say the least:

```
PS C:\>Get-ADGroup –Filter * | Select-Object –Property DistinguishedName
```

We can go a few different ways to find the Sales OU. First, we'll use the –**like** operator in a –**Filter** expression:

```
PS C:\> Get-ADGroup -Filter { Name -like "sales*" }


DistinguishedName : CN=Sales Users,OU=Sales,DC=company,DC=pri
GroupCategory     : Security
GroupScope        : Global
Name              : Sales Users
ObjectClass       : group
ObjectGUID        : b7bca69e-02ec-4106-8e54-51db96b550d2
SamAccountName    : SalesUsers
SID               : S-1-5-21-2869276075-3597274836-1290150734-1109
```

Now we'll bring out the RegEx heavy artillery. A bit of overkill here, I admit. Nonetheless, I need you to get as much practice with this stuff as possible:

```
PS C:\> Get-ADGroup -Filter * | Where-Object {$_.Name -match "^Sal*"}

DistinguishedName : CN=Sales Users,OU=Sales,DC=company,DC=pri
GroupCategory     : Security
GroupScope        : Global
Name              : Sales Users
ObjectClass       : group
ObjectGUID        : b7bca69e-02ec-4106-8e54-51db96b550d2
SamAccountName    : SalesUsers
SID               : S-1-5-21-2869276075-3597274836-1290150734-1109
```

Cool. So now we have an OU to house our Sales global security group. The next step in this trolley ride through PowerShell AD automation is to create a user account for a new Sales department employee.

Creating User Accounts

As you know, the Active Directory schema stores many, many attributes for user objects. So, I suggest that you open the Windows PowerShell ISE and script out the **New-ADUser** code for reuse. Check this out:

```
New-ADUser `
 -Name "Michelle Finch" `
 -Path "OU=Sales,DC=Company,DC=Pri" `
 -SamAccountName "michellef" `
 -DisplayName "Michelle Finch" `
 -AccountPassword (ConvertTo-SecureString "P@$$w0rd1" -AsPlainText -Force) `
 -ChangePasswordAtLogon $true `
 -Enabled $true
Add-ADGroupMember "CN=Sales Users,OU=Sales,DC=Company,DC=pri" "michellef"
```

TIP

Remember that if you use the backtick escape character as I did that you must not have any spaces between the backtick and the new line.

This particular example includes **Add-ADGroupMember**, which allows us to seamlessly pop the new user account into her appropriate global group.

Notice also how we cleverly handled the inclusion of a starter password for the user. The **ConvertTo-SecureString** accepts plain-text input, applies encryption, and stores the password hash safely in Active Directory.

I hope that the gears in your mind are turning and you're asking yourself how you can customize the above code by using variables and such. If so, congratulations on becoming a true-blue Windows PowerShell scripter!

You should open Active Directory Users and Computers to verify that you are indeed creating live AD objects using nothing more than Windows PowerShell code. Figure 21.2 shows my text environment.

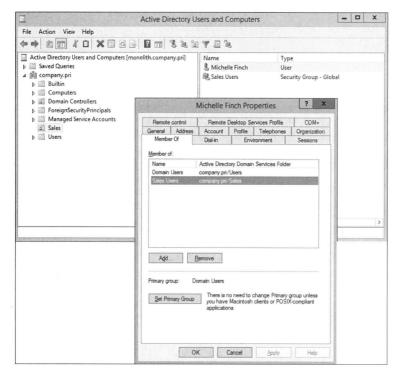

FIGURE 21.2
Can you believe it? We're actually managing Active Directory entirely through PowerShell code.

Managing User Accounts

In my experience, unlocking user accounts and resetting their passwords are the two most common tasks. First, let's assume that our Michelle Finch user mistyped her password enough times that her account is now locked. How can we unlock her account from the command line? There's a cmdlet for that:

```
PS C:\>Unlock-ADAccount -Identity "CN=Michelle Finch",OU=Sales,DC=company,DC=pri"
```

See, I told you that PowerShell-based AD administration requires that you "speak" in DN syntax.

To reset a user's password, we'll user **Set-ADAccountPassword**. This cmdlet has been a long time coming; prior to its introduction into PowerShell, resetting a simple password was a multiline, cumbersome task:

```
PS C:\>Set-ADAccountPassword "CN=Michelle Finch,OU=Sales,DC=Company,DC=pri" -Reset
➥-NewPassword (ConvertTo-SecureString -AsPlainText "p@ssw0rd1" -Force) -PassThru |
➥Set-ADUser -ChangePasswordAtLogon $True
```

The previous example is interesting because we use **–PassThru** to keep the **Set-ADAccountPassword** output in the pipeline. We do that so we can pass the password object into **Set-ADUser** and force the user to change her password during her next logon.

TRY IT YOURSELF ▼

Creating Domain User Accounts in Bulk

In this Try It Yourself exercise, you'll take a comma-separated value (CSV) containing user account information and import it into Active Directory by using PowerShell. This example is very "real world"; most Windows systems administrators face having to create several AD user accounts at once every once in a while.

To complete this exercise, you need a Windows Server 2008 R2 or later domain controller.

1. Use Excel, another spreadsheet application, or a simple text edit to create and save a CSV file named **domain-users.csv**. Populate the file with one or more user account entries as I've done in Figure 21.3.

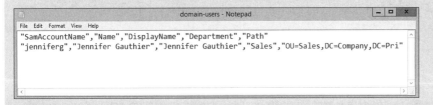

FIGURE 21.3
For a clean import, make sure that the CSV column headers are name-matched to legal parameter names of New-ADUser.

The trick here is to make sure that your CSV column headers match the user account properties supported by **New-ADUser**. Remember you can get those parameter names easily with PowerShell:

```
PS C:\> Get-Help -Name New-ADUser -Parameter * | Select-Object -Property Name
➥| Format-Wide -Column 2
```

AccountExpirationDate	AccountNotDelegated
AccountPassword	AllowReversiblePasswordEncryption
AuthenticationPolicy	AuthenticationPolicySilo
AuthType	CannotChangePassword
Certificates	ChangePasswordAtLogon
City	Company
CompoundIdentitySupported	Country
Credential	Department
Description	DisplayName
Division	EmailAddress
EmployeeID	EmployeeNumber
Enabled	Fax
GivenName	HomeDirectory
HomeDrive	HomePage
HomePhone	Initials
Instance	KerberosEncryptionType
LogonWorkstations	Manager
MobilePhone	Name
Office	OfficePhone
Organization	OtherAttributes
OtherName	POBox
PassThru	PasswordNeverExpires
PasswordNotRequired	Path
PostalCode	PrincipalsAllowedToDelegateToAccount
ProfilePath	SamAccountName
ScriptPath	Server
ServicePrincipalNames	SmartcardLogonRequired
State	StreetAddress
Surname	Title
TrustedForDelegation	Type
UserPrincipalName	Confirm

TIP
___

I understand that you may be tasked with creating a bunch of user accounts whose properties were exported to CSV from another system (perhaps your human resources database), and the column names may not match.

You can work around this problem by building a custom hash table that maps the CSV's column titles to appropriate New-ADUser parameters, but that procedure is beyond our scope for today.
___

2. Fire up the ISE and save a new script file named Create-Users.ps1. We'll begin by creating a variable to store our users' default starter password:

```
$pw = ConvertTo-SecureString -String "P@$$W0rd1" -AsPlainText -Force
```

That variable will come in handy during the next step.

3. Let's now leverage what we already know about importing CSV files and how the pipeline works to create ourselves one or more new AD user accounts:

```
Import-CSV -Path "C:\domain-users.csv" | New-ADUser -AccountPassword $pw
➥-Enabled True -ChangePasswordAtLogon $True
```

4. Next, let's ramp up the complexity a bit. Edit your domain-users.csv file to match what I show you in Figure 21.4. Do you see the problem? The "logon" and "DeptID" columns in the file aren't going to match parameter names of the New-ADUser cmdlet.

FIGURE 21.4
Unless you have a properly formatted input file, you may have to "massage" the data a bit in PowerShell for the pipeline to work.

5. We can fix this problem with some clever use of hash tables. Add the code found in Figure 21.5 into your script. I'll explain each line:

```
1  $pw = ConvertTo-SecureString -String "P@$$w0rd1" -AsPlainText -Force
2  $path = "OU=Sales,DC=Company,DC=Pri"
3
4
5
6  Import-CSV -Path "c:\domain-users.csv" |
7  Select @{Name="samAccountName";Expression={$_."Logon"}}, `
8  @{Name="Department";Expression={$_."DeptID"}}, * |
9  New-ADUser -AccountPassword $pw -Path $path -ChangePasswordAtLogon $true -Enabled $true
```

FIGURE 21.5
Source code for our Try It Yourself exercise.

Line 1: Here we store the generic password as a secure string, as usual.

Line 2: Here we store the OU path in a variable for easy reuse.

Line 6: Here we bring our CSV into our session again. I break lines in this script by using both the pipe and the backtick.

Line 7: We pipe the CSV data into **Select-Object**, first mapping the **samAccountName** parameter of **Get-ADUser** to the file's Logon column.

Line 8: Here we map the DeptID column in the CSV file to the properly named **Department** parameter. The asterisk at the end of the line is crucial because we want to pack the entire CSV file contents, not only our two custom remapped ones, into the pipeline.

Line 9: Finally, we run the output into **New-ADUser**, sweeping up the shavings by including references to the **$pw** and **$path** variables. Done and done.

Undertaking Various AD Administrative Tasks

We'll close this hour by examining some one-off AD management tasks. Some of these actions have wide implications for your domain and forest (messing with functional level, for instance). Therefore, I highly advise you to play with these cmdlets only in a safe, lab forest. Fair engouh? Alright, let's rock.

Managing FSMO Roles

The Flexible Single Master Roles (FSMOs) enable multiple domain controllers in a forest/domain to coexist without overwriting each others' data. For instance, all domain password changes go through the PDC Emulator domain role holder.

Let's enumerate the company.pri forest's forest FSMO role holders:

```
PS C:\> Get-ADForest –Identity company.pri | Format-Table –Property SchemaMaster,
➥DomainNamingMaster


SchemaMaster                          DomainNamingMaster
------------                          ------------------
monolith.company.pri                  monolith.company.pri
```

Now we'll use **Get-ADDomain** to see domain role holders:

```
PS C:\> Get-ADDomain company.pri | ft PDCEmulator, RIDMaster,
➥InfratructureMaster


PDCEmulator              RIDMaster               InfratructureMaster
------------             ---------               -------------------
monolith.company.pri     monolith.company.pri    {}
```

NOTE

Active Directory Administrative Center (ADAC) is a PowerShell host application that will eventually replace the Active Directory Users and Computers MMC console that Windows administrators around the world know and love.

As you can see in Figure 21.6, any action you take in ADAC is performed by the PowerShell runtime under the hood. What's more is that the PowerShell code is echoed directly in the interface; you are free to copy this code, paste it into your scripts, and automate AD management to your heart's content. Good stuff indeed.

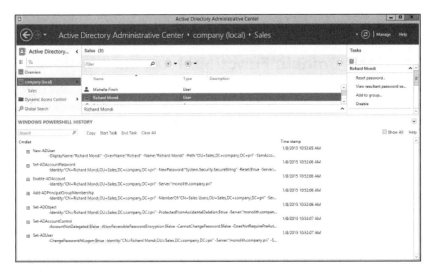

FIGURE 21.6
ADAC displays the underlying PowerShell code for every administrative action you take in the ADAC console.

Of course, my situation is about as boring as you can get because I have only one domain controller in a single domain forest. Note that because my monolith.company.pri domain controller hosts the global catalog, the infrastructure master role is effectively null.

Transferring FSMO Roles

For better performance and fault tolerance, you should transfer some or all FSMO roles off the forest root domain controller or the first domain controller promoted in each domain.

I think **Move-ADDirectoryServerOperationsMasterRole** is one of the...shall we say...longer cmdlets in existence. In the following example, I gracefully transfer the PDCEmulator and SchemaMaster roles off monolith.company.pri and onto a second domain contoller named xerxes.company.pri:

```
PS C:\>Move-ADDirectoryServerOperationMasterRole -Identity "xerxes.company.pri"
➥-OperationMasterRole PDCEmulator,SchemaMaster
```

When things go south and an FSMO role holder goes unexpectedly offline, you might need to perform a FSMO role seize operation. In this example, we force the PDCEmulator and SchemaMaster roles back to monolith.company.pri from xerxes:

```
PS C:\>Move-ADDirectoryServerOperationMasterRole -Identity "company.company.pri"
➥-OperationMasterRole PDCEmulator,SchemaMaster -Force
```

Pretty easy: A seize rather than a graceful move involves only the **–Force** switch parameter.

Handling Forest and Domain Functional Levels

AD administrators take advantage of Active Directory features by (a) installing one or more domain controllers running a new version of Windows Server, and (b) adjusting the forest or the domain functional level.

Let's start by using PowerShell to view the forest and domain functional levels:

```
PS C:\> (Get-ADForest).ForestMode
Windows2008R2Forest
PS C:\> (Get-ADDomain).DomainMode
Windows2008R2Domain
PS C:\>
```

The domain functional level can be set higher than the forest level; let's bring 'er on up to Windows Server 2012:

```
PS C:\>Set-ADDomainMode –Identity company.pri –DomainMode Windows2012R2Domain
➥-confirm:$false
```

If you're fortunate enough to have domain controllers running at least Windows Server 2008 R2, you can roll back a domain functional level. This may happen if you boost the level to Windows Server 2012 or 2012 R2 and realize that you still need 2008 R2 level. Whoops! No problem. All you have to do is run **Set-ADDomainMode** again, specifying the correct domain functional level. Note that some AD features, notably the AD recycle bin, make functional level rollback impossible.

To adjust the forest functional level, which sets the forest-wide functional level "floor," use **Set-ADForestMode**:

```
PS C:\>Set-ADForestMode –Identity company.pri –ForestMode WindowsServer2012R2
```

Administering Group Policy

The main thing I do from the command line concerning Group Policy is running good ol' GPUpdate.exe to refresh the local computer's assigned Group Policy Objects (GPOs):

```
C:\>GPUpdate /force
```

The difference between **Gpupdate** and **Gpupdate /force** is that the force switch reapplies every policy, new or old, whereas **Gpupdate** run alone applies new or modified GPO settings.

The problem with GPUpdate.exe is that it works only on the local computer. By contrast, we can force a Group Policy refresh of multiple computers by using **InvokeGPUpdate**. Check this out:

```
PS C:\>Invoke-GPUpdate –Computer (Get-Content "c:\domain-computers.txt")
```

The previous code refreshes Group Policy on all the computer names that are listed in my domain-computers.txt text file. Pretty handy, eh?

Summary

This hour of training comprises what's called a domain-specific application of Windows PowerShell. And no, I'm not speaking of Active Directory domains. Instead, you saw in this hour how you can apply the same Windows PowerShell syntax and behavior to a particular set of administrative job tasks.

Hour 22, "Managing SQL Server with Windows PowerShell," focuses our SharePoint energies on Microsoft SQL Server, one of the world's most popular relational database management systems (RDBMS).

Q&A

Q. How can I use PowerShell to manage Active Directory from my Windows 8.1 administrative workstation?

A. As long as you have the proper version of the Remote Server Administration Tools (RSAT) installed, you'll have the ActiveDirectory PowerShell module available to you. No problem!

Q. How can I browse my AD domain objects by using PowerShell?

A. Remember the concept of the PSDrive that we learned about earlier in this text? You'll find that an Active Directory PSDrive is created on your domian controllers. So, you can browse your AD directory partitions using typical navigation commands. See:

```
PS C:\> cd ad:
PS AD:\> dir


Name                ObjectClass          DistinguishedName
----                -----------          -----------------
company             domainDNS            DC=company,DC=pri
Configuration       configuration        CN=Configuration,DC=company,DC=pri
Schema              dMD                  CN=Schema,CN=Configuration,DC=comp...
DomainDnsZones      domainDNS            DC=DomainDnsZones,DC=company,DC=pri
ForestDnsZones      domainDNS            DC=ForestDnsZones,DC=company,DC=pri
```

Q. **Can I use PowerShell to interact with Active Directory by using ADSI?**

A. Wow, that's an advanced question! Yes, you can use the **ADSISEARCHER** type accelerator to query Active Directory by using the low-level Active Directory Services Interface (ADSI). You can look at a "type accelerator" as a shortcut method to directly access .NET objects.

First, you create an instance of the **ADSISEARCHER** object:

```
PS C:\>$searcher = [adsisearcher]""
```

You should pipe **$searcher** into **Get-Member** to see what's possible, property- and method-wise.

Second, you can start to query AD. The following example retrieves all Active Directory user objects:

```
PS C:\> ([adsisearcher]"objectCategory=user").FindAll()
```

```
Path                                    Properties
----                                    ----------
LDAP://CN=Administrator,CN=Users,DC=... {logoncount, codepage, objectcategor...
LDAP://CN=Guest,CN=Users,DC=company,... {logoncount, codepage, objectcategor...
LDAP://CN=krbtgt,CN=Users,DC=company... {logoncount, codepage, objectcategor...
LDAP://CN=Michelle Finch,OU=Sales,DC... {logoncount, codepage, objectcategor...
LDAP://CN=Richard Mondi,OU=Sales,DC=... {givenname, codepage, objectcategory...
LDAP://CN=Jon Nowell,OU=Sales,DC=com... {givenname, codepage, objectcategory...
```

Workshop

If you haven't yet taken the time to build yourself a virtual machine-based test lab, now is certainly the time. As long as you have a hardware (that is, "real") computer with at least 16GB of RAM, you can build yourself a two-node practice lab for no extra money—not kidding!

Here's what you need in order to get started:

▶ **Desktop virtualization software:** I recommend Oracle VM VirtualBox because it's free. If you're running Windows 8.1, you can actually use Hyper-V; you just need to activate the feature via Control Panel.

▶ **Evaluation software:** Search the Microsoft.com website for the download links for 180-day, fully functional evaluation software. You'll want Windows Server 2012 R2, Windows 8.1, SQL Server 2014, and SharePoint Server 2013.

▶ **External storage:** Virtual hard disks can occupy tens of gigabytes apiece. Although external USB drives aren't the fastest, they are inexpensive and will allow you to create far more VMs than you probably would otherwise.

Quiz

1. You must run **Import-Module ActiveDirectory** before you using AD cmdlets on your Windows Server 2012 R2 domain controller.

   a. True

   b. False

2. Which of the following statements describes the effect of this PowerShell statement?

   ```
   PS C:\>Remove-ADUser sarahg -WhatIf
   ```

   a. The user sarahg is notified that her account is being removed.

   b. The command will be evaluated but not executed.

   c. The script runner will be prompted for the user's distinguished name path.

3. Which of the following commands allows you to find the AD user with the last name Parker in the Marketing OU?

   a. Get-ADUser | where {surname –eq "Parker"}

   b. Get-ADUser -Filter {Lastname = "Parker"} -SearchRoot "DC=Marketing,DC=company,DC=pri"

   c. Get-ADUser -Filter {Surname -eq "Parker"} -SearchBase "DC=Marketing,DC=company,DC=pri"

Answers

1. The correct answer is B. This is a trick question. Remember that, as of Windows PowerShell v3, PowerShell autoloads modules as soon as you reference any of their enclosed commands. Of course, PowerShell has to know where to find these modules to autoload them. For that information, run the following:

   ```
   PS C:\>dir Env:\PSModulePath | fl *
   ```

2. The correct answer is B. This question tests your recall of the **–WhatIf** switch parameter. This parameter tests but does not actually execute the command. Many PowerShell administrators use **–Whatif** as a "sanity check" before executing potentially destructive PowerShell code.

3. The correct answer is C. The **–SearchBase** parameter is used with several Active Directory cmdlets and enables us to constrain how much of AD we're examining. You should spend time getting to know the most common AD schema attribute names (such as "surname" when you need someone's last name); in time, you'll use the names instinctively in your code.

HOUR 22
Managing SQL Server with Windows PowerShell

What You'll Learn in This Hour:

- ▶ Running PowerShell using SQL Server tools
- ▶ Interacting with SQL Server commands using PowerShell
- ▶ Automating common SQL Server DBA tasks

SQL (pronounced *sequel*) Server is Microsoft's enterprise-class relational database management system. If you work in a Microsoft shop and you run line-of-business (LOB) software, the chances are outstanding that you're running one or more SQL Server instances for data tier storage.

In this hour, you'll learn how to manage SQL Server instances and databases by using Windows PowerShell. As of this writing, SQL Server 2014 is the latest version of the software. However, I'll be using SQL Server 2012 because it's the platform I use in my data center. Don't worry, though; everything you'll learn in this hour of training applies equally to both versions.

NOTE

As I mentioned in Hour 21, "Managing Active Directory with Windows PowerShell," I don't have the space to give you detailed background on SQL Server itself. Instead, I defer to my Pearson colleagues Ray Rankins et al. and suggest that you read their comprehensive tome *Microsoft SQL Server 2012 Unleashed* (Sams Publishing, http://bit.ly/1xNat3y).

Oh, one more thing. For your practice purposes, you can get by just fine by downloading and installing the free SQL Server Express software from the Microsoft Download Center. If you do so, make sure to download the SQL Server Management Studio tools so that you can get both the graphical user interface (GUI) and PowerShell components. Let's get to work.

Running PowerShell Using SQL Server Tools

Let's start this discussion of PowerShell-based SQL Server management by investigating how to interact with the PowerShell runtime from within SQL Server.

A SQL Server instance is a separate installation of the SQL Server database engine. Within the instance are a number of built-in system databases, and you as the database administrator (DBA) are free to add as many user databases as you want.

SQL Server Management Studio, shown in Figure 22.1, is the primary SQL Server graphical administration tool.

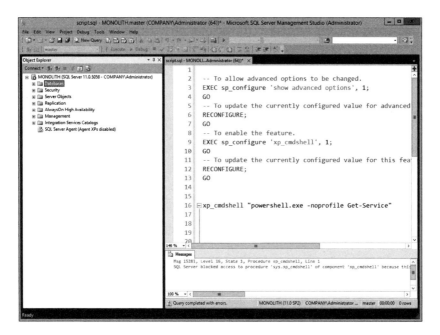

FIGURE 22.1
SQL Server Management Studio (SSMS) is a full-spectrum DBA and development environment for Microsoft SQL Server.

Installing the Management Tools

You'll need to install the SQL Server management tools and client software development kit (SDK) on your administrative workstation to interact with SQL Server.

As you can see in Figure 22.2, you'll want to run the SQL Server installation routine, choosing only to install the Client Tools SDK and the management tools. Doing this ensures that you have the SQL Server Management Studio, the sqlps module, and the SQL Server Management Objects (SMO).

By the way, SMO is a way to more directly address a SQL Server database instance by using .NET Framework namespaces instead of "raw" PowerShell or even T-SQL code.

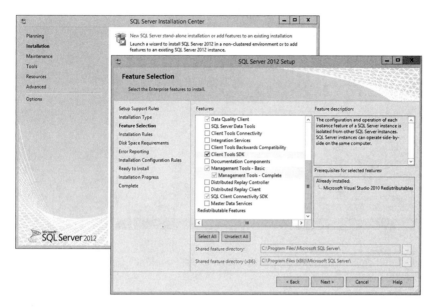

FIGURE 22.2
Preparing our environment for PowerShell-based SQL Server administration.

xp_cmdshell

SQL Server has a built-in stored procedure named **xp_cmdshell** that allows database administrators (DBAs) to run external executables from SQL Server scripts. For security reasons, SQL Server disables **xp_cmdshell** by default, and in my experiences most DBAs frown upon enabling it except for specific, ad hoc use cases.

To enable **xp_cmdshell**, run the following Transact-SQL code from the SQL Server Management Studio script pane:

```
EXEC sp_configure 'show advanced options', 1;
GO
RECONFIGURE
GO
EXEC sp_configure 'xp_cmdshell', 1;
GO
RECONFIGURE;
GO
```

What we're doing here is using another stored procedure, **sp_configure**, to enable the **xp_cmdshell** stored procedure.

Now that **xp_cmdshell** is enabled, we can call the PowerShell.exe executable and run simple PowerShell commands, as shown in Figure 22.3.

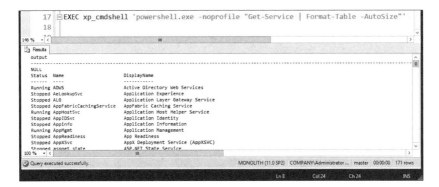

FIGURE 22.3
The xp_cmdshell system stored procedure allows SQL Server DBAs to call PowerShell scripts or commands directly from their T-SQL code.

NOTE

Structured Query Language (SQL, typically pronounced *ess-cue-el*) is a relational database data access language that's standardized by American National Standards Institute (ANSI). With SQL, DBAs run declarative commands like **SELECT**, **INSERT**, **UPDATE**, and **DELETE** to, well, select, insert, update, or delete records in one or more related tables.

Different database engine vendors put their own spin on SQL. For instance, Oracle's enriched procedural SQL is called PL-SQL. In SQL Server, Microsoft calls its SQL implementation Transact-SQL, with SQL pronounced as *sequel*.

Moreover, blah.

I hope you noticed in Figure 22.3 that we need to place quotes around our pipeline. To be honest, it's a bit tedious trying to run pipelines directly via the **xp_cmdshell** stored procedure.

TIP

A tip for getting easier-to-read output is to click **Query > Results To > Results to Text in SSMS**. You're welcome.

Instead of trying to construct pipelines in the SQL Server Management Studio (SSMS) query editor, I recommend that you use the **–Command** parameter and point to an honest-to-goodness PowerShell script in your file system. In the following example, I chose to bypass the system's PowerShell execution policy:

```
EXEC xp_cmdshell 'powershell -command "C:\myscript.ps1 -ExecutionPolicy Bypass"'
```

To once again disable **xp_cmdshell**, rerun the preceding code, changing the **1** value to **0** in the EXEC **sp_configure 'xp_cmdshell'** line.

Sqlps Minishell

Starting in SQL Server 2008, Windows PowerShell support was integrated into the product by means of the sqlps "mini shell." This is a self-contained Windows PowerShell v2 console that allows you acces to the SQL Server provider, cmdlets, and that's about it.

As you can see in Figure 22.4, we start the sqlps utility by right-clicking on a database object in SSMS and selecting **Start PowerShell** from the context menu.

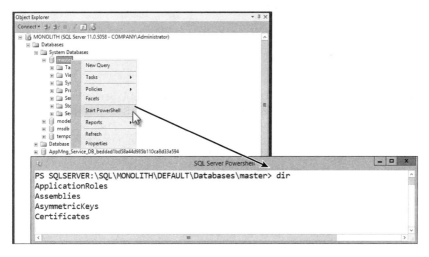

FIGURE 22.4
You can launch the Sqlps mini shell directly from SSMS.

As shown in Figure 22.5, the mini shell constrains your environment heavily. Because you're "trapped" in PowerShell v2, you don't have any flexibility to load other modules and do non-SQL Server stuff.

FIGURE 22.5
The Windows PowerShell team now admits that the sqlps mini shell was a mistake, given how limited its functionality is.

CAUTION
___

I highly advise you against using the sqlps utility. Even the PowerShell and SQL Server teams now admit that it was a mistake and contrary to the open spirit of Windows PowerShell. Microsoft keeps sqlps around even in the latest product release as of this writing (SQL Server 2014), but its status is officially "deprecated." This means that the utility is likely to be removed in a future version.
___

Interacting with SQL Server Using PowerShell

My preferred way to interact with SQL Server through PowerShell is to use the unfortunately named **sqlps** module. Yes, the module is named the same as the deprecated console utility; deal with it.

Start an administrative PowerShell console session (make sure that you're either on a SQL Server or have the management tools installed) and run the following to see what's there:

```
PS C:\> Get-Module -ListAvailable -Name SQL*

    Directory: C:\Program Files (x86)\Microsoft SQL
    Server\110\Tools\PowerShell\Modules
```

```
ModuleType  Version   Name                          ExportedCommands
----------  -------   ----                          ----------------
Manifest    1.0       SQLASCMDLETS                  {Add-RoleMember, B...
Manifest    1.0       SQLPS                         {Backup-SqlDatabas...
```

The **SQLASCMDLETS** module deals with SQL Server Analysis Services (SSAS), and isn't our concern in this hour of training. Instead, we want to know more about the **sqlps** module:

```
PS C:\> Get-Command -Module sqlps | Format-Wide -Column 2
```

```
SQLSERVER:                              Add-SqlAvailabilityDatabase
Add-SqlAvailabilityGroupListenerStat... Backup-SqlDatabase
Convert-UrnToPath                       Decode-SqlName
Disable-SqlAlwaysOn                     Enable-SqlAlwaysOn
Encode-SqlName                          Get-SqlCredential
Invoke-PolicyEvaluation                 Invoke-Sqlcmd
Join-SqlAvailabilityGroup               New-SqlAvailabilityGroup
New-SqlAvailabilityGroupListener        New-SqlAvailabilityReplica
New-SqlCredential                       New-SqlHADREndpoint
Remove-SqlAvailabilityDatabase          Remove-SqlAvailabilityGroup
Remove-SqlAvailabilityReplica           Remove-SqlCredential
Restore-SqlDatabase                     Resume-SqlAvailabilityDatabase
Set-SqlAvailabilityGroup                Set-SqlAvailabilityGroupListener
Set-SqlAvailabilityReplica              Set-SqlCredential
Set-SqlHADREndpoint                     Suspend-SqlAvailabilityDatabase
Switch-SqlAvailabilityGroup             Test-SqlAvailabilityGroup
Test-SqlAvailabilityReplica             Test-SqlDatabaseReplicaState
```

Sadly, many of the commands in the previous list deal with high availability and not (so much) daily administration. We'll use **Invoke-Sqlcmd**, though, and we'll also need to turn to SQL Server Management Objects (SMO) to take charge of some data definition language (DDL) and data manipulation language (DML) tasks.

Automating Common SQL Server DBA Tasks

Let's now have a look at how to accomplish a number of "bread and butter" SQL Server DBA tasks by using Windows PowerShell. To start, we'll use PowerShell to retrieve all databases from a given SQL Server database engine instance.

Listing Databases within an Instance

We'll use the SQL Server PSProvider to undertake this task. Notice the warning text that SQL Server gives you when you load the **sqlps** module:

```
PS C:\> Import-Module -Name sqlps
```

```
WARNING: The names of some imported commands from the module 'sqlps' include
unapproved verbs that might make them less discoverable. To find the commands
with unapproved verbs, run the Import-Module command again with the Verbose
parameter. For a list of approved verbs, type Get-Verb.
PS SQLSERVER:\>
```

We know by now that Get-Verb lists the 90-odd Microsoft "approved" PowerShell verbs. This warning lets us know that the SQL Server team must not have "gotten the memo" (more likely is they developed the cmdlets before the approved verb directed came down to them) and you may have discoverability problems when you use **Get-Command** –*Verb*.

For reference, you can supply a parameter to bypass the default warning:

```
PS C:\>Import-Module -Name sqlps -DisableNameChecking
```

Anyway, on to business. You should find yourself at the SQLSERVER:\> prompt after loading the **sqlps** module, so we can now enumerate the databases attached to your current instance. In the following example, I'm enumerating the databases on my default instance on my server named MONOLITH. I've piped the results to the grid view, which you can see in Figure 22.6:

```
PS SQLSERVER:\>Get-ChildItem -Path sql\monolith\default\databases | Out-Gridview
➥-Title "Database List: Monolith"
```

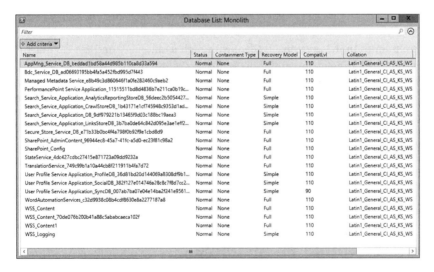

FIGURE 22.6
We used the SQL Server PSDrive and Out-Gridview to list all the many databases on my SharePoint Server 2013 / SQL Server computer. Lots o' databases.

Creating a New Database

In SQL, DDL commands like **CREATE, ALTER**, and **DROP** enable DBAs to, well, create, alter, and delete database objects; these objects range from the database itself, to the table, the column, the constraint, and so forth.

To create a new database I'd like for us to use the SMO interface.

NOTE

If you're a student of both Transact-SQL and Windows PowerShell, you need a comprehensive reference that covers both subjects together. I suggest that you pick up *SQL Server 2012 with PowerShell V3 Cookbook*, by Donabel Santos (Packt Publishing).

That book gives you lots of opportunity for practice with using SQL Server SMO and the **sqlps** PowerShell module to perform all the most common SQL Server DBA tasks.

In this example, we create a database named Test_Database in the default instance on the local SQL Server. If you're connecting remotely to SQL Server, make sure to supply the server name in the **$srv** variable declaration:

```
Import-Module –Name sqlps -DisableNameChecking
$srv = New-Object Microsoft.SqlServer.Management.Smo.Server("(localhost)")
$db = New-Object Microsoft.SqlServer.Management.Smo.Database($srv, "Test_Database")
$db.Create()
Write-Host $db.Name "created" $db.CreateDate
```

The **$srv** variable makes a server connection object by accessing the Smo.Server .NET SQL Server class, passing in the server name as a parameter.

The **$db** object defines a new database object named Test_Database, and the **Create()** method actually deploys the object on the server.

The **Write-Host** line is nothing more than feedback to you that the operation completed without errors.

Creating a New Table

We'll use a T-SQL script file and the **Invoke-sqlcmd** PowerShell cmdlet to create a sample table in our Test_Database database.

Start by creating a new file in Notepad, naming the file **products.sql**. You may need to

▶ Configure the Folder Options Control Panel to show file extensions.

▶ Use quotation marks around the full file name in Windows Notepad to create a .sql file and not a .txt file.

Save the .sql script file in the root of C: drive for easy access, and add the following T-SQL code:

```
use Test_Database
CREATE TABLE products
(
    product_ID int NOT NULL,
    productName varchar(100) NOT NULL,
    categoryName varchar(10),
    CONSTRAINT pk_productID PRIMARY KEY (product_ID)
)
```

We don't have the white space to describe the T-SQL code in terrific detail. Suffice it to say that we are creating a table named products that uses the product_id column as its primary key, and also includes productName and categoryName columns for added detail.

Now for the fun part: running the product.sql script from within PowerShell:

```
PS C:\>Invoke-sqlcmd -ServerInstance monolith -Database Test_Database -InputFile
➥"C:\products.sql"
```

Technically, we could have omitted the **–Database** parameter because we specify the database in our script file, but it never hurts to be explicit. As you can see, the key to the process is the **–InputFile** parameter of the **Invoke-sqlcmd** cmdlet.

Inserting Data into a Table

Let's continue using **Invoke-SQLCmd** with the **–query** parameter to insert row data into our products table:

```
PS C:\> Invoke-Sqlcmd -ServerInstance monolith -Database Test_SMO_Database -Query
➥"INSERT INTO dbo.products VALUES (1, 'spam', 'eggs')"
```

If you need to perform a bulk insert, you can feed comma-separated multiple rowsets (enclosed within parentheses) to the **VALUES** clause. Of course, there are several other ways to perform this or any other command using PowerShell cmdlets or the SMO objects, but we're just covering the basics here.

Let's do a multirecord insert using a query variable and a here string. A "here string" allows us to use line breaks and spaces in a way that would ordinarily present problems at a PowerShell command line. We construct here strings by placing at (@) signs before and after the quotes:

```
$query = @"
INSERT INTO dbo.products
VALUES (2, 'Widget', 'Category1'),
(3,'whatchamacallit','Category2'),
(4,"foo", "bar")
"@
```

Press **Enter** twice to exit the here string and return to your PowerShell prompt. If you write the here string in a script, you don't have to worry about it.

Now we can pass **$query** into **Invoke-sqlcmd**:

```
PS C:\> Invoke-Sqlcmd -ServerInstance monolith -Database test_smo_database
➥-Query $query
```

Running Select Queries Against Table Data

I've experimented with SMO to run **SELECT** queries, but believe me, the process is crazily cumbersome. Once again, **Invoke-SQLcmd** comes to the rescue:

```
PS C:\> Invoke-Sqlcmd -ServerInstance monolith -Database test_smo_database
➥-Query 'SELECT * FROM dbo.products'
```

```
product_ID productName              categoryName
---------- -----------             ------------
         1 foo                     bar
         2 spam                    eggs
         3 golly                   gee
         4 oh                      my
```

As I'm sure you can well imagine, SQL enables us to perform row filtering on our **SELECT** results (using **WHERE**) and sorting as well (using **ORDER BY**).

TRY IT YOURSELF ▼

Backing Up a Database on a Schedule with PowerShell

In this Try It Yourself exercise, you'll create a PowerShell recurring job that backs up the Test_ Database database that we've worked with so far in this hour of training. Once again, you're confronted with the question of whether to use T-SQL, SMO, PowerShell commands, or .ps1 script files. Here you'll combine the last three methods into a single procedure. The code I use in this script is adapted from an example in Donabel Santos's excellent *SQL Server 2012 with PowerShell V3 Cookbook*.

1. Open the Windows PowerShell integrated scripting environment (ISE) on your SQL Server computer and save a new script file named **backup-testdatabase.ps1** in the root of the C: drive.

2. Create a folder named **dbbackup** in the root of the C: drive to catch the database backups.

3. Add the code in Figure 22.7 to your backup-testdatabase.ps1 script file. As usual, I'll walk you through each part of the script.

```
     backup-testdatabase.ps1 ✕
 1   Import-Module sqlps -DisableNameChecking
 2
 3   $instanceName = "MONOLITH"
 4   $server = New-Object -TypeName Microsoft.SqlServer.Management.Smo.Server `
 5   -ArgumentList $instanceName
 6   $databasename = "TEST_SMO_DATABASE"
 7   $timestamp = Get-Date -Format yyyyMMddHHmmss
 8
 9   $backupfolder = "C:\dbbackup\"
10   $backupfile = "$($databasename)_Full_$($timestamp).bak"
11   $fullBackupFile = Join-Path $backupfolder $backupfile
12
13   Backup-SqlDatabase `
14   -ServerInstance $instanceName `
15   -Database $databasename `
16   -BackupFile $fullBackupFile `
17   -Checksum `
18   -Initialize `
19   -BackupSetName "$databasename Full Backup" `
20   -CompressionOption On
21
22   $smoRestore = New-Object Microsoft.SqlServer.Management.Smo.Restore
23   $smoRestore.Devices.AddDevice($fullBackupFile, [Microsoft.SqlServer.Management.Smo.DeviceType]::File)
24   $smoRestore.ReadBackupHeader($server)
25   $smoRestore.ReadFileList($server)
```

FIGURE 22.7
Our PowerShell script code to back up a SQL Server database.

Line 1: We can't do anything with **sqlps** unless we load the module.

Lines 3–9: In these lines, we define a bunch of variables to store the metadata of our SQL Server connection string and backup environment. In Figure 22.7, I back up my TEST_SMO_DATABASE; you can substitute that name for any database on your system that you want to back up. Remember in line 3 that MONOLITH is the name of my SQL Server instance; you'll want to substitute that with your own instance name.

Lines 10–11: This is some nifty code that serves both to timestamp our backup files and to prevent subsequent backups from overwriting the existing backup files in the C:\ dbbackup directory.

Lines 13–20: Here we use the **sqlps Backup-SQLDatabase** cmdlet, using the backtick (`) as a line escape to make the code more readable.

Lines 22–25: These lines are technically optional; I included them as a sanity check to give us confirmation data as to what happened during the backup procedure.

4. Now it's time to create our PowerShell scheduled job on the SQL Server. Open an administrative PowerShell console session and let's get this done. In this example, we'll take a full backup of the target database every morning at 2:00 a.m.

5. Let's create variables to store the trigger and job options. The job options here force the job to run even if the server is running on battery power. We also specify that the server needs to be "live" on the network for the job to continue:

```
$t = New-JobTrigger -Daily -At "2:00 AM"
$o = New-ScheduledJobOption -RequireNetwork -StartIfOnBattery
```

6. Now let's create the actual scheduled task, substituting in the variables for **–Trigger** and **–ScheduledJobOption**:

```
PS C:\>Register-ScheduledJob -Name BackupTestDB -FilePath
➡"C:\backup-testdatabase.ps1" -Trigger $t -ScheduledJobOption $o
```

7. You can find the scheduled job by opening Windows Task Scheduler and browsing to **Task Scheduler Library > Microsoft > Windows > PowerShell > ScheduledJobs**. Feel free to manually start the job to test it out, or delete it when you finish with this exercise.

TIP

You don't have to be an expert T-SQL programmer to develop quality .sql script files with SQL Server. Open SQL Server Management Studio, right-click a database, and click **Tasks > Back Up**.

Fill out the Back Up Database dialog box as usual, but when you finish, open the Script menu and select **Script Action to New Query Window**. Boom!

Now you have a .sql script file with all the relevant T-SQL code all laid out for you. You can script out most actions in SQL Server Management Studio by using the Script menu. That's an awesome trick, isn't it?

Summary

Interacting with SQL Server from Windows PowerShell definitely has more of a learning curve associated with it than, say, managing Active Directory with PowerShell.

Number one, we have the three-fold nature of the code: Transact-SQL, SMO, and PowerShell itself. Number two, doing any meaningful work with SQL Server requires that you know your way around the basics of database administration. Nonetheless, I hope that you are now more comfortable with both SQL Server and PowerShell.

In Hour 23, "Managing SharePoint Server with Windows PowerShell," we'll apply Windows PowerShell to another product that's intimately associated with SQL Server: SharePoint Server 2013, Microsoft's enterprise content management platform.

Q&A

Q. Given that the sqlps "mini shell" is deprecated and is so inflexible, why does it persist in SQL Server?

A. In my experience, there is generally a gap of several years between Microsoft deprecating a feature and actually removing it from the product. Strictly speaking, *deprecation* refers to the declaration that no more resources (namely, money and programmer hours) will be devoted to that particular feature, and it is subject to removal in a future version of the product.

I believe that Microsoft keeps deprecated features in the product to give administrators time to learn other avenues for accomplishing the tasks that they performed using the now-deprecated feature.

Q. Why are so many of the sqlps module cmdlets skewed toward stuff like high availability? There doesn't appear to be many "bread and butter" cmdlets that are of interest to the SQL Server DBA.

A. You would have to ask the Microsoft SQL Server team directly. My understanding is that although every Microsoft product team is required to build a PowerShell interface for their projects, the team has the latitude to choose which specific functionality makes the cutover to PowerShell. Please know that you can find some fantastic SQL Server community script resources at sites such as the Microsoft TechNet Script Center (https://gallery.technet.microsoft.com/scriptcenter) or the PowerShell Code Repository (http://poshcode.org).

Q. Can I run SQL Server stored procedures with PowerShell?

A. Indeed you can. A stored procedure is a compiled object that can be called and run in much the same way that we use PowerShell functions.

For instance, try the following PowerShell one-liner to retrieve a list of all databases in your SQL Server instance, sorted by decreasing database size:

```
PS C:\> Invoke-Sqlcmd -ServerInstance monolith -Query 'exec sp_databases' |
➡Select-Object -Property database_name, database_size |
➡Sort-Object -Property database_size -Descending

DATABASE_NAME                                                DATABASE_
SIZE
-------------                                                -----------
--
WSS_Logging                                                      1344512
Search_Service_Application_DB_9df979...                          151168
SharePoint_Config                                                143360
Search_Service_Application_CrawlStor...                           85312
SharePoint_AdminContent_96944ec8-45a...                           78848
WSS_Content1                                                      78464
```

Workshop

Combine your PowerShell, SMO, and SQL Server knowledge to perform the following tasks:

- ▶ Restart the SQL Server database engine service.
- ▶ Create a SQL Server login and give the user privilege on your test database.
- ▶ Back up, drop, and restore your test database, all programmatically.

Quiz

1. The SQL Server Management Objects (SMO) perform most SQL Server actions with much less code than by using the **sqlps** PowerShell module.

    a. True

    b. False

2. You must install the SQL Server Feature Pack to install SMO on a SQL Server computer.

    a. True

    b. False

3. The **sqlps** cmdlets typically use _____ as a noun prefix.

    a. ps

    b. sql

    c. cmd

Answers

1. The correct answer is B. With almost no exception, I'm able to use **Invoke-Sqlcmd** to manage SQL Server by using much more terse (and understandable) code than when I work with the SMO. By the way, you may want to check out the SQL Server PowerShell Extensions project at https://sqlpsx.codeplex.com/. SQLPSX consists of 13 modules that make accessing SMO much easier and streamlined.

2. The correct answer is B. Remember that as long as we install the Client Tools SDK and the Management Tools on a computer (regardless of whether the machine runs a SQL Server instance), we'll get access to the SMO.

    However, if you want the SMO and sqlps capabilities without installing any SQL Server bits, you should download and install the SQL Server Feature Pack from the Microsoft Download site.

3. The correct answer is B. Although we see the warning that the **sqlps** module uses unapproved verbs, at least most of the cmdlets use a descriptive prefix for the noun portion. Recall that these noun prefixes serve (a) to make the commands more identifiable by us administrators and (b) to prevent cmdlet name collisions when multiple modules are loaded into a session.

Managing SharePoint Server with Windows PowerShell

What You'll Learn in This Hour:

▶ Understanding the environment

▶ Deploying a service application

▶ Deploying a web application

▶ Deploying a site collection

▶ Setting permissions on a site collection

▶ Reporting on a SharePoint farm

Microsoft SharePoint is Microsoft's enterprise content management (ECM) and web content management (WCM) platform. SharePoint enables businesses to create dynamic, mobile-friendly intranet portals where users can share information, store documents, manage lists, and so forth.

This hour focuses on managing on-premises SharePoint Server 2013 by using Windows PowerShell and the SharePoint snap-in. You may know that Microsoft sells SharePoint as a public cloud subscription service known as SharePoint Online. You'll learn how to interact with SharePoint Online, Office 365, and Microsoft Azure in the final hour of training.

In the meantime, we have much to do, so let's get started.

Understanding the Environment

One reason why learning to manage SharePoint Server can be so complicated is that SharePoint is a three-tier ASP.NET web application architecture that embraces an entire stack of related Microsoft technologies:

▶ Windows Server running in an Active Directory domain

▶ Internet Information Services (IIS) web server

▶ SQL Server databases for back-end data storage and retrieval

As part of its prerequisite installation routine, SharePoint Server 2013 installs Windows Management Framework 3.0, which of course means that the SharePoint snap-in relies on Windows PowerShell v3. In this hour of training, we assume that you've installed SharePoint Server 2013 and created the farm configuration database and Central Administration web application.

SharePoint Management Shell

Some Windows systems administrators erroneously assume that they have to use the so-called management shells that come with some enterprise software.

For instance, you'll find a program shortcut for a SharePoint 2013 Management Shell on your SharePoint server computers. What's going on with that shell?

For grins, right-click the **SharePoint 2013 Management Shell** icon and select **Properties** from the shortcut menu.

In the **Target** field on the shortcut page, you'll see that launching the shortcut actually executes the following (long) line of code:

```
C:\Windows\System32\WindowsPowerShell\v1.0\PowerShell.exe  -NoExit  " & '
➥C:\ProgramFiles\Common Files\Microsoft Shared\Web Server
➥Extensions\15\CONFIG\POWERSHELL\Registration\\sharepoint.ps1 ' "
```

Here's what's happening under the proverbial covers:

▶ We launch the PowerShell.exe console environment with the **–NoExit** switch, which ensures that the console session stays onscreen when the commmand completes.

▶ The ampersand (&) is called an *invoke operator*, and simply executes the following command string in the context of PowerShell.exe.

▶ We load and run the sharepoint.ps1 startup script.

Of course, the salient question is this: "What does the sharepoint.ps1 startup script actually do?" That's fair. If you drill into the previously given file path and open up sharepoint.ps1 in a text editor, here is the source code you'll see:

```
$ver = $host | Select-Object -Property Version
if ($ver.Version.Major -gt 1)  {$Host.Runspace.ThreadOptions = "ReuseThread"}
Add-PsSnapin Microsoft.SharePoint.PowerShell
Set-location $home
```

You'll also see a big digital signature block because Microsoft signed this script file, but I omitted that from the previous output for obvious reasons.

Here's a breakdown of the four lines of code:

- ▶ We check the version of the currently running PowerShell console host.

- ▶ If the host version is greater than v1, we set the session runspace to reuse CPU execution threads and load the SharePoint snap-in.

- ▶ We set the console's present working directory to the user's home folder.

Ordinarily, every PowerShell command runs in a separate execution thread. By reusing the threads as the Management Console does, we reduce the amount of memory consumed by the PowerShell console session and also reduce the likelihood of memory leaks. It's a subtle performance improvement, too.

So do you need to use the Management Shell to do PowerShell-based SharePoint administration? Heck no. The wrinkle is that the SharePoint team elected to use the older snap-in model instead of the more, well, modular module model. Say that three times quickly, by the way.

After you've loaded the Microsoft.SharePoint.PowerShell snap-in manually several times, you'll memorize the long namespace:

```
PS C:\>Add-PSSnapin Microsoft.SharePoint.PowerShell
```

You might also consider adding the snap-in invocation to your PowerShell startup script.

Probing the SharePoint Snap-in

The SharePoint product team really knocked themselves out in developing cmdlets in the SharePoint snap-in. Let's count 'em:

```
PS C:\>Get-Command -PSSnapin microsoft.sharepoint.powershell | Measure-Object

Count    : 779
```

Almost 800 commands, just for SharePoint Server itself.

TIP

Note that the commands all have the SP noun prefix that obviously stands for SharePoint.

Creating a SharePoint Managed Account

SharePoint needs to have at least one managed service account that acts as a security context for what it does in the SharePoint farm. Every SharePoint-related Internet Information Services (IIS) application pool requires a service account, as does every SharePoint-related database user in SQL Server.

TIP

Best practice guidance says that you should create a separate Active Directory user account for each SharePoint-related service. These accounts should be standard users; Windows Server, SharePoint Server, and SQL Server will elevate the user rights to the appropriate level.

Let's use the ActiveDirectory module on one of our Windows Server 2012 R2 domain controllers to define a service account named spservice:

```
New-ADUser -Name "SharePoint Service" -SamAccountName "spservice" -DisplayName
➥"SharePoint Service" -Enabled $true -ChangePasswordAtLogon $false -AccountPassword
➥(ConvertTo-SecureString "P@$$w0rd" -AsPlainText -force) -PassThru
```

I've given you the most common options in the preceding code; you are free to add more if you so require. I included the **–PassThru** switch to push this operation, which normally falls out of the PowerShell pipeline, through so you can see some onscreen results feedback.

Next, you'll load the SharePoint snap-in on a SharePoint server and define a SharePoint managed account. To do this, you need to know the AD username and password; this shouldn't be a problem if you're an AD/SharePoint farm administrator:

```
$cred = Get-Credential -Credential "company\spservice"
$account = New-SPManagedAccount -Credential $cred
Set-SPManagedAccount -Identity $account -PreExpireDays 5 -AutoGeneratePassword
➥$true
```

A *SharePoint managed account* is an Active Directory user account for which SharePoint automatically controls password changes.

TIP

Another benefit of SharePoint managed accounts is that you can reference them in your code and you don't have to worry about remembering or specifying the account password.

In the preceding code, we store the spservice account credentials in the **$cred** variable, and then pass it to the **$account** object that defines the SharePoint managed account. Finally, we invoke **Set-SPManagedAccount** to specify that SharePoint automatically change the user's password five days before the domain password policy time interval expires.

NOTE

Whenever I recommend a book or online resource to you, please know that I have actually read that resource. I'm not shilling for anyone; I'm simply your instructor. For a comprehensive overview of SharePoint Server 2013, try Michael Noel's *SharePoint 2013 Unleashed* (Sams Publishing, http://amzn.to/1xCJXqC).

For a detailed recipe guide on managing all aspects of SharePoint Server 2013 with Windows PowerShell, get Steven Mann's *PowerShell for SharePoint 2013 How-To* (also by Sams Publishing, http://amzn.to/1xCK7Oz).

Deploying a Service Application

In SharePoint Server 2013, you deploy features and functionality through modular units called service applications. A service application typically involves the following parts and pieces:

▶ A service instance that can be started or stopped on any SharePoint farm server

▶ One or more SQL Server databases

▶ One or more IIS application pools

▶ An administrative user interface (UI)

The good news is that we as SharePoint farm administrators have unlimited flexibility and control in deploying the service applications when we use PowerShell to do so. The bad news is that each service application has its own cmdlets. Let's investigate:

```
PS C:\> Get-Command -PSSnapin microsoft.sharepoint.powershell -Noun *application
➥| Select-Object -Property Name | Format-Wide -Column 2
```

```
Convert-SPWebApplication                    Get-SPAccessServiceApplication
Get-SPAccessServicesApplication             Get-SPEnterpriseSearchServiceApplica...
Get-SPExcelServiceApplication               Get-SPMetadataServiceApplication
Get-SPPerformancePointServiceApplica...     Get-SPSecureStoreApplication
Get-SPServiceApplication                    Get-SPStateServiceApplication
Get-SPTopologyServiceApplication            Get-SPUsageApplication
Get-SPVisioServiceApplication               Get-SPWebApplication
New-SPAccessServiceApplication              New-SPAccessServicesApplication
New-SPAppManagementServiceApplication       New-SPBusinessDataCatalogServiceAppl...
New-SPEnterpriseSearchServiceApplica...     New-SPExcelServiceApplication
New-SPMetadataServiceApplication            New-SPPerformancePointServiceApplica...
New-SPPowerPointConversionServiceApp...     New-SPProfileServiceApplication
New-SPSecureStoreApplication                New-SPSecureStoreServiceApplication
New-SPSecureStoreTargetApplication          New-SPStateServiceApplication
New-SPSubscriptionSettingsServiceApp...     New-SPTranslationServiceApplication
New-SPUsageApplication                      New-SPVisioServiceApplication
```

I'm giving you only partial output there, to save white space. You'll want to spend some time looking over those commands and their help files to get a feel for how they work.

In the meantime, let's deploy an instance of the Managed Metadata Service (MMS) service application. We use MMS to support taxonomic tagging within a web application.

To begin with, we'll create a reference to our previously created SharePoint managed account. We'll also define a new IIS app pool that uses the managed account as its security context:

```
$servaccount = Get-SPManagedAccount -Identity "company\spservice"
$apppool = New-SPServiceApplicationPool -Name MMS_AppPool -Account $servaccount
```

Note by the SP noun prefix that we're dealing entirely with SharePoint PowerShell commands. Next, we'll create the new MMS service application instance and associated proxy:

```
$servapp = New-SPMetadataServiceApplication -Name "MMS Service" -ApplicationPool
$apppool -DatabaseName "SharePoint_MMS_DB" -DatabaseServer "monolith"
New-SPMetadataServiceApplicationProxy -Name "MMS Service Proxy"
➥-ServiceApplication $servapp -DefaultProxyGroup
```

TIP

It's important not to omit the proxy step because, as I hope you know, the proxy is the "glue" that ties a SharePoint service application instance to one or more target web applications.

To start the service instance on our SharePoint server (I'm assuming a single-server farm in this hour of training for simplicity's sake), we must first obtain the globally unique identifier (GUID) for that instance. (This isn't the MMS service application we just started; here we're referring to the underlying Managed Metadata Web Service that's present on all farm servers.)

```
PS C:\> Get-SPServiceInstance | Out-File -FilePath "C:\service.txt" |
➥Notepad "C:\service.txt"
```

You'll find the GUID in the ID property for the Managed Metadata Web Service; it's not enjoyable parsing through the text file. I challenge you to use your PowerShell skills to more efficiently filter the **Get-SPServiceInstance** output to find a particular service's ID value.

Now that we know the service ID, we can invoke **Start-SPServiceInstance**:

```
PS C:\> Start-SPServiceInstance -Identity 38576f10-7cee-40f4-ba4f-9dab74117b6c
WARNING: 'Managed Metadata Web Service' is already started on server
'monolith.company.pri'
```

Good. That's what we wanted to see. While we're at it, we probably should run the following command and take note of the MMS Service application's GUID for future reference:

```
PS C:\> Get-SPServiceApplication -Name "MMS Service" | Select-Object -Property
➥DisplayName, ID | Format-Table -AutoSize

DisplayName      Id
-----------      --
MMS Service      dc7c74af-2d10-42d1-bbb6-50a835b6cf36
```

Feel free to log into Central Administration to verify your work. Figure 23.1 shows my server's service application loadout.

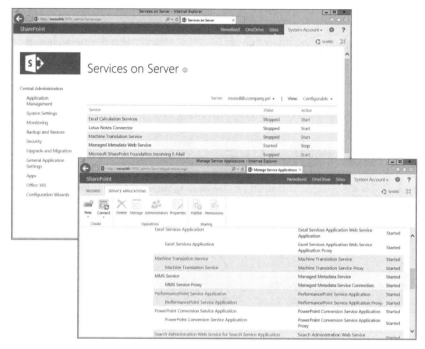

FIGURE 23.1
Our command-line PowerShell work manifests itself in the Central Administration GUI.

Deploying a Web Application

In the SharePoint object model, the web application is the entry point for your users. In Windows Server terms, a SharePoint web application is a SQL Server-backed ASP.NET website that's hosted by IIS:

```
$ap = New-SPAuthenticationProvider
New-SPWebApplication -Name "Corporate Intranet" -ApplicationPool "MMS_AppPool"
➥-ApplicationPoolAccount "company\spservice" -URL http://sharepoint.company.pri
➥-Port 80 -AuthenticationProvider $ap
```

In the first line, we create an instance of the SharePoint claims-based authentication provider. We use **New-SPWebApplication** to deploy the web app itself. Notice that we're reusing the same IIS application pool that we used for our earlier MMS service application.

About IIS Application Pools

IIS application pools provide a security and stability boundary for your web applications and service applications. At last check, Microsoft will support you only if your SharePoint servers have ten or fewer application pools per box.

So, your challenge as a systems administrator is to balance the isolation of your service/web apps with not overburdening your servers with too many app pools. It's a tough choice because IIS app pools isolate memory and serve to prevent a single crashed web or service app from bringing down the entire server.

Don't forget to update DNS to include the web application URL.

Deploying a Site Collection

A SharePoint web application all by itself is nothing more than a shell. The chief job of the web application is to receive HTTP/HTTPS connection requests and handle user authentication. The content comes from the site collection.

TIP

You probably know this, but the first site collection deployed inside of a Web application becomes the "root" or "top-level" site collection and exists at the same URL as its associated web application.

Depending on your SharePoint Server 2013 stock keeping unit (SKU), you'll have various site templates to choose from. In PowerShell, you need to know their formal names:

```
PS C:\> Get-SPWebTemplate | Where-Object { $_.CompatibilityLevel -eq 15 } |
➡Select-Object -Property Name, Title | Sort-Object -Property Name |
➡Format-Table -AutoSize
```

Name	Title
ACCSRV#0	Access Services Site
ACCSVC#0	Access Services Site Internal
ACCSVC#1	Access Services Site
APP#0	App Template
APPCATALOG#0	App Catalog Site
BDR#0	Document Center
BICenterSite#0	Business Intelligence Center
BLANKINTERNET#0	Publishing Site
BLANKINTERNET#1	Press Releases Site
BLANKINTERNET#2	Publishing Site with Workflow
BLANKINTERNETCONTAINER#0	Publishing Portal
BLOG#0	Blog

```
CENTRALADMIN#0            Central Admin Site
CMSPUBLISHING#0           Publishing Site
COMMUNITY#0               Community Site
COMMUNITYPORTAL#0         Community Portal
DEV#0                     Developer Site
DOCMARKETPLACESITE#0      Academic Library
EDISC#0                   eDiscovery Center
EDISC#1                   eDiscovery Case
ENTERWIKI#0               Enterprise Wiki
GLOBAL#0                  Global template
MPS#0                     Basic Meeting Workspace
MPS#1                     Blank Meeting Workspace
MPS#2                     Decision Meeting Workspace
MPS#3                     Social Meeting Workspace
MPS#4                     Multipage Meeting Workspace
OFFILE#0                  (obsolete) Records Center
OFFILE#1                  Records Center
OSRV#0                    Shared Services Administration Site
PPSMASite#0               PerformancePoint
PRODUCTCATALOG#0          Product Catalog
PROFILES#0                Profiles
PROJECTSITE#0             Project Site
SGS#0                     Group Work Site
SPS#0                     SharePoint Portal Server Site
SPSCOMMU#0                Community area template
SPSMSITE#0                Personalization Site
SPSMSITEHOST#0            My Site Host
SPSNEWS#0                 News Site
SPSNHOME#0                News Site
SPSPERS#0                 SharePoint Portal Server Personal Space
SPSPERS#2                 Storage And Social SharePoint Portal Server Persona...
SPSPERS#3                 Storage Only SharePoint Portal Server Personal Space
SPSPERS#4                 Social Only SharePoint Portal Server Personal Space
SPSPERS#5                 Empty SharePoint Portal Server Personal Space
SPSPORTAL#0               Collaboration Portal
SPSREPORTCENTER#0         Report Center
SPSSITES#0                Site Directory
SPSTOC#0                  Contents area Template
SPSTOPIC#0                Topic area template
SRCHCEN#0                 Enterprise Search Center
SRCHCENTERLITE#0          Basic Search Center
SRCHCENTERLITE#1          Basic Search Center
STS#0                     Team Site
STS#1                     Blank Site
STS#2                     Document Workspace
TENANTADMIN#0             Tenant Admin Site
visprus#0                 Visio Process Repository
WIKI#0                    Wiki Site
```

I filtered the site template output to show only SharePoint Server 2013 templates. Formally, SharePoint Server 2010 is version 14, and SharePoint Server 2013 is version 15.

The Team Site (STS#0) is the most popular site template in use nowadays; we'll use that for our new site collection:

```
$template = Get-SPWebTemplate -Identity "STS#0"
New-SPSite -Url "http://sharepoint.company.pri" -OwnerAlias
➡"company\administrator" -Template $template
```

Okay, now let's pop open a web browser and navigate to the web application/top-level site collection we just created. Figure 23.2 shows my team site.

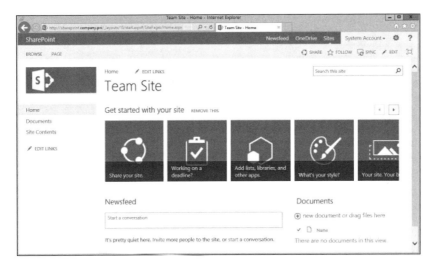

FIGURE 23.2
We built this cool intranet portal entirely with Windows PowerShell.

Setting Permissions on a Site Collection

A SharePoint portal isn't any good if your users and administrators cannot get access to the content. In this example, we want to grant our Domain Admins global group to have the Full Control permission level in our new site collection. We also want to grant our Domain Users global group the Contribute permissions level.

Run the following little script to enumerate the possible permission levels:

```
$site=Get-SPSite "http://sharepoint.company.pri:8080"
$web=$site.RootWeb
$roles=$web.RoleDefinitions
```

```
foreach($role in $roles)
{
  Write-Output $role.Name
}
```

For your reference, **foreach** is a common programming construct that loops (or iterates) through a data collection. Each detected role in the **$roles** collection is temporarily stored in the **$role** variable.

Dealing with Permissions in SharePoint

We hit a slight (okay, not so slight) snag when dealing with permissions in SharePoint, which are enormously complex. What makes it worse is that the PowerShell interface for creating and managing SharePoint users and groups is clunky, to say the least.

NOTE

I performed quite a bit of research, and finally settled on a PowerShell script made freely available by Ashley Feldon-Lawrence of the Full Circle Blog (http://bit.ly/1E7Pppn).

Download the CreateSPGroupAddADGroupSetPermissionLevel.ps1 script from that website and open it in Windows PowerShell ISE. This is actually a good thing because as PowerShell scripters it's not about reinventing the wheel, but in tweaking other users' scripts to suit our needs more effectively.

To that point, if you modify Ashley's script in a way that you think makes it better, please leave a comment on his blog and share your source code. Once again, we PowerShell scripters love to learn from others, and we always share our knowledge.

To sum it up, Ashey's script accepts a CSV file containing all your Active Directory groups and associated SharePoint permissions, and "plugs and chugs" the CSV data into a target site collection. At the end of the process, you'll have SharePoint groups that contain your relevant AD groups and are associated with your specified permission levels.

Reporting on a SharePoint Farm

What do you think the most common SharePoint verb is? Here, let's investigate the question ourselves:

```
PS C:\> Get-Command | Group-Object -Property Verb | Select-Object -Property Count,
Name | Sort-Object -Property Count -Descending

                           Count Name
                           ----- ----
                             676 Get
                             423 Set
                             278 Remove
                             256 New
                             106 Add
                              66 Enable
                              64 Disable
```

You're not surprised, I presume. Get is the most popular verb for a reason; it's how we gather intelligence by using PowerShell code.

Let's now go through a "lightning round" of SharePoint-related **Gets**. The thing to keep in mind here is that the SharePoint object model uses a wacky nomenclature, with site collections called *sites* and individual sites within a site collection called *webs*.

Viewing Web Applications

In the following example, we put a web application into a variable, and then enumerate the members. Spend time examining what's possible in terms of methods and properties for SharePoint web applications:

```
PS C:\> $webapp = Get-SPWebApplication -Identity "http://monolith"
PS C:\> $webapp | Get-Member
```

For instance, if you need to know which IIS application pool and SQL Server content database is associated with the service app, simply use dot notation and away you go:

```
PS C:\>$webapp.ApplicationPool
PS C:\>$webapp.ContentDatabases
```

Viewing Site Collections

Let's enumerate the site collections that exist within a given web application. Stay in the same session so that you can still access the **$webapp** variable:

```
PS C:\> Get-SPSite -WebApplication $webapp | Select-Object -Property Url

Url
---
http://monolith
http://monolith/my
http://monolith/my/personal/administrator
```

```
http://monolith/my/personal/tony
http://monolith/sites/ceoblog
http://monolith/sites/old
http://monolith/sites/old-eval
http://monolith/sites/search
```

Of course, remember to pipe the site collection object to **Get-Member** to examine methods and properties.

Viewing Sites

Within a site collection, we have at least one root or top-level site where the actual content (lists and libraries) exist. Let's enumerate the webs within my http://monolith top-level site collection:

```
PS C:\> Get-SPWeb -Site "http://monolith"

Url
---
http://monolith
http://monolith/bi
http://monolith/hr
```

If you need to obtain a reference to a particular subsite in your PowerShell script, try the following. In this example, we call SharePoint object model methods to change the file path of the site logo image:

```
Start-SPAssignment Global
$w = Get-SPWeb http://monolith/hr
$w.set_SiteLogoUrl(http://resources/hr_dept_image.png)
$w.Update()
Stop-SPAssignment -Global
```

The **Start-SPAssignment** and **Stop-SPAssignment** cmdlets are technically optional, but useful because they ensure that all the memory that SharePoint reserves for those big objects (after all, your **$w** variable may represent a humungous SharePoint site) is properly disposed of when it's no longer needed.

You'll call the **Update()** method a lot when you make configuration changes from PowerShell. Specifically, we're updating the content database that stores all site data and metadata.

Viewing Lists and Libraries

As you saw earlier regarding SharePoint permissions, accessing SharePoint lists and libraries programmatically is messy. Therefore, we'll again turn our attention to the PowerShell community and how those kind individuals help us out of a jam.

Adnan Amin from mstechtalk.com published a script named Generate Document Info Report.ps1 at the Microsoft Office TechCenter (https://gallery.technet.microsoft.com/office/Get-detail-report-of-all-b29ea8e2) that performs an excellent inventory of all document libraries within a site collection.

As usual, expect to tweak the source code a bit to suit your needs. When I was ready to invoke Adnan's **Get-DocInventory** function, I did this:

```
Get-DocInventory "http://monolith" | Where-Object {$_.list -eq "Documents"} |
➥Out-GridView -Title "MONOLITH Document Library Inventory"
```

Figure 23.3 shows my GridView results.

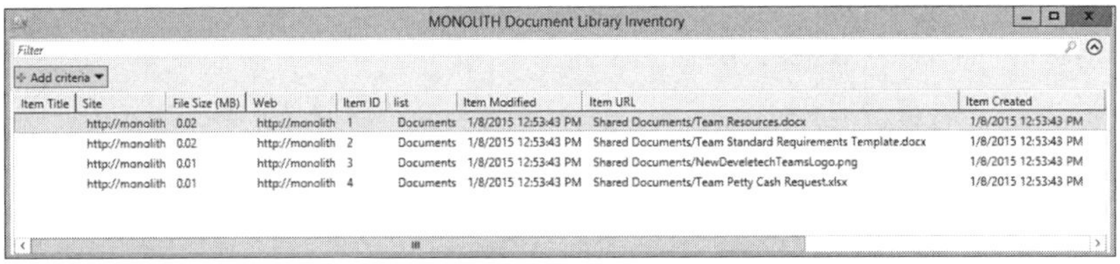

Item Title	Site	File Size (MB)	Web	Item ID	list	Item Modified	Item URL	Item Created
	http://monolith	0.02	http://monolith	1	Documents	1/8/2015 12:53:43 PM	Shared Documents/Team Resources.docx	1/8/2015 12:53:43 PM
	http://monolith	0.02	http://monolith	2	Documents	1/8/2015 12:53:43 PM	Shared Documents/Team Standard Requirements Template.docx	1/8/2015 12:53:43 PM
	http://monolith	0.01	http://monolith	3	Documents	1/8/2015 12:53:43 PM	Shared Documents/NewDeveletechTeamsLogo.png	1/8/2015 12:53:43 PM
	http://monolith	0.01	http://monolith	4	Documents	1/8/2015 12:53:43 PM	Shared Documents/Team Petty Cash Request.xlsx	1/8/2015 12:53:43 PM

FIGURE 23.3
With PowerShell, we get by with a little help from our friends.

▼ TRY IT YOURSELF

Creating a SharePoint List with PowerShell

In this Try It Yourself exercise, you'll use PowerShell and the SharePoint object model to create a new custom list. Use the PowerShell ISE editor and save your work in a .ps1 script file for future reference.

1. Let's start by loading the SharePoint PowerShell snap-in, obtaining a reference to our top-level site collection, and enumerating all the list templates that are available within it:

```
Add-PSSnapin microsoft.sharepoint.powershell
$web = Get-SPWeb "http://monolith"
$web.ListTemplates.Name
```

2. Now we'll invoke the **Add()** method of the **Lists** object to build a new list using the built-in custom list template:

```
$listID = $web.Lists.Add("My New List","A custom list.",
➥$web.ListTemplates["Custom List"])
```

3. We'll need to "move down a level" to interact with our new list. (Echo the contents of **$listID**, for instance, and all you'll get back is the object's GUID.) Try this:

```
$mylist = $web.Lists[$listID]
$mylist.Title
$mylist.Items
```

Of course, there are no items in this list. For that matter, we haven't even defined fields (columns) yet.

4. Now we'll create two text columns, relying heavily on our **$mylist** variable:

```
$spFieldType = [Microsoft.SharePoint.SPFieldType]::Text
$mylist.Fields.Add("Task",$spFieldType,$false)
$mylist.Fields.Add("Priority",$spFieldType,$false)
$myList.Update()
```

5. Finally, we'll add a couple rows of sample data to our My New List SharePoint list. If you've been following the code, you know that our list has two columns: Task and Priority.

```
$newItem1 = $mylist.AddItem()
$newItem1["Task"] = "File expense report"
$newItem1["Priority"] = "Medium"
$newItem1.Update()

$newItem2 = $mylist.AddItem()
$newItem2["Task"] = "Finish PPT presentation"
$newItem2["Priority"] = "High"
$newItem2.Update()
```

Good job! Figure 23.4 shows my results.

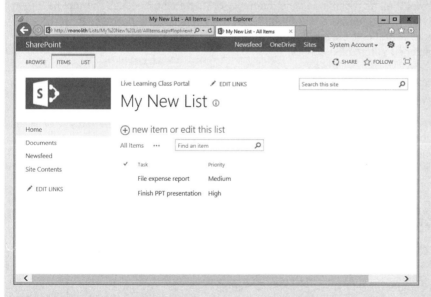

FIGURE 23.4
Our shiny new SharePoint tasks list, compliments of Windows PowerShell.

Summary

I hope by now you're pleased with your progress. Well done. You've been able to apply PowerShell to some real-world situations, to excellent results. In this hour of training, you saw that even robust SharePoint modules require you to "dip into" the lower levels of abstractions to interact with the SharePoint object model in much the same way that .NET developers do.

In the final hour, we focus our PowerShell energies at the Microsoft public cloud.

Q&A

Q. **You said that SharePoint uses SQL Server and Active Directory as part of its infrastructure. Does that mean I use the SharePoint cmdlets to perform AD and SQL tasks?**

A. Mostly no. What I mean is, in using the SharePoint cmdlets, you are indirectly performing operations in Active Directory, IIS, and SQL Server. However, you need to use those product-specific commands to perform honest-to-goodness administration on those platforms. For instance, I hope it makes sense to you that we'd need to use **sqlps** or SMO to back up SharePoint content or service application databases on a SQL Server computer.

Q. **Why can't I use Stsadm.exe to do this SharePoint stuff?**

A. A fair question, but one with a brief answer: You should avoid using Stsadm.exe, which predated PowerShell as a command-line interface to SharePoint, because the tool has been deprecated and will be removed in a future SharePoint version. The only reason we have Stsadm.exe in SharePoint Server 2013 is because some administrators still rely on it in their old-fashioned automation scripts.

Q. **Why did the SharePoint team bundle their cmdlets in an old-school snap-in? I hate typing the long assembly name.**

A. Me too. I believe the reason may be historical, or may be tied to the fact that because SharePoint command-line administration reaches so broadly and deeply across a server's hardware and software, making a low-level dynamic link library (DLL) probably offered more performance than deploying a traditional binary script.

Workshop

It will take some research, but use PowerShell and the SharePoint object model to accomplish the following tasks in your development farm:

▶ Create a document library named **PowerShell Scripts**.

▶ Create a couple sample .ps1 script files.

▶ Programmatically upload the documents to the library.

▶ Bonus: Set custom permissions on the library such that domain users can upload documents but not delete them.

Quiz

1. Which of the following commands shows you all of the SharePoint PowerShell commands that pertain to site collections?

    a. Get-Command –PSSnapin Microsoft.SharePoint.PowerShell –noun *SPSiteCollection*

    b. Get-Command –PSSnapin Microsoft.SharePoint.PowerShell –noun *SPWeb*

    c. Get-Command –PSSnapin Microsoft.SharePoint.PowerShell –noun *SPSite*

2. In the following statement, what is signified by the word **Add**?

   ```
   $mylist.Fields.Add("Task",$spFieldType,$false)
   ```

    a. Method

    b. Property

    c. Trigger

3. Make sure to adjust the PowerShell _____ on your system before attempting to run any helpful scripts that you downloaded from an online script repository.

    a. session configuration

    b. execution policy

    c. remoting settings

Answers

1. The correct answer is C. In the SharePoint object model, site collections are sites, and individual sites or subsites are webs.

2. The correct answer is A. Remember that in object-oriented programming, an object has both properties that describe attributes, and methods that define actions that the object can perform. The SharePoint object model is no different from any other .NET namespace.

3. The correct answer is B. The script execution policy on your system may be configured such that you are unable to run unsigned scripts downloaded from the Internet. Remember that you can run **Set-ExecutionPolicy** to make this change, and do so at one or several different scopes.

Managing Microsoft Azure with Windows PowerShell

What You'll Learn in This Hour:

▶ Defining Microsoft Azure

▶ Preparing Your Azure-PowerShell environment

▶ Working with Azure virtual machines

▶ Managing Office 365 and SharePoint online with Azure

I often tell my students that the two skills they need to have to ensure their value in the ever-changing IT marketplace are Windows PowerShell and Microsoft cloud computing. We're obviously covering the first task in this book; in this hour, I'd like to give you a taste of Microsoft Azure.

We have two challenges as we work through this material together in this final hour of training. First, the Azure platform changes on almost a daily basis. Azure CTO Mark Russinovich said in a 2014 keynote that his development teams add several new features to Azure *every single day*. Wow. That's a good thing because we customers get more toys to play with, but it's a bad thing because the technological sands are always shifting, requiring us to remain committed students of the platform.

NOTE

The other challenge is trying to cover a topic this broad and deep in 4,000 words or so. To that point, I recommend that you pick up Mitch Tulloch's excellent *Introducing Windows Azure for IT Professionals* (Microsoft Press, http://amzn.to/1yzL6oe). Mitch will fill in all the conceptual details that we have to pass over lightly in this space.

All that being said, let's get to work!

Defining Microsoft Azure

Microsoft Azure is Microsoft's public cloud platform. In cloud computing, the subsystems that we normally provision with on-premises hardware:

▶ CPU

▶ RAM

▶ Disk storage

▶ Network connectivity

are virtualized in a service provider's data center. Because we don't know exactly where the Azure data centers exist or what hardware is being used on the provider's side, we use the term *cloud* to describe this abstraction.

Microsoft Azure is called a *public cloud* because they make their compute resources available to the general public. You can combine your on-premises environment with the Azure public cloud; this configuration is known as a *hybrid cloud deployment*.

Microsoft Azure has grown a lot in the past few years; their chief competitors in this space are Amazon Web Services and the Google Cloud platform.

Microsoft Azure Features

With Azure, you pay for what services you need on a subscription-based usage model. The Azure platform as a whole embraces an incredible array of services. Here is a noncomprehensive list:

▶ Virtual servers

▶ Websites

▶ SQL Server Databases

▶ Active Directory directory services

▶ Large-scale data analysis (Hadoop) and business intelligence

You might have heard of Office 365 and SharePoint Online; those services are part of the Microsoft Azure public cloud as well. Office 365 gives individuals and businesses browser-based access to the Microsoft Office applications.

SharePoint Online is a cloud-based SharePoint Server 2013 platform. The features and functionality of cloud-based SharePoint are not the same as on-premises, but the feature sets are getting more in line with each other as time marches forward.

As a Microsoft Azure subscriber, you are what Microsoft calls a tenant in their cloud. Microsoft takes care of the day-to-day "back-end" stuff such as ensuring that your Azure services exist redundantly across several data centers around the world, that your virtual servers are backed up regularly, and so forth.

The idea with cloud services is that you, the Windows administrator, should focus on stuff like improving the efficiency and experience of the end users you support instead of horsing around with building fault tolerance, performing backups, and the like.

Azure Management Portal

As you'd expect, you can manage Microsoft Azure either by using Windows PowerShell or through a web-based console. The public URL for the current-generation web console is https://manage.windowsazure.com. Figure 24.1 shows the user interface.

FIGURE 24.1
The Microsoft Azure platform sure has a lot of moving parts, doesn't it?

As of this writing, the Azure team is previewing a next-generation web console, which exists at the URL https://portal.azure.com and I show you in Figure 24.2.

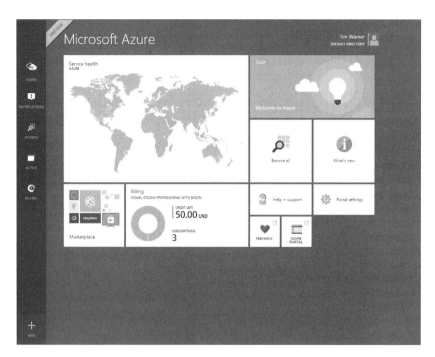

FIGURE 24.2
The next-generation Azure Management Portal takes a leaf from the Windows 8.1 Start Screen layout.

Security Implications of the Microsoft Public Cloud

One Achilles heel of any public cloud service is that you always wonder about the sovereignity of your data. You think you own your data—but do you with the public cloud?

Consider this: One of your public cloud provider's data centers likely resides in another country. Is your hosted data accessible to that country's government and/or police?

I'll leave further discussion of this important topic for another time. Nonetheless, it's one aspect of the public cloud that simply rules out the technology for some businesses.

Preparing Your Azure-PowerShell Environment

The first thing you need to do is to visit the Windows Azure home page at https://azure.microsoft.com and sign up for a free trial. Microsoft often runs promotions such as $200 of free service credit, so be on the lookout for those.

Don't be too nervous about giving Microsoft your credit card number. I've found that Azure is especially friendly to the cost-conscious administrator. Not only can you configure alerts when you are about to incur charge, but you can configure Azure to turn off services instead of charging your credit card.

Obtaining the Microsoft Azure PowerShell Module

Remember that, after all, we're concerned with Windows PowerShell-based Azure administration. After you have your Azure account squared away, it's time to download and install the Microsoft Azure PowerShell module.

NOTE
_____

Visit the Azure Downloads page at https://azure.microsoft.com/en-us/downloads, scroll down to Command-Line Tools, and click the **Install** link for the Windows PowerShell module.
_____

The Azure PowerShell module uses the Web Installer framework. This means that you're downloading a tiny stub program that orchestrates the actual download and installation of the software. Figure 24.3 shows the user interface.

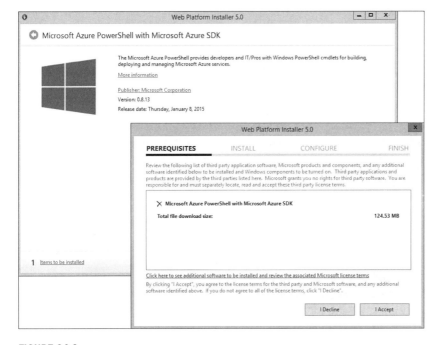

FIGURE 24.3
The Microsoft Azure PowerShell module is a component of the Microsoft Azure software development kit (SDK).

Don't be surprised when you see other components besides the Windows PowerShell module come down to your administrative workstation. The Microsoft Azure SDK gives you the (nearly) full toolbox that you need to manage Azure resources from your local premises.

Ever-Changing URLs

You know how it works with the World Wide Web: Uniform resource locators (URLs) tend to spontaneously change or go dead from time to time. To that point, don't be worried if you try one of the links I give you and you receive an unexpected result.

My best advice to you is simply to run a Google or Bing search for what you're looking for and let the search engine take care of the tedious task of locating the proper URL. For instance, to download the Microsoft Azure PowerShell module, run a Google search for just that: **download azure power-shell**. It pays to have developed your Google muscles.

Testing the Module Installation

Fire up an administrative command prompt, and let's peek inside our shiny new Microsoft Azure PowerShell module. The following represents partial output on my Windows 8.1 administrative workstation:

```
PS C:\> Get-Command -Module Azure -CommandType cmdlet |
↪Select-Object -Property Name | Format-Wide -Column 2
```

Add-AzureAccount	Add-AzureCacheWorkerRole
Add-AzureCertificate	Add-AzureDataDisk
Add-AzureDisk	Add-AzureDjangoWebRole
Add-AzureDns	Add-AzureEndpoint
Add-AzureEnvironment	Add-AzureHDInsightConfigValues
Add-AzureHDInsightMetastore	Add-AzureHDInsightScriptAction
Add-AzureHDInsightStorage	Add-AzureInternalLoadBalancer
Add-AzureNetworkInterfaceConfig	Add-AzureNodeWebRole
Add-AzureNodeWorkerRole	Add-AzurePHPWebRole
Add-AzurePHPWorkerRole	Add-AzureProvisioningConfig
Add-AzureTrafficManagerEndpoint	Add-AzureVhd
Add-AzureVMImage	Add-AzureWebRole
Add-AzureWorkerRole	Clear-AzureProfile

If you remove the formatting instructions from the previous statement and swap in **Measure-Object**, you'll see that the Azure module includes nearly 500 cmdlets (474 as of this writing). Can you say, "Holy PowerShell, Batman"?

Other than that, you should see no surprises: the Azure PowerShell cmdlets use the approved verbs, and the noun prefix starts with *Azure*. You'll find the documentation is complete as well. The Azure team put time into ensuring that we tenants have a "Cadillac" experience in administering Azure assets with the shell.

Connecting to Your Azure Subscription

You can connect to your Azure subscription via the command line in several ways, but I like using PowerShell to retrieve and install your Azure management digital certificate.

From your elevated PowerShell console session, run the following command:

```
PS C:\> Get-AzurePublishSettingsFile
```

You'll see your default browser open, and it will initate a download of your Azure .publishsettings file. If you aren't already logged in to Azure, you'll be prompted to log in with your organizational Microsoft account.

Make a note of the filename and location of that downloaded file; you'll need it in the next step.

Next, import your publish settings file:

```
PS C:\> Import-AzurePublishSettingsFile -PublishSettingsFile "C:\Visual Studio
➥Professional with MSDN-credentials.publishsettings"

Id          : 6e90210-39c2-321d-88b3-37621da1abd
Name        : Visual Studio Professional with MSDN
Environment : AzureCloud
Account     : B77AD2BB4B3283F39ADC97EFDA0A316B3C3C9876
Properties  : {[SupportedModes, AzureServiceManagement], [Default, True]}
```

The output lists the metadata associated with your subscription. Before you try any funny business, please know that the ID and account data in the previous output is *munged* (changed to dummy values).

Cool! Now that we've hooked into our Azure subscription, let's examine a couple honest-to-goodness use cases to give you a feel for how the process works.

Working with Azure Virtual Machines

To be perfectly candid with you, I strongly suggest that you avoid using Windows PowerShell to create Azure assets until you've mastered the graphical methods. In my experience, it's too easy to leave out important parameters when you attempt to, say, create a new virtual machine entirely from Windows PowerShell.

My suggestion applies to learning any technology. First you learn the technology and its capabilities, and then you learn how to automate it.

Creating a VM in the Cloud

Log in to the Azure Management Console and use the Gallery to build out a new virtual machine (VM). To get to the gallery, click the **New** button at the bottom of the screen and navigate to **Virtual Machines > From Gallery**.

Before you create your VM, you may also want to deploy a virtual network, which is a private IP subnet range that your Azure VMs will use to communicate internally.

Figure 24.4 shows some screenshots from the Create a Virtual Machine Wizard. Compare how easy it is to browse the various VM templates in the portal as compared to doing the same with programmatically with **Get-AzureVMImage**:

```
PS C:\> Get-AzureVMImage | Select-Object -Property ImageName | Where-Object
➡ImageName -Like "*Windows-Server-2012-R2*" | Format-List

ImageName : a699494373c04fc0bc8f2bb1389d6106__Windows-Server-2012-R2-201410.01-
➡en.us-127GB.vhd

ImageName : a699494373c04fc0bc8f2bb1389d6106__Windows-Server-2012-R2-201411.01-
➡en.us-127GB.vhd
```

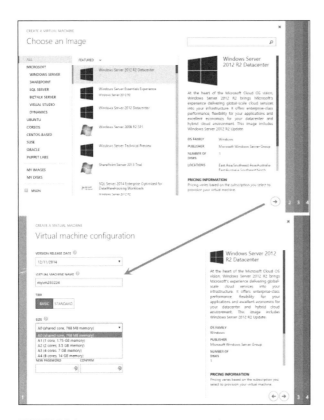

FIGURE 24.4
The Azure management portal makes it super easy to build VMs based on gallery templates.

The PowerShell output is enough to make your eyes cross, am I correct? Now look again at Figure 24.4, particularly at the lower portion of the image. After you choose a base operating system, your next steps are to select a service tier and VM size.

TIP

It's important to note that your per-minute runtime cost for each VM is based on (a) how much virtual hardware you need to consume and (b) the service level, which governs stuff like availability metrics and overall performance.

CAUTION

Note that if you shut down an Azure VM by using the shut down command from within the guest OS, Azure doesn't truly release its hold on your VM. This means you may incur usage fees that you don't intend.

To actually stop your VM, log in to the management portal and click **Shut Down**. Even though your VMs will show up as deallocated in your account, you can always restart them and recapture their original private IP addresses at your convenience.

Interacting with Azure VMs

Once Azure provisions your new VM, you can use Remote Desktop Protocol (RDP) to establish a remote desktop session with the VM. In fact, the portal generates a Remote Desktop .rdp file for you!

Let's assume that you have two cloud-based VMs in Azure. In my test environment, I have three Windows Server 2012 R2 VMs: DSCSERVER01 is already running, and DSCCLIENT1 and DSCCLIENT02 are stopped:

```
PS C:\> Get-AzureVM

ServiceName              Name                  Status
-----------              ----                  ------
DSCCLIENT02              DSCCLIENT02           StoppedDeallocated
dscserver01              dscclient01           StoppedDeallocated
dscserver01              dscserver01           ReadyRole
```

Let's see what we can do programmatically with our running (ReadyRole) VM by examining its members:

```
PS C:\>$s1 = Get-AzureVM -ServiceName "dscserver01" -Name "dscserver01"
PS C:\> $s1 | Get-Member

    TypeName:
```

```
Microsoft.WindowsAzure.Commands.ServiceManagement.Model.PersistentVMRoleContext

Name                          MemberType  Definition
----                          ----------  ----------
Equals                        Method      bool Equals(System.Object obj)
GetHashCode                   Method      int GetHashCode()
GetInstance                   Method      Microsoft.WindowsAzure.Commands.Servi...
GetType                       Method      type GetType()
ToString                      Method      string ToString()
AvailabilitySetName           Property    string AvailabilitySetName {get;set;}
DeploymentName                Property    string DeploymentName {get;set;}
DNSName                       Property    string DNSName {get;set;}
GuestAgentStatus              Property    Microsoft.WindowsAzure.Commands.Servi...
HostName                      Property    string HostName {get;set;}
InstanceErrorCode             Property    string InstanceErrorCode {get;set;}
InstanceFaultDomain           Property    string InstanceFaultDomain {get;set;}
InstanceName                  Property    string InstanceName {get;set;}
InstanceSize                  Property    string InstanceSize {get;set;}
InstanceStateDetails          Property    string InstanceStateDetails {get;set;}
InstanceStatus                Property    string InstanceStatus {get;set;}
InstanceUpgradeDomain         Property    string InstanceUpgradeDomain {get;set;}
IpAddress                     Property    string IpAddress {get;set;}
Label                         Property    string Label {get;set;}
Name                          Property    string Name {get;set;}
NetworkInterfaces             Property    Microsoft.WindowsAzure.Commands.Servi...
OperationDescription          Property    string OperationDescription {get;set;}
OperationId                   Property    string OperationId {get;set;}
OperationStatus               Property    string OperationStatus {get;set;}
PowerState                    Property    string PowerState {get;set;}
PublicIPAddress               Property    string PublicIPAddress {get;set;}
PublicIPName                  Property    string PublicIPName {get;set;}
ResourceExtensionStatusList   Property    System.Collections.Generic.List[Micro...
ServiceName                   Property    string ServiceName {get;set;}
Status                        Property    string Status {get;set;}
VM                            Property    Microsoft.WindowsAzure.Commands.Servi...
```

If you don't see any output that's specific to your Azure VM, Azure may be "confused" as to your subscription details. First get the names of your Azure subscriptions:

```
PS C:\> Get-AzureSubscription | Select-Object -Property SubscriptionName
```

Next, manually load your subscription details into your current session:

```
PS C:\> Select-AzureSubscription "My Subscription"
```

I re-created my **$s1** variable, and then saw what I needed when I accessed object members directly:

```
PS C:\> $s1 | Select-Object -Property Name, DNSName, InstanceSize, IPAddress,
➥OperationStatus | Format-List


Name             : dscserver01
DNSName          : http://dscserver01.cloudapp.net/
InstanceSize     : Basic_A1
IpAddress        : 10.0.1.4
OperationStatus  : OK
```

Starting and Stopping Azure VMs

Fortunately, the Azure PowerShell module includes native cmdlets to handle programmatic starting and stopping. For instance, let's start up my stopped and deallocated dscclient01 VM:

```
PS C:\> Start-AzureVM -Name "dscclient01" -ServiceName "dscserver01"


OperationDescription        OperationId             OperationStatus
--------------------        -----------             ---------------
Start-AzureVM               89f9ed46-855f-6d4b-9b42... Succeeded
```

TIP

By the way, in case you wondered: the Service Name represents one or more "pods" of VMs that share the same metadata; I'm talking about stuff like virtual networks, geographic locations, and so forth. It's confusing because in my test environment I gave one of my services the same name as one of my VMs. Another tip: Don't do that! Give your services descriptive names that differ from your VM hostnames.

As I said earlier in this hour of training, you need to stop and deallocate your VMs when you're finished testing so that you don't incur unexpected usage charges. The **–Force** switch of the **Stop-AzureVM** ensures that deallocation occurs:

```
PS C:\> Stop-AzureVM -Name "dscclient01" -ServiceName "dscserver01" -Force


OperationDescription        OperationId             OperationStatus
--------------------        -----------             ---------------
Stop-AzureVM                522d6440-908d-618f-b604... Succeeded
```

Creating SQL Databases in Microsoft Azure

In this Try It Yourself exercise, you'll "play with" the SQL database functionality in Microsoft Azure. Many businesses use Microsoft Azure to stage and present their n-tier web applications because you can host all layers of the stack (web servers, application servers, and database servers) natively in the Azure public cloud. Azure even provides high availability and network load balancing.

Make sure that you start an elevated PowerShell session and use **Set-AzureSubscription** to bring all your subscription settings into the session.

1. First, let's undertake some command discovery to see what's available from the PowerShell environment:

```
PS C:\> Get-Command -Module Azure -Noun *sql* | Select-Object –Property Name |
➡Format-Wide -Column 2
```

```
Get-AzureSqlDatabase                    Get-AzureSqlDatabaseCopy
Get-AzureSqlDatabaseImportExportStatus  Get-AzureSqlDatabaseOperation
Get-AzureSqlDatabaseServer              Get-AzureSqlDatabaseServerFirewallRule
Get-AzureSqlDatabaseServerQuota         Get-AzureSqlDatabaseServiceObjective
Get-AzureSqlRecoverableDatabase         Get-AzureVMSqlServerExtension
New-AzureSqlDatabase                    New-AzureSqlDatabaseServer
New-AzureSqlDatabaseServerContext       New-AzureSqlDatabaseServerFirewallRule
New-AzureVMSqlServerAutoBackupConfig    New-AzureVMSqlServerAutoPatchingConfig
Remove-AzureSqlDatabase                 Remove-AzureSqlDatabaseServer
Remove-AzureSqlDatabaseServerFirewal... Remove-AzureVMSqlServerExtension
Set-AzureSqlDatabase                    Set-AzureSqlDatabaseServer
Set-AzureSqlDatabaseServerFirewallRule  Set-AzureVMSqlServerExtension
Start-AzureSqlDatabaseCopy              Start-AzureSqlDatabaseExport
Start-AzureSqlDatabaseImport            Start-AzureSqlDatabaseRecovery
Start-AzureSqlDatabaseRestore           Stop-AzureSqlDatabaseCopy
```

Aha! I hope you see that there are cmdlets for both SQL database and SQL database server.

2. Let's create a new SQL server in our current Azure subscription:

```
PS C:\> New-AzureSqlDatabaseServer -AdministratorLogin "sqladmin" -Administrator
➡-LoginPassword "P@$$w0rd" -Location "East US"
```

```
ServerName        Location        AdministratorLogin  Version
----------        --------        ------------------  -------
eoonvvn8k7        East US         sqladmin
```

3. Now we'll create a new SQL database inside our new virtual SQL Server VM:

```
PS C:\> $database1 = New-AzureSqlDatabase -ServerName "eoonvvn8k7"
➥-DatabaseName "TestDB" -Edition Standard -MaxSizeGB 2 -Collation
➥"SQL_Latin1_General_CP1_CI_AS"
```

TIP

Notice that I captured the database into a variable for future reference. I also specified a database edition; remember to press **Tab** to cycle the options within that data enumeration.

4. By browsing the Azure SQL database cmdlets, you probably saw that we don't have easily identifiable options for actually working with the database. You can use the Azure management portal, though. Browse to the SQL Databases node, select your database, and click **Manage** from the bottom toolbar. As shown in Figure 24.5, the Azure team gives you a SQL Server Management Studio-ish administrative surface to work with.

FIGURE 24.5
Here we're creating a new table in our cloud-based SQL Server database by using the web administration console.

5. Although the Azure management portal is good and will get even better over time, you might instead prefer to manage your cloud databases by using an on-premises tool like SQL Server Management Studio itself. You can do that.

6. Retrieve the name of your target Azure SQL Server database server, and copy that name to your Clipboard:

```
PS C:\> Get-AzureSqlDatabaseServer

ServerName          Location          AdministratorLogin  Version
----------          --------          ------------------  -------
eoonvvn8k7          East US           sqladmin ·          2.0
```

Note that you may need to relax Windows Firewall rules on your SQL administrative client machine because the cloud connection uses nonstandard ports for security reasons.

7. Now open SQL Server Management Studio and log in by using the following parameters in the Connect to Server dialog box:

   ▶ **Server name:** <yourservername>.database.windows.net

   ▶ **Authentication:** SQL Server Authentication

   ▶ **Login:** <yourlogin>

   ▶ **Password:** <yourpassword>

   Figure 24.6 shows a composite of the login/cloud database in SSMS.

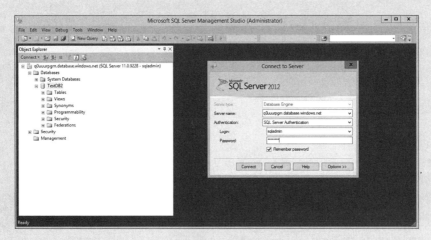

FIGURE 24.6
You can perform the same management on your Azure cloud SQL databases as you can on your on-premises databases, and with the same management tools, to boot.

I've verified that this SSMS-based management approach works with SQL Server 2012 and SQL Server 2014. You'll have to perform some research to see whether you can connect to Azure SQL databases by using older versions of SQL Server on-premises.

Look, if you plan to become expert in cloud technology (and I certainly hope you do), you need to get one piece of terminology absolutely clear. When we speak of our local data center, we reference our "on-premises" environment.

It amazes me when I see people who work on cloud technology all day—including cloud providers themselves—refer to on-premises as "on-premise." Please recall that *premises* means a physical location, whereas a *premise* is an idea. Do you get and appreciate the difference? Good. Now that we have that squared away, let's continue with our regularly scheduled programming.

Managing Office 365 and SharePoint Online with Azure

Although the Office 365 and SharePoint Online services rely on Microsoft Azure on the back end of things (that is to say, beyond the reach of you, the tenant customer), you use separate tools to manage these services with Windows PowerShell.

What's confusing to some is that SharePoint Online is included with most Office 365 subscription levels (check out the options by visiting the Office 365 site at http://bit.ly/1yAWLmP), but is also available as a standalone subscription (pricing reference: http://bit.ly/1yAWS1H). Personally, I would always need Office Web Apps with my SharePoint deployment, so the first option is a no-brainer for me.

Downloading and Installing the Prerequisite Software

To connect from on-premises PowerShell session to an Office 365 tenant, you need to download and install two components:

▶ Microsoft Online Services Sign-in Assistant for IT Professionals (http://bit.ly/1yAX5Sk)

▶ Windows Azure Active Directory Module for Windows PowerShell (http://bit.ly/1yAX5Sk)

Connecting to Your O365 Subscription

Okay. Having done that, make sure that you're still in an administrative PowerShell session. Import the **MSOnline** module, and check out what commands are available as usual:

```
PS C:\> Import-Module MSOnline
PS C:\> Get-Command -Module msonline | Select-Object -Property Name | Format-Wide
➡-Column 2

Add-MsolAdministrativeUnitMember        Add-MsolForeignGroupToRole
Add-MsolGroupMember                     Add-MsolRoleMember
Add-MsolScopedRoleMember                Confirm-MsolDomain
```

```
Confirm-MsolEmailVerifiedDomain            Connect-MsolService
Convert-MsolDomainToFederated              Convert-MsolDomainToStandard
Convert-MsolFederatedUser                  Get-MsolAccountSku
Get-MsolAdministrativeUnit                 Get-MsolAdministrativeUnitMember
Get-MsolCompanyInformation                 Get-MsolContact
Get-MsolDirSyncProvisioningError           Get-MsolDomain
Get-MsolDomainFederationSettings           Get-MsolDomainVerificationDns
Get-MsolFederationProperty                 Get-MsolGroup
Get-MsolGroupMember                        Get-MsolPartnerContract
Get-MsolPartnerInformation                 Get-MsolPasswordPolicy
Get-MsolRole                               Get-MsolRoleMember
Get-MsolScopedRoleMember                   Get-MsolServicePrincipal
Get-MsolServicePrincipalCredential         Get-MsolSubscription
Get-MsolUser                               Get-MsolUserByStrongAuthentication
Get-MsolUserRole                           New-MsolAdministrativeUnit
New-MsolDomain                             New-MsolFederatedDomain
New-MsolGroup                              New-MsolLicenseOptions
New-MsolServicePrincipal                   New-MsolServicePrincipalAddresses
New-MsolServicePrincipalCredential         New-MsolUser
New-MsolWellKnownGroup                     Redo-MsolProvisionContact
Redo-MsolProvisionGroup                    Redo-MsolProvisionUser
Remove-MsolAdministrativeUnit              Remove-MsolAdministrativeUnitMember
Remove-MsolApplicationPassword             Remove-MsolContact
Remove-MsolDomain                          Remove-MsolFederatedDomain
Remove-MsolForeignGroupFromRole            Remove-MsolGroup
Remove-MsolGroupMember                     Remove-MsolRoleMember
Remove-MsolScopedRoleMember                Remove-MsolServicePrincipal
Remove-MsolServicePrincipalCredential      Remove-MsolUser
Reset-MsolStrongAuthenticationMethod...    Restore-MsolUser
Set-MsolADFSContext                        Set-MsolAdministrativeUnit
Set-MsolCompanyContactInformation          Set-MsolCompanySecurityComplianceCon...
Set-MsolCompanySettings                    Set-MsolDirSyncEnabled
Set-MsolDomain                             Set-MsolDomainAuthentication
Set-MsolDomainFederationSettings           Set-MsolGroup
Set-MsolPartnerInformation                 Set-MsolPasswordPolicy
Set-MsolServicePrincipal                   Set-MsolUser
Set-MsolUserLicense                        Set-MsolUserPassword
Set-MsolUserPrincipalName                  Update-MsolFederatedDomain
```

Assuming you know your Office 365 username and password, we'll capture those credentials by storing a **Credential** object in a new variable:

```
PS C:\>$credential = Get-Credential
```

Next, we'll make an Internet pipeline, as it were, from PowerShell to the Office 365 service, passing in our stored credential:

```
PS C:\>Connect-MSOLService –Credential $credential
```

We'll now verify our O365 tenant domain by using **Get-MsolDomain**:

```
PS C:\> Get-MsolDomain

Name                             Status       Authentication
----                             ------       --------------
testdomain.onmicrosoft.com       Verified       Managed
```

Adding SharePoint Online to the Mix

Before we can PowerShell our way into our SharePoint Online subscription (whether it's part of an Office 365 subscription or standalone), we'll have to...wait for it...download and install the SharePoint Online Management Shell (http://bit.ly/15r5SJg).

After you finish installing the product, we can import the module into our session:

```
PS C:\>Import-Module -Name Microsoft.Online.SharePoint.PowerShell
```

TIP

You may see a warning regarding unapproved verbs that's almost identical to the warning text you saw when loading the SQL Server sqlps in the "Listing Databases within an Instance" section of Hour 22, "Managing SQL Server with Windows PowerShell."

Here's the commands form the SharePoint Online module so that you can get a feel for what's possible:

```
PS C:\> Get-Command -Module Microsoft.Online.SharePoint.PowerShell | Select-Object
➥-Property Name | Format-Wide -Column 2
```

Add-SPOUser	Connect-SPOService
Disconnect-SPOService	Get-SPOAppErrors
Get-SPOAppInfo	Get-SPODeletedSite
Get-SPOExternalUser	Get-SPOSite
Get-SPOSiteGroup	Get-SPOTenant
Get-SPOTenantLogEntry	Get-SPOTenantLogLastAvailableTimeInUtc
Get-SPOUser	Get-SPOWebTemplate
New-SPOSite	New-SPOSiteGroup
Remove-SPODeletedSite	Remove-SPOExternalUser
Remove-SPOSite	Remove-SPOSiteGroup
Remove-SPOUser	Repair-SPOSite
Request-SPOUpgradeEvaluationSite	Restore-SPODeletedSite
Set-SPOSite	Set-SPOSiteGroup
Set-SPOTenant	Set-SPOUser
Test-SPOSite	Upgrade-SPOSite

We are now free to connect into our SharePoint Online instance. To do this, we'll need our **$credential** variable as defined earlier. We'll also need our Office 365 domain, which we already examined earlier in this hour when we ran **Get-MsolDomain**.

Note in the following connection string that the SharePoint Online administrative URL takes the unique part of your Office 365 domain and prepends it to the string **–admin.sharepoint.com**:

```
PS C:\> Connect-SPOService -Url "https://testdomain-admin.sharepoint.com"
➡-Credential $credential
```

Cool! Now we can experiment with cloud-based SharePoint site collections, sites, and subsites by using very similar syntax to what you already now know, having worked with on-premises SharePoint Server:

```
PS C:\> Get-SPOSite | Select-Object -Property URL | Format-Table -AutoSize

Url
---
https://testdomain.sharepoint.com/
https://testdomain.sharepoint.com/search
https://testdomain.sharepoint.com/sites/appcatalog
https://testdomain.sharepoint.com/sites/Authoring
https://testdomain.sharepoint.com/sites/ITQandA
https://testdomain.sharepoint.com/sites/mos77419
https://testdomain.sharepoint.com/sites/publishing
https://testdomain.sharepoint.com/sites/records
https://testdomain.sharepoint.com/sites/search
https://testdomain.sharepoint.com/sites/teamsite
https://testdomain.sharepoint.com/teams/Jacob
https://testdomain.sharepoint.com/teams/Sarah
https://testdomain-my.sharepoint.com/
http://testdomain-public.sharepoint.com/
```

Summary

My goal as your instructor and guide in this hour of training was to get you far enough in the process that you have a solid connection between a local PowerShell session and various Microsoft Azure cloud-based resources. If you're hungry to know more, that's awesome! If you've learned nothing else by reading this book, you know how important curiosity and plain old research are in becoming effective with Windows PowerShell.

It's been an absolute pleasure teaching you how to use Windows PowerShell. I hope that you have some confidence with the technology now, and that you are able to discuss PowerShell intelligently with other IT professionals. I thank you so much for taking the time to buy and read this book, and I wish you all the best in life. Take care, and more power to the shell!

Q&A

Q. This "Managing Office 365 by using PowerShell" stuff can get complex quickly. Where can I go online to find quality helper scripts?

A. As you'd expect, capable PowerShell scripters all over the world are willing to share their work with you for fun and for free. Start with o365info.com; you'll find many, many PowerShell scripts that are all geared at accomplishing specific Office 365 management tasks.

With regard to Microsoft Azure, I suggest you visit the Microsoft Azure Script Center (http://azure.microsoft.com/en-us/documentation/scripts/), where you can download not only Windows PowerShell scripts specific to Azure but also System Center Orchestrator runbooks. Neat stuff.

Q. Why would anyone want to create Azure VMs from PowerShell when the online gallery is so informative and robust?

A. Well, you have to remember that one of the ideas behind the hybrid private/public cloud is automation. Remember that when you script out a process in PowerShell, you're ensuring absolute consistency. Sure, the initial testing and debugging of your PowerShell scripts might be a pain in the short term, but for software development companies who stand up and tear down VMs dozens of times per day, using the PowerShell interface makes a lot of sense.

Q. Can I use Windows PowerShell to download cloud-based VMs?

A. You sure can. Not only can you download Azure VMs, but you can also upload virtual hard disk files from your on-premises private cloud to the Azure public cloud.

The first thing you'd do is run Sysprep to generalize your Azure VM. (You also need to make sure that you can legally activate the Azure VM once it comes online on-premises.) Then do a full shutdown/deallocation by using **Stop-AzureVM –Force**.

Here's some sample code that shows how I'd download my Azure VM VHD file named DSCSERVER01 to my local environment.

```
PS C:\> Select-AzureSubscription "mysubscriptionname"

PS C:\>$sourceVHD =
➥"https://mylocation.blob.core.windows.net/uploads/mydatadisk.vhd"

PS C:\>$destinationVHD = "D:\LocalVHDs\mydatadisk-downloaded.vhd"

PS C:\>Save-AzureVhd -Source $sourceVHD -LocalFilePath $destinationVHD
➥-NumberOfThreads 5
```

You can use the portal or PowerShell to get the full path to your Azure VM's .vhd file. Note that as of this writing in early 2015 that Azure VMs don't support the generation 2 (.vhdx) file type. This means that you'll need to convert your .vhdx image files to .vhd in order to upload them to the Azure cloud.

Workshop

One Azure component we didn't cover formally in this hour of training is Azure Active Directory. As unbelievable as it may sound to "old salt" Active Directory administrators, you can bring up new Active Directory domains with just a few mouse clicks or keystrokes.

My challenge to you here is to perform some background research on Azure AD. (Here's where you can find Microsoft's online documentation to get you started: http://bit.ly/15r7eDP.)

Once you're up to speed, perform the following Azure AD tasks in your Azure subscription tenant:

- ▶ Create a new Active Directory instance.
- ▶ Create a new Azure AD group.
- ▶ Create a new Azure AD user, and populate the user into your group.
- ▶ Grant the new group access to an interesting application from the application gallery.
- ▶ Open another web browser and try to access the Azure-hosted application by using the new Azure AD user account.

Quiz

1. Which of the following commands retrieves your Microsoft Azure subscription settings file?

    a. Get-AzurePublishSettingsFile

    b. Import-AzurePublishSettingsFile

    c. Add-AzurePublishSettingsFile

2. Which of the following commands gives you the full name of the SharePoint Online module?

    a. Get-Pssnapin *sharepoint*

    b. Get-Module *sharepoint*

    c. Get-Command *sharepoint*

3. You're attempting to connect to an Azure VM, but you're receiving incomplete and unexpected results. Which of the following represents a solution to this problem?

    a. Start another PowerShell session

    b. Define a new PowerShell session configuration

    c. Attach your Azure subscription to your PowerShell session

Answers

1. The correct answer is A. First we retrieve the publish settings file, and then we import it by using **Import-AzurePublishSettingsFile**.

2. The correct answer is B. Although SharePoint Online uses a traditional .NET naming method, it's actually a module and not a snap-in. Choice C fails because **–Name** is the position 1 parameter for **Get-Command**, not **–Module**.

3. The correct answer is C. Make sure that you run **Set-AzureSubscription** so you can explicitly link your Azure subscription with your local PowerShell session.

Index

Symbols

& (ampersand) operator
  running external commands, 84-85
  running scripts, 390
  in SharePoint Server management shell, 454
< > (angle brackets), **405**
* (asterisk) wildcard character
  finding cmdlets, 57, 77-78
  as Kleene star, 316
  as placeholder, 125
  in regular expressions, 320
  in searches, 313-314
@ (at) signs, **446**
\ (backslash), 320
^ (caret), 318-320
: (colon), **156**
{ } (curly braces)
  for expressions, 214
  in functions, 384
  in regular expressions, 322
$ (dollar sign), **318-320**
$_ (dollar sign underscore) variable, **129**
` (grave accent), **128, 224, 406**
> (greater than)
  for output redirection, 142, 187
  in WQL, 302
< (less than), 302
(octothorpe), 129, 393
( ) (parentheses), **165**
% (percent sign), 302

. (period), 320
.\ (period backslash) notation, **390**
| (pipe), **20, 113, 128**
? (question mark)
  as alias, 138-139
  as wildcard character
    in regular expressions, 320
    in searches, 315
" " (quotation marks)
  in directory path, 84
  double quotes versus single quotes, 385
  in regular expressions, 321
; (semicolon), **73**
–% (stop parsing symbol), **85-86**
~ (tilde), **314**
7-Zip, installing, **340-341**

A

About help files, **60, 119, 167**
accessing command history, **33**
Active Directory
  child domains, installing, 422-423
  domain controllers, promoting, 421-422
  domains
    joining, 418-419
    testing for membership, 418

  Flexible Single Master Roles (FSMOs)
    managing, 430-431
    transferring, 431-432
  functional levels, setting, 432
  Group Policy administration, 432-433
  groups, creating, 424-425
  installing, 417-423
  organizational units (OUs), creating, 423-424
  user accounts
    creating, 425-426
    creating in bulk, 427-430
    managing, 426-427
Active Directory Administrative Center (ADAC), 17, 430
Active Directory Cookbook (Svidergol and Allen), 423
Active Directory provider, 169-170
activities for workflows, 283-284
  CheckPoint-Workflow cmdlet, 284-285
  Resume-Workflow cmdlet, 284-287
  Sequence, 284, 287-288
  Suspend-Workflow cmdlet, 284-287
ADAC (Active Directory Administrative Center), 17, 430
Add-ADGroupMember cmdlet, 425
Add-Computer cmdlet, 418
Add-Content cmdlet, 164
add-ons
  Commands add-on, turning on/off, 40

X

Z